MEDICAL ANTHROPOLOGY IN ECOLOGICAL PERSPECTIVE

Also of Interest

†*Women in Third World Development,* Sue Ellen M. Charlton

†*Theories of Comparative Politics: The Search for a Paradigm,* Ronald H. Chilcote

†*Theories of Development and Underdevelopment,* Ronald H. Chilcote

†*The Gap Between Rich and Poor: Contending Perspectives on the Political Economy of Development,* edited by Mitchell A. Seligson

†*Human Adaptability: An Introduction to Ecological Anthropology,* Emilio F. Moran

The Ecosystem Concept in Anthropology, edited by Emilio F. Moran

Rethinking Human Adaptation: Biological and Cultural Models, Rada Dyson-Hudson and Michael A. Little

Unfinished Agenda: The Dynamics of Modernization in Developing Nations, Manning Nash

Comparative Social Dynamics: Essays in Honor of S. N. Eisenstadt, edited by Erik Cohen, Moshe Lissak, and Uri Almagor

The Dilemma of Amazonian Development, edited by Emilio F. Moran

Village Viability in Contemporary Society, edited by Priscilla Copeland Reining and Barbara Lenkerd

The Transformation of a Sacred Town: Bhubaneswar, India, edited by Susan Seymour

Resource Managers: North American and Australian Hunter-Gatherers, edited by Nancy M. Williams and Eugene S. Hunn

†Available in hardcover and paperback.

MEDICAL ANTHROPOLOGY IN ECOLOGICAL PERSPECTIVE

Ann McElroy

Patricia K. Townsend

Westview Press / Boulder and London

The paper used in this publication meets the minimum requirements of the American National Standard for Permanence of Paper for Printed Library Materials Z39.48-1984.

Published in 1985 in the United States of America by Westview Press, Inc., 5500 Central Avenue, Boulder, Colorado 80301; Frederick A. Praeger, Publisher

First published in 1979 by Wadsworth, Inc.

Library of Congress Catalog Card Number: 85-50150
ISBN: 0-8133-0175-0
ISBN: 0-8133-0176-9 (pbk.)

Printed and bound in the United States of America

10   9   8   7   6   5

TO ROGER AND ALISON

CONTENTS

Preface   xiii
Introduction   xvii

CHAPTER 1 The Ecology of Health and Disease   1

Preview   2
STUDYING THE YANOMAMO: An Example of
Medical Ecology   3
ENVIRONMENT, CULTURE, AND HEALTH:
The Scope of Medical Anthropology   6
Anthropological Subdisciplines and Medical
Anthropology   7
A Focus on Adaptation   12
A Working Model of Ecology and Health   13
PROFILE: ARCTIC ADAPTATIONS   16
Resources   29

CHAPTER 2 Interdisciplinary Research in Health
Problems   32

Preview   34
The Nature of Collaboration   35
Environmental Data   37
Population Interactions and Energy Flow   39
Carrying Capacity and Population Regulation   41
Studying Environmental Factors in Health   43
PROFILE: CANNIBAL MOURNERS   43
Clinical Data   48
Epidemiological Data   50

PROFILE: THE EPIDEMIOLOGY OF HIGH
BLOOD PRESSURE   52
Behavioral, Social, and Cultural Data   57
Field Work in Medical Anthropology   58
Labeling Disease   60
PROFILE: THE EVERYDAY LIVES OF
RETARDED PERSONS   62
Conclusions   66
Resources   67

CHAPTER 3   The Meaning of Adaptation   70

Preview   72
Adaptation in Biological Evolution   76
Genetic Codes   77
Selective Compromise   80
Selection and Disease   83
PROFILE: MALARIA AND AGRICULTURE   85
Physiological Adaptation   93
High-Altitude Adaptation   94
Cold Adaptation   96
PROFILE: LACTOSE TOLERANCE   97
Cultural and Individual Adaptation   100
Culture Learning   101
Variability and Change in Cultural Systems   103
Cultural Adaptation and Health   104
Direct Medical Control Strategies   106
PROFILE: INDIVIDUAL AND CULTURAL
ADAPTATIONS TO SICKLE CELL ANEMIA   109
Limits to Adaptation   117
Conclusions   119
Resources   121

CHAPTER 4   Evolving Patterns of Birth, Disease,
             and Death   124

Preview   126
Hazards in the Cultural Environment   127
The Population Equation   131
Natality   131
PROFILE: INFANT MORTALITY IN A NEW
GUINEA SOCIETY   134
Mortality   139
Migration   142
Population Density   143

Life and Death in Hunter-Gatherer Camps   144
Life and Death in Farming Villages   147
Life and Death in the Preindustrial City   152
PROFILE: THE BLACK DEATH   153
Life and Death in the Industrial Society   158
PROFILE: PESTICIDE TRAGEDY IN VIRGINIA   162
Methods for Studying the Evolution of Disease
Patterns   165
Conclusions   168
Resources   170

CHAPTER 5   The Ecology and Economics of
             Nutrition   172

Preview   174
Human Foodways and Nutritional Needs   175
Subsistence by Hunting and Gathering   176
PROFILE: SUBSISTENCE ECOLOGY OF THE
!KUNG SAN   177
Subsistence by Farming   185
Tropical Farmers   185
Peasant Farmers   190
The Anthropology of Food Habits   195
All That Goes into the Mouth Is Not Food   199
PROFILE: COCA CHEWING AND HEALTH IN
THE HIGH ANDES   200
A Hungry World   205
Hunger in the United States   207
Overnutrition and Other Problems of Affluence   211
Conclusions   216
Resources   217

CHAPTER 6   Nutrition Throughout the Life Cycle   220

Preview   222
Prenatal Nutrition   223
Infant Feeding   225
Weaning and the Critical Second Year   229
Nutrition in Childhood and Adolescence   234
Nutrition Throughout Adult Life   238
Nutrition and Old Age   243
PROFILE: LIVING PAST 100 IN THE CAUCASUS   244
Assessing Diet and Nutrition   250
Famine   252
PROFILE: THE SAHEL DROUGHT AND FAMINE   253
The Social Cost of Malnutrition   259
Conclusions   263
Resources   264

CHAPTER 7   Stress and Disease   266
            Preview   268
            The Concept of Stress   269
            A Model of Stress   271
            Individual and Cultural Variation in Tolerance of
            Stress   274
            Seeking out Stress   276
            Understanding the Physiology of Stress   278
            Selye's General Adaptation Syndrome   278
            The Role of Hormones in Stress and Disease   281
            Cannon's Concept of the Fight-or-Flight Response   284
            The Body's Response to Symbolic Danger   286
            PROFILE: MAGICAL DEATH   288
            Stress and Healing   294
            Stress in the Physical and Biotic Environment   298
            Nutritional Stress   298
            Climatic Stress   299
            Cumulative Stressors   300
            Biological Rhythms   301
            PROFILE: ARCTIC HYSTERIA   303
            Stressors in the Sociocultural Environment   307
            Urban Environments   308
            Role Conflict   311
            PROFILE: DEPRIVATION DWARFISM   314
            Alcoholism   320
            Conclusions   322
            Resources   324

CHAPTER 8   Health Repercussions of Culture
            Contact   326
            Preview   328
            The Story of Ishi   330
            Stressors of Contact   331
            Types and Degrees of Contact   334
            Diffusion   334
            Acculturation   335
            Assimilation   336
            Ethnic Revitalization   337
            PROFILE: CULTURE CHANGE AND INUIT
            HEALTH   338
            Models for the Study of Contact Processes   349
            Health Risks of Acculturation   351
            EPIDEMIOLOGICAL CHANGE: Malaria in the
            New World   354
            DEMOGRAPHIC CHANGE: The Asmat of New
            Guinea   359
            NUTRITIONAL AND HEALTH CARE
            CHANGE: A Rural Health Center in South
            Africa   362
            Migration and Changes in Health Status   368
            Involuntary Migration   368

Voluntary Migration   370
Conclusions   372
Resources   373

CHAPTER 9   Health Costs of Modernization   376

Preview   378
New Roads and Old Diseases   380
What Modernization Means   382
Economic Development   385
Approaches to Evaluating Modernization and
Health   388
Agriculture and Development   388
PROFILE: IRRIGATION AND SCHISTOSOMIASIS   389
Repercussions of Technological Change   395
Strategies for Health Care Development   399
Anthropologists in Developing Areas   405
Values and Change   405
Anthropologists as Community Mediators   407
Evaluating Economic Development—No Free
Lunch?   409
Minority Health in Developed Nations   412
PROFILE: ARABS AND BLACKS IN AN
INDUSTRIAL AMERICAN CITY   415
Conclusions   423
Resources   427

Appendix: Projects in Medical
Anthropology   429
References Cited   433
Index   460

PREFACE

As an introduction to the anthropological study of health and disease patterns in human populations, this text takes an ecological perspective. The major theme of the book, influenced greatly by the writing of René Dubos and Alexander Alland, Jr., is that the distribution of disease over time and across geographic space is directly related to a population's role in its ecosystem. A community's health closely reflects the nature of its adaptation to the environment. Through this emphasis on the ways ecological concepts contribute to the theoretical development of medical anthropology, we attempt to give unity to an interdisciplinary science that uses clinical, epidemiological, and ethnographic approaches to health problems. The organization of the book reflects, we believe, the organization of medical anthropology itself—a new and growing field, strongly eclectic, yet in search of one or more theoretical frameworks to give it direction and a sense of identity.

Medical Anthropology in Ecological Perspective is for undergraduate students. We have discovered that undergraduates planning careers in health-related professions are interested in taking a course in medical anthropology, especially if the course stands alone and requires no prerequisite general anthropology course. Typically, about 65 percent of the students in McElroy's undergraduate medical anthropology course are majors in a nursing, premedical, or other health science program, while only 25 percent are anthropology, sociology, or psychology majors. Up to 70 percent of those enrolled in the course have taken no previous course in anthropology. We have tried to develop a textbook that allows beginning students to understand what anthropology is and the meaning of some key concepts in anthropology such as evolution, adaptation, cultural systems, and ethnography. At the same time, advanced students can apply their knowledge of general anthropology to problems of health maintenance and population dynamics. Anthropology majors will be familiar with many concepts and terms used in the text, but they will find their comprehension of these concepts enriched as they learn about the contributions of the anthropological subdisciplines to the development of medical anthropology.

In teaching medical anthropology and cultural ecology to undergraduates, we have found students to be concerned about national and global problems of maternal and child health, malnutrition, overpopulation, and pollution. A perspective that integrates anthropological and ecological concepts makes sense to these students, and they report that it makes increasing sense in continuing years of training as nurses, doctors, public health workers, anthropologists, and community organizers.

Not only has the ecological framework worked well in teaching medical anthropology, but we have also found interdisciplinary "case studies" to be a productive way of showing students how health scientists work. In the classroom, materials for this approach include films, slides, guest speakers, journal articles, and monographs—each study chosen to enrich the student's understanding of health processes in the context of cultural systems. In this text, we have attempted to replicate this teaching strategy in studies we call health profiles. The profiles illustrate how anthropologists and other scientists do research on health problems, thus giving the student exposure to methodological as well as substantive material.

The topics most emphasized in this book, such as reproduction, nutrition, culture change, and modernization, reflect our general training and special research interests. McElroy's interests in the cultural antecedents and consequences of stress, the dynamics of culture contact, and the health impact of modernization are especially reflected in the last three chapters. These interests developed out of training by James A. Clifton in studies of Potawatomi contact history and modern reservation communities and by John J. Honigmann and Dorothea Leighton in studies of acculturating Inuit on Baffin Island. More recent projects by McElroy on rural development in northern Iran and in health facilities in West Germany and the United States also contribute to ideas developed in the last three chapters of the book. Townsend's grounding in an ecological–evolutionary approach as a student at the University of Michigan is reflected throughout the text but most strongly in chapters 4 through 6. Her field work in Papua New Guinea and Peru was concerned with the cultural adaptation of peoples living in tropical forest regions. Postdoctoral study in the Mental Retardation Center at UCLA helped Townsend in thinking through some of the methodological issues discussed in this text as well as turning attention to health problems in the United States.

We would like to acknowledge and thank the persons who helped in producing this text. We appreciate our students' evaluations of drafts of chapters. We are also indebted to the following individuals who reviewed the manuscript at various stages and made many helpful suggestions: George Armelagos, University of Massachusetts; Marcha Flint, Montclair State College; Gail Harrison, University of Arizona; Edward E. Hunt, Jr., The Pennsylvania State University; Marshall Hurlich, University of Washington; Michael H. Logan, University of Tennessee; Pertti J. Pelto, University of Connecticut; and A. T. Steegmann, Jr., State University of New York at Buffalo. Bill Townsend and Roger Glasgow were a great help as friendly critics; their confidence in our project provided the support we needed at crucial points. And special thanks and appreciation go to Jeremiah Lyons.

Without the energy and assistance of many people this book would not have been finished, and we are grateful. We hope our ideas will prove a useful framework for learning. The text is an experiment in introducing an eclectic field of study within a given theoretical perspective, and we welcome response from those who use the text.

Ann McElroy

Patricia K. Townsend

INTRODUCTION

Bones in a Mayan tomb, blood pressure records in rural Mississippi, crowding in Calcutta, and bottle-fed Eskimo babies are among the diverse concerns of medical anthropology that this text will consider. Reaching widely across space and time for its materials, medical anthropology builds a bridge between the health sciences and anthropology. Crossing the bridge in one direction are persons trained in the health sciences who have come to sense a need to see health and disease in the broad context of a total way of life. Anthropology's comparative framework helps medically trained people avoid a limited one-culture perspective, to see how social and environmental factors affect health, and to be aware of alternative ways of understanding and treating disease.

Coming from the other side, persons trained in anthropology have found that strategies for maintaining health are an especially significant and revealing part of the cultures they seek to understand. The holistic approach of medical anthropology views humans as multidimensional: as biological organisms, as social persons, and as beings who communicate and maintain cultural systems. Each of these dimensions includes aspects of health maintenance that reflect larger cultural patterns.

Anthropology has usually emphasized that health and healing are best understood in terms of a given society's system of ethnomedicine, and the "insider's view" is necessary to understand how a society defines and diagnoses disease. Western medicine, on the other hand, usually considers disease as a clinical entity that can be diagnosed and treated while ignoring the cultural context. To strike a balance between these two points of view, this text will emphasize a multidimensional view of health and disease.

A type of research recently emerging in medical anthropology offers the kind of broad, holistic, and interdisciplinary framework that we seek. This research approach, medical ecology, emphasizes the health implications of interactions between human groups and their physical and biological environments (Fabrega 1974:46, 59 ff.). With its interest in how human populations adapt to environmental problems, maintain health, and persist over time, medical ecology provides a useful balance to the clinical preoccupation with disease and the anthropological focus on ethnomedicine. When the unit of analysis is a total ecosystem, rather than simply the individual or the society, health and disease become indicators of the group's effectiveness in dealing with the environment (Dubos 1975: xvii).

The ecological approach is relatively new in medical anthropology, and its potentially great contribution has not yet been fully realized. We have found that the dynamic concept of ecosystems helps in understanding how environmental changes and fluctuations affect rates and patterns of disease. Using this systems model, one can see how human technology sets off environmental changes that affect health. Cultural beliefs, rituals, and taboos further affect the use of technology, the exploitation of resources, population growth, and other components of human ecology related to health and survival.

In chapter 1 we trace the linkages in this systems approach, constructing a general framework for thinking about how health, community, and environment are related. We discuss how this framework can be applied to both simple and complex societies, including our own, and how each of the anthropological subdisciplines has contributed to the development of medical anthropology.

The special contributions to medical ecology made by the various disciplines in the clinical sciences, the environmental sciences, and the social sciences are outlined in chapter 2. Field work—intensive, on-the-spot observational study—has a prominent place in medical anthropology. The methods of field work used in distant locales such as Papua, New Guinea are put to equally good use in locales as close to home as southern California, as extended examples in this chapter illustrate.

A primary concern of medical anthropology is the way health and disease are related to the adaptation of human groups over a wide geographic range and across a broad span of time, from prehistory to the future. The third chapter explains and illustrates the adaptive processes of adjustment and change that enhance a population's survival in a given environment. These adaptive processes include genetic change, physiological adjustments, and cultural responses to problems.

Chapter 4 explores the changing patterns of birth, disease, and death that have accompanied the evolution of ever-larger societies and more complicated cultures. Death in infancy and early childhood from infectious disease is frequent in agricultural societies; death in old age from heart disease and cancer is typical of industrial societies. These contrasting patterns are founded in altered relationships to the environment.

Food is basic to health, but the kinds and amounts provided to people vary greatly in different cultures and environments, as discussed in chapters 5 and 6. Chapter 5 follows an evolutionary framework like that of chapter 4, dealing with food in hunting-gathering societies, agricultural societies, and industrial societies. Nutrition through the life cycle from infancy to old age is the subject of chapter 6.

Chapter 7 introduces a topic often neglected in medical anthropology, the factor of stress in health and disease. From laboratory studies by psychologists and physiologists, we have learned how important a role stress plays in the health of urban people. We need to know more about how environmental stress affects people in all types of culture and how it has influenced human evolution; this chapter discusses initial efforts by medical anthropologists to study those questions.

The last two chapters deal with the health problems of culture contact, modernization, and economic development. Culture change sparked by the introduction of new economic systems or by conquest and colonialism often disrupts ecosystems and affects health. Continuing change exerts stress on native peoples and ethnic minorities throughout the world. We hope that the information in chapters 8 and

9 will increase the understanding of how rapid, poorly planned change can create critical health problems, and how applied medical anthropologists can help alleviate some of these problems.

ORGANIZATION OF THE TEXT

Each chapter begins with a *preview,* a short summary of the content of the chapter. The preview can serve as a study guide, allowing the reader to anticipate the basic concepts and major examples of the chapter. The student wishing to review for class discussion or exams will find the previews and the *conclusions* of each chapter a useful combination. While the previews provide an overview of content, the conclusions highlight controversies in the field and discuss questions of relevance.

Following the conclusions in each chapter, we provide a set of *resources* for further study, an annotated list of recommended readings and films for classroom use. Many of the resources listed expand and illustrate ethnographic cases introduced in the chapter. The readings recommended are useful for students planning papers and projects, an integral part of learning medical anthropology. In addition, a list of recommended *student projects* is provided as an appendix to the text. Each of these projects has been carried out by students in McElroy's medical anthropology course, who report that the opportunity to do "field work" in their own community greatly enriches the learning process and helps in career planning.

The text also includes twenty *health profiles,* distributed throughout the chapters. In anthropology courses, students usually read ethnographies, descriptions of the way of life of a people written by anthropologists who have participated in that life for an extended period. Similarly, a course in medical anthropology should have a set of medical ethnographies, but very few are available. Courses in this subject have only recently been developed, and most studies of health written by anthropologists are geared to a professional audience rather than to students. In preparing this series of short health profiles for use by students, we hoped to provide the kind of ethnographic detail and comparative perspective that is essential in communicating how health and culture are related.

The health profiles have a range of purposes. Some illustrate how research in medical anthropology is carried out. For example, a health profile of *kuru*, a mysterious disease in New Guinea that killed women and children but spared adult males, shows how research collaboration among neurologists, physicians, and cultural anthropologists revealed an explanation of the disease. In chapter 4 you will read about coauthor Pat Townsend's methods of studying family size regulation in a New Guinea group, and in chapter 9 a profile of health in an industrial United States city describes how an East African anthropologist, Simeon Chilungu, compared American blacks with Arab immigrants.

Other health profiles—on hypertension, or high blood pressure, mental retardation, and sickle cell anemia—explore health problems of significance to modern society from a holistic viewpoint. Our interest in how people live past the age of ninety and beyond in full health is explored in a profile on the peoples of the Caucasus Mountains in Russia, while a profile on famine in the Sahel of Africa documents the ecological and economic factors that drastically reduce life expectancy.

Some of the health profiles illustrate the health risks of the transition to modern ways of life. A profile of the health problems of contemporary Inuit, or Eskimos, of Arctic Canada in chapter 8 contrasts with a profile of traditional Inuit adaptation in the first chapter. A study of schistosomiasis in chapter 9 shows that attempts to increase food production through irrigation can lead to increase in diseases caused by water-borne flukes.

The health profiles are designed to carry forward the essential points of each chapter, and they function as an integral part of each chapter. They are not supplementary readings in any sense of the word. Although the profiles may draw on materials that were not collected by researchers who identify themselves as medical anthropologists, each views a problem in the way a medical anthropologist would, simultaneously looking for the big picture or whole context and for the small ecological and physiological details that help in understanding the context.

Thus while the health profiles vary in their specific purposes, encompassing methodology, disease explanations, descriptions of the health of a group of people, or discussion of a research controversy, the overall purpose of these studies is to carry the text forward with ethnographic vehicles for learning. We have attempted to include many of the examples that anthropologists consider to be classic in the field: the link between agriculture, malaria, and the sickle cell trait in West Africa; schistosomiasis and irrigation; arctic hysteria and the calcium-deficiency hypothesis; the ecology and nutrition of the !Kung San of the Kalahari Desert in Africa. Other examples have been selected because they represent new directions in medical anthropology or topics that have been neglected until recently.

Many of the health profiles can serve as models for student projects; for example, the study of Kepone poisoning in chapter 4. Even the health profiles that deal with people who seem very distant and isolated provide working models for student projects on concerns closer to home. The study of infant mortality among the Inuit of northern Canada and the Sanio-Hiowe of New Guinea, for example, may suggest ways the student might look at relationships between infant mortality and economic and environmental factors in the student's own city.

THE PURPOSE OF THE TEXT

We often hear students ask about the relevance of medical anthropology for their lives and careers. The first chapter, for example, discusses two isolated groups, the Inuit and the Yanomamo, a tropical forest people in South America. Why study those people, when our own health problems need attention?

Our answer is that a comparative perspective helps us understand the problems of our own society. By studying a small community whose medical history is documented or whose nutrition, blood types, and immune responses to disease can be studied directly, anthropologists can better understand relations among technology, ecology, and health in larger, more complex populations. By looking at the impact of technological change on a natural ecosystem, we can reconstruct the kinds of changes that transformed our own environment. When we look at how arctic hunters, African farmers, and Japanese industrialists solve certain survival problems and inadvertently create new ones, we realize that we are not alone in paying health costs to maintain a certain way of life. Each society pays certain "costs" in order to survive, and these costs are often exacted in terms of human suffering and deprivation.

A central purpose of this text, then, is to demonstrate the value of the comparative perspective in health studies and the value of a holistic, ecological framework for learning medical anthropology. We hope to start a dialogue between students in different disciplines. Students of the health sciences and the social sciences have much to learn from each other, in spite of departmental boundaries and curricular fragmentation. Medical anthropology thrives on interdisciplinary stimulation. It is a research-and-teaching approach that allows people from different disciplines to plan research together and students with different majors to share their knowledge and work on problems together. It is exciting, for example, when nursing students who understand the dynamics of disease transmission can exchange information with anthropology majors, who can in turn explain social networks in a community. As they discover together that the lines of disease transmission parallel the lines of social communication in a given case study, a unique kind of learning is taking place. This is the very same kind of interdisciplinary collaboration that is at the core of medical anthropology, and it is only through such collaboration that we can begin to understand and solve the critical environmental problems that face North Americans today and threaten the future of peoples all over the world.

The Ecology of Health and Disease

CHAPTER 1

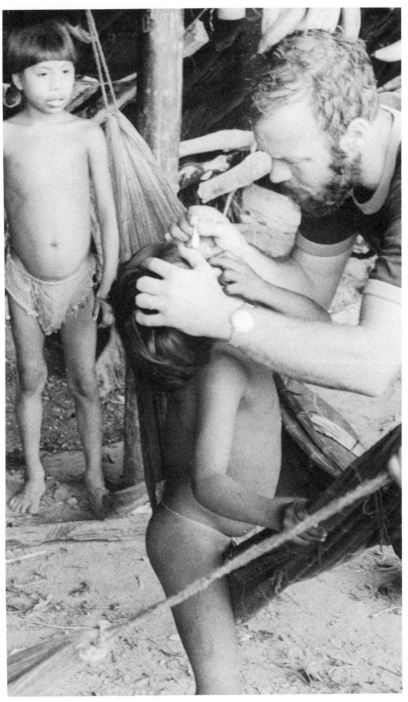

PREVIEW

Medical anthropology, the study of human health in cultural and environmental context, compares health and disease patterns of both isolated and modern populations through a variety of interdisciplinary research approaches. The field of *medical ecology* is a new approach in medical anthropology that views health and disease as reflections of ecological relationships within a population, between neighboring populations, and among the life forms and physical components of a habitat. Medical ecology considers health to be a measure of how well a population has adapted to its environment.

To illustrate how health can be studied through ecological concepts, this chapter discusses two isolated populations, the Yanomamo of Venezuela and Brazil and the Inuit of arctic North America. We consider the response of the Yanomamo to a measles epidemic and discuss the factors that contributed to transmission of the disease. The Inuit study describes how an arctic people traditionally used available raw materials, derived maximal nourishment from an all-meat diet, managed to stay warm, and kept the population size within environmental limits.

Medical anthropology has developed through studying the survival strategies of small, isolated populations like the Yanomamo and Inuit, but it is also productive for understanding the health problems of more complex societies. People living in cities modify their environments extensively, but they share with all societies the basic problems of allocating space, food, and other resources. The comparative perspective of medical anthropology, combined with the interdisciplinary teamwork of medical ecology, allows us to consider a wide range of human solutions to environmental problems and the health repercussions of those solutions.

As an academic subdiscipline, medical anthropology incorporates research techniques and theoretical concepts from each of the four major fields of anthropology: archaeology, human biology, cultural anthropology, and linguistics. Each of these fields contributes to the study of human adaptation, one of the central concerns of medical ecology.

STUDYING THE YANOMAMO: AN EXAMPLE OF MEDICAL ECOLOGY

In 1968 a team of scientists preparing an expedition to study the health of a group of South American Indians received word that measles had broken out in the study region. Through analysis of antibodies in blood samples taken earlier, the scientists knew that many of these Indians had never been exposed to measles. Thus there was a chance of a serious epidemic.

This was the third trip that the research team, headed by the geneticist James Neel, had made to study the Yanomamo, a population of about 10,000 Indians living in tropical forests along the Brazil–Venezuela border. With the collaboration of the cultural anthropologist Napoleon Chagnon, the team collected data on genetic inheritance, reproduction, nutrition, growth, disease resistance, and many other health characteristics (Neel 1970). Other tribes in the region were also being studied by United States and South American scientists in a multidisciplinary effort to understand and compare the evolutionary history, health, and general adaptation of isolated peoples who have been exposed to civilization only recently.

A measles epidemic among other Indians in Brazil in 1954 had been devastating. Among those groups receiving no medical care, 26.8 percent had died. Concerned about the susceptibility of the Yano-mamo, the research team had planned to vaccinate every village systematically, keeping careful records, monitoring individual reactions to the vaccine, and conducting other medical tests. (The chapter-opening photo shows Dr. Chagnon at work.) Neel and his associates had not expected to be fighting an epidemic, but under the circumstances they felt responsible to help medical auxiliaries and missionaries in a rapid effort to vaccinate unexposed people and to treat those suffering from measles already (Neel et al. 1970). Had measles been as common among the Yanomamo as malaria was, the research team might not have chosen to spend time immunizing people, but the Yanomamo had not been exposed to contagious infectious diseases like measles, rubella, or polio and had no immunities to these diseases.

The 1968 epidemic began at missions where Yanomamo were visiting. It was the dry season, a time of traveling to missions as well as trading and feasting between Indian villages. Some Indians contracted the disease from Brazilians at the missions and returned home to entertain visitors during the highly contagious eight- to thirteen-day incubation period. When these people finally developed symptoms, their Yanomamo visitors left in alarm, but they had already been exposed and unwittingly carried the virus with them. Concerned kinsfolk, hearing of the illness, rushed to visit sick relatives and became exposed themselves. Even enemies passed the disease on— warriors who raided a village of sick people and captured one of the women of the village were suffering from measles within a few weeks. The disease spread to fifteen villages in two months.

Medical care and antibiotics to treat respiratory complications helped hold the death rate to only 9 percent of all patients. A later study of blood samples showed that Indians exposed to measles during the epidemic had developed normal antibody levels. Their reaction was similar to the typical immune reaction of Caucasian populations. There is little evidence that these Indians are genetically more susceptible to measles than whites, as was previously believed. Neel believes that the high death rates in other groups exposed to measles have been partly due to the collapse of village life and lack of medical care at a time when everyone is weak, feverish, dehydrated, and unable to get food.

The impact of measles or any other pathogen on a group of people depends on several factors. How the community organizes to care for the sick is as important as the ability to form antibodies or the pattern of transmission between communities. Through the study of the Yanomamo responses to a newly introduced disease, the research team gained a better understanding of how social, biological, and environmental factors interact and influence health.

The Yanomamo research is an example of **medical ecology,** a special approach to doing medical anthropology that emphasizes the *study of health and disease in environmental context.* Medical ecology is concerned with one basic question, whether it is asked about hunters in a South American forest, Egyptian farmers, or Manhattan city dwellers: How do these people survive in this particular environment? How do they cope with disease? And how do they solve problems that affect their health?

To understand survival processes, one must ask many questions about the resources of the environment that affect survival. The medical ecologist asks: What are the sources of energy, including nourishment, in this environment? How do humans interact with animals and plants, microbes and fellow humans, who must also derive energy from this environment? Must people remain dispersed in small villages of allies and relatives, like the Yanomamo, to support themselves and protect their territory? Or can they crowd together in dense cities, allocating resources along ethnic boundaries and through a complex market economy and food industry? Is the population growing, and how rapidly will it exceed its resources if growth is not checked? Or is the population declining, and why? The answer to each of these questions will reflect a system of relationships among health, community, and environment.

Medical ecology is a new field of study that meshes three established disciplines: anthropology, medicine, and ecology. It provides a framework for understanding medical problems that differs from the usual approaches of clinical and statistical investigations. One difference is that medical ecology, as described by Fabrega (1974:46 ff.), is **holistic,** that is, it deals with the entire system of factors that affect health. A second feature of medical ecology is that it is **multi-disciplinary,** drawing on theoretical concepts from many fields. Medical ecology projects often involve teamwork by specialists, as in the Yanomamo study. Most projects have been done among small, isolated populations, but the basic approach of medical ecology can readily be used by medical anthropologists in studies of environment and health in larger societies.

Medical ecology is one of many approaches that medical anthropologists use to study health problems holistically. Medical anthropologists are eclectic, drawing on the data and research methods of many sciences. Their flexibility derives from the fact that medical anthropology is a new field of study. There is no formula for doing a medical anthropology study, no single type of training for a professional career in medical anthropology. To explain this unusual degree of flexibility, we will sketch how the field has developed through the contributions of each of the traditional subdisciplines of anthropology and how it bridges the biological, cultural, and linguistic specializations of the discipline.

ENVIRONMENT, CULTURE, AND HEALTH: THE SCOPE OF MEDICAL ANTHROPOLOGY

Like all anthropological subdisciplines, medical anthropology is concerned with human ways of life, with special emphasis on the maintenance of health in human populations. Medical anthropology has emerged as an identified subdiscipline only in the last twenty years or so, although concern with health has long been a part of anthropological studies. The national Society for Medical Anthropology was founded in 1968; by 1978 the membership numbered over 1700, including not only anthropologists but also many health professionals.

Anthropology has four traditional subdisciplines: physical anthropology, archaeology, cultural anthropology, and anthropological linguistics. Ideally, each anthropologist receives training in all four subdisciplines. To be truly holistic in studying human behavior, one needs to know something about human biology, prehistory, cultural systems, and language processes. But in the last few decades, the subdisciplines have been drifting farther apart into increasing specialization, and in practice most anthropologists have specialized research training in only one or two areas of the discipline. Medical anthropology, with its emphasis on viewing humans as both biological and cultural creatures, is one of the few fields that bridges the subdisciplines. Although each of the subdisciplines has many interests unrelated to health problems, each can contribute to medical anthropology. An unexpected dividend of recent work in medical anthropology has been that focusing on problems of medical ecology has brought the subdisciplines back together.

Anthropological Subdisciplines and Medical Anthropology

Physical anthropology, also called biological anthropology or human biology, studies the physical origins and variation of the human species. To study human origins, physical anthropologists interpret the fossil record as well as studying the behavior of living nonhuman primates. Physical anthropologists also describe physical variation—such as in skin color, blood type, hair form, bone structure, and stature—between contemporary human groups. *Anthropometry*, the statistical measurement of the external dimensions of the human body, contributes to research on human growth and development (see figure 1.1). More often, though, the variation that gives the most information about human adaptation is not these surface characteristics but rather characteristics like blood groups that are observable only in the laboratory. The physical and biochemical characteristics of humans are shaped by the genes, which direct the processes of growth and development at the cellular level in interaction with the environment during development. James Neel's studies of Yanomamo genetics and population structure exemplify the work of biological anthropology, as do studies on sickle cell trait and lactase deficiency, which we discuss in chapter 3.

Prehistoric archaeology reconstructs the way of life of prehistoric peoples by analyzing artifacts and other material remains, including

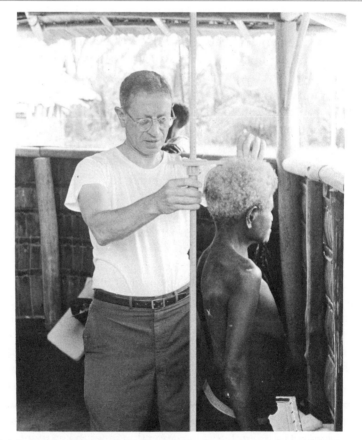

FIGURE 1.1   Human biologist Dr. Albert Damon measuring a Solomon Islander.
Photo courtesy of Fitchburg Art Museum (Fitchburg, Massachusetts).

human skeletons. Although its methods of excavating, recording, and analyzing data are similar to those of classical archaeology, prehistoric archaeology normally lacks historical documents that give clues to interpreting findings at the site. However, other anthropologists' studies of the cultures of living populations give archaeologists help in interpreting the remains of past cultures. Of all the subfields of anthropology, archaeology would seem least likely to contribute to medical ecology, but in studying the evidence of the material culture and social organization of past populations, one can see how health, culture, and environment are related. Some of the most interesting studies are comparisons between populations living in the same area at different times. For example, between A.D. 550 and 900, Mayan culture in Central America was at its peak. The skeletal remains of Mayans who lived during this same period show that people of the common class were getting shorter, while the elite—those who were buried in tombs—remained the same average height. Simultaneously, certain food remains, such as snail shells and animal bones, also became more scarce. The evidence suggests that nutrition was declining during this period, at least for the working class (Haviland 1967).

By far the most important subdiscipline in the development of medical anthropology has been *cultural anthropology*. According to the pioneer in this field, George M. Foster (1978:3 ff.), three types of studies by cultural anthropologists form the roots of contemporary medical anthropology:

1. the study of primitive medicine, witchcraft, and magic
2. studies of personality and mental health in diverse cultural settings
3. involvement in international public health and planned community change programs

Anthropologists who describe primitive and traditional cultures have always included accounts of medical practices and beliefs about disease in their writings. Shamans who appear to suck foreign objects from a patient in pain, herbal medicines, and drug-induced trance are all part of the cultural sphere studied by ethnographers, who categorized these patterns as ritual or magic. Medical anthropologists study healing rituals as a part of *ethnomedicine*. While ethnomedicine began as the study of health practices and beliefs of non-Western peoples and of folk medicine within Western culture, the concept is now expanding to mean any health maintenance system operating within a given cultural matrix. We explain this concept further in chapter 3.

Another long-term concern of cultural anthropology that is now part of medical anthropology is the study of culture and personality. Anthropologists with this interest study relationships between child-rearing practices and adult personality, family relations and larger societal institutions. Culture and personality specialists also study *folk illnesses* or ethnic psychoses, that is, categories of mental illness specific to particular cultures. Some of the best known of these are *susto* in Hispanic America, *wiitiiko* psychosis among the Cree and Ojibwa of Eastern Canada, and *latah* in Southeast Asia. Each is a culturally patterned form of mental illness.

Anthropologists have long been interested in the process of culture change from a theoretical point of view, but particularly in the years during and since World War II, *applied anthropology* has developed to put this understanding of change to work in practical ways. International public health programs made use of anthropological findings to attempt to improve the effectiveness of communication and the introduction of new types of health care into developing countries. More recently, applied anthropologists have become involved in much the same kind of cross-cultural trouble-shooting within our own society. They have worked in urban programs that provide health care to people of divergent cultural backgrounds.

Two other areas of anthropology have more recently influenced the development of medical anthropology. *Ecological anthropology,* like early studies in ethnomedicine, has not focused on health problems directly but rather on culture and environment. Nevertheless, there are implications for health in what cultural ecologists have learned about techniques of food production, settlement patterns, and population growth. Medical ecology overlaps considerably in method and theory with ecological anthropology.

Evolutionary theory is a fifth influence in the development of medical anthropology, providing a time depth not present in ethnographic, psychological, and applied studies. The long-range view helps us understand how evolutionary mechanisms affect health and, ultimately, survival. The concept of environmental adaptation through evolutionary mechanisms is a key concept of medical ecology.

Anthropological linguistics, like archaeology, seems at first glance to have little relevance to medical anthropology. Most of the work of linguists analyzing the sound systems and grammars of the 5000 or so languages of the world has little to do with health. However, a major contribution to medical anthropology has been the development of a methodology called *ethnoscience* or *ethnosemantics,* an approach to culture that attempts to find out how the participants in that culture categorize their experience. Ethnographic field work using participant observation is combined with specific techniques derived from linguistics to elicit culturally significant categories and to get at the native's or insider's point of view.

You Owe Yourself a Drunk, a study of skid road alcoholics in Seattle by James P. Spradley (1970), is an outstanding example of the use of ethnosemantics in studying a problem of concern to medical anthropology. One of the earliest findings of the study was that the concept of "skid road alcoholic" was not a culturally appropriate term. The men did not consider themselves alcoholics; rather, they had other, nonmedical conceptions of their own identity. In jail, they categorized themselves as *inmates,* but out of jail they classified themselves within a system of fifteen different kinds of *tramps.* The fifteen terms, shown in figure 1.2, are used by the men themselves. For example, both a box car tramp and a ding travel by freight train, but a ding is specialized in begging for a living while a box car tramp gets a living by a wide variety of strategies such as working, selling his blood, searching for discards, or taking a mission handout. An airedale is much like a box car tramp, but he walks rather than riding the trains. Each of these terms describes survival strategies important to these urban nomads. Ethnosemantic methods allow us to get the perspective of the participant in the culture rather than imposing outsiders' categories.

Spradley's study, like other ethnoscience studies of categories of disease and diagnostic procedures (cf. Frake 1961; Fabrega 1974:223 ff.), is concerned with more than just linguistic categories. The terminology of identity used by Seattle tramps also reflects ways they have adapted to a difficult environment. The study goes beyond the issue of health to a focus on how humans adapt to adversity—in this case, poverty, addiction to alcohol, and continual involvement with legal authorities.

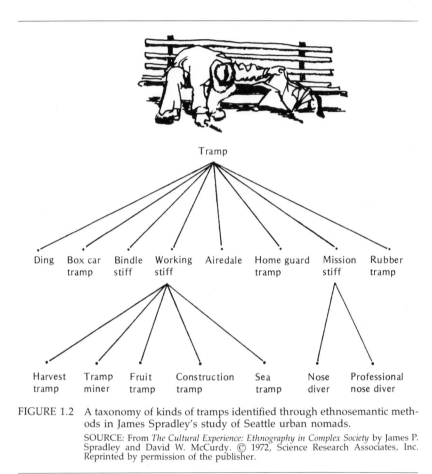

FIGURE 1.2   A taxonomy of kinds of tramps identified through ethnosemantic methods in James Spradley's study of Seattle urban nomads.

SOURCE: From *The Cultural Experience: Ethnography in Complex Society* by James P. Spradley and David W. McCurdy. © 1972, Science Research Associates, Inc. Reprinted by permission of the publisher.

A Focus on Adaptation

Whatever their subdisciplinary orientation, whether ethnosemantics, human biology, or ethnomedicine, most medical anthropology studies deal in some respect with **adaptation,** that is, changes and modifications that enable a person or group to survive in a given environment. Like any other animal, humans adapt through a variety of biological mechanisms and behavioral strategies, but they depend on cultural patterns of adaptation more than do other species. They use cultural adaptive mechanisms in banding together and coordinating their efforts to get food, in protecting themselves from the weather, in training their young. However harsh or dangerous the environment, humans usually have the flexibility to survive, but only in groups. And so pervasive is the human dependence on learned rather than innate or instinctive strategies that it makes sense to consider human culture as a mechanism of adaptation specific to human evolution.

As humans hunt animals and cultivate crops, find protection against arctic blizzards and desert sandstorms through clothing and dwellings, teach their young about the environment, form alliances and exchange goods with neighbors, and so on, they create survival-promoting relationships within an environmental system. These are relationships within the group, with neighboring groups, and with the plants and animals of the habitat. A central premise of medical anthropology is that the group's level of health reflects the nature and quality of these relationships. As Lieban (1973) says, "health and disease are measures of the effectiveness with which human groups, combining biological and cultural resources, adapt to their environments" (p. 1031).

A key idea of the book is that *health is a measure of environmental adaptation,* and that health can be studied through ecological models. We organize this text around some fundamental ideas about how ecological systems operate, how energy is acquired and consumed by organisms in a food web, and which factors affect population size and density. Although sometimes we do not talk about health and illness directly, but rather about energy flow, subsistence strategies, population control, and similar concepts, all the material we cover ultimately deals with the question of how ecology affects the health of the individual and of the group.

A WORKING MODEL OF ECOLOGY AND HEALTH

In this text, we use the working model shown in figure 1.3. A model like this is a visual aid that suggests some important relationships

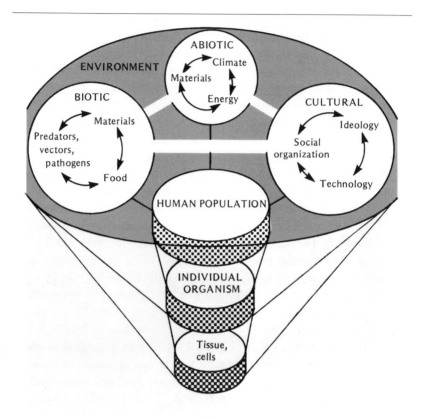

FIGURE 1.3   The environment that impinges on a human population is made up of
physical, biological, and cultural components forming a total ecosystem.

among variables. It shows that the environment that impinges on
people can be broken down into three parts: the physical, or abiotic,
environment; the biotic environment; and the cultural environment.
The parts are interdependent and continually in interaction; a change
in one variable frequently leads to a change in another. Although we
usually focus on the separate parts and think of them as causes and
effects of change processes, it is also possible to imagine all these
individual spheres and variables functioning as a single unit. If you
look at the whole this way, you have a model of an **ecosystem,** a set of
relationships among organisms and their environments.

The model shows that in analyzing the impact of people on their environment and the impact of environment on people, we can focus on the individual or the population, the latter including individuals as cultural and biological beings. For certain purposes, we may want to lower our focus to events and processes on the level of the organ system, tissue, cell, or even molecule.

Let's take an example of the variables we consider as we shift levels of focus. An arctic hunter puts on his snow goggles to protect his eyes from the glare of sun on snow and ice, which is especially intense in the spring months. The goggles are a material artifact, a part of the cultural environment that impinges on the hunter, modifying the impact of the physical environment on his vision and preventing snow blindness. The goggles themselves are made from bone, a material coming from the biological environment. As we look at this simple act of putting on snow goggles, we can focus on the effect on the whole person's functioning, or we can lower the level of focus and consider effects on his eyes, his pupils, and his retinas. We can also raise the level of focus to the population and consider the effects of this artifact on the group's success in stalking seals and finding enough food to survive.

Where do health and disease fit into this model? A change in any one of these variables can lead to certain ecological and physiological imbalances. Too severe an imbalance will be defined as disease or stress. For instance, change in climate may lead to a sharp decrease in human food supplies. Adaptive responses within the cultural sphere—say, a shift in food production techniques—can easily change relationships with other organisms in the ecosystem, and this change may involve an increase in disease.

Our model delineates several points about the ecology of health and disease. First, there are no single causes of disease. The immediate, clinically detectable stimulus for disease may be a virus, vitamin deficiency, or an intestinal parasite, but disease itself is ultimately due to a chain of factors related to ecosystemic imbalances. Second, health and disease are part of a set of physical, biological, and cultural subsystems that continually affect one another. The holistic approach in medical ecology attempts to account for as many of these variables as possible. But the analysis of so many variables is difficult conceptually and not always possible in research design: our brains can handle only so much information, and research is always limited by time and money. The model allows us to look at only part of the overall system; for example, we can look at how technological change directly leads to increase in disease. While remaining aware that many ecosystemic variables are involved in this change, we can choose to study only a few variables at a time.

The model presented here provides a framework for the study of health in environmental context. It does not specify what factors maintain health other than to suggest that change in ecological relations may adversely affect health, but not invariably, for adaptation to disease inherently involves ecological changes also. A systems approach precludes easy explanations, but it does allow you to think about health and disease in ways that are both realistic and challenging. With this open model, you can analyze many of the specific ethnographic cases discussed in this text, assessing the relative impact of one or another variable on health and comparing the adaptive strategies of various populations in terms of health benefits and disease risks.

The following health profile describes how traditional arctic peoples survived in the past through an unusually high-protein diet, remarkable ways of keeping warm, and maintenance of almost zero population growth. A parallel profile in chapter 8 shows how modernization has affected the health and population growth of these people. Both studies illustrate the holistic and multidisciplinary approach of medical ecology. The first depicts the adaptive patterns of the traditional Central Arctic Eskimo as recorded by early ethnographers, explorers, and physicians and as reconstructed through archaeology and ethnohistory. The profile in chapter 8 traces changes in patterns of disease, nutrition, and birth rates during contact and modernization, as documented in history, in clinical findings, and by cultural anthropologists.

PROFILE: ARCTIC ADAPTATIONS

Eskimos tell a story of a woman who raised a polar bear cub as her son. She nursed him, gave him a soft warm bed next to hers, and talked to the cub as if to a child. When the bear grew up, he brought seals and salmon home to his adopted mother. Because of his skill in hunting, the people in the camp became envious and decided to kill him. The old woman offered her own life in place of the bear's, but the people refused. In tears she told him to go away and save his life. The bear gently placed his huge paw on her head and hugged her, saying "Good mother, Kunikdjuaq will always be on the lookout for you and serve you as best he can" (Boas 1964:230–231).

Of all the arctic animals, the polar bear is the most admired by Inuit, as Eskimo call themselves. (The singular form is *Inuk*.) They point out how much the bear's hunting techniques resemble their own: slowly stalking seals who lie sunning themselves on ice floes or waiting quietly at the seal's breathing-holes in the ice. Because they admire and envy the bear and compete with it for food, Inuit feel a sense of ambivalent kinship with the bear, and sometimes they even name a child *nanook,* or "bear."

The symbolic closeness of the two species, bear and human, reflects their ecological relationship. They face similar problems: to get enough to eat in an ecosystem that supports relatively few species of animals and almost no edible plants, and to conserve body heat in a harsh climate. Both bears and humans are large animals with high caloric needs. Because food resources are dispersed and only seasonally available in varying locations, both bears and humans must also remain dispersed in small mobile units. Neither was seriously subjected to predation until humans acquired rifles about seventy years ago. Avoiding predators was far less a problem than finding food, keeping warm, and keeping population size within the limits of available food.

Bears have evolved solutions to these problems such as thick fur, semihibernation in winter, and social units not larger than three animals. Human solutions to the same problems are quite different. Lacking fur, they know how to turn animal fur into clothing for protection against cold. Unable to swim in icy arctic waters, the Inuit make boats. Rather than eating only a few species of large marine mammals, humans use nearly all species of both land and sea habitats (see figure 1.4).

Humans and bears live in the same habitat, but their total adaptation is very different because of the cultural component in

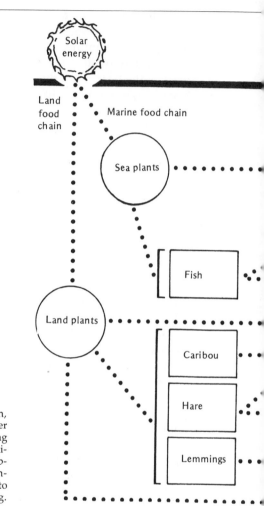

FIGURE 1.4 In the arctic food chain, humans differ from other mammals in exploiting nearly all species of animals in land and sea habitats. The species not consumed as food are fed to dogs or used for clothing.

human behavior. This health profile will describe traditional human adaptive patterns in the Central Arctic and discuss how these patterns affected the Inuit's health.

ALLOCATING ENERGY: SELECTIVITY IN EXPLOITATION The Arctic is depicted in movies and novels as a barren, frozen land where famine constantly threatens and people must eat everything available just to stay alive. The arctic tundra does have

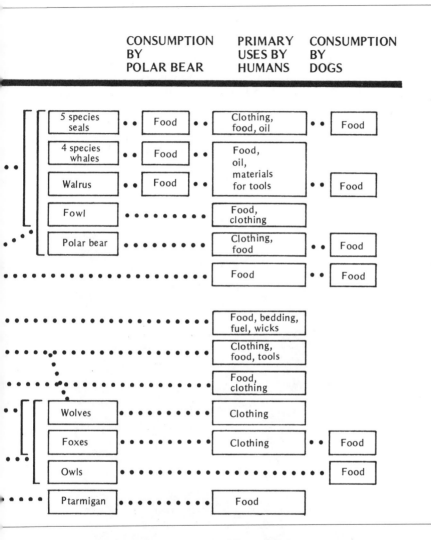

relatively few species of plants and animals, and it is a simple ecosystem compared with the complex tropical rain forest. But at least twenty species of game are available to Inuit for food, and they need to exploit heavily only four categories: fish, seals, whales, and caribou. Some animals are not eaten at all except during severe shortages, but as figure 1.4 shows, every animal and plant has some use. Before contact with traders, Inuit manufactured all artifacts from natural resources, mostly from animal products because wood and appropriate kinds of stone were scarce. Bone, ivory, sinew, antler, skin, fur, feathers, blubber—every part of the animal was used for something, from sewing needles to harpoons, water buckets to boats, snow shovels, lamp fuel, and boots. Even snow goggles were made to reduce the risk of snow blindness, one of the greatest hazards of spring hunting.

Inuit pursue game that provide maximal yield for minimal energy output or relatively low risk. They prefer species such as the seal and whale that provide a good return of meat and by-products such as skin, bones, and oil. Arctic char, a fish similar to salmon,

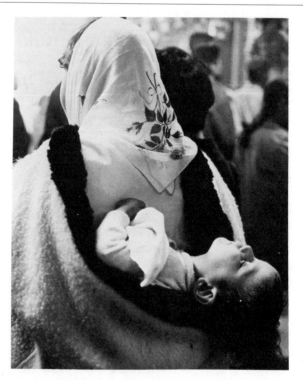

FIGURE 1.5   An Inuit child sleeps in an *amaut* or mother's parka. Store-bought duffel cloth has replaced traditional caribou fur, but the form of the garment continues to allow the woman free use of her hands and provides the child warmth and security.
Photo by Ann McElroy.

is an important seasonal resource because the return is excellent for the time and energy invested in netting and spearing as runs of char swim upstream to spawn. Migratory caribou herds also return a good yield and provide material for clothing.

Musk ox herds, in past centuries reliable sources of food and by-products, no longer figure in arctic ecosystems because the few remaining animals are protected by law from being hunted. The hunting of polar bears is also regulated by government quotas, but polar bears were never an important source of food, for several reasons. Hunting the bears was risky because a wounded bear would maul humans and dogs. Also, cooking polar bear meat, which is necessary to prevent trichinosis, is wasteful of fuel since most foods can be eaten raw. Finally, bear liver is so rich in vitamin A that it is dangerous to humans and dogs. Dogs, foxes, and wolves carry a tapeworm that can be transmitted to humans and cause severe effects if lodged in the brain, bone marrow, or kidney (Oswalt 1967:79). We have no evidence that Inuit were aware of the risk of tapeworm, but it is interesting that they ate these three animals only in times of great need.

The fact that some species such as the tiny and unpalatable lemmings are rarely eaten by humans supports the view of ecological anthropologists that food was normally fairly abundant in the traditional ecosystem (Kemp 1971). Only rarely were starving Inuit forced to cannibalism. What was more likely during shortages was that the small hunting group, usually fifteen to fifty people, would split into smaller units of one or two families and disperse in search of food. They would eat their dogs long before they would consider killing a person for food, which is an abhorrent idea to Inuit. Thus dogs provide not only transportation but also a reserve food supply.

Human relationships with dogs are as ambivalent as they are with polar bears. This is reflected in tales of dogs who married women. Their offspring became the ancestors of Indians, the traditional enemy of Inuit. Inuit have no love for their dogs, who can viciously maim a child, but they do depend on them for travel and as beasts of burden, and so they must feed them. Much energy goes into providing food for dogs. A Banks Island trapper annually brings in an average of 6226 pounds of meat;

4627 pounds will feed his nine dogs, while only 1599 pounds will go to his family (Usher 1971:85).

CONSUMING ENERGY: DIETARY PATTERNS Life in the Arctic requires consistently high energy levels. Both the intake and the output of energy are high. Traveling by dogsled means much running, pushing, and pulling; rarely is there a chance to ride. Each evening, a new snowhouse or tent must be erected, and in summer, water is hauled from inland pools and willow and

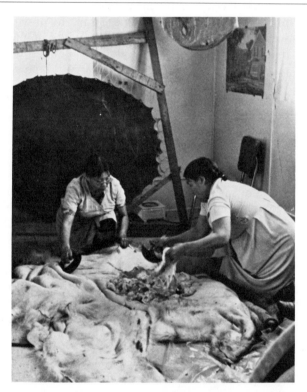

FIGURE 1.6   These Baffin Island women use a traditional *ulu*, woman's knife, to clean a polar bear skin. Lashed to the rack is the skin of a bearded seal, used to make boot soles. Hanging from the rafter is the soft, fine skin of the ringed seal, used for boot tops and clothing.

Photo by Ann McElroy.

heather are gathered for bedding. Men construct fish weirs by carrying hundreds of boulders, and women scrape animal skins for hours to soften them for sewing. Babies are nursed and carried on their mother's backs up to three years. Breast milk production requires extra calories, and it takes energy to carry a growing child five to ten hours a day. To help keep warm, Inuit enjoy strenuous wrestling, acrobatics, and races.

Inuit look stocky or even fat because of their bulky clothing and relatively short limbs, but they are actually lean and muscular and have little body fat to burn during food shortages. Adult men expend about 2700 calories per day and require between 2800 and 3100 calories to maintain a weight of about 140 pounds (63 kg) at an average height of 5 feet 3 inches (160 cm) (Rodahl 1963:103). Women's caloric needs are somewhat less. Because they do not hunt and stay in camp preparing skins and tending children, they conserve calories. But when they are nursing a child, digging for clams, chasing ptarmigan, or traveling, they need almost as many calories as the men do.

Inuit consume an average of 200 grams of protein per day, about 32 percent of their total caloric intake. This is far more than the average daily consumption of protein in the United States, 75 grams and 12 percent of intake (Draper 1977:311). Even a group of African hunters, the !Kung Bushmen of the Kalahari Desert, consume only an average of 93 grams of protein daily per person, 15 percent of total caloric intake (Lee 1968:39).

In contrast, Inuit carbohydrate consumption is very low, 10 grams daily and 2 percent of total intake (Draper 1977:311). Because of the cold and the long months of little daylight, it is not possible to raise food plants or to gather sufficient quantities of wild plants. Small portions of berries, sourgrass and sorrel, and sea kelp gathered in summer add variety but not enough vitamins to meet nutritional needs. As figure 1.4 shows, nearly all available food comes from animals, fish, and birds—all high-protein and high-fat foods. Fat consumption is very high: an average of 185 grams daily, representing 66 percent of the diet. The average American consumes less fat than this, about 117 grams daily as 42 percent of caloric intake (Draper 1977:311).

With this unbalanced diet of high protein, high fat, and low carbohydrates, we would expect health problems. And yet Inuit are well nourished, without deficiency diseases like scurvy and rickets or heart disease from cholesterol build-up. How do they manage to thrive on this diet?

In large quantities, meat can provide adequate amounts of all vitamins except ascorbic acid, vitamin C. Seal oil and fish are especially rich in vitamins A and D. Inuit prepare and eat meat in ways that maximize its nutritional value. For example, by eating meat raw, they preserve small quantities of vitamin C that would be lost in cooking. This was shown by the anthropologist-explorer Stefansson, who ate meat raw, frozen, or only lightly cooked just as the Inuit do in order to avoid developing scurvy (Draper 1977).

By eating the soft parts of animal bones, as well as dried fish and bird bones, Inuit compensate for the lack of other sources of calcium in their diet. Their molars are so hard and their jaw muscles so strong that they can crunch through bones easily. Nevertheless, some of them suffer from mild calcium deficiency, especially in winter when the lack of vitamin D from sunlight inhibits calcium absorption. This puts a particular strain on nursing women. The elderly are prone to a condition called osteoporosis, a decrease in bone mass that increases the risk of fractures. But rickets is very rare in children, probably because they are nursed for long periods.

Because of the low proportion of carbohydrates in the Inuit diet, the glucose needed for quick energy and for brain functioning is not readily available, but additional glucose can be synthesized from amino acids released from digested protein. Laboratory tests and medical records show that present Inuit populations have very efficient glucose metabolism and rarely show signs of diabetes except in cases of high carbohydrate consumption and obesity (Mouratoff, Carroll, and Scott 1967).

Inuit diets are high in fat, yet they have neither high cholesterol levels in the blood nor frequent heart disease. It is thought that the meat they eat is significantly lower in saturated fats than is commercial beef. For instance, caribou meat has a much higher proportion of polyunsaturated fatty acid content, 21 percent as compared to only 3 percent in beef (Draper 1977:312). A comparison of the diets of the Danes, who consume large amounts of saturated fats from dairy products, and of the Greenland Inuit, who eat mostly whale and seal, showed differences in the proportion and types of polyunsaturates in the food and blood samples from both groups (Bang, Dyerberg, and Hjørne 1976).

CONSERVING ENERGY: STAYING WARM   How can humans cope with the severe arctic cold, working, traveling, even playing games out of doors in −30°F (−34°C) or colder? Do the Inuit have an extra layer of body fat to resist cold? Or perhaps an unusually high metabolism to increase body heat production?

The extra fat idea has been disproved by skinfold measurements. Inuit are no fatter than racially similar people like Chinese and Japanese living in temperate climates (Laughlin 1964). Their basal metabolism, however, is between 13 and 33 percent higher than among people in temperate climates. Diet contributes to higher metabolic rates. When some Alaskan Eskimos were placed on a white man's diet, lower in protein and higher in carbohydrates than their own diet, their basal metabolism fell. Another group of Eskimo hunters had a metabolism rate 25 percent higher than a group of Eskimos living in a city (Hammel 1969:335–336).

Because of this higher metabolism, Inuit have excellent blood circulation and resistance to cold in the hands and feet (Laughlin 1969:414). This is also more related to diet than to genetic inheritance. It is an important physiological adaptation because the hands are the only part of the body frequently exposed to wet cold. Many tasks like untangling dog harnesses, spearing fish, or butchering seals are done more efficiently without mittens.

Under normal circumstances, only the hands and face are exposed to extremely low temperatures. Out of doors, Inuit are clothed in double-layered caribou furs, which provide three or more inches of excellent insulation, and waterproof sealskin boots lined with caribou fur. Traditionally, Greenlandic people used bear skins for leggings, and some Alaskans used dog skins or sealskins. But most groups preferred caribou because the hairs are hollow and very dense, providing good insulation, light weight, and softness. This creates a microclimate as warm as a person could desire, sometimes even too warm during strenuous activity.

Inuit take advantage of body heat to keep their infants warm on the mother's back in the spacious pouch of the mother's parka, or *amaut*. The waistband of the *amaut* can be loosened to allow the naked infant to be shifted around to the front to nurse without being exposed to the air. Indoors on the sleeping platform, Inuit sleep in close body contact, sharing the warmth of thick caribou furs.

Heated only by melted seal blubber and small flames from a length of moss wick in a stone lamp, plus the heat of human bodies, snowhouses, or *igluit*, become remarkably warm, often 30 to 60°F (−2 to 16°C) higher than outside temperatures. Drafts are prevented by attaching entrance tunnels with openings at right angles. Sleeping areas are well insulated with skins and elevated to take advantage of the fact that warm air rises.

CONTROLLING ENERGY: LIMITING POPULATION GROWTH
Food resources are a critical factor limiting population size and density in the Arctic. The number of fish or caribou one could expect to take was always unpredictable. When hunting was good, it was hard to accumulate surplus against hard times because of the mobile lifestyle and the need to travel lightly. In winter, frozen caches of meat were stored under rocks, but never in large quantities. When there was surplus, people simply feasted until the food was all gone. Food supply was rarely dependable enough to allow people to settle in one place for long.

Thus population density was very low: an average of four persons per 36 square miles (100 square km) in Alaska and even lower in Greenland and Canada. Total population was low also, estimated as 25,000 in Alaska (Oswalt 1967:113–114) and approximately 35,000 in Greenland and Canada combined (Guemple 1972:95). If population size in any given region exceeds the area's resources, starvation threatens. Inuit avoided this by keeping well under the upper limits, usually less than a hundred persons per camp, with a social structure that allowed easy fissioning of groups.

Several factors can maintain stability in population size: predation, starvation, disease, accidents, and social mortality. Humans were rarely preyed on in the Arctic, although polar bears were said to stalk people occasionally. Starvation was not a frequent cause of death, but it is certain that mortality increased among old people and small children during serious food shortages. Disease was also rare, for two reasons. One is that a simple ecosystem like the tundra has few parasitic and infectious organisms and few species of animals or insects that transmit diseases to humans (Dunn 1968:226). The second reason is that communities were too small to sustain epidemic diseases before the days of European whaling and trading stations.

Inuit did have health problems, but rarely were these acute conditions leading to death. Rather, they were chronic problems like arthritis in the elbows, spinal defects and inflammation, deficiency in enamel formation on the teeth, loss of incisors, and osteoporosis. Hunting hazards included snow blindness and sensory overload due to glare and isolation in a one-man boat, the kayak. There was a risk of contracting tapeworm and trichinosis. Eating aged meat, considered a delicacy, posed a risk of fatal botulism.

By far the major cause of natural death was accidents, especially drowning or freezing to death after capsizing, but including house fires and attacks by sled dogs. Hunting accidents among men accounted for 15 percent of the deaths of a southern Baffin Island group (Kemp 1971).

Another important regulator of population is "social mortality" (Dunn 1968). Few Inuit groups feuded or conducted warfare, but murders did occur. Suicide was frequent, sometimes by old people who could not keep up with the group and wished not to be a burden, sometimes because of blindness or other crippling disability, guilt, or despair. Among the Netsilik Eskimos of Canada, in fifty years there were thirty-five successful and four unsuccessful suicides in a group of only 300 people (Balikci 1970:163).

A final important form of social mortality was infanticide, usually of newborn females. In 1902, one group, the Netsilik, included 66 girls and 138 boys; in 1923 the tribe numbered 109 females and 150 males altogether (Balikci 1970:148). Infanticide keeps population down in several ways: it is a direct check on the effective birth rate and reduces the number of potential reproducers in the next generation, and it makes the mother's milk available for her older child. Also, infanticide is far less risky to the mother's health than abortion would be, given the limitations of the native medical system.

Not all Inuit groups had such high infanticide rates as the Netsilik. A census in 1912 on Baffin Island showed 89 females per 100 males among people younger than nineteen (Kemp 1971). For those older than nineteen, there were 127 females per 100 males, reflecting the high mortality of hunters from accidents. Thus in populations with high adult male death rates, female infanticide served to reduce the ratio of non-food-producing women to food-producing men, while limiting future birth rates.

HUMAN RESOURCES FOR SURVIVAL   The resources for survival that distinguished Inuit from other mammals of the Arctic included the ability to make tools, to use speech, to coordinate and plan hunting activities, to teach their young necessary skills, and to exploit the total environment. They exploited the resources of the ecosystem, yet they remained a part of the system without changing it or threatening its overall equilibrium. Their health was a reflection of their ecology. Inuit lived for 5000 years or more in a relatively unchanging way of life, as a part of nature rather than separate from it. They could feel a kinship with *nanook*, the bear, yet because of their tools, their language, and their creativity, they also felt a sense of competition and separation.

An old Inuit man once showed Ann McElroy a chess set he was carving from ivory. He had chosen *nanook* to be king of all the animals and *inuk* (the man) to be king of a whimsical ensemble of dogs, children, sleds, and snowhouses. The set was skillfully carved and would bring a fine price in Toronto. But somehow it was more than just a tourist item. It seemed as symbolic of the human role in the arctic ecosystem as the myth of a bear cub who grew up with humans and then was rejected by them. It seemed fitting that bear and human would be both equals and opponents, setting nature against culture, in this old man's conception of the game.

RESOURCES

Readings

Balikci, Asen
1970 The Netsilik Eskimo. Garden City, New York: Natural History Press.
This book is one of the most comprehensive ethnographies available on the traditional subsistence patterns and social organization of Canadian Inuit. Sections on conflict resolution, infanticide, and suicide are especially fascinating.

Chagnon, Napoleon A.
1977 Yanomamö—The Fierce People. Second ed. New York: Holt, Rinehart and Winston. Case Studies in Cultural Anthropology. George Spindler and Louise Spindler, gen. eds.
Chagnon's ethnography on the Yanomamö vividly portrays what it is like to do field work among a volatile, aggressively organized people. The central topics are adaptation to the physical and sociopolitical environment, social organization, political alliance, and warfare. The final section, about contact with Westerners, is especially pertinent to medical ecology.

Kemp, William B.
1971 The Flow of Energy in a Hunting Society. Scientific American 224 (3):104–115.
Kemp compares the energy inputs and energy yields of a modern and a traditional Inuit household on southern Baffin Island, including data on imported energy sources such as kerosene, store food, ammunition, and wages. Energy flow diagrams showing the integration of traditional subsistence with modern alternatives provides a useful contrast to figure 1.4 in the profile on Inuit adaptations.

Landy, David, ed.
1977 Culture, Disease, and Healing: Studies in Medical Anthropology. New York: Macmillan.

Logan, Michael H., and Edward E. Hunt, Jr.
1978 Health and the Human Condition: Perspectives on Medical Anthropology. North Scituate, Massachusetts: Duxbury Press.
These two books are useful collections of readings in medical anthropology, most of them reprinted from various journals. They cover the same general areas as this text, but they also include anthropological studies of ethnomedicine and health care systems.

Neel, James V.
1970 Lessons from a "Primitive People." Science 170 (3960):815–822.
This article describes research with the Yanomamö, Makiritare, and Xavante Indians by a multidisciplinary team and discusses the relevance of findings to the population problems of modern societies.

Spradley, James P.
   1970   You Owe Yourself a Drunk: An Ethnography of Urban Nomads.
   Boston: Little, Brown.
   A lively account of anthropological field work that gives the participants'
   view of their culture. Spradley's study of skid road tramps in Seattle
   provides a basis for reevaluating existing approaches to alcoholism.

Journal

Medical Anthropology, which began publication in 1977, is a quarterly journal of
   studies in health and illness. It is published by Redgrave Publishing
   Company, Pleasantville, New York.

Films

Yanomama: A Multidisciplinary Study. 43 minutes. Available for purchase
   through National Audiovisual Center, Washington, D.C., and for rental
   through various university film libraries.
   This film portrays the 1968 expedition to study the Yanomamo by
   Chagnon, Neel, and other members of the research team. The ecology
   and social organization of the Yanomamo are described, along with
   scenes of the medical team at work, taking samples, examining subjects,
   eliciting microlinguistic data, assessing reproductive patterns, and
   administering the measles vaccine.
Netsilik Eskimo Series. 30 minutes. Available through Universal Education and
   Visual Arts, Inc., New York.
   This series shows the traditional annual cycle of the Netsilik Eskimo of
   the Pelly Bay–Arctic Coast area of northern Canada. Modern Netsilik
   worked with anthropologists Asen Balikci and Guy Mary-Rousseliere to
   reconstruct the traditional way of life for the film record.
   The films include: Autumn River Camp, I and II; Caribou Hunting at the
   Crossing Place, I and II; Fishing at the Stone Weir, I and II; Winter Sea Ice
   Camp, I, II, III, IV.

Interdisciplinary Research in Health Problems

CHAPTER 2

Photo: Patricia Townsend

PREVIEW

Health problems, whether they are as exotic as the fatal neurological disease *kuru* or as familiar as hypertension or mental retardation, have no respect for disciplinary boundaries. As we will see in this chapter, an understanding of each health problem in an ecological context requires at least four different kinds of information:

1. environmental data
2. clinical data
3. epidemiological data
4. behavioral, social, and cultural data

Biology and other environmental sciences contribute ecological concepts as well as data on the environmental factors affecting health. Clinical medicine, concerned with the diagnosis and treatment of individual patients, contributes an understanding of the disease process. Epidemiology shows how diseases are distributed in space and time and uses disease statistics as clues to the determinants of disease. The social sciences focus on human behavior patterns that have implications for health.

The interdisciplinary approach of medical anthropology is useful not only for field researchers, but also for people who want to understand the ecology of health and disease in the community where they live—parents, nurses, physicians, social workers. To do this effectively, the student of medical anthropology needs to learn something of the basic concepts, the core vocabulary, the research techniques, and the capabilities and limitations of each of these disciplines.

Interdisciplinary research collaboration is illustrated in this chapter by the profile of *kuru*, a neurological disease found in a small ethnic group of highland New Guineans, and by the study of high blood pressure in the southeastern United States. The research methods used by medical anthropologists were developed in exotic settings like New Guinea, but they can be applied in our own culture as well, as the health profile of mental retardation in southern California demonstrates.

THE NATURE OF COLLABORATION

Seals are sea mammals who must come to the surface and breathe every fifteen or twenty minutes. In winter, when ice covers the sea, seals keep several funnel-shaped breathing holes open by scratching from beneath with their sharp claws. Their warm breath melts the snow that accumulates over the holes. The hunting dogs of the Inuit locate these breathing holes. The hunter must wait motionless for hours at the hole, harpoon ready to strike when a seal appears. If one hunter watches a single hole, his chances of harpooning a seal are slight, for the seal uses many different holes as he covers the area where he feeds. But if a group of hunters watches several nearby holes, their chances of catching a seal are greatly increased (Balikci 1970:55–57, 74–77). This kind of communication and cooperation are the adaptive skills that human beings have developed most fully.

Just as Inuit subsistence depends on collaboration between hunter and hunting dog and between hunter and kin, so do medical anthro-

FIGURE 2.1   An Inuit hunter waits at a seal breathing hole. This illustration came from
a very early anthropological study by Franz Boas (1888).

SOURCE: Franz Boas, *The Central Eskimo,* Sixth Annual Report of the Bureau of
Ethnology (Washington, D.C.: Smithsonian Institution, 1888).

pology and medical ecology depend on collaboration among epidemiologists, parasitologists, entomologists, nutritionists, clinicians, and
anthropologists. Though none of these researchers think of themselves as watchers at seal breathing holes, they frequently use similar
metaphors such as medical "detective work" and research "targets."
The elusive quarry that makes such collaboration essential is an
understanding of the maintenance of health in human populations.

In working in a small, isolated population, the medical anthropologist may become a jack-of-all-trades, collecting environmental, medical, and cultural data. In doing research in Papua New Guinea, coauthor Pat Townsend, trained as a cultural anthropologist, found that she needed to take on tasks as varied as compiling a dictionary for an unwritten language, diagnosing and treating skin diseases, measuring rainfall, and collecting plants to be sent to the herbarium for identification.

Sometimes it is possible for a multidisciplinary research team of specialists to collect the data needed to describe the health status of a population. The Yanomamo research expedition reported at the beginning of chapter 1 illustrates this situation. More often, the understanding of health problems in their environmental and cultural context is built up piece by piece, as investigators with training in different disciplines work, publish their findings, and stimulate later researchers to fill in the gaps, using the concepts and methods of other disciplines. The information in the Inuit case study accumulated in this manner.

ENVIRONMENTAL DATA

Ecology is the field of study concerned with the interrelationships between populations and their environments which constitute ecosystems. The popular use of the word "ecology" to refer to picking up beer cans and planting petunias gets at only a tiny segment of what ecology is all about. Ecologists have developed very sophisticated models for describing the flow of energy and materials in ecosystems. At one time, social scientists were content to borrow whichever of these concepts seemed useful to them and to apply the concepts rather loosely to the human scene. The present trend, however, is for ecologically oriented anthropologists to work toward a more rigorous application of this approach to ecosystems involving human beings.

By doing so, they hope to unify human ecology with general ecology (Vayda and Rappaport 1968:492).

The basic unit of study in ecology is a **population.** The Yanomamo, for example, are a population of humans. The stands of *ediweshi* palms from which they gather fruits are a plant population, and the wild pigs, deer, tapir, and armadillos they hunt are animal populations in that habitat, in that place. The term "population" has been defined in many ways for different purposes, but a very general definition would simply say that a population is composed of all the organisms of a single species or group that inhabit a given area. We may want to define that area very broadly, as when we talk about the world population of 4 billion people, or very narrowly, as when we talk about the people living in a single river valley in New Guinea or the population of a species of microorganism living in someone's intestines. A **species** is a biological classification of organisms with shared genetic characteristics, a common origin, and the ability to interbreed.

All human beings belong to a single species, and yet the total world population divides into many groups with different cultural, physiological, and genetic traits. Consider the Italian and Spanish Catholic missionaries, the North American and Venezuelan scientists, mixed-blood settlers, and the Yanomamo tribes all found in the Orinoco River region. All are members of the same species, and yet it is not useful to consider them all a single population. Their environmental adaptations differ, their evolutionary history is separate, and only the Yanomamo are truly at home in this ecosystem. Therefore, we will define a **human population** as a group of individuals living in a given habitat with the same pattern of environmental adaptation.

Each population has an **ecological niche,** that is, a specialized role in the habitat. Populations of different species share the same habitat by using slightly different resources or by using the same resources at a different season or time of day (Boughey 1973:91). Niche differentiation allows the coexistence of two species populations that would otherwise be competitors. The concept of niche has been applied to human ecology in a way that is only partly consistent with its use in biology. If one human population farms while another group herds cattle in the same habitat, the two populations are said to have two ecological niches, even though they are one biological species.

Population Interactions and Energy Flow

There are several kinds of possible relationships between populations coexisting in a single habitat. One possibility is that the two populations may be in *competition* for some of the same resources, as are the Inuit and the polar bear. When populations use the same food resources in this way, their niches tend to diverge in other respects, reducing the competition between them (Boughey 1973:91).

Another type of coexistence is the **predator-prey** relationship in which one population serves as a food resource for the other. For example, the Eskimo and caribou coexist as predator and prey. It is in the interest of the predator not to deplete the population of prey. Instead, the two populations mutually regulate each other. This principle is recognized by the Nunamiut Eskimo of Alaska, who claim that the number of Nunamiut in the Brooks Range fluctuates with the number of caribou (Gubser 1965:321).

A more intimate form of coexistence is **parasitism,** where individuals of a population feeding on another population live on or inside individuals of the second population, which are called **hosts.** Eskimos often found themselves hosts to lice, about whom they told many joking tales, such as the one about Mrs. Louse who made fancy sealskin trousers for Mr. Louse to go from their home on the back of the head to the forehead for a big dance (Gubser 1965:254). The louse-human relationship is a very simple and direct form of parasitism. Other parasites require one or more **vectors,** which are insect species that serve as hosts to another stage in the parasite's life cycle before transmitting the parasite to its human host.

Symbiosis is a kind of interaction between populations that benefits both populations involved. The relationship between the Inuit and their hunting dogs is of this sort. Other populations living symbiotically with humans are the normal intestinal bacteria, which help humans digest food and resist infection (Dubos 1965:129, 135 ff.).

These relationships among populations can be viewed as a flow of energy and mineral nutrients through a living system. All organisms require energy—that is, the capacity to do work—in order to carry out biological processes. In fact, ecosystems run on energy, which origi-

nates from sunlight. Energy is never destroyed; rather, it is transformed by various levels of consumers into other forms of energy.

A plant receives radiant energy from sunlight and converts it into
chemical energy through photosynthesis. Plants are called *producers* in
an ecosystem. This energy from organic material is then transferred to
animals (called *primary consumers*) when they eat the plants and then
later to animals (*secondary consumers*) who eat those animals. Thus
energy is transferred along a food chain. At each successive level of the
pyramid, only part of the productivity of the previous level can be

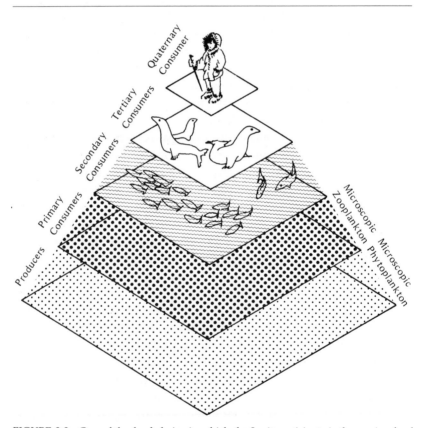

FIGURE 2.2   One of the food chains in which the Inuit participate is the marine food
chain. Each successive consumer derives energy from organisms a step
below in the food chain. The higher steps in the ecological pyramid have
fewer individuals and less total biomass.

harvested; therefore each successive level has a smaller total biomass, that is, energy stored by growth and reproduction of the animals on that level.

One of the food chains in which the Inuit participate is shown in figure 2.2. In this marine food chain, the Inuit are *carnivores,* or meat eaters, eating very high on the food chain as tertiary or quaternary consumers. Inuit also participate in other food chains, which are not shown in figure 2.2. When the Inuit eat berries, they are acting as primary consumers or *herbivores,* eaters of plants. When they eat caribou, which in turn eat plants such as lichens and grasses, the Inuit are acting as secondary consumers.

Humans vary in their role in food chains. Some, like the Inuit, are primarily carnivores, while other groups mostly consume plants. Most human populations exploit a wide range of food resources at all consumer levels, however. Unlike many animals who occupy a specialized ecological niche, humans tend to be generalized. This contributes to their success, but it also entails the risk of population growth that depletes the resources on which the population depends.

Carrying Capacity and Population Regulation

All life forms reproduce themselves, and under optimal conditions each organism can reproduce well beyond simply replacing itself. Each population has the potential to multiply very rapidly in a pattern called *exponential growth,* increasing by a percentage of the whole over time. Exponential growth is like compound interest in a savings account; the increase from interest becomes part of the balance, which continues to earn more interest.

Ecologists define *carrying capacity* as the maximum size or biomass of a population that can be sustained by an environment over a given period without degrading environmental resources. Such a limit is commonly set by food supplies or space (Boughey 1973:5). Attempts have been made to calculate the carrying capacity of environments for human populations, but they are complicated by people's ability to change their subsistence technology and with it the potential carrying capacity. Even with a specified technology, there are uncertainties about what the limiting factors are. For the Yanomamo, for example, the limits to growth are surely not set by food energy; more bananas and plantains could easily be grown. Some anthropologists conclude that the limiting factor there is the supply of protein from game animals (Harris 1977:53). Others conclude that the limiting factor is the elbow room required by Yanomamo personality and politics. If population growth presses toward carrying capacity in one area, fissioning of the group and migration to another area relieves the pressure. Both Yanomamo settlements and Inuit camps are constantly fissioning and regrouping.

Despite the possibility of migration, if an animal population grew unchecked and ate up all its resources, it would crash. Most of the time, though, populations stay in equilibrium with their resources. We have already mentioned how predation and parasitism contribute to population regulation. Death and disease are only one kind of check on population, however; fertility control is equally important. Most animals have some seasonal regulation of reproduction. Females come into estrus, a period of sexual and reproductive receptivity, only at certain seasons of the year or, in higher primates, only during a fraction of the monthly cycle. Breeding periods are in synchrony with maximal resources during birth seasons, thus ensuring that females have enough food while they nurse their young.

When reproduction has been too successful and animals become overcrowded, conditions are less than optimal for the survival of young. In fact, animals that are overcrowded in experiments or otherwise stressed often do not breed at all or else kill off their young. Hormonal regulators also help space births and thus check population. For example, nonhuman primates usually do not ovulate or become sexually receptive while they are nursing young. Such birth spacing ensures that the considerable investment of energy put into rearing each offspring has a maximum chance of success. In chimpanzees, the period between births is around five years, which allows for slow population growth and optimal care of the young (Hunt 1978b).

Human fertility tends to be regulated less by natural checks than by cultural restraints, however. Human females do not go into estrus, and the sexual bond serves a number of psychosocial needs in addition to reproduction. Cultural practices regulating marriage and sexual activity function to space births, to ensure care of each child, and to check population growth. These practices are described in greater detail in chapter 4.

Studying Environmental Factors in Health

The concepts just presented are central to the discipline of ecology, and they provide a theoretical framework for the study of health and disease. In addition to this conceptual framework, however, the more specific techniques and findings of the many environmental sciences are needed in medical ecology.

Environmental sciences such as geology, meteorology, and geography make their contribution to medical ecology by describing and analyzing the physical environment. Differences in underlying rock strata affect health by influencing the mineral content of drinking water, for example. Fluorine that is naturally present in excessive amounts mottles the teeth, but when it is present in insufficient amounts, tooth decay is more prevalent. A change in rainfall patterns, recorded by meteorologists, may be critical in understanding why an epidemic of pneumonic plague, which has very narrow temperature and humidity requirements, broke out in a particular time and place.

Biologists contribute specialized information about the habits of the plants and animals with which humans interact. These include the plants and animals used for food and other economic purposes, as well as the viruses, bacteria, fungi, protozoans, helminths, and arthropods that are parasites of humans and the vectors of disease.

The following health profile illustrates multidisciplinary collaboration in medical anthropology. Many different environmental factors were considered in attempting to understand the puzzling disease *kuru,* and the sophisticated laboratory methods of virology made a key contribution.

PROFILE: CANNIBAL MOURNERS

Kuru began with tremors. Despite her trembling and jerking, a South Fore woman could lean on her digging stick as she went about the work of a woman in highland New Guinea—weeding her sweet potato garden and caring for her children. In several months, her coordination was worse; she could not walk unless someone supported her. Her eyes were crossed. Excitement made the symptoms worse, and she was easily provoked to foolish laughter. Within a year, she could no longer sit up and was left lying near the fireplace in her low grass-roofed house. Death was inevitable.

FIGURE 2.3   A young Fore girl with advanced *kuru*.

Photo by Dr. E. R. Sorenson from *Edge of the Forest: Land, Childhood and Change in a New Guinea Protoagricultural Society* (Washington, D.C.: Smithsonian Institution Press, 1976).

After her funeral was over, other women of the village prepared her body for cooking. The flesh, viscera, and brains were steamed with vegetables in bamboo tubes or in an earth oven with hot stones. Only close friends and kinsfolk would eat, as a sign of their love and respect (Sorenson 1976:32). Maternal kin had a special right to their kinswoman's flesh, and specific kin had rights to certain body parts. A woman's brain was eaten by her son's wife or her brother's wife, for example (Glasse 1967). A woman's flesh was not eaten by her own parents, children, or husband. South Fore warriors generally avoided eating human flesh, believing it made them vulnerable to the arrows of enemies. But in any case, they avoided women's flesh because women were believed to be a danger to men. It was mostly women who were cannibals, and they shared the funeral meal with their children of both sexes. They would not eat a victim of certain diseases like dysentery and leprosy, but the flesh of *kuru* victims was acceptable.

His wife dead of *kuru*, the Fore man would not find it easy to remarry, for men outnumbered women in the area, as a result of the higher death rate from *kuru* among women. He had lost his first wife to *kuru*, and a young son and daughter as well. Almost half the deaths in this village and nearby villages were due to the trembling disease.

Kuru is the name not only of the disease but also of the kind of sorcery that the Fore believe causes it. Divination rituals helped identify the suspected sorcerer, a man in a nearby but distrusted group of Fore. The sorcerer was accused of stealing bits of the woman's old skirt, hair, food scraps, or feces, despite her carefulness in disposing of these things. These or other personal leavings were wrapped up with magical charms and a spell was chanted:

> I break the bones of your legs,
> I break the bones of your feet,
> I break the bones of your arms,
> I break the bones of your hands,
> And finally I make you die. *Lindenbaum (1971:281)*

Buried in mud, the bundle rotted, and as it rotted, the disease progressed. The victim's kinsmen might kill the accused sorcerer, ritually marking his corpse so that all would recognize his guilt.

In the 1950s, Australian administration reached the Fore territory. The Fore were remarkably receptive to changes introduced by government officials, missionaries, and scientists. Eager to please, the Fore quickly abandoned cannibalism and warfare, and by 1967 they were making a quarter of a million dollars a year from growing coffee for sale (Sorenson 1976:15). The early medical officer in the area, Vincent Zigas, encountered *kuru* in his patients. Puzzled by the fatal neurological disease, which was limited to this one ethnic group of about 12,000 people and a few neighboring tribes, Zigas consulted D. Carleton Gajdusek of the U.S. National Institutes of Health. Gajdusek began an intensive program of research that engaged scientists of many disciplines for more than a decade before the etiology of *kuru* was understood.

Zigas and Gajdusek did intensive field work in 1957 to 1959, traveling from village to village and bringing patients to the bush hospital built for this purpose. They observed the clinical course of the disease and attempted treatment. They also worked at mapping the epidemiological patterns, of which the distribution of the disease by age and sex was especially striking. Of the 416 *kuru* deaths recorded in 1957–1958, 63 percent were adults and 37 percent were children and adolescents. Among the adults dying, women outnumbered men dramatically, about twenty-five to one. Among the children and adolescents, the sex ratio was more nearly equal (Alpers 1970).

Many different hypotheses were explored as possible explanations of *kuru*. In the early 1960s, the most widely accepted explanation was a genetic one. Specialists thought that a lethal mutation had arisen in this population. Analysis of genealogies showed that *kuru* did tend to run in families, though there were some odd, unexplained patterns. Most disturbing was the combination of high lethality and high incidence. How could the gene maintain itself in the population despite the high death rate from *kuru*, which would have been removing the gene from the population systematically? The gene must have conferred some powerful, but unknown, advantage to carriers of the gene who did not themselves develop *kuru*. Those who questioned the genetic hypothesis explored other possibilities, such as nutritional deficiencies, toxic substances, and psychosomatic causes (Fischer and Fischer 1961).

Even as the *kuru* studies were continuing, the epidemiological patterns began to change: the incidence and mortality declined,

first among the younger age groups and later in all age groups
(figure 2.4). It began to look as though *kuru* might eventually

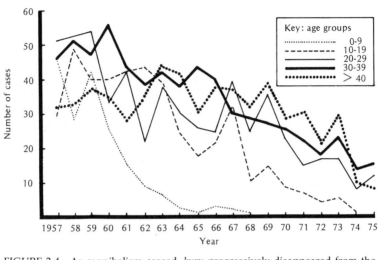

FIGURE 2.4   As cannibalism ceased, *kuru* progressively disappeared from the
Fore population, beginning with the lowest age groups.

SOURCE: Reproduced, with permission from D. C. Gajdusek et al. (1977),
"Urgent Opportunistic Observations," in *Health and Disease in Tribal Societies,*
Ciba Symposium #49 (Amsterdam, Elsevier), p. 96.

disappear, although no treatment had yet been found. Although
the Fore lacked written history or a system of dating events,
cultural anthropologists Robert Glasse and Shirley Lindenbaum
were able to probe the memories of older informants during
field work in 1961–1962. They found that both cannibalism and
kuru were relatively new to the Fore. The custom of cannibalism
had been adopted in about 1910, and the first cases of *kuru* had
occurred some time later, with the disease becoming increasingly
prevalent until the 1950s. They suggested that *kuru* was transmitted by cannibalism (Mathews, Glasse, and Lindenbaum
1968). As cannibalism had declined, the disease was not being
transmitted to children who had never tasted human flesh.

Laboratory research also contributed to unraveling the mystery.
After an incubation period of eighteen to thirty months, laboratory chimpanzees inoculated with the brains of women who had
died of *kuru* developed the disease. Other chimpanzees inocu-

lated with material from their brains developed experimental cases of *kuru,* too (Gajdusek, Gibbs, and Alpers 1967). It was now known that the disease was transmissible by a substance assumed to be a virus, although its structure was not yet known. In 1976, the Nobel Prize in Medicine was awarded to Gajdusek for this work. (The award was shared by Baruch Blumberg, who had done related research dealing with another infectious disease, hepatitis.) The study of *kuru,* a slow or latent virus, had opened up a whole new area of medical research. Concepts and methods were developed in working with one exotic disease that could be applied to many other more familiar, but poorly understood, neurological diseases such as multiple sclerosis.

CLINICAL DATA

Clinical medicine is concerned with the diagnosis and treatment of disease in individual patients. Disease as defined biomedically is a deviation from normal functioning, observable and measurable by biomedical techniques. It goes without saying that clinical medicine is one of the basic sources of data about health and disease for the study of medical anthropology. The clinician's identifications and descriptions of the disease process are an essential starting point of our study. Since this is so fundamental and obvious, it is more to the point to note the *limitations* of clinical data. One such limitation is the clinician's preoccupation with pathology, with the abnormal. In medical anthropology, we are concerned with health as well as with disease. We are often frustrated to find that seemingly more is known about deficiency disease, for example, than about normal nutritional requirements. More seems to be known about gynecological disease than about normal pregnancy, menstruation, and menopause.

Another limitation of the clinical sciences is that they look at the individual patient from the perspective of Western biomedical science. Thus they do not tell us about the social context in which disease occurs, nor do they necessarily tell us how the individual or family members and community perceive and experience the illness. *Kuru,* defined from a biomedical perspective, is a disease process characterized by progressive degeneration of the central nervous system caused by a slow virus transmitted by cannibalism. However, the Fore concept of *kuru* also refers to a kind of sorcery, which from the viewpoint of biomedical science is not part of the disease entity at all. Further, the Fore conception of *kuru* also includes some people who suddenly develop tremors and get better just as quickly. From a biomedical standpoint, these persons, lacking the characteristic central nervous system degeneration, exhibit still another disease entity, hysteria, a mental illness that mimics the symptoms of *kuru.* Thus we need to make a distinction between disease, illness, and sickness. *Disease* is defined from the perspective of biomedical science. It may be defined narrowly, as a deviation from clinical norms, or it may be defined more broadly, as an impairment in the ability to rally from an environmental insult. *Illness* is a cultural category applied to individual experience, and *sickness* is a category of social behavior. This opens the possibility that an individual may have an illness without any corresponding disease, or a disease without an illness. For example, many persons with hypertensive disease go untreated because they do not experience symptoms that would lead them to regard themselves as ill or to take on the sick role.

Clinicians are concerned with the *treatment* of patients. While researchers in medical anthropology are not callous about the people suffering from disease, their chief concern is not with treatment but with a better understanding of health, which will ultimately feed back into *prevention* of disease as well as treatment. From this point of view, neither the failure to find a cure for *kuru* nor the small and declining numbers of *kuru* patients are relevant to judging the importance of that research.

The clinical sciences can contribute to the study of health and disease even among remote, isolated people without access to modern health care. By taking blood samples and sending them out to laboratories for study, it is possible to obtain much information. Biochemical tests can be used to assess nutrition. Testing serum for persisting specific antibodies shows what infectious diseases the individual has experienced. Laboratory tests also reveal the presence of genetic diseases such as the abnormal hemoglobins.

EPIDEMIOLOGICAL DATA

Epidemiology is the study of the distribution of disease in populations and of the factors that explain disease and its distribution: the population rather than the individual is the unit of study. Epidemiology depends on input from the clinical sciences. Using birth certificates, death certificates, medical records, and surveys as sources of data, epidemiologists use statistical methods to identify subgroups that are at especially high or low risk of acquiring a particular disease. Epidemiologists observe how the frequency of occurrence of a disease is related to age, sex, ethnic group, occupation, marital status, social class, and other variables.

Health statistics can also be arranged to show the distribution of health and disease in space—by contrasting rates between countries, states, or cities—and in time—by comparing rates from day to day, month to month, or year to year. Long-term trends such as the trend toward taller, heavier, earlier-maturing children or the marked increase in mortality from lung cancer among males in the United States in the last fifty years are sometimes called *secular* trends.

If a large number of people are affected by a disease in a short period, the disease is an **epidemic** disease. In contrast, if the disease is present in the community at all times but in more moderate numbers, it is said to be **endemic.** In describing the frequency of disease, epidemiologists use the terms **prevalence** and **incidence.** The prevalence is the proportion of individuals in a population who have a particular disease at one particular time. For example, if a survey of a village in Egypt found that 46.9 percent of the people showed symptoms of the parasitic disease schistosomiasis, the prevalence rate of schistosomiasis was 46.9 percent at the time of the survey. The incidence, in contrast, is the rate at which new cases of a disease occur in a population over a given period, that is, the proportion of people at risk of developing a disease who actually do so in that period. For instance, the annual incidence of newly reported civilian cases of gonorrhea among males aged 20 to 24 was 2593 per 100,000 population in this age group in the United States in 1972. Disease statistics may be expressed in terms of **morbidity,** the number of cases of disease per unit of population occurring over a unit of time, or **mortality,** the number of deaths per unit of population in a unit of time.

Epidemiologists have mostly worked in large populations with modern health care systems. In principle, however, the statistical methods of epidemiology are applicable to other kinds of data as well. Even in paleopathology, the study of disease in the skeletal remains unearthed by archaeologists, scientists now attempt to say more than simply "arthritis and dental caries were present." Instead, they work toward statistical statements of the proportion of the skeletal population showing the disease in question and ultimately to an understanding of process.

Epidemiologists go beyond describing the distribution of disease to analyze the **etiology,** or the determinants, of disease. Etiology involves not only well-defined primary causes, such as a parasite or a toxic substance or a deficiency of some nutrient, but the whole chain of factors that contribute to the disease process. When epidemiologists are employed by state or county departments of public health, much of their epidemiological detective work is concerned with investigating outbreaks of food poisoning and acute communicable diseases. In these diseases, the causal chain is simple. However, most diseases have a much more complex etiology—multiple causes in the social, biological, and physical environment interact with factors within the individual that increase or modify his or her susceptibility to the disease.

The following health profile deals with high blood pressure, which, unlike *kuru,* is neither rare nor exotic but is widespread in Westernized populations. To give a focus to the report, we will deal primarily with blacks in the American South, a population in which the prevalence of hypertension is especially high. As the report will show, a great deal of research has been invested in the clinical and epidemiological aspects of hypertension. Yet despite the deceptively familiar setting so close to home, we really do not know very much about the social and behavioral pieces of the puzzle.

PROFILE: THE EPIDEMIOLOGY
OF HIGH BLOOD PRESSURE

In the poor rural community of Holmes County in central Mississippi, 40 percent of all black adults of ages 18 through 79 have definite hypertension. In addition, many have borderline hypertension, and others show normal blood pressures only because they are already taking prescribed medication (Eckenfels et al. 1977). On the small farms along dirt roads in the hill country of central Holmes County and in other communities like it, several factors that are associated with high blood pressure coincide, escalating the prevalence of hypertension. Epidemiological studies have shown that hypertension is generally more prevalent with advancing age, more common among blacks than whites, and more common among the poor than the rich. It is also found more among the less educated than the better educated, and more among the obese than the thin. More men than women show it up to the age of 45, but after the age of 45, it is more common among women than men. Geographically, it is more prevalent in rural than in urban areas in the Southeast and more prevalent in the Southeast than in other regions of the United States, but these geographical patterns partly reflect racial patterns of residence.

At least 15 percent of white American adults and 28 percent of black American adults have definite hypertension. Although these high percentages make it a health problem of major magnitude, hypertension is widely ignored. Its mention does not strike fear into an American or motivate him or her to contribute to a fund drive. Although medication is available to control hypertension, patients frequently fail to take it consistently. One reason for this indifference is that high blood pressure is a quiet disease; it is present for many years without symptoms before it visibly and irreversibly damages the arteries feeding heart, kidneys, eyes, and brain. Damage to the arteries feeding the brain results in stroke, and the death rates from stroke are one of the most reliable indicators of the prevalence of hypertension in a population. When all the damage resulting from hypertension is taken into account, it clearly merits designation as the number one health problem of American blacks, and it seriously affects Westernized populations throughout the world.

Although blood pressure varies from day to day and is affected by activities and emotions, a fairly normal blood pressure reading for a young adult is 120/80. This ratio refers to the systolic (upper) and diastolic (lower) blood pressure, the height in millimeters (mm) of a column of mercury in a tube as it is pushed up by the force of flowing blood against the walls of the arteries. The systolic pressure, the larger number, is the pressure when the heart is contracting. The diastolic pressure is the pressure between heartbeats, when the heart is at rest. Blood pressure readings persistently above 140/90 are generally taken to be a warning signal or the borderline of mild hypertension. A systolic

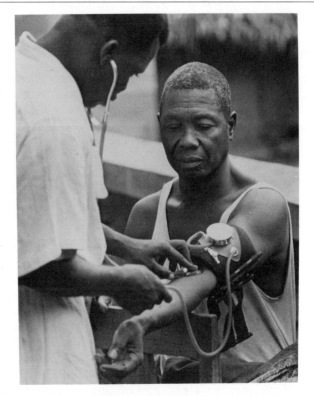

FIGURE 2.5   Screening for high blood pressure is necessary because hypertension can do a great deal of damage before any symptoms are noticed.

Photo: World Health Organization.

blood pressure of at least 160 mm or a diastolic pressure of at least 95 mm is regarded as "definite hypertension" by World Health Organization criteria.

In the United States, Europe, and Westernized segments of non-Western societies, it is considered a normal part of aging for the blood pressure to rise throughout life (figure 2.6). However, studies of some isolated, traditional societies have shown a different pattern: blood pressures that remain low throughout life. The Yanomamo Indians of Venezuela typically have blood pressures of 100/65 at all ages from the teens until age 50 and older (Oliver, Cohen, and Neel 1975). The Bushmen of the Kalahari Desert also maintain low blood pressures during aging (Truswell and Hansen 1976).

Since blood pressure does tend to rise with age in Americans, hypertension is more prevalent among older Americans. This does not mean that it is not of direct concern to young people, however, since the pattern of rising blood pressure begins early. Even very young people may suffer from hypertensive disease. In a major epidemiological survey of Evans County, Georgia, 50 of the 435 adolescents surveyed in 1961 had blood pressures of 140/90 or higher. Seven years later, 30 of these young people were recontacted. None had received treatment. Some of them now showed normal blood pressures. But already, by their early twenties, two had died of cerebral hemorrhage, another had developed hypertensive heart disease, three had other symptoms of damage from hypertensive disease, and five others had blood pressures of 160/95 or higher but had not yet developed other symptoms (Heyden et al. 1969).

The etiology, or causation, of hypertension is complex and not very well understood. Recent research into the mechanisms that regulate blood pressure indicates that different physiological mechanisms produce high blood pressure in different individuals (Marx 1976). Certainly some of the factors that enter into the etiology of hypertension are genetic, but it is not clear how much of the tendency for high blood pressure to run in families is due to a shared family environment and how much to shared genes. It is probable that the increased susceptibility of blacks to hypertension is partly genetically determined; blood pressures also

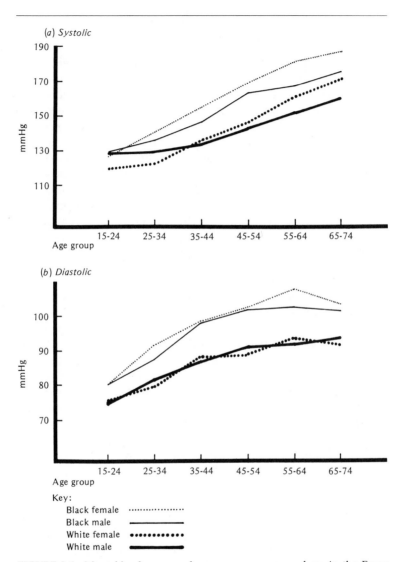

FIGURE 2.6   Mean blood pressure by age group, race, and sex in the Evans County, Georgia, study: (a) systolic pressure; (b) diastolic pressure.

SOURCE: John R. McDonough et al., "Blood Pressure and Hypertensive Disease Among Negroes and Whites in Evans County, Georgia," in *The Epidemiology of Hypertension*, eds. Jeremiah Stamler et al. (New York: Grune and Stratton, 1967), p. 172. Reproduced by permission.

tend to be high in West African and Caribbean blacks, though not as high as among blacks in the United States (Akinkugbe 1972).

The complex of causes also includes environmental factors such as diet and stress. One way to study these factors is through experiments, which allow researchers to manipulate the environment in controlled ways and to observe the effects on blood pressure. High blood pressure can be produced in genetically susceptible laboratory rats by feeding them salt, giving them coffee as their only fluid, or repeatedly exposing them to stressful stimuli. The question remains whether these rises in blood pressure are equivalent to the way primary hypertension develops in humans. Blood pressure does rise temporarily when people are under stress, ranging from the mild stress of a medical examination to the severe stress of battle or disaster. But these transitory elevations may not be equivalent to the long-term disease process of hypertension.

One kind of evidence that social stress contributes to hypertension comes from comparing non-Western peoples leading a traditional way of life with genetically related groups who are in the process of becoming urbanized or Westernized. This presumably stressful adaptation has been associated with blood pressure changes in many different countries. For example, when farmers move from more isolated highland villages to lowland areas near cities in Chile, hypertension appears (Cruz-Coke, Donoso, and Barrera 1973). Urban Nigerians show blood pressures that rise more steeply after age 45 than do rural Nigerians (Akinkugbe 1972). It is not simply the stress of living in cities that is everywhere the critical difference, however, since in the southeastern United States, Jamaica, and Japan, hypertension is more prevalent in rural than in urban areas. When behavior patterns learned early in life do not fit with the circumstances people face later in life, their expectations are constantly frustrated. This dissonance is a critical component of the lifelong stress that leads to rising blood pressure with age, according to the comparative studies of Henry and Cassel (1969).

Salt in the diet is another environmental factor involved in some way with hypertension, for populations that use little salt tend to show lower blood pressures than populations—such as the U.S. population—that use much salt (Page 1976; Dahl 1972). Studies that examine differences in salt use *within* populations have not been very successful in demonstrating relationships with blood pressure, however. This indicates that individuals differ in their tolerance for high-sodium diets. Soul food, which is traditional Southern fare, is especially high in salt because it includes many smoked or processed pork products. Rather than sodium alone being the culprit, it seems more likely that a complex of nutritional factors is involved, including the balance of sodium to potassium and calcium. One test case for the role of diet in hypertension has been Japan, where rates of hypertension and stroke are very high, especially in farming villages in northeastern Japan, where the inhabitants eat more salt and fewer vegetables than do people in other parts of the country.

To develop an understanding of the epidemiology of high blood pressure, it is clear that we have to work with a *multicausal* model rather than expecting to come to a neat correspondence between a single cause and a single effect. The causal mosaic includes both genetic and environmental factors, and the environmental factors of diet and stress interact with each other in ways not yet fully understood.

BEHAVIORAL, SOCIAL, AND CULTURAL DATA

To understand the ecology of hypertension, we drew primarily on epidemiological data. What is missing from the picture that a medical anthropologist could add? Medical anthropologist Norman A. Scotch studied this health problem among the Zulu of South Africa. He found that urban Zulu show average blood pressures higher than American whites though not as high as American blacks. Rural Zulu have the lowest blood pressures of these four groups. Under the South African system of apartheid, urban life for the Zulu is undoubtedly stressful, but Scotch identified some additional, very specific factors that were stressful in the urban environment. These factors were correlated with hypertension in the city but not in the rural area. He found that "the individuals most likely to be hypertensive were those who maintained traditional cultural practices and who were thus unable to adapt successfully to the demands of urban living" (Scotch 1963:1212). For Zulu women in the South African city, hypertension is statistically associated with traditional patterns such as living in an extended family rather than a nuclear family, having many children, and believing in sorcery, while normal blood pressure is associated with modern patterns such as attending a medical clinic and being a member of a church.

Scotch's work illustrates some main dimensions of medical anthropology, which is both a **field work** discipline and a **comparative** discipline. It was intensive field work that allowed Scotch to move from abstract or general statements about social stress to identifying specific stressful conditions. If similar research were to be done in rural and urban communities in the United States, Jamaica, and Japan, the understanding of hypertension might be greatly advanced. Field work in many cultures builds a basis for comparative studies. The comparison between urban and rural Zulu was built into the design of Scotch's study. More often, however, the field work is conducted in just one community, and the systematic comparisons draw on a sample of other cultures studied by other investigators.

Field Work in
Medical Anthropology

Anthropological field work usually means traveling to the study region and living there for an extended period, often six months to two years at a stretch. If possible, anthropologists try to live in the village or neighborhood they wish to study, perhaps even with a local household. Simply by staying throughout the year, a field worker can notice seasonal changes, such as variation in infant nutrition as their mothers' agricultural work load varies, that a quick survey might miss. Field workers who return to the research site at intervals over the years accumulate longitudinal data on personal and social change.

Because of the long stay, the researcher can form friendships with local people, learn the language, and get a total picture of how the physical and social environment affects health. Chances are good that the anthropologist will learn about health and ecology through first-hand experiences with stinging insects, parasites, native herbs prescribed to cure diarrhea, moldy shoes, frozen camera shutters, or other inevitable inconveniences. The field worker's own efforts to adapt to the situation become part of the data, which is why this kind of work is called **participant observation.**

The method of participant observation has become the hallmark of cultural anthropology in much the way that the use of documents typifies the historian; the use of maps, the geographer; and the use of survey interviews, the sociologist. Although the field-work techniques of anthropology were developed in exotic settings, they have been applied in settings closer to home such as slum neighborhoods, state hospital wards, and school classrooms. The intensive, face-to-face methods of anthropology produce somewhat different insights than do the large-scale surveys characteristic of other kinds of social research usually applied in our society.

The trained observer is the key factor, though still and movie photographs, video tape, and tape recordings may supplement note taking as a way to record data. Later, the films may be given frame-by-frame analysis. Field work may have a very general goal to produce an **ethnography,** which is a detailed, systematic account of a whole culture. It may have one or more specific goals to collect information of specific kinds or to test a hypothesis.

In addition to the general technique of observing while participating in community activities, the field worker can use many specific data-gathering techniques. Most field workers conduct a household census and map the village or neighborhood. They may draw up formal questionnaires to assure that they obtain the same kinds of information from many individuals on some subject of critical importance in the study, whether it be child rearing, the ownership of pigs or cows, or the use of herbal contraceptives.

These interviews may seek to gain information organized in categories that the observer brings to the research setting from outside. Alternatively, the researcher may try to find out how the participants in that culture categorize their experience, by means of the ethnoscientific, or ethnosemantic, techniques discussed in chapter 1. A classic study exemplifying ethnoscientific methodology is Charles Frake's study of disease diagnosis among the Subanun of the Philippines (1961). One portion of the Subanun disease classification is shown in figure 2.7. This chart shows the terms for skin disease, which tends to be prevalent in tropical areas. When Frake developed an infectious swelling on his leg, he asked all his visitors the name of his ailment. Some replied with the very general term for skin disease, *nuka* ("eruption"); others used a very specific term, *pagid* ("inflamed quasi-bite"). Frake studied the way in which the social and linguistic context determined the choice of terms.

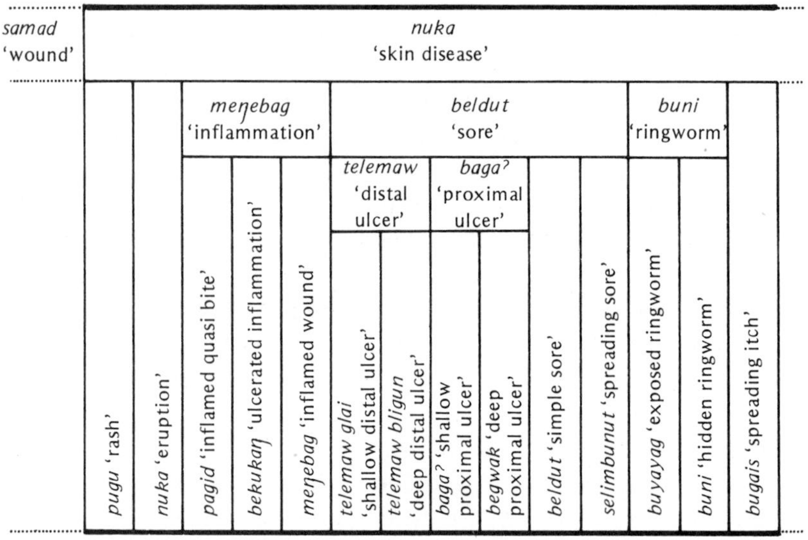

samad 'wound'	*nuka* 'skin disease'		
	meɲebag 'inflammation'	*beldut* 'sore'	*buni* 'ringworm'
		telemaw 'distal ulcer' / *baga?* 'proximal ulcer'	

Leaf terms (left to right): *pugu* 'rash'; *nuka* 'eruption'; *pagid* 'inflamed quasi bite'; *bekukaŋ* 'ulcerated inflammation'; *meɲebag* 'inflamed wound'; *telemaw glai* 'shallow distal ulcer'; *telemaw bligun* 'deep distal ulcer'; *baga?* 'shallow proximal ulcer'; *begwak* 'deep proximal ulcer'; *beldut* 'simple sore'; *selimbunut* 'spreading sore'; *buyayag* 'exposed ringworm'; *buni* 'hidden ringworm'; *bugais* 'spreading itch'.

FIGURE 2.7 The Subanun of the Philippines diagnose and classify skin diseases by means of an ethnoscientific terminology analyzed by Charles Frake.

SOURCE: Charles O. Frake, "The Diagnosis of Disease Among the Subanun of Mindanao." Reproduced by permission of the American Anthropological Association from the *American Anthropologist* 63:118, 1961.

Labeling Disease

The system by which people classify diseases is influenced by their observation and understanding of disease processes. Compared with the Subanun, many other cultures have simpler classification systems that reflect much less detailed attention to medical matters. The classification used can sometimes limit or obscure further understanding. This is as true of scientific systems or classification as it is of folk systems. Changes in disease terms over the last few centuries both reflect and generate new understanding. For example, who suffers any longer from dropsy or phthisis? Both were once common terms, but "dropsy" obscured the differences between different types of fluid accumulation, and "phthisis" has similarly gone out of fashion as a term for tuberculosis. Currently, when researchers on hypertension begin to talk about "low-renin hypertensives" as being significantly different from others, it is an indication that an existing category has combined phenomena that now need to be separated.

Epidemiological research is also influenced by the disease-labeling process, since the kinds of categories entered into medical records or death certificates shape the statistics that epidemiologists work with. Epidemiologists always have to worry whether an apparent rise in prevalence of a disease is simply a result of a change in classifying or reporting.

Social scientists have been especially concerned with the ways in which diagnostic labeling influences the person who is labeled. Once labeled as diseased, the person may take on a sick role with great relief at the opportunity to rest from normal responsibilities. Or the labeled individual may be stigmatized, as when a successfully treated cancer patient has difficulty finding a job. Once labeled, all a person's subsequent behavior may be interpreted in relation to the label. In a psychological study, eight sane people faked their way into mental hospitals (Rosenhan 1973). Once they had been admitted, they ceased acting abnormally. Yet despite acting sanely, none of them was detected as a fake. The label of mental illness stuck, remaining on their records even after discharge. While in the hospital, they took notes for the research, and even this was interpreted as irrational behavior. While some fellow patients suspected that these pseudopatients were sane, none of the staff came to doubt the diagnosis of mental illness.

Labeling is an especially touchy issue when the condition is one that is not simply present or absent in an individual, but continuously distributed along a scale. Blood pressure and intelligence test scores are distributed in this way in a population. How high does blood pressure have to be in order to be labeled hypertension? How much below the average score of 100 does IQ have to be in order to be labeled mental retardation? Generally, the answer is that the cutoff point is arbitrary, chosen because it has proved useful as a screening device, and that single test readings must be interpreted only in the context of other kinds of evidence.

The formal criteria for labeling mental retardation are shown in table 2.1. The IQ test is the formal measure, although the individual's

TABLE 2.1   Classification of mental retardation by IQ tests.

IQ range	Description
70–84	Borderline
55–69	Mildly retarded
40–54	Moderate
25–39	Severe
Below 25	Profound

SOURCE: After R. Heber, "Modifications in the Manual on Terminology and Classification in Mental Retardation," *American Journal of Mental Deficiency*, 1961, vol. 65, p. 500.

adaptive behavior in society is also taken into account. The more severely retarded are usually labeled early by medical personnel; the mildly retarded are most often labeled by the school system. Many of these may be considered "situationally retarded," that is, retarded in the context of school but unimpaired in their home and neighborhood life. Once they get past school age, the situationally retarded are able to lose their label (Mercer 1973).

The following health profile is concerned with people who were labeled as retarded. In reading their case histories, one is struck by how often they came to be labeled only because they were a problem to someone, as an orphan or an illegitimate child or a sexually truant adolescent. Because they had been hospitalized for many years, the label stuck, and it was something they continually had to be able to explain to themselves and to others.

PROFILE: THE EVERYDAY LIVES OF RETARDED PERSONS

"I've got a tendency of an ailment, but it isn't what it seems," says Martha, who is thirty-nine years old and has an IQ of 72. Martha is "pathetically unattractive." Her hair is unkempt, her eyes are crossed, and her yellowed teeth protrude. Her part-time work as a maid in a motel provides her with a room where she lives isolated in bare surroundings. Her low level of competence, her anxiety, and her irritability make it hard for her to keep a job to provide for her other needs, but she saves money when she can work. Surprisingly, she has accumulated $1800 in a savings account, which makes her feel more secure. As an illegitimate child, Martha was shifted from an orphanage to a succession of foster homes. She was committed to a state hospital for the mentally retarded when she was a teen-ager and spent eighteen years there before she was discharged (Edgerton 1967:57–74).

In contrast to the tearful anxiety of Martha, Fred presents an image of happy-go-lucky bravado. A heavy-set man in his early thirties, he works nights cleaning up in a skid row cafe and bar. Although his IQ tests in the low 50s, he is articulate and eager to convey an image of competence and independence. Fred's chief interest is his health; he takes great pleasure in eating well and sleeping well, and these subjects dominate his conversation. He claims to have many important friends, including his former social worker, and it is these benefactors who have carried him through periodic crises and periods of unemployment since his release from the state hospital for the mentally retarded (Edgerton 1967:41–57).

Of all the diagnostic labels that can be applied to a person, the label "mentally retarded" is one of the most profoundly stigmatizing. Unlike a disease process that is somewhere out there attacking a person, mental retardation is a defect near the core of the self, a defect in one's intelligence and competence. Unlike mental illness, which also affects the center of one's personality, retardation is not seen as a curable episode but as a lifelong state (Edgerton 1967:207).

The epidemiology of mental retardation is complex. It is relatively easy to determine the prevalence of the more severe forms of retardation and those with an identifiable organic etiology, such as Down's Syndrome (mongolism), in which a person has an extra chromosome. For the great majority of cases of retardation, however, no organic etiology can be identified. Also, the great majority of the retarded are only mildly affected. Many people whose IQ would place them in the category of borderline, mild, or moderate retardation never come to the attention of any agency that would label them as retarded. They may muddle along with help from family and friends or even be quite successful in their adaptation.

What of those who are identified as mentally retarded? How does this condition affect their lives? Anthropologist Robert B. Edgerton and his coworkers have studied a sample of retarded adults over more than a decade. The study began with a sample, or cohort, of 110 persons who had been residents of Pacific State Hospital for the mentally retarded in southern California. The largest percentage of them had IQs in the mildly retarded range, some were moderate, and others were borderline. Between 1949 and 1958, they were released from the hospital, under a program of vocational rehabilitation, to live and work in the community. When Edgerton and his assistants contacted them in 1960–1961, they had been out of the hospital for an average of six years. It was possible to locate 98 of the original 110 patients. Only the 53 ex-patients who were living within fifty miles of the hospital were included in the study. These 53 people had an average age of 34 and an average IQ of 65. Because it was not possible to get adequate data from 5 of the 53, they were dropped. The final, detailed study thus included 48 people. In the 1972–1973 follow-up, 30 of these people were studied again, some twenty years after they had left the hospital.

How does an anthropologist study 48 people scattered throughout metropolitan Los Angeles? Certainly the image of pith helmet, mud hut, and notebook is inappropriate. Yet the basic techniques of field work still apply: participant observation supplemented by indirect, open-ended questioning that encourages people to talk about their own concerns. Several field workers were involved. Besides visiting the informants in their homes, they participated in shopping and sightseeing trips, parties, and other activities. An average of seventeen hours was spent with each of the 48 former patients.

The study focused on the central concerns of the former patients: their jobs, leisure activities, and sex and marriage. Holding a job was important to them—all had been released from the hospital because they were successfully employed and a job was seen as essential to being like other people, except for married women, whose homemaking roles exempted them from the labor force. Twenty-one of the 28 women in the cohort were married, most of these to men who were not retarded, although many of these men either had other problems such as alcoholism or were much older than their wives. The kinds of jobs usually available were semiskilled work in sanitariums, kitchen jobs in restaurants, domestic work, and odd jobs. The 6 persons who were unemployed at the time of the 1960–1961 study were anxious and despondent.

Recreation was an important interest of the former patients, whose lives before and during hospitalization had been so lacking in fun and good times. Conversation and television were the usual leisure activities; some individuals had special interests such as bicycling and handicrafts. Their experiences of sex and marriage were diverse, though they seem representative of lower socioeconomic groups generally. Almost all of them had been sterilized before leaving the hospital, but this seemed to have more destructive impact on self-esteem than on sexual or marital relationships.

Maintaining self-esteem, in the face of the massive threat to self-image that a diagnosis of mental retardation implies, was indeed a central concern for these former patients. In order to cope, they denied to themselves that they were retarded and were careful to avoid exposing to others their history of hospitalization. To pass as people of normal intelligence, they developed strategies to avoid their difficulties with telling time, dealing with numbers, and reading. ("My watch stopped. Is it nine o'clock yet?" or "Can you read this for me? I forgot my glasses.") This attempt to cover themselves with a "cloak of competence" gave Edgerton the title for his book. But according to him, their attempts to manage stigma "are in reality such tattered and transparent garments that they reveal their wearers in all their naked incompetence" (Edgerton 1967:218). In their efforts to adapt to life outside the hospital, they sought help from various benefactors such as landladies, social workers, employers, and nonretarded husbands. Although the 48 ex-patients varied a great deal in their degree of independence and ability to manage their own affairs, all were eager to locate benefactors who could bolster self-esteem as well as offer practical aid.

When they were contacted twelve years later, the former patients were much less concerned with stigma or passing (Edgerton and Bercovici 1976), as the hospital experience had receded farther into the past. Although health and employment had worsened, these changes were taken as signs of aging, which also affect normal people and are not so stigmatizing. The satisfactions of their leisure activities were more important to them and anxiety about work was less than it had been in 1960–1961 although only 8 were employed and more were on welfare.

Edgerton's *Cloak of Competence* study has been helpful to those planning rehabilitation programs and delivering social services. The anthropological approach it used lets the informants speak for themselves and looks at their everyday lives in the context of home, work place, and community. Other, nonanthropological studies of retarded persons have been less holistic, and they have more often listened to social workers, teachers, employers, or parents rather than to the retarded persons themselves.

CONCLUSIONS

Traditionally, anthropologists have worked outside their home cultures. In fact, it can be argued that special insights come from crossing a cultural boundary; an outsider may fail to understand much that insiders know, but he or she may also see things they are too close to notice. This is why some of the keenest observers of American culture have been anthropologists from France, England, China, and India. The techniques anthropologists have developed for listening to and learning from other peoples are also useful for the middle-class professional person who needs to learn from the culturally diverse population that he or she serves.

In this chapter we have contrasted the research orientations of several disciplines. Few readers of this text will master the methodological intricacies of more than one of these disciplines. Yet at the core of each discipline is at least one principle of method that can be applied to good effect by any health professional, any student tackling one of the term projects suggested at the back of this book, or anyone concerned with understanding a health problem. What are some of these principles? From the clinical sciences, to be precise in observing symptoms and cautious in interpreting them, a caution that comes from experience in making life-and-death decisions. From epidemiology, to respect the judicious use of statistics. From the environmental sciences, to be curious about the wider context of health, a counterweight to medicine's preoccupation with internal events. From anthropology and the other social sciences, to *listen*. The specific methods of the social sciences are mostly ways to make that listening more effective.

Sensitivity to cultural differences within our own pluralistic culture is important, but in a shrinking world, responsible citizenship demands some understanding of worldwide health problems as well. In the following chapters, you will explore the problems of population growth, world food supply, and the public health implications of economic development and industrialization. Rather than the helpless hand wringing that accompanies most discussions of world problems, we want to set you to work at building a cultural and ecological framework for understanding these problems that can provide a basis for informed action.

RESOURCES

Readings

Boughey, Arthur S.
    1973   Man and the Environment. N.Y.: The Macmillan Co.
    This introduction to human ecology takes an evolutionary perspective and incorporates anthropological data on primates, human evolution, the origin of agriculture and cities, and cross-cultural variations in contemporary ecologies. A problem-oriented text, it provides valuable information on pesticides, water pollution, and resource management.
Cassel, John
    1974   An Epidemiological Perspective of Psychosocial Factors in Disease Etiology. American Journal of Public Health 64:1040–1043.
    This article provides a short sample of the work of an epidemiologist who has pioneered in considering the social factors in disease.

Edgerton, Robert B.
    1967   The Cloak of Competence: Stigma in the Lives of the Mentally
    Retarded. Berkeley: University of California Press.
    This book gives a fuller account of the study of mentally retarded persons
    described in this chapter.
Fabrega, Horacio, Jr.
    1974   Disease and Social Behavior: An Interdisciplinary Perspective.
    Cambridge, Massachusetts: M.I.T. Press.
    Fabrega, who is both a medical anthropologist and a psychiatrist, gives a
    systematic and critical review of studies of the social and cultural factors
    in disease.
Goldman, Ralph
    1973   Principles of Medical Science. New York: McGraw-Hill.
    Students who come into medical anthropology from the social sciences
    will find this a helpful general introduction to disease processes. Cover-
    age is given to genetics and birth defects, malnutrition, physical injury,
    immunity, infection, circulatory disorders, cancer, and aging.
Little, Michael A., and George E. B. Morren, Jr.
    1976   Ecology, Energetics, and Human Variability. Dubuque, Iowa: Wm.
    C. Brown.
    Oriented to beginning students, this short book is the most consistent
    application of the methods of general ecology by anthropologists. It
    includes case studies dealing with Eskimos, East African pastoralists,
    Peruvian high-altitude peoples, and New Guinea highlanders.
Spradley, James P., and David W. McCurdy
    1972   The Cultural Experience: Ethnography in Complex Society. Chi-
    cago: Science Research Associates.
    Undergraduate students can do their own field-work projects with the
    guidance of this book on selecting a project, working with informants,
    discovering cultural categories, and writing an ethnographic description.
    Several sample student papers included in the book deal with U.S.
    cultural scenes such as a jewelry store, a second grade recess, and
    hitchhiking.

Films

Rock-a-Bye Baby. 30 minutes. Available for rental through University of Cali-
    fornia Extension Media Center, Film #8507.
    This film shows interdisciplinary approaches to research on the problems
    of mental retardation and childhood autism.

The Meaning of
Adaptation

CHAPTER 3

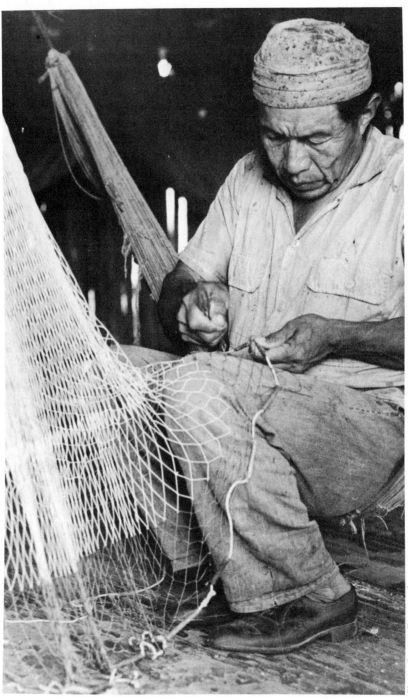

PREVIEW

A central concept of medical ecology is adaptation, the processes of adjustment and change that enable a population to maintain itself in a given environment. Because environments and ecological relationships change over time, adaptation is a continual process. Environmental pressures—such as climatic extremes, seasonal fluctuations, and natural or man-made disasters—evoke adaptive responses. Some responses are quickly made and quickly reversed if the environmental pressures are alleviated. Other responses take generations to become established in a population and are relatively irreversible.

The slowest and least reversible adaptive mechanisms are genetic changes. Natural selection, occurring through differences in mortality rates and reproductive success of individuals exposed to a specific disease such as malaria, brings about genetic adaptation to that disease. The chapter's first profile, concerning adaptation to malaria, discusses one of the best examples of how ecological change—in this case, development of agriculture in West Africa—is related historically to genetic change in a population.

A second type of adaptive mechanism is the constellation of physiological responses made within an individual life span. Some of these responses are very rapid, as when a person begins to sweat in a hot room. Others are incremental results of developmental processes, for example, the development of large chests and lungs by people who grow up at high altitudes. Because individuals must have the genetic potential for physiological adaptation, it is difficult to discriminate between physiological and genetic forms of adaptation, as the profile describing lactose tolerance in milk-drinking populations shows.

A third type of adaptive response highly developed in human beings is the use of cultural information shared by a social group and transmitted through learning to each generation. Medical systems are one aspect of cultural adaptation to health problems. Cultural customs, beliefs, and taboos also have an indirect effect on health.

The capacity of the group and the individual to adapt to environmental circumstances is very broad, but certain limits exist and compromises are often necessary between what is desired and what is possible. Adaptation is never perfect and often involves inherent risks along with potential benefits. Technological changes may increase the environment's carrying capacity, but these changes may also increase the risk of disease or hazard. Evolutionary changes giving resistance to disease in certain environments may create genetic difficulties for future generations, requiring new kinds of adaptive responses, as shown in the health profile on sickle cell anemia in the United States.

Now, here, you see, it takes all the running you can do, to keep in the same place.
—The Red Queen, in Lewis Carroll, *Through the Looking-Glass*

The Red Queen's explanation to Alice reflects a basic premise of medical ecology: ecosystems are dynamic, and living things are continually in processes of change and response to change. Organisms that cannot respond flexibly to change may not survive, and populations lacking variability in response potential can tolerate only limited change. These principles apply to human groups as well as to plants and animals, and in this chapter we consider the mechanisms that allow for human flexibility in adaptation.

Adaptation can be defined as a set of processes that increase a population's chances of continuing to exist through successive generations in a given environment. Adaptation occurs within two time frames: short-term adjustments and long-range evolution. The physiological and behavioral adjustments that a person makes in his or her lifetime in response to specific environmental problems are one component of adaptation. When the population itself undergoes genetic or cultural changes that enhance the group's success within its ecological niche or in new niches, it is adapting through evolutionary processes.

Adaptation occurs in response to a variety of environmental problems and challenges. Some habitats sustain life rather precariously, with poor soil, little rainfall, and extremes of heat and cold, and yet humans manage to live in these places. The diverse processes by which people manage to survive, even to thrive, in such environments indicate the human capacity for adaptation. Some of these adaptive processes are indicated in a comparison of the two men in figure 3.1.

The differences in the body size and shape of the two men, largely inherited but also influenced by diet and variable growth patterns, are related to the different climates of their home environments. The arctic hunter's short limbs and compact, bulky body help him conserve heat, while the long limbs and greater body surface of the East African help him dissipate body heat (Howells 1960; Steegmann 1975).

Even more important than body type in coping with temperature extremes is the capacity to adjust physiologically to variations in temperature. As the dry heat of the grasslands increases during the day, the African maintains a fairly constant body temperature through sweating. The Inuk is also capable of throwing off excess body heat through sweating during exertion and when the microclimate of his fur parka or crowded snowhouse becomes too warm.

Both arctic and grasslands dwellers are able to respond to a decrease in air temperature through the constriction of peripheral blood vessels. This prevents loss of heat from the warm body core area. However, the blood vessels of the Inuk's hands and feet quickly dilate again, allowing rewarming and giving protection against cold injury. The heat-adapted African's fingers and toes usually do not rewarm

FIGURE 3.1   Differences in body size and shape reflect genetic adaptation to climate. The African's long limbs help dissipate heat, while the arctic hunter's bulky body conserves heat. The dwellings constructed by these men illustrate cultural adaptation to climate.

quickly, and he is more susceptible to injury if exposed to severe cold (Steegmann 1975:144–146).

The houses that these people build also provide protection against the environment. The snowhouse insulates against wind and heat loss, while the mud-and-thatch house insulates against heat. Both dwellings make good use of principles of insulation and air convection. The snowhouse uses thick blocks of dense, dry snow, air pockets between hanging skins and outer walls, raised sleeping platforms, and right-angle tunnel entrances. The thick mud walls of the grasslands house have good insulating properties also. They absorb solar radiation during the day and radiate it during the cooler night, leveling the daily temperature variation.

Body type, sweating and vasodilatation, and housing all give protection against the environment. They result from very different processes, yet each contributes to adaptation. Body type is highly influenced by heredity, which sets fairly narrow limits on variability. Sweating and cooling are flexible responses that occur automatically within a fairly wide range of external variation. The ability to build houses is not inherited, of course. People must learn from others which raw materials are appropriate and which tools are needed for construction. The human ability to use tools and raw materials to create buffers against the environment is very flexible and is limited only by available materials, technology, and human energy.

Not all habitats are as harsh as the Arctic or the hot, dry grasslands, but each habitat requires certain modifications and variations in human physiology and behavior. Every ecosystem has periodic fluctuations in temperature, precipitation, food supply, and pressure from predators and pathogens. Long-term or permanent changes occur, including those resulting from natural or man-made disasters. With these changes, new opportunities may arise for competition or cooperation between populations, and humans themselves modify their technology in ways that change their ecological niche or increase their effectiveness in their present niche. Any of these changes—whether they are natural fluctuations, unexpected catastrophes, or human-induced changes—act as challenges for adaptation. They evoke a variety of human responses, some automatic and influenced by heredity, others the product of learning and innovation.

As human populations respond to environmental pressures, one of the ways they change over time is in their patterns of genetic inheritance. These are evolutionary changes, to be discussed in the following section.

ADAPTATION IN BIOLOGICAL EVOLUTION

Evidence of evolutionary change can be found in the fossil record and in historical sources, as well as in the fact that populations in various geographic regions vary in height, skin color, blood types, resistance to certain diseases, and other physical characteristics. Populations differ over time and across space in part because of the adaptive process of biological evolution, defined as change over time in the genetically inheritable characteristics of a population. A population is a group of people, usually but not always of common ancestry, who live in the same general region and type of environment and who form mating relationships. They may or may not share a single cultural system, but they do share similar genetic characteristics. It is the population that evolves, not the individual, through changes in its genetic characteristics.

Genetic Codes

Genetic characteristics are derived from biochemical codes or instructions for life processes of the body—self-maintenance, repair, growth, use of energy. These instructions are contained within the set of twenty-three pairs of chromosomes found in the nucleus of each primary cell of the human body. Chromosomes contain molecules of DNA (deoxyribonucleic acid), double structures of alternating sugar and phosphate groups joined by chemical base pairs. The structure of DNA is shown in figure 3.2. Bases always bond in pairs, and the sequence of base pairs provides the chemical instructions for synthesis of amino acids. The instructional codes are called **genes.** A gene is a length of DNA that codes for a complete chain of amino acids determining protein structure (Damon 1977:68). Each gene corresponds to a certain *locus,* or position, on the chromosome. Since chromosomes function in pairs, the genes are also paired, one inherited from the individual's father and one from the mother. The two genes may be almost identical or they may be slightly different, expressing two variants, or *alleles,* of the gene.

If you inherit allele A from your father and allele B from your mother, your *genotype* would be AB. If A is dominant and B is recessive, on laboratory tests you would show up as type A, and your *phenotype* would be A. A genotype expresses the actual genetic makeup, while the phenotype is the expressed or visible trait. Having two different alleles at a locus is called a *heterozygous* condition; thus the AB individual is a heterozygote. The person who inherits A from

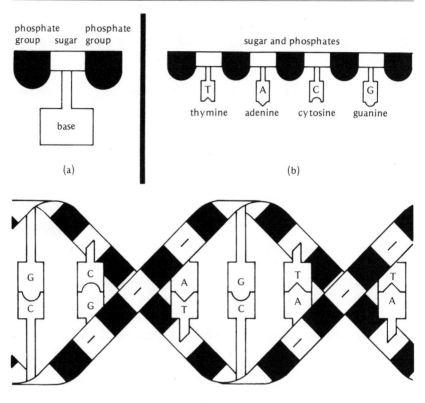

FIGURE 3.2 Each unit of DNA contains three parts shown in (a): a base, bonded to a
sugar, bonded to a phosphate, making the chain shown in (b). DNA has
four types of bases, which always bond in pairs, thymine (T) with adenine
(A) and cytosine (C) with guanine (G), shown in (c). It is the bonding of
the bases that holds the DNA double helix (c) together.

both parents is *homozygous* for that trait and is designated AA. Because
A is dominant over B, AB and AA are phenotypically similar even
though they are genotypically different (Birdsell 1972:54–55).

Many genes exist without variants; about two-thirds of all loci in the
gene pool of a population (and about seven-eighths in an average
individual) are nonvariant loci. About one-third of all chromosomal
loci are variable, and it is this variation that is the raw material for
evolution (Birdsell, 1972:55, 396). While some elements of the genetic
pool are standardized, others are variable, or *polymorphic,* in a popu-

lation. Traits that vary polymorphically in populations are especially suitable for the study of factors that influence changes in allele frequencies in a gene pool.

Genetic changes occur partly because of *mutations,* small and abrupt changes in base pair sequences in the DNA molecules or breaks in chromosomes leading to rearrangements of gene positions and code sequences. Mutations create small changes in biochemical activity, but these small changes can have a significant metabolic effect on the individual. *Point mutations,* involving the substitution of a single base in a code sequence, seem particularly insignificant, but these tiny alterations are the most important source of genetic variation. Most mutations are harmful, particularly in the homozygous condition. However, sometimes it is actually an advantage to be heterozygous for a trait, with one normal allele and one variant form. The first profile in this chapter will show how this can be so in the case of adaptation to malaria.

Mutation maintains variation within a species, but by itself, mutation is not inherently adaptive. It is simply a random process, only rarely producing a change that happens to be of any adaptive value. Like mutation, the other genetic processes (for example, meiosis, crossing over, and genetic drift) that introduce variability are random, that is, undirected and not inherently adaptive.

The major directional force in evolution is called **natural selection.** Selection occurs through differences in survival to reproductive age and differences in reproduction. To paraphrase the explanation given by George G. Simpson (1969a:81), natural selection is based simply on differential reproduction and differential mortality associated with genotype. If some individuals in a population have more surviving offspring than others, if these offspring in turn reproduce more than others, and if there is some degree of difference between the genotypes of those who have more offspring and those who have fewer offspring, natural selection is operating. These are the key factors:

1. Some types of people leave more descendants than others.
2. This happens when some individuals respond more effectively to environmental pressures than others, in ways that enhance their own survival, their fertility, and the survival of those who carry their genes in the next generation.
3. When differences in the effectiveness of response to the environment are significantly a function of inherited varia-

tion, the genes that govern that variation will increase in frequency in the population over time.

Genotype differences are the basis of selection, and what changes through selection are gene frequencies. But selective forces—climate, predation, famine, and especially diseases—actually operate on the phenotype, the inherited characteristics as modified by the environment in the individual's lifetime. It is the human being, not a single gene, who manages or fails to survive the hazards of life, manages or fails to reproduce children. Some failures to survive, such as fatal accidents in childhood, may have nothing to do with genetic factors and do not affect selection. Some genetic factors—say, whether a person has blue or brown eyes—do not affect survival or reproduction and also are not part of natural selection. It is only the phenotypic characteristics that give some advantage or degree of **Darwinian fitness** that are subject to selective action. Darwinian fitness, so called because Charles Darwin first developed the concept that variation in fitness was the key factor in evolution, is simply the ability to contribute one's genes to the next generation. Fitness need not have anything to do with strength, intelligence, or aggressiveness.

How does one measure Darwinian fitness? Take an example of two hypothetical phenotypes, A and B, which differ in a single genetic characteristic. Equal numbers of A and B are born, but only 999 B's reach reproductive maturity, while 1000 A's do. The difference in fitness is one in a thousand, or .001. This difference seems small, but in large populations it is enough to bring about changes in the gene pool over time (Birdsell 1972:397).

A measurable difference in fitness occurs between persons of normal height and achondroplastic dwarfs, whose condition is caused by a mutation. Healthy adult dwarfs produce about twenty surviving children for every hundred produced by kin of normal height, as shown in figure 3.3. The Darwinian fitness of these dwarfs is .2; the selection coefficient against the mutated gene is .8 (Dobzhansky 1960).

Selective Compromise

Selection operates at the same time on many genetic traits that affect survival and reproduction. When selective forces counteract each

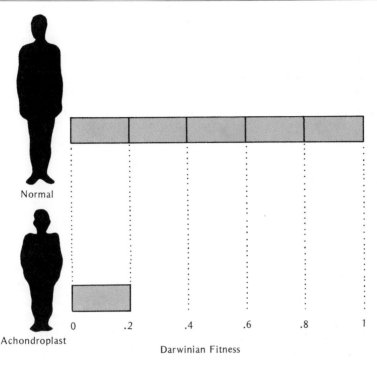

Normal

Achondroplast

Darwinian Fitness

FIGURE 3.3 Healthy achondroplastic dwarfs have only one-fifth as many surviving children as do people of normal height. This is an example of difference in Darwinian fitness.

other, they set limits on genetic change. For example, selection for an optimal birth weight is continually operating. A seven-pound baby has a far better chance of surviving after birth than a three-pound one. If there were no balancing forces operating, birth weights might continue to increase. But in fact the optimal limits are rather narrow, for most women are more likely to have difficulty delivering a ten-pound baby. Such a high birth weight poses a hazard both to the infant and to the mother. The opposed selective forces stabilize a range of about five to eight pounds as optimal birth weight in most populations.

Many selective forces operating on many traits affected the evolution in humans of upright walking, female pelvis size, brain and skull size of infants, and birth weight. The earliest hominids could walk upright, but perhaps not too gracefully or efficiently. It took millions of years of natural selection for the structural changes that perfected the human stride. In the transition to comfortable bipedalism through selection for a series of changes in the structure and mechanics of the pelvis (figure 3.4), selection for larger brains was also occurring. Cranial capacity doubled in the transition from australopithecines, hominids living 2 to 4 million years ago, to early humans (called *Homo*

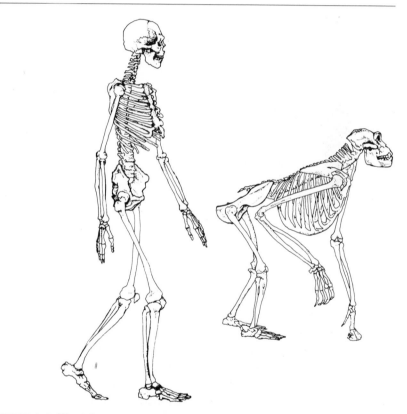

FIGURE 3.4   The differences in the pelvis of the bipedal human (left) and the quadrupedal gorilla (right) reflect structural changes in the evolution from
quadrupedalism to upright walking. Humans did not evolve from goril-
las, but both kinds of primates evolved from quadrupedal ancestral
forms. The human pelvis represents a new type of adaptation to grasslands, while the gorilla pelvis retains a successful adaptation to tropical
forest.

erectus or pithecanthropines), and it almost tripled through the evolutionary transition to true humans *(Homo sapiens)*.

Simultaneous selection for change in pelvis structure and change in brain size operated within certain constraints. The female pelvis had to be wide enough to permit the delivery of large-brained infants, but not so wide as to inhibit the woman's ability to walk and run. The major selective factors were mortality rates of women and infants at childbirth, as affected by pelvis size, head size, and birth weight, and survival rates for individuals with increased brain size and increased mobility. Perhaps one of the most important *selective compromises* coming out of this situation was selection for brain and skull growth after birth rather than before. The human infant's brain has reached only one-third of its total growth capacity at birth. In contrast, the rhesus monkey, another contemporary primate, is born with a brain almost three-fourths of adult size. Not only was there selection for increased brain size and delayed brain growth, but also for elaboration of the cerebral cortex, which facilitates learning, memory, imitation, and cognitive processing of environmental input.

Not all selective compromises are as advantageous as the example just discussed, however. Genetic adaptation often involves less than ideal evolutionary outcomes. The size and shape of the pelvis is not ideal; if it were, childbirth would be an easier and faster process, and backaches would not be such a common complaint. But the usual range of pelvis size is adequate. Infants do get born, and humans can walk long distances with their hands free to carry tools, weapons, and supplies of food. Compromise between opposing selective forces allows for relative, not total, adaptedness.

Selection and Disease

Disease has played an important selective role in human evolution. Infectious diseases can be especially potent selective factors, depending on mortality rates or the effect of the disease on reproduction. Diseases with low mortality rates, and those affecting mostly older people (such as cancer, diabetes, and arteriosclerosis) are less subject to selection because the people affected by them usually have already reproduced when the disease develops.

Resistance to disease can develop in two ways: (1) through physiological mechanisms such as active immunity responses of the body or passive immunity received from antibodies transmitted through the placenta or the mother's milk, and (2) through genetically inherited traits that promote resistance.

Genetic resistance, unlike the immune system, is specific to a given disease or category of diseases, and it plays an important role in childhood in the transition between passive immunity and active immunity. Genetic resistance is controlled by a specific gene or set of genes and does not promote overall adaptability in the way the immune system normally does.

The dynamics of genetic resistance to disease have been thoroughly studied in laboratory mice, rabbits, and other mammals. For example, a single gene protects mice from a group of yellow fever–type viruses, although the mice are still susceptible to other viruses such as polio and rabies (Motulsky 1971:225). In principle, genetic resistance probably operates in a similar way in humans, but obviously the process cannot be studied as easily as it can with mice. Human health should not be jeopardized by laboratory experiments, and genetic changes take so many generations to develop that it is difficult to reconstruct the role of disease factors in these genetic changes.

Genetic factors may be responsible for increased resistance of populations over time to tuberculosis, plague, smallpox, yellow fever, and other high-mortality diseases, but we have no conclusive evidence. Resistance to tuberculosis, for example, depends a great deal on diet, overall health, and even degree of emotional stress. Although genetic factors may contribute to resistance, environmental factors appear to play an equally influential part in increasing resistance over time.

Natural selection does affect disease resistance indirectly through evolutionary change in the virus or parasite responsible for the disease. The organism undergoes adaptive change in response to the mortality rates of the host population, and there may be selection favoring microorganisms whose metabolic requirements inflict less harm on the host population. Laboratory studies using rabbits highly susceptible to myxomatosis, a viral disease, have shown definite evolutionary changes in the virus. Controlling the factor of host resistance, the experiments showed that the virus strain became less harmful with each epidemic (Motulsky 1971:226). We presume that this process of mutual adaptation over time between parasite and host operates in human populations as well. Human intestinal bacteria, which are normally harmless, may have evolved from more debilitating forms.

When a disease organism has two hosts in its life cycle, it may be harmless for one and damaging to the other. This is the case of the malaria parasite, which has adapted to coexisting with the mosquito vector without harming it. As McNeill (1976) explains, in order for the parasite to reach a new human host, "the mosquito carrying it must be vigorous enough to fly normally. A seriously sick mosquito simply could not play its part in perpetuating the malarial cycle by carrying the parasite to a new human host successfully. But a weak and feverish human being does not interfere with the cycle in the slightest" (p. 11).

Of the many parasitical diseases that affect humans, malaria is one of the most ancient, and populations living in endemically malarial environments have evolved certain genetic characteristics that contribute significantly to malaria resistance. These characteristics include many hemoglobin variants. Some are relatively rare or localized, such as hemoglobin E in Southeast Asia and hemoglobin C in West Africa. Hemoglobin S, which is more widespread, is discussed in the following health profile.

PROFILE: MALARIA AND AGRICULTURE

Ancient Chinese mythology describes three demons who bring malaria. One demon carries a hammer to cause a pounding headache, the second carries a pail of icy water to chill its victims, and the third carries a stove to produce fever. Thus each demon afflicts humans with the three major symptoms of a disease that plagued the ancient civilizations of China, India, and Mesopotamia, afflicted Renaissance England and nineteenth-century America, and continues to kill millions of children every year (Russell et al. 1963; Motulsky 1971:235).

Malaria is caused by a protozoan parasite of the genus *Plasmo-dium*, which lives in red blood cells. The protozoa cannot survive outside their hosts and completely depend on the enzymes and metabolism of red cells, consuming the glucose and enzymes needed by the cell for its own functioning. When the protozoa destroy the cells, usually at two- or three-day intervals, the release of waste products and pigment brings on severe inter-mittent bouts of chills and fever.

The name for the disease comes from the Italian words *mala* ("bad") and *aria* ("air"). For centuries, people believed that marsh air caused the illness, and a Roman author advised his readers against building a house near a marsh, which "always throws up noxious and poisonous steams during the heats, and breeds animals armed with mischievous stings . . ." (Russell et al. 1963:2).

The "mischievous stings" come from mosquitoes, the vectors that transmit malaria from one person to another. A female mosquito of the genus *Anopheles* bites a person who is already infected and who carries male and female *Plasmodium* gameto-cytes (sexual forms in the life cycle) in the blood stream. The mosquito ingests the gametocytes and becomes infected, al-though with no negative effect on her health. Gametes develop in the mosquito, undergo fertilization, and release sporozoites (asexual forms in the life cycle of *Plasmodium*), which travel to the mosquito's salivary glands. When the mosquito feeds, she injects sporozoites into a new victim, thus completing the cycle of disease transmission. Each parasite depends on both an insect vector and a mammal host to live out its full life cycle, although it can reproduce asexually for an indefinite time in the host.

Four species of *Plasmodium* affect humans. The most severe of the four species is *P. falciparum*, which causes acute symptoms in victims, especially among small children. When untreated, the death rate among nonimmunes is about 25 percent. Since well-adapted parasites do not kill their hosts, falciparum protozoa may have begun to affect humans fairly recently. In contrast, the less severe forms *P. vivax*, *P. malariae*, and *P. ovale* have probably had a long evolutionary association with humans.

Two major groups of vector mosquitoes for falciparum malaria in sub-Saharan Africa are *Anopheles gambiae* and *Anopheles funestus*.

The two species have very different ecological niches. Funestus mosquitoes breed along shaded river edges and in heavily vegetated swamps in undisturbed tropical forest. Gambiae mosquitoes breed best in open, sunny pools and in ditches with slow-running water. When African forest dwellers lived as small groups of hunters without permanent village sites and with no need to cut down trees, there were relatively few breeding or habitation areas for gambiae mosquitoes. Nor were humans in frequent contact with funestus mosquitoes, who fed on other mammals. Although the two vectors were present in the ecosystem, the incidence of malaria for humans was not high.

The introduction of agriculture into sub-Saharan Africa about 2000 years ago set off a migration by Bantu tribes, which greatly changed the ecology of the tropical forests. Iron tools and iron-working techniques made it possible to clear the vegetation effectively (Livingstone 1958:549). Clearing of forests and cultivation of root and tree crops greatly increased the breeding opportunities of gambiae mosquitoes. Domestication of plants and storage of surplus meant that far more people could be supported in one place than had been possible with hunting-gathering subsistence. This shift in settlement pattern also benefited mosquitoes. Agricultural villages provided not only sunlit, stagnant pools for breeding, but also a feast of human blood.

The malaria parasites also benefited from these changes, and the disease increased in prevalence. This may have been the period in which *P. falciparum* began to adapt to human red blood cells. Previous mammalian hosts decreased in number as human activities altered the ecosystem. With rapid population growth, theorizes Frank Livingstone (1958), the human being became "the most widespread large animal" in West Africa and thus "the most available blood meal for mosquitoes and the most available host for parasites" (p. 556).

The changes in the mosquito and parasite niches created serious disease problems for the human population. With death rates as high as 25 percent and the debilitation of those chronically infected, the health costs of the new subsistence strategy were high. The death rate from malaria is highest among small children, and it also causes intrauterine death, premature birth and spontaneous abortion, and serious disorders of pregnancy.

Responsible for both high mortality and reduced birth rates, falciparum malaria operated as a major agent of natural selection (Russell 1963:391).

Infants in malarial areas are born with passive immunity to malaria acquired prenatally from their mothers. This immunity lasts about six months. Then they are highly susceptible until age 3, when they begin to develop active immunity to the parasite. Older children are frequently infected without experiencing severe symptoms (Motulsky 1971:236). Thus the age of six months to three years is especially critical, and any genetic factor that gives resistance to children during this age period is favored by natural selection. In fact, up to 40 percent of the people of West Africa do have an inherited characteristic that provides a certain amount of resistance to malaria: the sickle cell trait for abnormal hemoglobin in the red blood cells.

Hemoglobin is a molecule of two alpha and two beta protein chains, which binds, carries, and releases oxygen and carbon dioxide in the tissues. Because the hemoglobin molecule is large, there is considerable potential for point mutations to occur. At some time in the past, a point mutation occurred in certain individuals in one of the DNA base pair codes for the hemoglobin protein chains. The copying error affected the synthesis of the amino acid at the sixth position on two of the four protein chains, that is, on the beta chains. A simple reversal in the order of the base pairs changed the instructions for the sequence of amino acids, substituting valine for glutamic acid at the sixth position, as shown in figure 3.5.

The substitution of valine affected the hemoglobin's level of oxygen affinity. Glutamic acid has a negative charge, allowing easy change from high to low oxygen affinity, depending on the external environment of the red blood cell. But valine has no electrical charge and is structured differently, so that in certain conditions the hemoglobin molecules containing valine at the sixth position tend to clump together. When there is a deficiency of oxygen, the molecules combine and form rigid bundles of needle-like crystals that distort the cell membrane into an irregular, sickled or curved shape (Stini 1975b:37; Brodie 1975:453; Milner 1973). This hemoglobin is designated hemoglobin S (Hb^S) because of the sickle shape of these red blood cells.

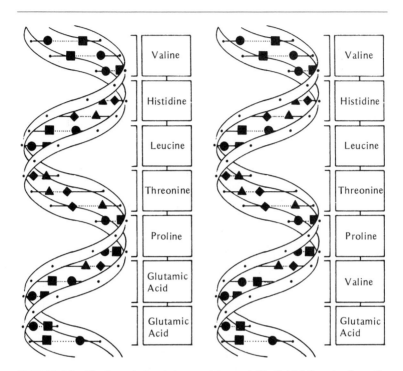

FIGURE 3.5   The beta chain of abnormal hemoglobin S (right) varies from the
normal hemoglobin beta chain (left) by a single amino acid. The
substitution of valine for glutamic acid in the beta chain of the
molecule, due to a point mutation, is responsible for the sickling
trait.

This type of hemoglobin in the red blood cell greatly inhibits the
metabolism and reproduction of the malaria parasite. The normal
red blood cell lasts about 120 days, while a cell with a combination of both genetic characteristics, Hb^A and Hb^S, may last only
two to three weeks, which is not enough time for the parasite to
reproduce. The parasite is also not well adapted metabolically to
the type of red blood cell that contains both hemoglobins (Stini
1975:39).

Because they have the sickling trait, which is disadvantageous for
Plasmodium, heterozygotes are unlikely to suffer greatly from
malaria. Having the sickling trait does not give them immunity to

the disease, but it does reduce the severity of infection and increases their chance of surviving and of reproducing normally.

Individuals heterozygous for the sickle cell condition have both normal and abnormal hemoglobin in every red blood cell. Persons homozygous for sickling also resist malaria, but their red cells contain only abnormal hemoglobin. This causes excessive sickling and severe anemia. Without medical care, sickle cell anemia is usually fatal for children, who rarely survive long enough to reproduce.

The shift to agriculture in Africa had far-reaching ecological repercussions. The new human ecological niche changed the adaptive opportunities of many animals and plants, including those of anophelines and *Plasmodium*, who both moved into new niches created by human activities. We can see a series of concomitant adaptations operating in this situation of ecological change. As humans adapted culturally through new and more efficient methods of subsistence, *A. gambiae* adapted behaviorally to the presence of humans in sedentary villages. Both the malaria parasite and the human population then underwent certain genetic adaptations. The parasites evolved into forms biochemically suited to the metabolism of the human red blood cell, while selection for mutant hemoglobin types resistant to the parasite affected the population's genetic makeup.

Two principles are illustrated in this chain of adaptations among interacting organisms. First, adaptation must always be assessed in the context of a specific environment. The sickling trait proved adaptive in a malarial environment. In regions where malaria has been eradicated, the sickling trait no longer gives any special advantage. This is why the frequency of the trait has declined sharply among blacks in the United States. Second, adaptation is rarely without costs. The occurrence of sickle cell anemia in about 4 percent of West African populations was one of the costs of genetic adaptation, a negative effect that would continue to pose medical problems for people of African ancestry long after they had migrated to other continents.

Hemoglobin S is just one of several mutations that act as genetic buffers against malaria. The distribution of several of these traits is shown in figure 3.6. Hemoglobin C, resulting from a substitution of

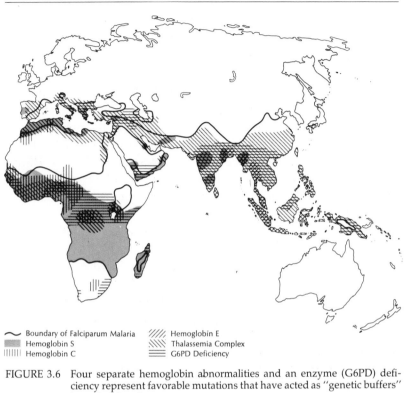

~ Boundary of Falciparum Malaria   //// Hemoglobin E
▓ Hemoglobin S   \\\\ Thalassemia Complex
||||||| Hemoglobin C   ≡ G6PD Deficiency

FIGURE 3.6   Four separate hemoglobin abnormalities and an enzyme (G6PD) deficiency represent favorable mutations that have acted as "genetic buffers" in malarial regions.

SOURCE: J. B. Birdsell, *Human Evolution*, 2nd edition, p. 452, Fig. 16–5. © 1975 Rand McNally College Publishing Company. Reprinted by permission.

lysine for glutamic acid at the sixth position of the beta chain, provides resistance to the malaria parasite without causing severe anemia in homozygotes. Two other types of defects produce some anemia in heterozygotes but also increase their resistance to malaria: the thalassemia complex, found in the Mediterranean countries, India, and the Middle East, and G6PD deficiency, found in Italy, Greece, and the Middle East.

G6PD deficiency produces anemia only under special circumstances, as when persons with this deficiency eat raw fava beans, commonly grown in southern Europe and the Near East, or inhale fava pollen. Anemia also develops if the person is given primaquine, an antimalarial drug, or if the person is suffering from certain bacterial or viral infections. The adaptive value of this deficiency may be that malaria parasites do not grow well in red cells lacking the enzyme. The parasites require glutathione for growth, and enzyme-deficient cells have less glutathione than do normal cells. But this is just a hypothesis; tests have given inconclusive results.

Evidence of the differential fitness provided by the sickling trait is far more conclusive. Calculating the difference between the statistically expected and the actually observed frequencies of the normal hemoglobin in homozygous form ($Hb^A Hb^A$) and the sickling trait in heterozygous form ($Hb^A Hb^S$), the Darwinian fitness of $Hb^A Hb^A$ is .943 and that of $Hb^A Hb^S$ is 1.238. The heterozygous condition gives a slight selective advantage over the normal homozygous condition (Stini 1975b:42).

If having the sickling trait is advantageous, why hasn't this variant completely replaced the normal gene? The answer is that there is one chance in four that heterozygous parents will reproduce children who are homozygous for the trait ($Hb^S Hb^S$). The affected child has double dose instructions for abnormal hemoglobin in each red blood cell and suffers from sickle cell anemia. Homozygotes have high mortality before adolescence, and about 16 percent of the sickle cell genes in the population are lost each generation.

The heterozygote has a selective advantage over *both* types of homozygote. $Hb^A Hb^A$ has higher mortality and lower fertility because of malaria, while $Hb^S Hb^S$ is normally a fatal condition. Heterozygotes usually do not exceed 30 to 40 percent in a population, however, because selection against allele A by malaria is counterbalanced by even stronger selection against allele S by anemia and complications. When two selective forces oppose one another in this manner, the frequencies of the two genes stabilize. This situation is called *balanced polymorphism* because the disadvantage for some in the population who have anemia is balanced by the advantage to others who can resist malaria. The system is in equilibrium, with more than one allele persisting over time.

Note that the mutations responsible for hemoglobin changes occurred before malaria became a severe problem. It is important to understand that selection operates on traits that already exist in the gene pool. Until these mutations proved advantageous because of some environmental change, they were without value and even deleterious for some individuals. But when human technological and demographic change led to an increase in malaria, individuals who had inherited the variant allele with the normal allele had an adaptive advantage. Not only did more of them survive childhood malaria, but they also suffered less from the disease as adults. Because of generally better health, their reproduction rates were slightly higher. They may have had lower nutritional needs than $Hb^A Hb^A$ individuals who had to feed, as it were, both themselves and the parasites in their blood. With better health, heterozygotes could also be more productive in agriculture, compensating for losses in human productivity due to increased disease following the shift to agriculture (Wiesenfeld 1967).

PHYSIOLOGICAL ADAPTATION

Step out of your air-conditioned room and jog along the pavement on a hot day, and your body makes certain adjustments to the heat. You begin to sweat: evaporative cooling is taking place. Your face reddens as an expanded flow of blood through the capillary bed allows more heat to be lost. The body is working to maintain **homeostasis,** the return to inner balance that keeps an organism within tolerable limits despite external change.

We all have the capability to maintain homeostasis and to respond to different **stressors** such as climatic extremes of heat and cold, high or low humidity, ultraviolet radiation, excess or deficient nutrients, toxic substances, or disease-producing organisms. Some people are clearly more flexible than others in responding to different stressors. Some do better in heat and others in cold, for complex reasons of diet, physique, metabolism, and adjustments since infancy. But all people can tolerate a wide range of environmental conditions; our adaptability is part of our genetic programming.

In contrast to the adaptive changes in gene frequency, discussed in the previous section, which require more than a generation to develop, physiological adaptation occurs within a lifetime. Some changes are instantaneous, as when the pupil of your eye narrows in response to light. Other changes take longer, such as skin tanning after exposure to ultraviolet rays. Most types of physiological adaptation are reversible, but certain ones that develop over a long time are irreversible, such as the barrel-chested physique that develops in people who grow up at high altitudes in the Andes and the Himalayas. Many scientists question whether all these physiological changes should even be called "adaptation." They try to reserve that term for evolutionary, genetic change.

Physiological changes occur more rapidly than do genetic changes, and they are often more reversible. They form a graded response system in which short-term and long-term adjustments of different kinds are made by individuals, who vary in their genetically endowed ability to make those adjustments successfully. Three levels of physiological adaptation can be distinguished. *Acclimation* is rapid, short-term adjustment to an environmental stressor. *Acclimatization* is a more pervasive but still reversible response to change over a more extended period. This acquired acclimatization can be contrasted with native or *developmental acclimatization*, which is the radical, irreversible result of exposure during growth to a given set of environmental stressors (Stini 1975b:9). The differences among these concepts are seen in the ways people adapt to high altitudes.

High-altitude Adaptation

Reduced oxygen pressure at high altitudes is one of the most severe forms of environmental stress that people tolerate. Lowlanders who visit the mountains at 10,000 feet (3000 meters) above sea level may suffer mountain sickness due to *hypoxia*, insufficient oxygen reaching the tissues, especially if they exert themselves physically. The symptoms are nausea, shortness of breath, and headaches.

In adjusting to low oxygen pressure, faster breathing and a more rapid heartbeat are immediate responses. Later there is a gradual increase in the number of red blood cells circulating, which makes more hemoglobin available for carrying oxygen to the tissues. The capacity to adapt to high altitudes varies individually. Some people never do become successfully acclimatized, while others adjust but are not capable of full work effort. Most athletes participating in the 1968 Olympics in Mexico City, at 7500 feet (2300 meters), adapted well enough to compete, but only after a period of acclimatization at high-altitude training camps.

Lifetime residents of high altitudes make a set of characteristic anatomical and physiological adjustments that give them the capacity for sustained work in thin mountain air (Stini 1975b:53–64; Mazess 1975; Baker 1978; Baker and Little 1976). They tend to be short-legged, to grow slowly, and to have a large thoracic volume. A rounded rib cage and long sternum increase the chest volume, which accommodates larger lungs. They also have more red marrow, a tissue that produces red blood cells, in the ribs and sternum.

High-altitude populations also differ from sea level populations in

FIGURE 3.7   By studying people living at high altitudes, such as these Sherpa from a village in central Nepal, anthropologists attempt to understand developmental adaptation to altitude.

Photo by John M. Bishop.

their greater blood volume, red cell volume and concentration, total and relative hemoglobin, and greater acidity of the blood. Pumping this more viscous blood enlarges the heart muscle, especially the right ventricle, which pumps blood to the lungs.

Like all adaptations to environmental extremes, these adaptations to high altitudes are neither perfect nor without costs. Higher levels of adrenocortical stress hormones seem to predispose high-altitude men to gastric ulcers (Stini 1975b:62). Another cost is the high rate of stillbirths and a tendency for babies to have low birth weights. But in these populations, babies weighing less than 2500 grams (about $5\frac{1}{2}$ pounds) and thus technically considered premature (whether they are full-term or not) survive considerably more than expected among sea-level populations. Thus it appears that natural selection favors low birth weights in hypoxic environments (Stini 1975b:63). This selection may ultimately contribute to adaptive genetic changes in populations long-resident at high altitudes, but there is little evidence that unique genetic traits play as large a role in adaptation as do flexible homeostatic adjustments over the span of the individual's lifetime.

Cold Adaptation

People who live at high altitudes must adapt to cold as well as to hypoxia, but adaptation to cold has been more thoroughly studied in arctic and subarctic regions. In experiments on cold response, Inuit and Indians perform better than do Europeans. The skin of natives' fingers, hands, and feet remains warmer for a longer period, and the tissues and joints are better protected (Steegmann 1975:145). Adults do better on these tests than children do, though, indicating that physiological adaptation to cold develops over one's lifetime.

Most tests of cold response are conducted in laboratory situations simulating natural conditions, for example, immersing the person's fingers in ice water and measuring his responses. Recent studies of cold adaptation by Marshall Hurlich (1976) among Cree Indians and by A. T. Steegmann, Jr. (1977) among Ojibwa Indians in northern Ontario (also see Hurlich and Steegmann 1979) combined these standard techniques with additional measures conducted outside the laboratory, while men were riding snowmobiles, cutting firewood, hunting, and trapping. These human biologists found that adaptation to cold stress involves more than just physiological responses. Coping with the cold is affected by the kind of food consumed, by methods of handling equipment during travel, by knowledge of weather patterns, and by intelligence and judgment. In other words, response to an environmental stressor is never purely physiological in human beings; cultural patterns and individual behavioral variation also influence the chances of survival. Physiological responses prove critical, however, in the unexpected emergency. The body's ability to conserve heat, to resist frostbite, and to keep active with very little food serves as a kind of emergency reserve, allowing the habitual response repertoire to stretch well beyond the usual limits.

Culture has a dual role in relation to the process of physiological adaptation. Cultural patterns buffer environmental extremes and create artificial microclimates. Properly speaking, Inuit do not live in the Arctic so much as they live in tents or snowhouses and in tailored skin clothing. On the other hand, while culture protects humans from many environmental stressors, it can create new ones also. Rock music or air hammers create noise levels greater than the human ear is normally required to adapt to in nature. In his book *Man Adapting* (1965), René Dubos explores the high price of human adaptability. He expresses dismay that people can adapt to the noise, pollution, and crowding of industrial cities and come to consider this kind of environment as normal. This acceptance is the tragic side of adaptability.

The following health profile shows the dual role of culture as both creating stresses and as providing a repertoire of adaptive responses to a problem with a genetic basis: intolerance to lactose in milk.

PROFILE: LACTOSE TOLERANCE

It is not always easy to discover whether a particular adaptation is genetic or physiological. The problem of milk drinking and lactose tolerance illustrates this. Humans, like other mammals, are able to digest lactose (milk sugar) during infancy. And like other mammals, most humans lose this ability as they grow up. In later childhood and adulthood, they show very low levels of activity of *lactase,* the enzyme in the small intestine that breaks down lactose into the simple sugar glucose. However, in some human populations in which dairying is practiced, most adults retain sufficient lactase activity to be able to digest lactose. After drinking milk or a laboratory solution of lactose, tests of their blood show a rise in glucose, indicating that the lactose has been transformed into a usable energy source. These individuals are said to be *lactose tolerant.*

Lactose tolerance tends to be prevalent among populations who have used milk products for a long time, especially among people from northern and western Europe, as well as among some African herding peoples such as the Bahima of Uganda. But in populations in which adults do not drink milk, *lactose intolerance* is prevalent. The lactose is not broken down to glucose, and in large amounts it may cause the symptoms of fermentative diarrhea: cramps, flatulence and belching, and a watery, explosive diarrhea (Lerner and Libby 1976:327).

Lactose intolerance is common among Orientals; the indigenous peoples of North and South America, Australia, and Oceania; and the African peoples who were not traditionally herders, including their American black descendants. In the United States, Orientals are about 95 percent intolerant, blacks around 75 percent, Native Americans around 60 percent, and Caucasians quite variable, between 2 and 24 percent in various samples.

Some populations seem to be exceptions to the neat correspondence between dairying and lactose tolerance. Some groups, such as Mexican-Americans, show intermediate frequencies, reflecting a complex ancestry or too recent a history of milk drinking for adaptation to have occurred. Mediterranean and Near Eastern peoples such as Greeks, Italians, and Jews have a long history of milking animals, yet they have high rates of intolerance. In these and many other cultures, however, milk is used in ways that reduce the lactose content—as cheese, yogurt, and fermented milk products in which some of the lactose is converted to lactic acid. The milking of domesticated animals is an important cultural adaptation to nutritional stress, and techniques of preparing fermented milk products are cultural adaptations that facilitate the use of milk by lactose-intolerant populations.

A simple hypothesis to explain the distribution of lactose tolerance and intolerance in human populations would be that a physiological adaptation enables individuals who continue to drink milk throughout life to maintain lactase activity and digest lactose. In this view, the continual challenge to digest lactose keeps the enzyme active. This hypothesis can be tested by feeding lactose regularly to lactose-intolerant individuals or by withholding milk from lactose-tolerant individuals. Changes in their lactase activity are then measured over a period of weeks or months. The result of this kind of study so far suggests that adult lactase activity does not change much either way. If physiological adaptation does occur, it must be a long-term process during childhood development, since adults are not very flexible in this regard.

Although the evidence is not all in, most researchers accept a second hypothesis: that lactose tolerance is a genetic adaptation of dairying populations. In populations where dairying is absent, there is no selective advantage to lactose tolerance, but where adults do drink milk, the lactose-tolerant individual has some selective advantage. Just what the mechanism of natural selection is in this case is still an open question, however. McCracken (1971) and Simoons (1970) both suggest that the lactose-tolerant individual might be better nourished and thus able to reproduce more effectively. It is true that lactose is an added source of carbohydrate for those who can digest it, but carbohydrates are usually abundantly available from cereal grains in dairying areas. Even those who are lactose intolerant can use the protein and fat in milk, unless they drink large enough quantities to produce diarrhea, so it is hard to see that lactose intolerance would be a serious nutritional disadvantage. More recently, it has been suggested that the selective advantage of lactose tolerance for Europeans is that lactose facilitates calcium absorption, helping prevent rickets and osteomalacia, which have been significant health problems for these northern peoples (Flatz and Rotthauwe 1973).

Further research is clearly needed. The mechanism of inheritance is not yet known. Even researchers who accept the genetic hypothesis are not sure whether a single gene or multiple genes are involved (Harrison 1975). Some conclusions are based on testing very few individuals, and some on laboratory techniques that have not been standardized. Many populations have not been tested at all. Most studies have dichotomized people into two groups—lactose tolerant and lactose intolerant—but in fact some people are more intolerant than others, and this variability needs to be explored.

One practical implication of the research on lactose tolerance is that milk is clearly not good for everybody, and it is ethnocentric for Americans to assume that dried or condensed milk would be of benefit to people in Africa or South America. Knowing that milk can cause digestive upsets helps us understand why recipients of powdered milk as emergency aid have used the milk to whitewash their buildings and have even accused aid programs of being U.S. plots to poison them (Lerner and Libby 1976:327).

Because most populations of the world are lactose intolerant as adults, it seems unwise to encourage every developing nation to give priority to the costly expansion of a dairy industry. Nutrition programs in the United States and in other countries where a significant minority are lactose intolerant might also offer milk substitutes. Yet overreaction is also unwise. The appropriate use of milk in amounts and forms in which it can be tolerated can make an important nutritional contribution, even in populations where lactose intolerance is prevalent.

CULTURAL AND INDIVIDUAL ADAPTATION

When environmental change occurs, humans can respond rapidly and flexibly by change in their behavior: they can come in out of the rain. Behavioral adaptation ranks along with genetic and physiological adaptation as a major type of response to environmental alterations. Some behavioral adaptations are idiosyncratic, or specific to the individual regardless of cultural background. These *individual adaptations* are studied, for the most part, by psychologists. Other behavioral adaptations are shared by members of a society and are traditional; these *cultural adaptations* are the special focus of anthropologists (Carneiro 1968a).

A culture is often casually defined as a way of life, but inherent in this phrase is an ambiguity. On the one hand, it implies a lifestyle with a set of behavioral symbols full of meaning for some subgroup of humanity. On the other hand, the emphasis can be shifted to a culture as a way *of life,* in the sense of a strategy for survival, a population's means of staying alive under the pressures of natural selection. Depending on the balance between these two perspectives—the symbolic and the ecological—different anthropologists' priorities in cultural analysis may be very different.

Each culture, whether simple or complex, is comprised of *technology, social organization,* and *ideology.* These components of culture evolve in interaction with each other and with the environment. The cattle-herding peoples adapted to the grasslands of East Africa, for example, share patterns of subsistence technology, settlement patterns, and religious beliefs that differ systematically from those of the West African tropical forest farmers mentioned in the malaria profile earlier in this chapter.

Culture Learning

Many of the adaptive processes used by humans to cope with environmental problems are based on information and skills that have been learned. In growing up, children learn how to get food, to avoid danger, to secure protection against the weather, to use raw materials for tools. They have not inherited this information genetically, and if one is abandoned by the group, he or she would find it almost impossible to learn all this through trial-and-error learning. Each generation has to learn basic survival techniques from the previous generation in the context of problem-solving interaction and communication. This process is called *cultural transmission.*

The culture of a group is an information system transmitted from one generation to another through nongenetic mechanisms. The information units are very diverse. Some are material objects, others are ideas and beliefs, and yet other units are ways of doing things—instructions or "recipes" in a broad sense. Tools, clothing, houses, weapons, music, laws, medicine, farming, raising children, regulating conflict—these and many more human behaviors and products of behavior form a complex informational system that each group member must draw on in attempting to solve problems.

Although culture is nongenetic, three genetically based characteristics underlie the human capacity for culture. First, humans have evolved extensive and complex neural connections in the cerebral cortex of the brain, with considerable overlap between specific association areas for vision, hearing, touch, and motor coordination. This overlap allows learning to occur through transfer and correlation of information between association areas. A part of this learning is the acquisition of language in early childhood, made possible by neural connections between a portion of the auditory association area and an area controlling the motor actions of speech. Without some form of language, human groups could not maintain the complex informational systems through which they adapt, nor could they easily transmit this information to children.

Second, the human hand and fingers facilitate the manipulation of objects and making of tools. Our prehensile hands can grip, lift, and throw objects with no difficulty, and our opposable thumbs allow us to pick up and work with very small tools. Evolution of this type of hand accompanied evolution of fine visual-motor coordination in the brain; the selective factor may have been differential survival of individuals and groups that used tools.

Third, humans are born as altogether dependent beings, unable to walk, to hold onto the mother, or actively to search for food. The child remains dependent on the group for many years, and this allows a long time for learning. It also allows for intense attachments to form between infants and their caretakers, usually the parents. This *bonding* behavior occurs in other animals, especially primates, and in birds as well. Humans normally form social bonds throughout their lives—with peers, coworkers, mates, their children—and they work together, creating and coordinating group strategies for meeting problems.

Some anthropologists believe that the bonding trait of humans has been selected in evolution because it is highly advantageous for survival. Since learning to be sociable is fairly easy and satisfying for humans, most people probably have innate tendencies or predispositions to affiliate with others rather than living solitary lives, even if social bonding is not fully instinctive. '

These three characteristics—a brain capable of complex learning and speech, the ability to use and make tools and other objects, and social bonding—have allowed humans to generate an impressive diversity of cultural systems and to survive in a wide range of ecological niches. Each of these characteristics provides only a generalized framework for adaptation; that is, they do not specify what people must learn, how they must use tools, or how to organize themselves socially. The content of cultural adaptation varies from population to population and from generation to generation. We have few genetic instructions on how to live effectively in a given environment, but we do have a complex cultural pool of ideas, techniques, strategies, and rules developed over many generations by group experiences in that environment. This pool encompasses far more knowledge and ideas than any one individual could learn or needs to learn. The group knows more than one person knows; people have at their disposal diverse sets of knowledge, skills, and innovative ideas.

Variability and Change in Cultural Systems

Just as the genetic pool of a population contains varied genotypes, some of which may prove over time to be more adaptive than others to environmental changes, so the informational pool of a cultural system contains considerable variation. Each person learns and replicates what he or she is taught imperfectly. Young people reinterpret rules they have learned from elders in terms of their own experiences and problems. Changes occur also through selective retention of new ideas and techniques that promote the effectiveness of the group or of the individual in dealing with problems, including situations that threaten the integration of the group and the self. These new ideas may be innovated within the group, but frequently they are borrowed from neighboring groups, travelers and traders, allies and enemies. Adaptation in this sense extends beyond ecological systems. It also involves adjustments and changes that increase the group's competence and security, maintain the community's physical and emotional health, and protect the individual and defend the ego.

We come to understand individual adaptation through psychological concepts, giving attention to how the mind works, how the person learns from his or her cultural system to cope emotionally with pressures exerted by that cultural system. The individual uses culture but is always a bit separate from it. A cultural system emerges from the interaction of two or more people. Thus the study of cultural adaptation focuses on the community or population rather than on the individual.

As a population process, cultural adaptation is analogous to genetic adaptation. Cultures evolve—that is, they undergo directed adaptive changes in response to environmental pressures and challenges—just as biological populations evolve, although the mechanisms that bring about the two types of evolution differ. Further, biological evolution in humans has paralleled cultural evolution; there has been natural selection for traits underlying the human ability to learn, to communicate, and to work together, the fundamental requirements for a cultural system. In turn, cultural patterns have affected biological evolution, at times protecting humans against the selective forces of disease and climatic extremes, at other times intensifying natural selection through ecological changes that increase disease.

Cultural Adaptation and Health

Cultural adaptation to health problems involves both conscious, intended efforts to control disease and unconscious, unintended effects of certain customs on health. The latter type of adaptation is particularly of interest because positive biological feedback may contribute toward the selective retention of certain customs. Male circumcision, for example, has been practiced for thousands of years in Middle Eastern countries. Although it is done for religious and social reasons, it may bring about unintended health benefits. An uncircumcised male is more likely to introduce smegma, a thick, bad-smelling genital secretion, into contact with the cervix. Smegma is thought to be a possible factor in the causation of cancer of the cervix. The rates of cervical cancer are in fact extremely low among Jewish, Moslem, and Parsee women (Wynder et al. 1954 and Graham 1963, as cited in Lieban 1973:1041).

Many cultural patterns affect health indirectly. When the effect is positive, the pattern is considered to be adaptive even though people may not be aware of the adaptive value of what they are doing. In other words, a custom may have **adaptive functions** even though it is not consciously developed to solve a health problem. For example, some of the staple crops raised in Africa contain the chemical compound thiocyanate, which many researchers believe will inhibit the sickling of red blood cells. Eating these crops—which include cassava, yams, sorghum, and millet—may reduce the severity of symptoms of sickle cell anemia and decrease the chances that heterozygotes will sickle under conditions of stress (Haas and Harrison 1977:78–79).

Medical ecologists are especially interested in how populations have limited birth rates. Many societies have postpartum sex taboos, which prohibit a couple from having sexual intercourse for an extended period after the woman gives birth. People who practice this custom do not justify it in medical terms; rather, they consider it a way of protecting the individuals involved, including the child, from the mysterious forces associated with sexual and reproductive processes. But one adaptive function of the custom is birth spacing.

The subincision of males at puberty, a traditional custom of Australian Aborigines, is also thought to reduce birth rates. Subincision alters the penis so that semen is ejaculated high in the urethra, from the base rather than the tip of the penis, thus reducing the chances of conception. This ritual ordeal has more than one function. The more readily observable function is the way it bonds the young male to the group, acknowledging that he is now an adult who has access to sacred knowledge. The ritual also asserts his sexual and masculine identity, functioning to enhance individual adaptation while also functioning socially by reaffirming the group's role structure. The ritual's indirect adaptive function to reduce the birth rate—a continual problem for nomadic people—was probably not consciously intended by the Aborigines.

Dietary taboos are another aspect of culture that may have latent health functions. Although it is possible that many taboos once had very pragmatic bases, over many generations people came to consider them sacred without fully understanding their original purpose. For example, southeastern American Indians had taboos against the use of salt by menstruating and pregnant women, by adolescents during puberty rituals, and by warriors. Thomas Neumann (1977) suggests that the restriction of salt intake could be of benefit in reducing hypertension and water retention in women and reducing complications of pregnancy and childbirth.

Direct Medical Control Strategies

Functional interpretations of the adaptive value of customs and taboos contribute to considerable controversy in medical anthropology. Somewhat less problematic is the study of adaptive mechanisms that are directly intended to control disease and improve health. Each population has access to a cultural system of information, roles, and skills specifically developed to maintain health, however the society defines the concept. As mentioned in chapter 1, we call such a system an **ethnomedical system.** Ethnomedical systems include all the beliefs and knowledge held both by health specialists and by nonspecialists about sickness and health, childbirth, nutrition, and death. They include rules for the behavior expected of healers and patients, and the skills, implements, and medicines used by healers and by patients.

Ethnomedicine need not be considered to be exclusively folk or primitive medicine. For comparative purposes, it is useful to define ethnomedicine as the health maintenance system of any society, operating in "a matrix of values, traditions, beliefs, and patterns of ecological adaptation" (Landy 1977:131). Each medical system reflects the core values of the people who use that system.

Cosmopolitan medicine is the ethnomedical system that most Americans use much of the time. It is often called Western medicine because of its historical origins, but the term "cosmopolitan medicine" more accurately reflects its distribution in most of the cities of the world. This ethnomedical system operates within a cultural matrix that stresses the value of technology, control over the environment, and hierarchical, specialized healing roles. The values of this matrix support a medicine that tries to control and eradicate disease through surgery, drugs, public health measures, and a perplexing array of highly specialized medical personnel and procedures.

Humoral medicine, practiced for thousands of years in the Mediterranean and Middle East and brought to Latin America by Spaniards, has a different set of values, derived from a philosophy of balance between the fundamental qualities of nature. To deal with sickness, the practitioner attempts to restore the body's equilibrium in its hot and cold, wet and dry qualities. Diagnosis, therapies and medicines, and prevention must take into consideration the principle that foods, drugs, and even types of illnesses have innate qualities. In Guatemala, for example, diarrhea is classified as a cold disease, and therefore penicillin, a cold medicine, is not appropriate for treatment. But if the disease is dysentery, it is considered hot because of the presence of blood, and then penicillin is acceptable because the hot disease and the cold medicine counterbalance (Logan 1978:365–371).

In some societies, healing and religion overlap and the people themselves do not distinguish between the two. The Navaho religious system is concerned almost exclusively with healing ceremonies and maintaining health through spiritual harmony. In other societies, specialized healing systems coexist and sometimes compete. In the United States, for example, one can go to a practitioner of cosmopolitan medicine, to a spiritualist healer, to an acupuncture specialist, to a teacher of transcendental meditation, and to a naturopath who heals through nutritional change. Which system is likely to be most effective depends partly on the nature of the illness and partly on the patient's expectations. If the patient has faith in the healer, the anxiety and stress associated with (or causing) the illness will be reduced, thus increasing the chance for the prescribed therapy to be effective.

Every ethnomedical system has some empirical components—including systems that heavily rely on ritual and magic—and these treatments are often quite effective. The Navaho use sweat baths and emetics in their ceremonies; the Inuit used confession as a means of alleviating guilt and reducing group tensions. Widespread empirical techniques include the use of minerals, plants, and animal products as medicines. Tannins in bark and tea are effective in treating hemorrhage, ulcers, burns, and diarrhea. Oils can be used as cathartics, and as treatment for worms, burns, and frostbite. Chemicals in willow leaves provide a medicine similar to aspirin. Marijuana, opium, and hashish are widely used as medicines, as is rauwolfia, an effective tranquilizer (Alland 1970).

Therapies intended to benefit the patient vary greatly in their empirical value, and we can find negative effects and maladaptive aspects of every ethnomedical system. Cosmopolitan medicine as practiced in the United States relies heavily on surgery for therapy, which at times is not the most effective approach to treatment. Purging, blistering, and bleeding were standard treatments in eighteenth-century America; they contributed to the death of George Washington when physicians tried to treat him for an infection (Landy 1977:130). Dietary taboos in Southeast Asian medical systems restrict women from eating fruits and vegetables for forty days after childbirth, for these foods are considered dangerously cold to a body weakened by childbirth. These taboos can make existing anemias worse and lower the level of nutrients that lactating mothers need (Wilson 1977:303).

Ethnomedical systems also vary in their definitions of what conditions should be considered an illness and be treated. The Chinese of Hong Kong traditionally believed that everyone must have measles, and they treated it not as a disease but as a transition from one life stage to another, accompanied by ritual. Even though mortality from measles was high, they accepted the condition as an inevitable fact and not something to be treated medically (Topley 1970).

In some cases, a physical impairment may be defined as a disease, but for social and political reasons it may not be recognized as worthy of special treatment. For instance, sickle cell anemia has not had the status of a legitimate social problem in the United States until quite recently. Organized concern required political action by the ethnic group most affected by the disease, black Americans. Communication, publicity, and lobbying for federal funds were necessary for cultural adaptation to this disease (Kunitz 1974).

In the first health profile of this chapter, sickle cell anemia was mentioned only in passing as a disease related to genetic adaptation to a malarial environment; the malarial environment itself shaped by cultural adaptation of farmers. The following health profile discusses sickle cell disease from the perspective of cultural adaptation, examining the range of medical, political, and individual adaptive processes available for dealing with a disease once a society decides that it requires action.

PROFILE: INDIVIDUAL AND CULTURAL ADAPTATIONS TO SICKLE CELL ANEMIA

During my childhood I had frequent abdominal and leg pains, severe headaches, and upset stomach, and my eyes became very jaundiced, though nobody knew why. When I was twelve years old my legs hurt so badly that Mother thought I had polio. She took me to a family physician who told me I had growing pains and sent me home.

> —Ozella Keys Fuller, in Olafson and Parker (1973:4)*

About three out of every thousand black children born in the United States suffer from sickle cell anemia, a chronic hereditary disease in which many of the red blood cells become rigid in sickle or crescent shapes and clog the capillaries. Many children with sickle cell anemia do not survive through adolescence, dying from infections, heart failure, and strokes. Patients suffer painful crises at unpredictable intervals and are typically underweight, slow to mature, and dependent on protective, anxious parents. There is no fully effective treatment, and many physicians, like the one who dismissed Ozella Keys's symptoms as "growing pains," are not trained to diagnose and treat this disease.

Until very recently, far fewer government funds and private

---

*This excerpt and those on the immediately following pages are reprinted from Ozella Keys Fuller, in Freya Olafson and Alberta W. Parker, *Sickle Cell Anemia—The Neglected Disease* (Berkeley, California: University Extension Publications, University of California, 1973), pp. 4–5.

donations have been available for research on sickle cell anemia than for other hereditary childhood diseases. Black clinicians and researchers hold that the lack of government and public concern stems from the fact that the disease primarily affects minority children. They see a reflection of health politics in the paradox that the genetic and molecular bases for hemoglobin abnormalities are quite well understood, while research on treatment and diagnosis has lagged.

It is not possible to detect the disease through the diagnostic procedure of amniocentesis, and diagnosis is also very difficult during the first six months after birth. The infant's red cells contain mostly fetal hemoglobin, and sickling does not occur until most of the fetal hemoglobin is lost after six months.

The first sign of sickle cell anemia in a small child is swelling and pain in the hands and feet due to the blockage of blood vessels.

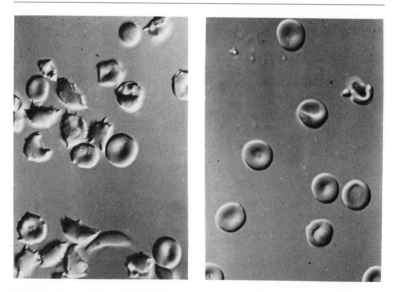

FIGURE 3.8   Red blood cells with abnormal hemoglobin molecules (left) tend to clump and sickle under low oxygen tension, in contrast to normal red blood cells (right).

Photos: The Rockefeller University.

Each attack of this "hand-foot syndrome" lasts one to two weeks and recurs periodically until the child is three or four years old. Another symptom is an enlarged spleen. A spleen congested with destroyed, sickled cells cannot carry out its usual function of clearing bacteria from the blood stream, and the child resists infection poorly (Pearson 1973:247).

Sickling of red cells is due to abnormal hemoglobin molecules that tend to clump and damage the red blood cell membrane during conditions of low oxygen tension. The genetic factors responsible for this abnormality, discussed earlier in this chapter, are summarized in figure 3.9.

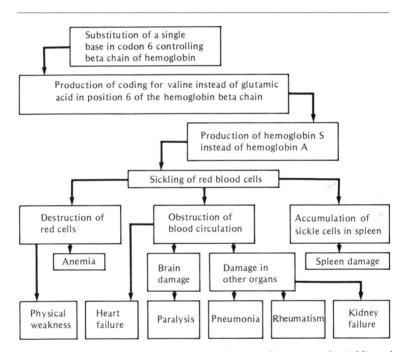

FIGURE 3.9 A single molecular change in DNA coding causes the sickling of red blood cells and can lead to a variety of physiological problems shown in this chart.

SOURCE: Modified from Michael Lerner and William J. Libby, *Heredity, Evolution and Society*, Second edition (San Francisco: W. H. Freeman, 1976), p. 109; originally developed by James V. Neel and William J. Schull, *Human Heredity* (Chicago: University of Chicago Press, 1958).

Can you imagine how it would feel to have a knife going through your bone marrow? Or imagine that someone is constantly stabbing you in the chest with a knife, or that you have a tourniquet around your arm that is cutting off all circulation? I have fainted many times, unable to bear the pain, even with the large amounts of pain medicine that were given to me.
—Ozella Keys Fuller, in Olafson and Parker (1973:5)

Ozella Fuller is describing a sickle cell crisis, an acute phase of the disease usually precipitated by infection. The most painful type of crisis is caused by the obstruction of blood flow, which cuts off oxygen from tissues. Other causes of crisis include failure by the bone marrow to produce enough red cells, and accumulation of blood in the spleen. These crises are not as painful, but they require blood transfusions and can be fatal. Crises are difficult to manage; the toxic effects of sickling trigger continued sickling, and transfusions are not always effective.

Children have an average of four crises per year up to age 6, and the highest death rate among patients occurs during these first six years of life. Before medical care became available, the average life expectancy for patients was twenty years.

Crises are less frequent during middle childhood, and the child's chances of surviving are reasonably good. But because of poor circulation, there are risks of damage to tissues, bone deformities, blood clots, ulcers on the surface of the leg that are difficult to heal, and lesions on the retina.

Medical intervention is needed to deal with crises, but certain physiological adaptations allow the child to function fairly normally in spite of chronic anemia. The heart becomes enlarged, and cardiac output increases. The level of phosphate compounds in the red cells increases also, changing the oxygen affinity of the hemoglobin and increasing oxygen delivery to tissues (Gorst 1976:1437).

Along with these physiological responses, the child must learn to cope with a variety of social and psychological problems. Because ordinary childhood bruises and scrapes can precipitate a crisis, the child must be cautious in play and sports; thus she or he becomes identified as "different" by neighbors and schoolmates. The very real possibility that the child could die reminds teachers and friends of their own vulnerability, and their normal denial or avoidance responses serve to inhibit discussion about the disease with the child, maintaining the "conspiracy of silence" that so often surrounds a fatal childhood disease.

Children with sickle cell anemia find it difficult to discuss their condition with family members also. Parents may feel guilty because their child has a hereditary disease. During early crises when the child's condition is critical, family members may have experienced "expectant mourning" for the child, anticipating death or preparing emotionally for the possibility of death. This kind of emotional preparedness for loss creates tension (Olafson and Parker 1973:26). To cope with these feelings, parents and family members use certain psychological defenses.

One common defense is to pretend that the child does not really have sickle cell anemia, to repress thoughts about death, and to take an optimistic view of the child's future. This is a valuable adaptive response for parents. But it allows the child no outlet for discussing fears about death, which become very real at each crisis or hint of a crisis. Parents also adapt by overprotecting the child. Any sign of physical discomfort creates anxiety; both children and parents find it hard to distinguish between ordinary pains and the pain that signals the onset of a crisis (Vavasseur 1977:337).

> I was 19 before I seriously realized that I had to give up things. I had to give up the idea of going to nursing school, which I dearly loved, and go to work to pay my hospital bills. Later I learned that the normal eight-hour work day would be overexertion for me and would very likely lead to a serious attack. I have been forced to give up work altogether. I must also be very careful to avoid minor accidents. A small bruise or bump, which most people can brush off, might send me to the hospital.
> —Ozella Keys Fuller, in Olafson and Parker (1973:5)

Adolescence is particularly difficult because the young person is pessimistic about getting a good job, continuing in school, or planning on marriage. During adolescence, the frequency of crises increases; hospitalizations and the frequent need for Demerol or morphine to reduce pain make it impossible to maintain a normal schedule.

The adolescent with sickle cell anemia usually feels unattractive sexually, typically being underweight and slow to mature, with jaundiced eyes and leg ulcers. Female patients feel hostile toward normal women who can plan to have families, and this hostility may be directed toward their own mothers as a normal defense against dependence on the mother, who typically has been very protective of the sick child (LePontois 1975:73–74).

An effective approach to helping adolescents cope with depression and family tensions is group psychotherapy. The sense of isolation and hopelessness breaks down as group members share feelings and information (LePontois 1975). Parents also benefit from group counseling and information sessions given by teams of nurses and social workers.

The trend toward psychological support for sickle cell patients and their families began in the early 1970s through the development of comprehensive care programs at fifteen Comprehensive Sickle Cell Centers supported by federal funds (Vavasseur 1977:335). In 1972, Congress appropriated $143 million for research, screening, counseling, and public information programs to be administered through various federal agencies. Implementation of the bill, the National Sickle Cell Anemia Control Act, sparked a number of community action programs, fundraising efforts, camps for children, and conferences of clinicians and other health personnel.

> *I have just gotten married, and knowing my disease, we have no intention of having a child. That is an individual decision, and I am not telling others with sickle cell anemia to do the same. But because I know exactly what my condition is, how serious and chronic it is, it would be ignorant of me to bear a child. There is a fifty-fifty chance that I would not survive giving birth. If I did survive, I would still run the risk of bearing an injured child.*
> —Ozella Keys Fuller, in Olafson and Parker (1973:5)

One of the more controversial aspects of managing sickle cell anemia is in the area of genetic counseling. Not everyone agrees with Ozella Fuller that the sickle cell patient should give up hope of having children, and many resist the idea of sterilization in hopes that an effective treatment will be developed.

Genetic counseling is of particular concern in screening programs. Electrophoresis, an inexpensive test that passes a blood sample through an electric field, is used not only to diagnose the disease but also to detect whether a person carries the sickling trait. Between 8 and 10 percent of all black Americans have inherited the sickle cell trait that gave their African ancestors an advantage in resisting malaria. These 2 million or so people do not suffer from anemia; however, when two people with the trait mate, there is a one in two chance that their child will also carry the trait as they do, and a one in four chance that their child will have sickle cell disease.

In an effort to prevent sickle cell anemia through genetic counseling of trait carriers, twenty-eight states had passed sickle cell testing laws by the mid-1970s. Fifteen states require compulsory testing either of black schoolchildren or of all blacks applying for marriage licenses. Some people view both kinds of screening as discriminatory and a violation of civil rights, since Caucasians may also have the sickling trait but are not required to be tested.

Critics question the timing of either type of screening. Genetic counseling of school-age carriers is inappropriate; as Gary (1977) says, "a child of seven . . . should not be expected to deal with the notion that he might give his future children a fatal disease unless he selects a marriage partner who is not a carrier" (p. 366). If, on the other hand, screening is not done until the time of marriage, the emotional impact can be traumatic for a man and woman who plan to have a family but discover that they are both trait carriers. The impact is doubly traumatic when the discovery is made only after the woman is pregnant.

Laws requiring genetic screening for the trait have led to confusion about whether the trait is a mild form of the disease. For example, the federal bill passed in 1972 erroneously states that sickle cell anemia "afflicts approximately two million American citizens." This is the number of trait carriers, but certainly not all of them are debilitated with the disease. It is only very special circumstances—such as heavy exercise at high altitudes, deep sea diving, or deep anesthesia—that pose serious problems for the trait carrier's health.

Confusion between the trait and the disease continues to be perpetuated in the media, by fund raisers who inflate statistics, and even by lawyers who hope to exempt clients from military duty (Bowman 1974:50). Carriers are discriminated against by life insurance companies, and they are rejected for employment by airlines because of the slight possibility of sickling if oxygen pressure is not maintained properly at high altitudes (Johnson 1974:60). Given these discriminatory attitudes, it is not surprising that blacks resent compulsory screening and insist that confidentiality be improved in screening programs.

To compound the level of controversy that surrounds the sickling trait and the actual disease, black leaders are divided on the issue of using federal funding for research. Some leaders encourage continued work on new treatments such as the use of sodium cyanate to increase the oxygen affinity of hemoglobin S (Cerami and Peterson 1975) or the use of zinc or procaine to inhibit calcium formation in the red cell membrane (Brewer 1976:125).

But other leaders question the importance of the disease in comparison to other health problems of blacks in the United States. They point out that in 1975 approximately 13,500 blacks died from complications of hypertension, while only 340 died from sickle cell anemia (Gary 1977:363). Simple iron deficiency is far more prevalent among blacks than is sickle cell anemia. The health of blacks in this country is poor not because of genetic disabilities, but because of discrimination, inadequate health care, poverty, and psychological stress. Too great an emphasis on a single genetic disease could simply feed racist ideas about biological inferiority and serve to deflect attention from other health problems.

LIMITS TO ADAPTATION

In this chapter, we have seen that the relationship between adaptation and health is complex. Adaptation is an ongoing series of adjustments to environmental problems, and not all adjustments guarantee the health of each individual. The history of sickle cell anemia, itself an evolutionary by-product to adaptive mechanisms operating in malarial environments, shows a series of cultural adjustments over time to this health problem. These adjustments have not been completely satisfactory to all individuals involved. Various treatment approaches, for example, pose additional health risks for patients. Prevention efforts, such as screening and counseling, create emotional stress in carriers of the sickle cell trait. Efforts to deal with disease usually carry certain built-in risks. Adaptation is never perfect; it involves compromises between what is desirable and what is possible, given social and technological limitations.

Another example of how adaptation involves a series of adjustments between desired and undesired outcomes is the use of "night soil," human feces, as a source of fertilizer by subsistence farmers in many areas of the world. In areas with high population density and scarcity of land, this recycling of organic matter increases soil fertility and food production. In an ecological sense, the use of human feces as fertilizer is an adaptive response to the problem of low soil fertility. But from a medical viewpoint, this agricultural practice poses health risks, since human feces often contain the eggs and cysts of parasites. Roundworm, hookworm, and amoebic dysentery are especially likely to be transmitted to people working in the fields and consuming the plants (Alland 1970:13; Cockburn 1977:88). However, the risk of disease can be reduced by storing the feces for several days. Combustion occurs in the manure during storage, reducing the number of eggs (Alland 1970:95, 131).

Anthropologist Alexander Alland, Jr., applies the mathematical term "minimax" to cultural practices that minimize the risk of disease and maximize the benefit to the group (Alland 1970:2–3). The idea here is that environment and population are adversaries in a game of survival;

each player works to maximize its advantage and to anticipate the opponent's "moves." The game rarely ends, of course, and a population must continue to "make do" through a series of minimax strategies rather than try to achieve absolute success. At any point, the adaptation attained is often an uneasy compromise, and changing historical and ecological circumstances assure that no adaptation is ever complete or final.

The So of Uganda are a case in point (Laughlin 1978). These mountain people have a long history of coping with periodic droughts. In rainy years they traditionally raised crops and gathered honey, and in drought years they hunted. Around 1880 they began trading ivory from elephant tusks, and by 1910 they had decimated the elephant population in the region. In effect, the So had eliminated their major source of food in drought periods, and they quickly overhunted and depleted other game animals too. At this point, the So could not maintain their cycle of farming and hunting, and they shifted to herding cattle and goats. In the 1950s, neighboring tribes began raiding their large herds. The So had to move closer to administrative centers for protection, thus increasing population density and competition for crop land, water, and grazing land.

During drought years, nutritional pressure on the population is severe, and a series of social responses are evoked. Households hoard food and do not share with their kin. Young men travel long distances to hunt, bringing little of the game back to the household. Wage labor and trade increase, with decreasing interdependence and reciprocity among kin, who quarrel about conflicts over grazing and water rights and debt payments. Acting in counterbalance against these fissioning tendencies is an acceleration of the ritual cycle for rainmaking ceremonies, blessing of crops, and exorcism of spirits that cause sickness. These rituals maintain some degree of community solidarity.

This history of successive adaptations by the So reflects the fact that human groups modify their habitats through their subsistence patterns. Too much success in hunting creates ecological imbalance, as does overgrazing by cattle. It is not unusual for humans to create the very problems to which they must adapt.

Every human community has a remarkably wide and varied response repertoire, or reaction range, to deal with problems, but this range is not infinite. The human body has limits, and illness and stress are indications that those limits are being exceeded. People can work as high as 19,000 feet (5900 meters) in a mine in the Andes mountains of Peru, but they cannot live at such high levels, suffering loss of appetite and weight and difficulty in sleeping. At 17,500 feet (5700 meters), however, they can live comfortably with none of these symptoms (Hock 1970).

The Peruvians' ability to adapt to high altitudes is an example of lifetime adjustments and local genetic differences in response potential. The wide response range is a product of the evolutionary past of the human species, but the Highlanders' specialized anatomy and physiology are products of lifetime development rather than of clearly evident evolutionary change. If human adaptation operated primarily through biological evolution, hominids might have differentiated into several species—one adapted to high altitudes, another to arctic climates, another to deserts, and perhaps more recently even a *Homo urbanus,* a creature adapted to the crowding and pollution of cities. But this has not happened. Humans have moved into a large number of ecological niches and environments while remaining a single species, relatively unspecialized in anatomy and physiology. Our major specialization is that we are more dependent on group organization and information sharing than any other species, with the possible exception of social insects. As Stini (1975b:72–74) says, the major adaptation of the human species is our *adaptability,* our plasticity in coping with a wide range of conditions.

CONCLUSIONS

The concept of adaptation presented here has been greatly influenced by Darwin's theory of selection. According to his theory, adaptation involves the differential survival and differential reproduction of individual organisms within the context of a specific habitat. Traits that facilitate either a homeostatic plateau within a relatively stable environment or flexibility in a changing environment are more likely to be transmitted through differential reproduction to new generations. Adaptation involves both continuity and change, retention of survival-promoting traits and selection for advantageous variants. Mechanisms that work to retain advantageous traits, and select advantageous modifications need not be exclusively genetic processes. Directional change operates on both the cultural and genetic levels.

An important component of adaptation is the structuring of relationships within an ecological system, especially relationships that affect health. Organisms affect one another, and when feedback contributes to changes in levels of health, mortality, and reproduction, informational codes develop that reflect this feedback. In humans, these are both genetic codes for biochemical processes and cultural codes for technological, social, and cognitive processes. Both kinds of codes are mechanisms for survival.

The mode of inheriting cultural codes differs from genetic inheritance, but in both cases information is transmitted, and modification of information becomes possible in the transmission process. The "poor copying" of culture that occurs when children make errors or innovate in the learning process is analogous to variation in encoding point mutations. These and other types of modifications that occur in the process of transmitting genetic and cultural materials from one generation to the next allow for flexibility and variability within populations.

An unresolved question is whether variability and change are always adaptive. Are all societies informed and prescient enough to make technoeconomic choices that maximize their chances of success over the long run? The example of the So of Uganda shows how certain choices may bring brief prosperity and future hardships. Our present dependence on chemicals in industry similarly may prove maladaptive for future generations. Are all responses to the environment adaptive? The answer is probably no. Although one could say that a society that has survived at all must have maintained at least a minimal level of adaptability, to say that "what is, is therefore adaptive" is circular reasoning.

In considering the variety of primate adaptations, Hans Kummer (1971) observes that "discussions of adaptiveness sometimes leave us with the impression that every trait observed in a species must by definition be ideally adaptive, whereas all we can say with certainty is that it must be tolerable since it did not lead to extinction" (p. 90). Although Kummer refers to nonhuman primates, the point is well taken in assessing the adaptive value of the customs and choices of human populations. Some ethnomedical practices do as much harm as good; agricultural practices can leave soil eroded or full of parasites; some people are malnourished because of poor dietary choices or lack of information about proper food preparation. Yet in spite of these problems, humans usually maintain a close margin of success in balancing poor or shortsighted choices against wise or fortuitous choices of response to environmental problems. How humans have managed to maintain that narrow margin at each stage in cultural evolution will be the question explored in the following chapter.

RESOURCES

Readings

Alland, Alexander, Jr.
    1970 Adaptation in Cultural Evolution: An Approach to Medical Anthropology. New York: Columbia University Press.
    This is an informative and provocative introduction to the concept of adaptation from the perspective of both medical ecology and ethnomedicine. The book develops a game-playing model of population-environment relationships and views technological and medical changes in terms of minimax strategies.
Alland, Alexander, Jr., and Bonnie McCay
    1973 The Concept of Adaptation in Biological and Cultural Evolution. *In* Handbook of Social and Cultural Anthropology. John J. Honigmann, ed. Pp. 143–178. Chicago: Rand McNally.
    Alland and McCay discuss many definitions and models of adaptation and provide a useful history of evolutionary theory and extensive bibliography.
Birdsell, Joseph B.
    1972 Human Evolution. Chicago: Rand McNally.
    This intermediate-level text explains the principles of evolution and genetics with particular application to human prehistory, evolutionary forces at work today, and issues of racial variation. A series of focused supplements on selected topics, similar in purpose to the health profiles

used in this text, increases the interest and relevance of the text for medical anthropology students.

Damon, Albert, ed.

1975   Physiological Anthropology. New York: Oxford University Press. This moderately technical book contains articles by specialists on human responses to various stressors, including heat, cold, high altitude, light, noise, nutritional deprivation, infectious disease, and sensory deprivation and overstimulation.

Olafson, Freya, and Alberta W. Parker, eds.

1973   Sickle Cell Anemia—The Neglected Disease: Community Approaches to Combating Sickle Cell Anemia. Berkeley: University Extension, University of California. These proceedings of a symposium on sickle cell anemia held January 14–15, 1972, in San Francisco, contain speeches and articles by a variety of clinicians, social workers, community workers, and legislators.

Stini, William

1975   Ecology and Human Adaptation. Dubuque, Iowa: Wm. C. Brown. This introductory text by a physical anthropologist is concerned with both genetic adaptation and acclimatization. It includes excellent information on the genetics of sickling, on nutritional stress, and on adaption to hypoxia.

Evolving Patterns of Birth, Disease, and Death

CHAPTER 4

Photo: William H. Townsend

PREVIEW

Culture is the distinctively human strategy of adaptation. At the same time that specific cultures have adapted to specific environments, there has been a general trend for culture to become more complex. This process of sociocultural evolution has had several facets:

1. an increasingly large inventory of cultural artifacts and ideas
2. the use of increasingly large amounts of energy from new sources
3. the growth of population

All these facets of sociocultural evolution have influenced patterns of health and disease.

As technology has evolved, the major sources of environmental trauma have changed. Falls from trees are displaced by automobile accidents, arrow wounds by bullet wounds. The use of new sources of energy also presents new hazards; for example, burns and eye irritation from the smoke of cooking fires are replaced by the dangers of air and water pollution and radiation. One of the health profiles in this chapter shows how a pesticide, Kepone, affected health in a modern community.

As technology has evolved and population has grown, the characteristic human settlement has changed from a small, mobile hunting-gathering band to a farming village and then to a preindustrial and industrial city. In each of these environments, human populations enter into characteristic relationships with populations of other organisms. Among these are the organisms causing infectious and parasitic diseases. As far as we can tell from contemporary peoples, hunter-gatherers tend to suffer mostly from chronic, endemic infections. As settlements increase in size and more people are in face-to-face contact, epidemics of acute infectious disease become more significant. Mortality from epidemics became massive in preindustrial cities and their rural hinterlands, as the health profile of plague in fourteenth-century Europe illustrates. In developed industrial nations, infectious diseases have ceased to be a major factor in mortality, although they still cause much minor illness.

Changes in population patterns have not simply been due to these changes in mortality, however. Even in hunting-gathering societies, people have attempted to regulate reproduction by practices such as sexual abstinence and infanticide. These practices are related to high death rates among infants and young children in a New Guinea society profiled in this chapter. The growth, stability, or decline of a population results from the shifting balance between births, deaths, and migration. All these terms in the population equation are markedly influenced by culture.   ⬡

HAZARDS IN THE CULTURAL ENVIRONMENT

Admitted to the emergency room of a busy city hospital: a driver injured when his van hit a utility pole, a child poisoned by drinking paint thinner stored in a soft drink bottle in the garage, a woman with a gunshot wound from a family fight. Each of these patients has met with **environmental trauma,** a physical or chemical injury. Each of the examples happened to be an injury caused by a cultural artifact: automobile, paint thinner, bullet. To a great extent, culture creates the environment in which people live.

Far from the city, another cultural environment presents people with different resources and different hazards. The Hadza are hunters and gatherers of wild foods in the dry scrublands of East Africa. The greatest number of severe accidental injuries is to Hadza men who fall from trees they have climbed in search of wild honey. Another environmental hazard is the dust of the camps and the smoke of cooking fires, which are a constant irritation to the eyes of Hadza children. Conjunctivitis is another result of environmental trauma that is prevalent among the Hadza (Bennett et al. 1973).

Although automobiles and honey trees are hazards limited to certain cultures, some environmental hazards would seem nearly universal in their human impact. Earthquakes, for example, endanger people in several geologically unstable zones, the largest of these extending in a narrow band all the way around the Pacific rim from the east coast of Asia to the west coast of the Americas. In parts of this area, tropical palm-thatched houses, built of small timbers with flexible rattan joinings, simply sway with the force of a quake. The people who live in them are likely to come through unscathed unless they get in the way of a mountain landslide or a tidal wave. In densely populated agricultural areas, such as the high valleys of the Andes, timber is scarce and houses are built of clay bricks with heavy tile roofs. When these houses collapse under the force of an earthquake, their inhabitants are buried. In industrial societies, engineers can design buildings to withstand moderate earthquakes, but the existing buildings of a city are shaped as much by economic and political factors in the culture as by technological know-how. People at work in a tall office building may be safe, while nearby pedestrians may be struck by bricks falling from the facade of an old store. Even though a natural force is constant from place to place, such as an earthquake of a given magnitude, culture modifies its human impact.

Each culture defines a specific environment with a unique set of hazards and opportunities for the people who follow that way of life. At the same time, cultures are shaped by their environments. This idea of a continual dialogue between culture and environment is not new in anthropology; Julian H. Steward began to apply this approach in his research in the 1930s and summarized it in his *Theory of Culture Change* (1955). Steward's "method of cultural ecology," as he called it, places special emphasis on the technology for producing food because he found subsistence systems to be conspicuously related to the environmental resources. Ecological studies in anthropology have continued to be strongly identified with the study of subsistence; we will be discussing some of these studies in chapters 5 and 6, which deal with nutrition. Here in chapter 4 we will focus not on resources but on hazards: aspects of the physical, biological, and cultural environment that present dangers to human life. The diseases emphasized in this chapter will be primarily the result of physical and chemical trauma, infection, and parasitism, those in which environmental agents are especially prominent.

As culture has evolved, different categories of environmental agents have come into prominence; hence this chapter will have an evolutionary framework. The cultures discussed will range from simple to complex, the societies from small scale to large scale. This concept of evolution as progressive increase in complexity over time is often called *Spencerian evolution*, for Herbert Spencer, the nineteenth-century exponent of this theory. This perspective on evolution contrasts with and complements the evolutionary perspective emphasizing natural selection that is associated with another nineteenth-century evolutionist, Charles Darwin.

One aspect of the process of cultural evolution is the increase in the inventory of artifacts and ideas. This process is cumulative and accelerating, and it is the aspect in which evolution is most likely to be termed "progress." Over time, footpaths evolved to graveled roads, which evolved to paved highways. Collecting edible seeds from wild grasses evolved to grain farming. The folk healer's collection of herbs evolved to a vast pharmacopoeia.

From the point of view of the total system, complexity has increased. However, any individual participant in culture is cut off from much of this by increasing specialization. An assembly-line worker tightening the same few bolts hundreds of times experiences less varied activity in an eight-hour day than a hunter who repairs a bow, prepares arrow poison, and stalks small and large game in a work day. The factory worker controls a fraction of an enormous cultural inventory; the hunter controls virtually all of a much smaller inventory of tools and knowledge.

Another dimension of sociocultural evolution is the flow of energy through the system, measured in kilocalories (White 1969). In the simplest cultures, heat from firewood and food energy transformed into the muscle power of a small group of people represent the entire energy flow through the cultural system, no more than 5000 kilocalories per person per day. As culture evolved, animal power, wind power, and water power were added, and energy use increased about fivefold in agricultural societies. In industrial societies, fossil fuels vastly expand the flow of energy through the system. A person in the United States consumes at least 230,000 kilocalories per day, only a fraction of it as food, most as electricity and gasoline (Cook 1971).

As this chapter moves from low-energy, hunting-gathering communities to high-energy industrial society, the implications of this aspect of evolution emerge. The high-energy system has a more severe impact on its physical and biological environment; the low-energy system modifies and disturbs its environment less. At the price of high energy consumption, individuals can be protected from the necessity to adapt to environmental fluctuations such as those in temperature or food supply.

Cultures evolve as the inventory of artifacts and ideas expands, the flow of energy increases, and population expands. The pressure of a growing population on limited resources of game, water, or land may be a motive force behind social or cultural evolution. According to this theory, under population pressure, people give up old, comfortable ways of doing things and organizing themselves for new, more productive ways. Not only population pressure but also population concentration is an important factor in social evolution. As the size of the largest settlements in society has grown from villages of a few hundred people to cities of thousands and even millions, there has been a corresponding social and political evolution that orders the relationships of the larger group.

Cultural evolution has the three facets discussed above: increase in *complexity*, increase in *energy flow*, and increase in *population*. Each of these has significant effects on health and disease, which will be explored in this chapter.

THE POPULATION EQUATION

The size and density of a human population is one of the most important factors that determine patterns of disease. Disease and death, in turn, help to keep population growth under control. This depressing conclusion is only part of the population story, however. A population is formed by the processes of natality, mortality, and migration. And each of these processes is markedly influenced by culture.

Population = Births − Deaths ± Migration

Natality

Differences in birth rates normally account for the larger share of the difference in growth rates among human populations, along with differences in mortality rates among infants and small children. Some societies have achieved high levels of natality by encouraging women to marry young and continue to bear children until menopause. Of entire societies, the Hutterites, a rural communal society living in Alberta, Canada, have the highest average natality: an average Hutterite woman has nine children.

Such high natality is unusual, however. Most societies place cultural constraints on reproduction. Table 4.1 shows the completed family sizes for a wide range of human societies. In general, the smallest family size is associated with industrial society. Only slightly larger families are found among hunter-gatherers. The largest families are found among farming peoples.

All cultures place some kinds of constraints of time, place, and person on sexual intercourse. Some of these constraints may have important effects on the frequency of conception. If intercourse is successfully restricted to married people, the number of births may be reduced. Delaying marriage for young people and delaying the re-marriage of widows and divorced people can also reduce the total

FIGURE 4.1   A Hutterite mother braiding the hair of her daughter (1963). Families are large in this communal agricultural society in western Canada.
Photo by C. Low, N.F.B. Photothèque.

number of pregnancies. The absence of husbands on long trips for hunting, trapping, raiding, or wage labor will lengthen the average spacing between their wives' pregnancies. An especially widespread cultural rule is the *postpartum taboo,* mentioned in chapter 3, which serves to space births by forbidding intercourse after the birth of a child for a few months or even years, while the child is being breast-fed. Even without the postpartum taboo, long lactation by itself suppresses ovulation by stimulating the secretion of the hormone

TABLE 4.1   Number of children born to women who have completed childbearing.

	Ave. no. of children
U.S. whites (1964)	2.2
U.S. nonwhites (1964)	2.7
Eskimo, a group hunting in northern Greenland	3.5
Yanomamo of Venezuela	3.8
!Kung, hunter-gatherers in South Africa	4.1
Five Aymara agricultural villages in the Andes of Chile	5.8–8.5
Eskimo, a settled group in Alaska	8.8
Hutterites	9.0

SOURCE: Data from James N. Spuhler, "The Maximum Opportunity for Selection in Some Human Populations," pp. 192–193, in *Demographic Anthropology*, ed. Ezra B. W. Zubrow (Albuquerque: University of New Mexico Press, 1976). A School of American Research Advanced Seminar book.

prolactin and reduces the chances of conception (Jelliffe and Jelliffe 1972).

Sexual intercourse is often prohibited for other specified intervals. Prohibiting intercourse with a menstruating woman will not reduce the birth rate because conception is very rare at that time, but prohibiting intercourse before a hunting trip or during a ritual may reduce the likelihood of conception effectively, though unintentionally. Very little is known about the frequency of coitus in different societies, but there is every reason to expect it to vary cross-culturally. Some cultures regard frequent sexual contact to be dangerous or weakening, while others value it as life-giving, symbolically as well as literally.

Although effective contraceptive technology is a modern phenomenon, people in less technologically complex cultures also regulate their fertility intentionally and unintentionally. Amazonian villagers use herbal contraceptives, for example, but their effectiveness is unproved (Hern 1976). Withdrawal, or coitus interruptus, is an ancient and widespread method of avoiding conception without complete abstinence. Chemically or mechanically induced abortion is known in the majority of human societies, though the cruder methods are often of uncertain success and safety (Newman 1972).

Like abortions, certain obstetric procedures, whether practiced in a modern hospital or in a hut built outside a tropical village, can affect a woman's subsequent ability to bear children. Hence they can be considered as an unintended form of birth control. More important, they affect the health and survival of both mother and child. Many traditional customs such as building a special hut for delivery improve sanitation. Cutting the umbilical cord with a freshly stripped sliver of bamboo offers far less risk of tetanus than the rusty razor blade that often replaces it in the course of culture change. In a large majority of the world's cultures, women normally give birth in an upright position—kneeling, squatting, or sitting (Naroll, Naroll, and Howard 1961; Cosminsky 1977). This position takes advantage of gravity, though it is less convenient for the physician or other birth attendant. Traditional birth attendants have developed a variety of manipulation techniques, but surgery for complicated deliveries tends to be limited to modern hospitals.

The method of last resort in case of unwanted pregnancy is *infanticide*. Most societies forbid it except in well-defined circumstances such as the birth of a deformed infant or twins. In the past, infanticide may have been an important means of spacing births, particularly in hunting-gathering societies where it was impossible for a woman to carry two children while going about her daily work or where the lack of appropriate weaning foods made long lactation important. It is usually not possible to gather direct and reliable statistics of infanticide because governments and missionaries have been quick to suppress it. Indirect evidence of female infanticide is present in many populations in the form of skewed sex ratios, males greatly outnumbering females especially in the younger age groups, before higher male mortality from warfare and disease begins to even out the ratio.

The following health profile includes a unique record of infanticide rates in a tiny New Guinea population. The population described is in some ways similar to both hunter-gatherers and tropical forest farmers; like these societies, it shows an intermediate level of natality, higher than industrial society but lower than most agricultural societies.

PROFILE: INFANT MORTALITY IN A NEW GUINEA SOCIETY

Life is full of hazards for Sanio-Hiowe infants in lowland Papua New Guinea. One infant out of ten is killed immediately after birth. Of those who remain, one out of three will die of infectious disease as an infant or toddler.

The Sanio-Hiowe live along the Wogamus River, a small tributary of the Sepik, which is a vast muddy river flowing through equatorial swamps. They live in communities of no more than forty people in one or more houses built on low hills rising out of swamp forest. Food is provided by the sago palm, which grows wild and abundantly in the swamp forest. Women process the pith of the palm into a starchy staple food (Townsend 1974). To balance the diet, men hunt and both men and women fish, gather wild fruits and vegetables, and grow a few vegetables and fruits. Pork from both wild and tame pigs is a main source of protein, though the tiny quantities of fish are more dependable on a daily basis. Plump white sago grubs are a source of fat.

Pat Townsend began a study of the Sanio-Hiowe infants, and the families and culture in which they live, in 1966. Townsend, then a graduate student in anthropology at the University of Michigan, and her husband Bill, a civil engineer, spent more than a

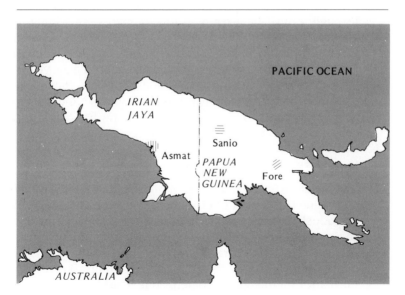

FIGURE 4.2 This map of the island of New Guinea in the South Pacific shows the location of the Sanio-Hiowe. The highlands location of the Fore, discussed in the *kuru* profile in chapter 2, and the location of the Asmat, to be discussed in chapter 8, are also shown.

year living with the Sanio-Hiowe and observing their way of life. The central purpose of the research was to describe food-getting activities and how they were related to culture and ecology. The study established closest contact with the 234 people speaking the western dialect of the Sanio-Hiowe language, but the whole language group includes only 500 or so people. The language had never been described by linguists, was unwritten, and has no written grammars or dictionaries. Much of the research time was spent simply establishing communication. At the time they were studied in the mid-1960s, the Sanio-Hiowe had just begun to encounter steel axes, money, Western medicine, and Christian missionaries. All these had been present for decades in less remote parts of Papua New Guinea along the coasts and in the densely populated highland valleys.

Through interviews, Townsend recorded complete reproductive histories for the twenty-five women whose child-bearing years were over. They might have neglected to mention a child who died many years ago if the Sanio naming system did not permanently record each child's order of birth. When a child who was present was called "number-five-daughter," daughters 1 through 4 must be accounted for. Women were willing to talk about births freely. These twenty-five New Guinea women had given birth to an average of 5.3 children, ranging from 1 to 10 (Townsend 1971). Marriage occurred within a few years after puberty. It was usually monogamous and very stable: none of their marriages had been disrupted by divorce. Nine women had been widowed and remarried. These nine had slightly fewer children than the average (4.8). They probably lost some reproductive time during the mourning period, before they were able to remarry, but the difference is not statistically significant.

In a society without a concept of dates and ages, it is difficult to determine the intervals between births or the total length of the reproductive span. Studies in other parts of New Guinea where census and medical records have been kept for many years show some of the latest average ages anywhere in the world for the menarche—as late as 18 at first menstruation. But records are fuzzier for middle-aged women, so it is hard to be sure at what ages childbearing ends and menopause occurs. Crudely estimating the ages of Sanio women and their children suggests that the reproductive span may last only about twenty years, which is about two-thirds as long as in populations living under better conditions of nutrition and health. If this is so, it is obviously a factor reducing the total number of births.

When a Sanio-Hiowe woman has only one child, gossip usually has it that someone has given her a drug to induce sterility. Nothing is known about the scientific or magical properties of this "barrenness ginger." One man was said to have given it to his wife because he was too crippled with yaws to want any children, and another was said to have given it to his sister out of pique at not getting a fair share of bridewealth for her marriage.

One major limit on fertility is the postpartum taboo. Until their infant is ready to be weaned, Sanio-Hiowe parents are not supposed to have sexual intercourse. This taboo seems to last at least two years, ideally, though it is difficult to know how carefully it is observed. People are concerned about the nutrition of older infants because of the scarcity of good weaning foods. In fact, the conventional question about a child is not "Does he walk yet?" or "Does he talk yet?" but "Does he eat sago yet?"

If births are not properly spaced and an infant is born before the older child is judged ready for weaning, the new infant may be killed. Twenty-one women were asked about causes of their children's deaths. In 104 births, they reported that 48 infants died before weaning, 11 of whom were killed. When a mother judged that her older child still needed breast-feeding, she strangled the newborn with a length of vine. A seriously deformed infant was also killed at birth.

Infanticide affected female infants more than males. Eight of the 11 killed were girls, though in one case a male infant was killed to spare his older sister. Although in other parts of the world infanticide may be concealed or punished, these women did not hesitate to report it, although they did regret that the killing was necessary. When one looks at the high rates of mortality from infectious disease, especially malaria and pneumonia, complicated by marginal nutrition, one cannot help but regard their assessment as accurate.

Of 132 children born to the 25 women, 57 died in infancy or early childhood (roughly under five years of age), a mortality rate of 43 percent. Mortality rates were significantly higher for firstborn

FIGURE 4.3   Sanio-Hiowe women and children talk to Pat Townsend, seated on the ground in the hamlet of Yapatawi. A baby pig forages for scraps of food.

Photo by William H. Townsend.

infants of either sex (51 percent versus 39 percent for later-born infants) even though firstborns are spared from infanticide. It is not clear whether this may be a result of the new mothers' lesser degree of physical maturity or experience in caring for infants. Even making allowance for infanticide, girls were more likely to die in infancy than boys, which makes one wonder whether boys get better care, though Townsend did not observe any neglect or abuse of infants.

Although they believe that all infants are vulnerable to harm from ghosts and evil spirits, the Sanio-Hiowe think that baby girls are especially vulnerable to the ancestral spirits whose voices are the sounds of secret flutes blown in the men's cult house. The death of a little girl is likely to be given this explanation. In fact, however, it is possible that the health of infants of both sexes may be affected by food taboos prohibiting some kinds of meat to women during pregnancy and during lactation at times when the infant is sick.

The result of the unbalanced infant mortality was that in the whole Sanio-Hiowe population of 234, males outnumbered females 130 to 104. Women marry at an earlier age than men, so there is no real shortage of marriageable women. Like other New Guinea societies, this one is male chauvinist in its ritual and ideology even though women make important contributions to family decision making. They also make an important economic contribution: they produce nine-tenths of the food.

High mortality in infancy and early childhood reduces the average number of surviving children to three for each of the Sanio-Hiowe women. Even this number would be enough to assure a steady growth in population except that fewer than half the children are females and not all of them survive a full reproductive life. Disease continues to take a toll, and warfare or homicide removes nearly as many women as men in this society.

One might ask whether it is the infanticide rate of 11 percent that keeps a population like this stable. Infanticide could have that effect, particularly since it tends to remove more females who have the babies in the next generation. This population impact is blunted in this case, however, because the likelihood is so great that the infant who is killed, and perhaps an older sibling as well, would have died anyway. It should be noted that early childhood deaths are not as numerous in coastal and highland areas of Papua New Guinea where malaria and other mosquito-borne diseases are less prevalent and in areas with better access to medical services.

Mortality

A discussion of natality must lead into a discussion of mortality, for the two population processes are interdependent. The New Guinea woman whose infant dies will abandon postpartum taboos and quickly become pregnant again. A couple in India who are reconciled to a high rate of child mortality will not consider their old age secure if they have only one son. A computer simulation showed that a family in India must have 6.3 children to be 95-percent certain of having a surviving son at the father's 65th birthday. The actual family size is very close to this (May and Heer 1968). This link between death and birth on the family level is also clearly observable on the level of the entire population: after an epidemic sweeps through a population, it can quickly rebound with high natality.

The causes of death vary in different environmental and cultural settings. The patterns in this variation are discussed throughout this book. Here we need only emphasize that the *timing* of death is of importance for population growth. The mortality that has the biggest demographic impact is death at an early age, before reproduction. And it is this infant and juvenile mortality that has been undergoing the biggest changes in the last century. Average life expectancy at birth in the United States increased from about thirty-five years in the 1780s to fifty years in 1900 and seventy in 1960 (figure 4.4). This change has been almost entirely due to the reduction of the death rate in infancy and childhood, through protection from infectious diseases and malnutrition, and not to improvements in the health of middle-aged and older people.

If the birth rate exceeds the death rate, a population will grow; if death rates exceed birth rates, the population will decline; and if the situation is not reversed, the population will eventually become extinct. The number of Native Americans of New England declined from about 36,500 to about 2400 in 300 years of European settlement on their lands. This decimation is most carefully documented for the islands of Martha's Vineyard and Nantucket, where the Native American population was reduced at a rate of about 1.5 percent per year during the colonial period (Cook 1973). Much of the mortality occurred in two severe epidemics: plague in 1617 and smallpox in 1633. Tuberculosis, dysentery, and warfare with settlers contributed to the year-by-year decline.

The Pacific island of Yap in Micronesia is another example of depopulation. As with Nantucket and Martha's Vineyard, the fact that it is an island defines its boundaries sharply and makes it easier to

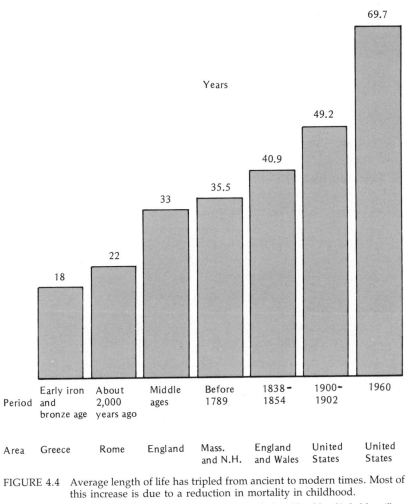

FIGURE 4.4   Average length of life has tripled from ancient to modern times. Most of this increase is due to a reduction in mortality in childhood.

SOURCE: Reprinted from Louis I. Dublin, *Factbook on Man* (New York: Macmillan, 1965), p. 394, by permission of the estate of the author.

conduct a demographic study. The island population declined steeply throughout the nineteenth century from a possible high of 51,000 to 7808 in 1899. Population continued to decline at a rate of about 2.3 percent per year until 1946, when the inhabitants numbered only 2582. Then medical treatment reversed the decline, and the population of

Yap began to increase again. Many different causes for the decline have been suggested, but the critical factor seems to have been sterility and reduced reproduction as a result of gonorrhea and yaws (Hunt 1978a; Underwood 1973).

Most of the populations observed today are growing rather than declining or holding steady, though they are growing at very different rates under different social and environmental conditions. The world population as a whole has been growing recently at a rate of about 2 percent per year. The industrialized nations have been growing at rates of 1 percent or less and the nonindustrialized countries have been growing at rates approaching 3 percent per year. Growth is very uneven within all these countries, as peasants move to the city or urban dwellers flee to the suburbs.

Migration

If we look at very small units, such as bands of hunter-gatherers or small farming villages, we find even greater potential for discrepancies in rates of growth. In a very small population, chance differences in fertility, sex ratio, and exposure to disease may contribute to one group's growing very rapidly while another declines. Migration in and out of such groups can help to even things out. Studies of contemporary hunter-gatherers show that the membership of local groups is constantly in flux, with people readily moving between groups. In addition, the camps change their size and location to respond to seasonal and long-term changes in resources. Julian Steward's classic study of the Great Basin Shoshoni of Nevada, done in the 1930s, described this kind of seasonal flux. One or two Shoshoni families foraged alone for seeds and hunted small game during the spring and summer, but several families were able to camp together to gather pine nuts in the fall and remain together throughout the winter (Steward 1955:101–121). Other anthropologists who have studied hunter-gatherers have found that they move between camps because of whim or illness or conflict with a campmate or for any of a dozen reasons in addition to moving for better access to food resources.

Migration is not uncommon among food-cultivating populations either, although their crops and possessions tend to make them less mobile. Individuals from a crowded community may join a community with more resources, or a community may fission and part of the population may colonize previously unused lands. Some anthropologists view tribal warfare as predominantly a mechanism that, like migration, distributes unevenly growing groups of people over the land. In this view, the most important demographic effect of warfare is that it allows expansion into the land of smaller, weaker groups, who may be driven off to settle elsewhere as refugees. This redistribution of population by war may be more important than the direct mortality that war causes.

Migration from rural areas to cities is one of the most conspicuous of recent demographic trends. It is particularly dramatic in Africa and South America, continents that are still predominantly rural, but where the overflow of people from rural areas go to seek their fortune in the cities. Cities in these regions are growing at stunning rates, for example, Lagos, Nigeria, at 14 percent per year recently and Bogota, Colombia, at 7 percent.

Population Density

The face of the earth is very unevenly covered with people. In 1976, there were 83 people per square mile (30 per square kilometer) of the world's land area (United Nations 1977). People were thinly scattered over deserts and arctic and subarctic lands at densities of less than 1 person per square mile or kilometer. They were squeezed into cities like New York and Tokyo at densities of 20,000 or more people per square mile (8000 per square kilometer). Even large countries like India, Australia, and the United States vary sharply in their overall population density, as shown in table 4.2.

Although it is easy enough to calculate population density for an area, it is far more difficult to judge from that whether people feel crowded, which is a subjective experience that differs between individuals and societies. It is even more difficult to determine whether **population pressure** on resources exists. Population pressure occurs whenever a population is growing to levels that are difficult to support under given conditions of environment, technology, and economy. It can occur at what might seem like very low actual densities to someone

TABLE 4.2 Population density.

Country	Per square mile	Per square km
Australia	5	2
Canada	5	2
Brazil	34	13
United States	64	23
Indonesia	179	69
Switzerland	400	154
India	484	186
Japan	788	303
Netherlands	876	337

SOURCE: Data recalculated from *Demographic Yearbook:* 1976 (New York: United Nations, 1977).

coming from a setting where land is used more intensively. This kind of evaluation of land has taken place, for example, when settlers or builders of roads or pipelines have viewed the lands of Native Americans as wide open spaces. The next section of this chapter will discuss a type of subsistence economy that can operate successfully only at very low population densities.

LIFE AND DEATH IN HUNTER-GATHERER CAMPS

Until about 10,000 years ago, all human societies were sustained by hunting and gathering. Nomadic hunter-gatherers represent only a tiny and decreasing fraction of the world's population today, less than 0.001 of 1 percent, but their ways of life are among the most important clues we have to some aspects of the human past. They also provide clues to the ways humans adapt to extremes of climate, because the peoples who have maintained themselves as hunter-gatherers into the twentieth century have lived in extreme environments—deserts, deep tropical forests, or arctic and subarctic cold. These, the remotest of all habitats, were inhospitable to expanding populations of farmers and herders. Still other nomadic hunter-gatherers managed to survive into the twentieth century as enclaves among settled peoples in such places as India, New Guinea, the Philippines, and Malaysia.

Regardless of environment, these food-collecting populations are alike in the small size and temporary nature of their settlements, a factor that has important implications for health. Camps of about 25 people drawn from regional populations of 500 or so seem typical for hunters (Birdsell 1968:245). When camps are small and briefly occupied, sanitation is not as serious a problem as it is in larger, more permanent communities. More important, in small isolated populations, epidemics of acute disease dependent on direct person-to-person contact cannot readily get going. If a disease such as measles were introduced into a camp, it would quickly spread through the group of people in face-to-face contact. Then, finding no more susceptible individuals, the disease-causing organism would die out unless the people were to visit other camps. Even ritual gatherings like the !Kung boys' initiation, which brings together up to 200 people for six weeks every four or five years, would give the disease organism only a temporary lease on life.

Given this limitation, what sorts of infectious diseases are likely to be prevalent in nomadic hunting-gathering populations? Certain parasites have probably been with humans throughout their evolutionary history since closely related forms are shared with the other primates. Some of these are head and body lice, pinworms, many intestinal protozoans, and the herpes virus that causes canker sores. Other diseases that would maintain themselves in small groups of hunters are *zoonoses,* diseases of wild animals that can be transmitted to people. For example, yellow fever is predominantly a disease of jungle monkeys that is incidentally transmitted to humans.

Organisms causing disease can also maintain themselves in small groups of people if the disease is chronic, so that the organism stays around a long time to infect newly susceptible individuals who are born into or join the group. Malaria is one of these diseases, as are many of the *helminthic* diseases, that is, diseases caused by worms. In other words, small isolated populations are more likely to avoid epidemic disease, occurring widely and suddenly throughout the community. Their diseases are more often endemic, occurring continuously at low levels.

The number and kinds of disease organisms present in different populations of hunter-gatherers can vary a great deal, depending on the environmental setting. Among tropical forest hunter-gatherers, such as the pygmies of Africa, there are very many more species of parasitic worms and protozoans than among desert hunter-gatherers or arctic peoples (Dunn 1968). Tropical forest ecosystems in general are characterized by small numbers of individuals of any one plant or animal species, but very many different species. This diversity, which is characteristic of the ecosystem as a whole, also is true of the parasites of humans.

It is not just the physical environment that influences the number and kinds of infections present in a population of hunter-gatherers; the social environment is important, too. Present-day hunters no longer live in a world of hunters. Instead, they live in close and prolonged contact with farming or herding peoples and the outposts of industrial civilization. Often they survive only in a kind of symbiosis in which they provide hunted or gathered products in exchange for agricultural and industrial products. Hence they are also subject to the diseases evolved in connection with these other ways of life.

As far as the hunting-gathering way of life free of these modern influences can be reconstructed, it seems to be a rather health-promoting lifestyle. Food is varied and nutritious, as we will see in chapter 5. People get good exercise. Infectious and parasitic diseases are less of a threat than in farming villages. Accidental injury may be more frequent among hunters than some other peoples, however, especially in the far north, where drowning, burns, and exposure add to the accident toll. Homicide plays a variable role in mortality as well, though large-scale warfare cannot be organized in small-scale societies. Most often, hunting peoples seem simply to move to avoid conflict.

If, as seems to be the case in contemporary hunting peoples, mortality was only moderate during the Pleistocene, or Ice Age, population growth must have been held in check by maintaining moderate levels of natality as well. The continuation of the hunting way of life depended on keeping human population low enough so that the populations of game animals were not threatened with extinction.

Cultural practices restricting family size, such as the postpartum taboo and infanticide, have probably served as population controls for a long time. It is difficult for a woman to carry more than one child while she gathers food or moves camp in a nomadic society. Because of the skills and environmental knowledge required for hunting and gathering, children remain an economic burden even after they can walk well enough to cease to be a literal burden. Hence hunter-gatherers are motivated to limit family size. On the basis of his research with Australian Aborigines and on theoretical grounds, Birdsell (1968) suggests that hunter-gatherers must have killed between 15 and 50 percent of their children to achieve adequate three- to four-year spacing and population regulation. At the other end of the life span, the abandonment of old people, *geronticide,* also sometimes occurred in hard times in hunting societies.

Hunting populations have probably not always succeeded in staying in balance with their resources, however. It has been suggested that Pleistocene hunters expanding into the New World were responsible for the extinction of the mammoth and other large mammals (Martin 1973). With the large game animals gone, the people turned to hunting small game and seed gathering, and eventually to plant domestication.

LIFE AND DEATH IN FARMING VILLAGES

Settled farming villages go back nearly 10,000 years in the Old World and nearly 5,000 years in the Americas. The shift from food gathering to food producing had important implications for human nutrition, which will be discussed in the next chapter. But simply from a population standpoint, the new circumstances had a significant impact on health. Farming allowed for increased population densities, more people per square mile of land. Villages could be larger. Farming called for more enduring settlements, tied to a site by stores of food from last year's crop and by the need to protect this year's plantings from predators. When small, frequently moved camps gave way to settled villages, new problems of sanitation arose.

As people settled down in villages, other animals settled down with them, too: animals ranging from purposefully domesticated cows, pigs, and chickens to unchosen companions such as rats, which fed on stored grain, and mosquitoes, which bred in water containers. Agricultural practices modified the landscape and created new and increased opportunities for transmitting old diseases. Clearing land made new breeding places for the mosquito vectors of malaria, as we saw in chapter 3. Irrigation ditches provided new homes for snails, which harbor the flukes that cause schistosomiasis. The use of animal and human manure on fields increased crop yields but also transmitted disease.

Settled life also opens up the possibility of a new set of transmissible diseases, which depend on direct contact between an infected person and a susceptible person, one who has not acquired immunity to the disease. These include the childhood diseases of measles, rubella, mumps, chicken pox, and smallpox. They are considered diseases of childhood because they sweep through an area in epidemics every few years, and most of the people who are not yet immune from a previous exposure are children. Any of these diseases can be devastating to adults and children alike when introduced for the first time into a community. This tragedy occurred many times as explorers from one continent opened contacts with previously isolated people on a new continent. The decimation of Native Americans by smallpox is the best known instance of this. The newly contacted populations had not yet evolved genetic resistance to the disease nor had individuals acquired immunity through childhood exposure.

Because these childhood diseases infect humans only briefly, they could be eradicated if there were no active infections anywhere in the world at some time. In this respect, they differ from chronic diseases, which persist in human carriers or animal populations. This is what makes it reasonable for the World Health Organization to set the goal of eradicating smallpox, for example, for which a vaccine has been available since 1798. However, eradication has been made more difficult by the fact that the virus causing smallpox can live for several months in the blankets or clothing before being passed on to a susceptible person and beginning the chain of transmission again.

Disease-causing organisms evolve just as other living things do. In fact, their short reproductive time makes it possible for them to evolve very quickly. Probably many of these strictly human diseases of settled life evolved out of closely related diseases of domestic animals. This seems especially likely in the case of the group of pox viruses and the influenza group (Cockburn 1963:96). New diseases are evolving all the time out of previously harmless or mild strains of microorganisms. Cholera, for example, seems to have emerged as a new disease in 1817 in Calcutta. And the influenza virus mutates to new strains frequently. Each new strain is especially severe because it finds a newly suscepti- ble human population, which in time adapts to the new disease by all the means available to it: genetic, physiological, and cultural.

The evolution of disease is especially noticeable in a group of very closely related organisms or a single organism that causes different symptoms under different conditions, such as the treponemas, sin- gle-celled spiral organisms causing yaws, pinta, and syphilis. Yaws, a disfiguring skin disease transmitted by skin contact generally found in moist tropical lowlands, was prevalent, for example, among the Sanio-Hiowe of Papua New Guinea when Pat Townsend studied them in 1966–1967. Syphilis, transmitted by sexual contact, tends to be more destructive of the internal organs than yaws and is more likely to be transmitted congenitally. It has been suggested that venereal syphilis may have evolved out of yaws or nonvenereal syphilis several centu- ries ago in Europe when changes in clothing and personal cleanliness reduced skin contact, so that people seldom came in direct contact with each other except during the sexual act (Cockburn 1963:159). Pinta, named for its white, blue, pink, yellow, or violet skin blotches, is the variant of treponematosis that occurs in Central and South America. Because it evolved in isolation from the other forms of treponema for so long, it is the most divergent of these diseases.

Although new types of disease evolved along with farming villages and mortality probably increased as a result of epidemics, natality increased even more, producing population growth. Agricultural peoples know about and sometimes practice many of the traditional techniques for family limitation already discussed, such as infanticide and abortion. Yet still other factors promote a high birth rate.

As people settled down and women no longer needed to cover as much ground in gathering food or moving between camps, more closely spaced children became less burdensome. Women continued to breast-feed as long as possible, but if another pregnancy forced early weaning at eighteen months or less, the child could be fed cereal gruel and animal milk. Social changes favored a more closely knit extended family, adding relatives to share household tasks and child care.

Although very young children are everywhere an economic burden, in agricultural society they begin to make a significant contribution to their own support earlier than in other economies. By the age of 6, children may be caring for animals or doing household chores, freeing older children and adults for more complicated tasks. Anthropologists who timed the work activities of children and adults in villages in Java and Nepal found that children six to eight years old spent an average of three and a half hours a day at household tasks and animal care (Nag, White, and Peet 1978). They found that girls worked more than boys at all ages because of their greater involvement in child care and food preparation. The authors concluded that children in these societies probably have a positive economic value to their parents as children and not only as old-age security.

Although settled agricultural life offers tremendous potential for population increase, this increase has not occurred everywhere to the same extent. On densely populated Java in Indonesia, for example, irrigated rice terraces are worked by labor-intensive methods, with painstaking attention to each seedling. In contrast, on the remaining Indonesian islands, where population density is only one-twentieth as great as in Java, land is used more lavishly. A fraction of the labor is put into each acre of land with consequently lower yields per acre (Geertz 1963).

British economist Ester Boserup (1965) has theorized that it is population pressure that leads to agricultural evolution, forcing farmers to adopt more intensive methods of using their land, methods that are less easy and less pleasant. Boserup turned around the old view that technological evolution led to population expansion, so she started a lively controversy in anthropology. What came first, the chicken (agricultural methods) or the egg (population growth)? Population growth does force people into using more intensive methods, such as irrigating or getting more than one crop per year from a field, but at the same time, the increasing demands for labor encourage them to have large families.

Although economic and motivational factors clearly play a part in higher birth rates, some researchers have sought more direct, biological factors that might influence reproduction. The various mechanisms suggested so far are highly controversial. For example, Frisch and McArthur (1974) suggest that the onset and maintenance of menstrual cycles require a critical level of body fat stores. If this is so, in food-producing societies, the carbohydrate staple foods may have made this easier to attain. This would mean not only that women could reproduce at a younger age, but that after childbirth, during lactation, they might resume ovulation sooner, thus reducing birth intervals.

Another controversial factor in the demography of farming people is warfare. It is too simplistic to claim that warfare reduces population pressure by killing off the excess, yet in certain societies war does have adaptive significance in regulating population and other variables. This process has been most thoughtfully analyzed by the anthropologist Andrew P. Vayda (1976), who has emphasized the way war redistributes population in relation to land. Vayda has also pointed out that warfare is a process in which earlier phases may serve different functions than later phases of hostilities. The reasons that people give for fighting, such as to avenge ghosts or capture women, may also be quite different from the functions analysts perceive.

A few anthropologists have had unique opportunities to study warfare in progress and to analyze its demographic effects. Among the Yanomamo of Venezuela, 24 percent of adult males are killed in warfare (Chagnon 1977:20). However, the killing of so many males does not have a direct role in controlling population growth, for a successful warrior will be married polygynously and father many children. The Yanomamo have their own demographic rationale for war: to capture women. The shortage of marriageable women stems in turn from the practice of infanticide. Although exact figures on Yanomamo infanticide are not available, the skewed sex ratio suggests that more female infants are killed, a bias that would be consistent with the cultural value placed on males, who grow up to be warriors. The Yanomamo have been widely used as an example to show the place of warfare in the population balance of tropical farmers. However, even such intense practice of warfare, coupled with infanticide, did not prevent the Yanomamo population from growing rapidly, until postcontact epidemics of malaria and measles decimated them (Lizot 1977:503).

It is a long way from a Yanomamo raiding party armed with arrows to World War I–style trench warfare to nuclear war. Yet each of these types of war has both a direct impact on mortality and, far more

FIGURE 4.5   Three Yanomamo shamans chant to their *hekura* demons while in a
drug-induced state. The evil spirits are enjoined to come out of a sick
villager or to descend on enemies, causing them illness.
Photo by Napoleon Chagnon.

difficult to assess, indirect effects on the health of entire populations.
War has everywhere been associated with both famine and epidemic
disease.

LIFE AND DEATH IN
THE PREINDUSTRIAL
CITY

With further social evolution, the emergence of cities brings even more
people into face-to-face contact. In consequence, epidemic disease

becomes even more serious than it is in villages. Cities grew to several thousand inhabitants in the Old World by 3000 B.C. and somewhat later in the Americas. These cities were made possible by an intensive agriculture that supported craft specialists, rulers, and bureaucrats who did not have to produce their own food but obtained it from the peasantry by taxation, rent, and trade. Supplying such large numbers of people with food and water and carrying away their wastes was a challenge; contamination of a single source of food or water could cause widespread illness. Typhoid and cholera are two of the diseases associated with mixing water supply and sewage in cities.

The emergence of cities is associated with increasingly marked social stratification, and differences between rich and poor lifestyles lead to differences in risks of illness and death. Such differences do sometimes occur in tribal societies. But in class-stratified societies, wealth differences and health differences become sharper. Sharp differences in infant and childhood mortality between rich and poor reflect the interaction of many factors: nutrition, exposure to infection, and availability of medical care. However, rich and poor alike were devastated by the great epidemic diseases such as plague, discussed in the following health profile.

PROFILE: THE BLACK DEATH

Bubonic plague has swept through cities and countryside in several *pandemics*, or great worldwide epidemics, throughout history. Possibly the earliest description of bubonic plague is the Old Testament account in the book of I Samuel of a plague of swellings and rodents that struck the Philistines. The plague later struck the crumbling Roman Empire under Justinian in the seventh century. And from 1348 to 1350, the "Black Death" swept across Europe and the Middle East, killing more than one quarter of the population. According to some estimates, England and Italy lost as much as half their populations.

Bubonic plague is fundamentally a disease of field rodents, but sometimes people accidentally get in the way of the normal

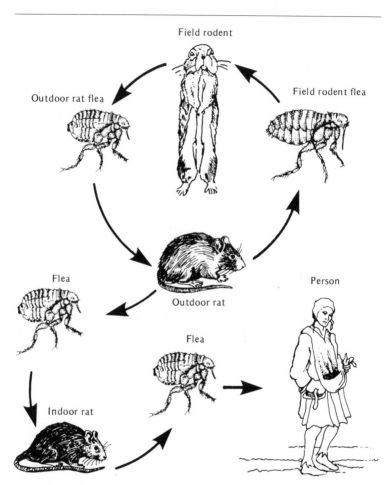

FIGURE 4.6   Cycle of plague transmission. Plague is transmitted from fleas to
mammals. The disease normally is maintained in populations of
wild rodents in the grasslands and in the populations of fleas
associated with them. Under certain conditions, outbreaks of the
disease can spill over into other rodent populations and affect
humans.

rodent-to-rodent transmission of the bacteria causing the disease, and it becomes a human disaster as well. Many different
kinds of rodents are infected with the plague bacillus, among
them marmots, ground squirrels, prairie dogs, chipmunks, ger-

bils, rats, mice, and rabbits (Hirst 1953). Sometimes the disease is spread from field rodents to species of rats that live in closer association with humans. The bacteria are spread from rodent to rodent by fleas. When a flea feeds on an infected animal, its gizzard becomes blocked with masses of plague bacilli so that it cannot suck blood effectively. In trying unsuccessfully to feed again, it regurgitates blood and bacilli into another animal.

Various species of fleas can transmit the plague bacillus, but one of the most effective is *Xenopsylla cheopis*, a flea of an indoor rat, the black rat. This species of flea is more likely to venture out and attack humans than some other flea species, which prefer to stay in the rat's nest. When a rodent dies of the plague, its fleas leave the cold body and look for another host. Now a human may accidentally be bitten and infected (see figure 4.6). The person develops the symptoms of bubonic plague—fever, pain, and a swollen lymph node in the groin or armpit, which is called a bubo—and unless treated with antibiotics usually dies within a few days as infection of the blood stream leads to heart failure. Under some conditions the plague infects the lungs; this pneumonic form is extremely infectious because the sick person's cough spreads the bacillus to other people.

Little is known of the outbreak of plague in Asia that led to the Black Death. Several rainy years in Southern Russia may have led to a buildup of the flea population (Watt 1973:246). The subsequent spread of plague across Europe from Italy north and west to England in the years 1348–1350 is documented in parish records. After two centuries of rapid growth of the economy and population, several years of famine and economic depression seem to have prepared the way for the epidemic. Small but crowded and unsanitary medieval cities like London provided ideal conditions for disease transmission. The wattle-and-daub houses of the time offered better hiding places for black rats than later brick architecture. Food was stored right in the houses rather than in separate granaries, so rats and their fleas were attracted into close association with people.

As the plague advanced across Europe, it was regarded as a judgment of God. Astrological observers noted the fateful conjunction of Saturn, Jupiter, and Mars. Jews were persecuted and killed as rumor claimed they had poisoned wells. People fled the

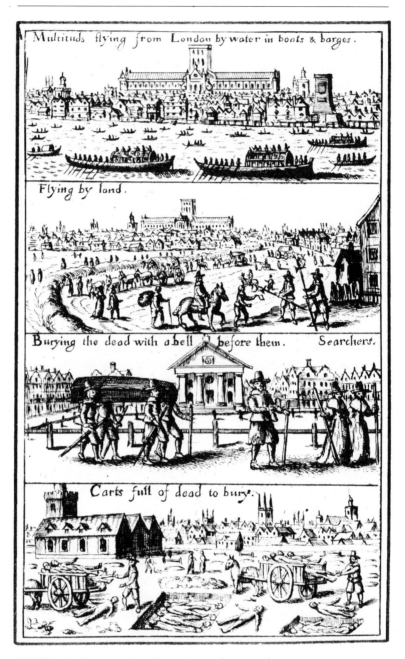

FIGURE 4.7   Scenes in London during a plague epidemic.

SOURCE: From a print in the Pepys Library (*London and Westminster* ii. 447d). Reproduced by permission of the Master and Fellows, Magdalene College, Cambridge.

plague-ravaged cities for the countryside. Medical interpretation was divided between those who thought the cause was miasma, corruption of the air, and those who assumed that direct contact was the cause and advocated quarantines. The quarantines were of little use, given the rat-flea transmission of the disease, but these complexities were not understood until research was conducted during the next great plague pandemic, which began in the 1890s.

Historians have argued over the social impact of plague (Langer 1964). The severe reduction in the labor force drove up wages and made farm workers more mobile, perhaps accelerating the disintegration of the manorial system. The Church lost prestige and authority as a result of the plague; though religious fervor increased, it found expression through dissident sects. The tragic pessimism of the times pervaded the arts as well—death became a dominant theme in paintings.

For two centuries after the Black Death, severe plague occurred every several years. In the Muslim empire of the Middle East, the Black Death and the recurring epidemics of the next two centuries led to population decline and disruption of the economy (Dols 1977). Several years of extremely high or low water levels on the Nile River combined with the shortage of agricultural workers to produce famine. Muslim beliefs prescribed rather different responses to the plague than did the Christian religion in Europe, though. While Christians interpreted the plague as God's punishment for their sins, Muslims tended to view it as a calamity decreed by an unknowable God. Death was not a punishment but, if anything, a martyrdom. Because the plague was fated by God, flight from it was discouraged, although some people did flee as the disease approached.

In the next plague pandemic, which began in the 1890s, over 13 million people died within forty years. Most of these deaths were in India, but the disease spread widely from one seaport to the next. Plague entered the port of San Francisco and spread to the rat-infested warehouses. Eighty-nine people died in San Francisco in the 1907–1908 epidemic, but perhaps more significant in the long run is the fact that plague became established for the first time in the wild rodent population of the United States.

Plague exists now in wild rodent populations throughout the

great grasslands of the world: the Asian steppes, the western United States, southern Africa, and the South American pampas. Sporadic cases of plague occur among hunters and other people who come into contact with wild rodents (Reed et al. 1970). Recently in the U.S. Southwest, several Navaho children playing around prairie dogs and several residents of a rural commune contracted bubonic plague. Most of these victims were successfully treated with antibiotics. A geologist working in the Southwest was not so fortunate. He flew back to his university in the Northeast and died before physicians discovered what was wrong with him.

With rural reservoirs of plague in so many parts of the world, epidemics spreading into populations of city rats are always a possibility. Plague broke out in Vietnam under the wartime conditions of the late 1960s. Wherever social conditions deteriorate even today people may get in the way of an outbreak of the disease in rats.

LIFE AND DEATH IN THE INDUSTRIAL SOCIETY

When the industrial age began to get underway, population was growing very rapidly. The population of Europe nearly doubled in the hundred years from 1750 to 1850 (Langer 1972:93). This population growth was made possible by the cultivation of potatoes in the north and maize in the south; both were highly productive crops introduced into Europe from America. In Ireland, especially, the potato went hand in hand with population growth. The population of Ireland grew from 3.2 million in 1754 to 8.2 million in 1845. In addition, another 1.75 million emigrated (Crosby 1972).

Historian William L. Langer (1972) has summed up the factors in the European population equation in the century from 1750 to 1850. Infectious diseases, especially smallpox, plague, tuberculosis, and typhus, were the major cause of death. Marriage practices were an important check on population growth, although natality was very high for married people. People married late, probably in their late twenties, and many were unable to marry at all. In addition to the voluntary celibacy of clergy, many of the poor were legally restricted from marrying or were unable to marry while employed as servants or soldiers.

Infanticide was another check to population growth. Though it was morally disapproved and legally penalized, it was frequently practiced and continued to increase steadily until the late nineteenth century. A common form of infanticide was the death by suffocation of a child who was in bed with his parents. It was impossible to be sure to what extent this "overlaying," as it was called, was accidental. Often newborn infants were abandoned. The foundling hospitals established to care for these children, despite all good intentions, contributed further mortality: 70 to 90 percent of the infants in some of these institutions died (Langer 1972:98).

By the mid-nineteenth century, the terms of the population equation had changed. Large-scale emigration from Europe to less densely populated frontiers had begun. Industrial development was having new effects on both natality and mortality. In the crowded, sooty industrial cities of the nineteenth century, infectious diseases were still the leading cause of death. Air pollution contributed to the prevalence of tuberculosis and respiratory diseases in the industrial environment. But at the same time, the accelerating pace of technological innovation began to help bring many infectious diseases under control. Sanitation improved, immunization methods were developed, and the insect vectors of some diseases were controlled. Much more recently, antibiotics have made treatment more successful, as well.

Somewhat after death rates fell and the life chances of individual children began to improve, birth rates began to fall as well. This two-stage shift to the modern pattern of low mortality and low natality is called the **demographic transition.** In the industrial nations, this drop in birth rates mostly preceded the widespread availability of effective low-cost contraceptives. It has most often been explained in terms of the high economic and educational cost of raising each additional child in industrial society.

Even modern low birth rates vary from year to year as cultural change occurs. The shift from the ideal of a four-child family in the 1950s to the ideal of a two-child family in the 1970s in the United States exemplifies this.

In Japan, industrialization has been mostly a post–World War II phenomenon, and with it birth rates have dropped steadily. But in 1966, the drop was sharp and mysterious. In the ancient Japanese lunar-solar calendar, the Year of the Fire coincided with the Year of the Horse in 1966, to begin a new sixty-year cycle. According to the calendar, any girl born in such a year "will be of harsh temperament and invite misfortune." Apparently the Japanese used birth control and abortion to avoid 1966 births, especially in traditional, rural areas (Azumi 1968). In 1906 there had been a slight decline, too, and an unusual excess of boys over girls. Azumi suggests that many household heads probably registered girls born that year as having been born in 1905 or 1907. Obviously, culture retains a powerful influence on human natality.

Just as the availability of contraceptive technology cannot by itself account for the reduction of the birth rate, the role of medical developments in reducing the toll of infectious disease should perhaps not be exaggerated. The most effective techniques to avoid disease in the nineteenth century came from social measures introduced to combat the injustices brought about by industrialization, to provide reasonable working hours, decent housing, pure water, and adequate nutrition (Dubos 1959; McKeown 1976). The laboratory sciences made their chief contributions later, well after the infectious diseases were already on a downward trend. Dubos has shown that tuberculosis declined long before vaccines and drugs were available (1965:169). Improved social conditions and acquired immunities were significant. Some genetic adaptation undoubtedly also occurred, as individuals especially susceptible to the diseases of the new industrial environment died young or failed to reproduce.

Although infectious diseases are not as frequent a cause of death as they were at one time, this is only the case as long as public health measures are maintained, for the pathogenic organisms are still around. Eradication proved elusive. By about 1900, infectious diseases were no longer the main causes of death in the United States. Rather, their place on the list was taken by the degenerative diseases: diseases of the cardiovascular system and cancer. As life expectancy increased, these diseases of old age were bound to become more important simply because there were more old people in the population. Nor are they any longer simply diseases of old age: they are diseases of affluence. Nutrition (chapter 5) and stress (chapter 7) seem to play an important role in their earlier onset in modern society.

Industry itself has shaped new environments to which the human body is not adapted. The most intense effects are often felt in the work place itself, but the products of industry offer new hazards to consumers as well. Most far reaching are the effects of the automobile. About 250,000 people throughout the world die in automobile accidents each year. Less directly, the automobile makes a major contribution to air pollution. Epidemiological studies are beginning to note statistically significant rises in lung diseases, including emphysema, chronic bronchitis, and cancer, in relation to exposure to air pollution.

Lead from auto emissions, added to the effects of sweet-tasting lead chips flaking from a tenement home, dangerously raises the levels of this heavy metal in the body of a city child. Lead poisoning damages the central nervous system as insidiously as the *kuru* virus in the radically different environment of highland New Guinea.

Mercury is another toxic heavy metal in the industrial environment. Mercury poisoning is called Minimata disease, named for the Japanese town where it was first described. People who ate fish from Minimata Bay developed numbness in their fingers, toes, and lips and constriction of the visual field. Several people died, and pregnant women who ate fish from the bay gave birth to children with abnormalities. The source of the mercury pollution was a factory that used inorganic mercuric salts in manufacturing plastic and discharged pollutants into the bay, where bacteria or tiny water animals probably converted it to the more toxic methyl mercury (Montague 1971).

In its basic outlines, the Minimata crisis resembles the sequence of events described in the Kepone health profile that follows. Each represents a blatant case of industrial pollution that ramified through the ecosystem with severe effects on the people exposed to the pollution. What is more difficult to sort out is the cumulative effect of hundreds of lesser environmental insults on each of us living in the industrialized ecosystem.

PROFILE: PESTICIDE TRAGEDY IN VIRGINIA

Kepone is an insecticide that is especially useful against fire ants, roaches, banana root borers, and tobacco wireworms. In 1975, it was produced in one plant in Hopewell, Virginia—a small company called Life Science Products. Life Science was making Kepone under contract for Allied Chemical, a much larger firm.

In summer 1975, a worker at the Life Science plant was found to be suffering from Kepone poisoning. The plant was closed and the firm went into bankruptcy. Within the next several months, twenty-eight employees had been hospitalized with traces of Kepone in their blood. The Kepone poisoning was said to have caused tremors, liver and brain damage, visual defects, and male sterility. The workers filed a civil suit for more than $29 million. At this point, the Kepone case seemed to be primarily a question of occupational health, calling for more careful enforcement of occupational health and safety standards.

In December 1975, the Environmental Protection Agency reported finding significant amounts of Kepone in air and water near Hopewell, and the issue became more hotly political. The governor of Virginia ordered the Kepone-polluted James River, an important oyster-growing area, closed to fishing. By summer 1976, the Food and Drug Administration had found Kepone residues in fish from Chesapeake Bay; the contamination probably came from the bottom sediments of the James River, which flows into the bay (Ricci 1976).

Even after the Life Science plant was closed, disposing of the left-over Kepone proved difficult. The old plant was completely dismantled and buried in a special landfill. Allied Chemical asked permission to dispose of nonburnable residues in abandoned missile silos in Idaho, but this request was denied. Disposal of the Kepone itself requires a special 2000°F (1093°C) furnace.

Kepone is a chlorinated hydrocarbon, as is DDT. The problems caused by these pesticides were first given wide publicity by

Rachel Carson's 1962 book *The Silent Spring*. Carson wrote of the effects of insecticides on birds that eat the poisoned insects. Like these birds, people tend to eat high on the food chain. We eat the big fish, who eat the little fish, who eat still smaller organisms, who have absorbed toxic chemicals. Or we eat cattle, who eat grain treated with pesticides. At each step in the food chain, the organisms retain and concentrate these chemicals in their bodies, so that the top meat-eating animal consumes the most concentrated dose (figure 4.8).

For a while, these pesticides had revolutionary effects on agriculture and on the control of mosquito-borne diseases. Those beneficial effects were dampened in time by the pests' tendency

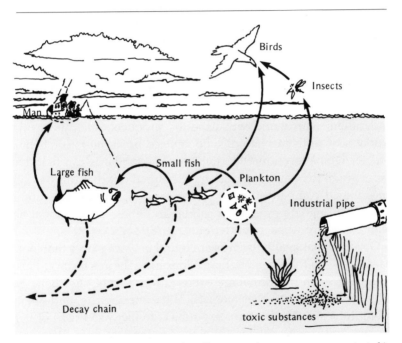

FIGURE 4.8   Toxic substances such as Kepone and mercury are concentrated in the aquatic food chain. The highest concentrations are found in the animals on the highest level of the ecological pyramid, here the fish-eating birds and humans. The bacteria involved in the decay chain, by which the bodies of all the organisms are decomposed, may also modify the pollutants, making them more toxic.

🔊 to adapt to the chemicals by evolving genetic resistance. Meanwhile, a new set of health problems was created through the tendency of the toxic chemicals to persist in the environment.

Workers in a given industry usually bear the brunt of damage from a hazardous substance. Long-term workers in a given industry often show a distinctive pattern of disease that gives a clue to possible risks to the rest of the population. Several occupations are linked to specific tumors: workers in the dye industry show higher-than-average rates of bladder cancer, as do miners with lung cancer and radiologists with leukemia. Often, different substances have effects that interact. For example, asbestos workers who smoke cigarettes have unusually high rates of lung cancer.

In addition to increasing the risk of lung cancer, asbestos fibers that lodge in the lungs produce scar tissue. The resulting condition, asbestosis, affects those who work in factories manufacturing asbestos and others who work with asbestos products, such as insulation workers or auto mechanics who replace brake and clutch linings. Stricter regulation of occupational health standards can help reduce exposure to the hazard. Critics have pointed out that this has simply encouraged companies to move the more hazardous operations to industrializing countries such as Mexico, where occupational health regulations are weaker (Butler et al. 1978).

Occupational health hazards are found in work places that look less hazardous, on the face of it, than a Mexican asbestos factory. Hospital operating room personnel are exposed to traces of anesthetic gases. Male and female anesthesiologists, nurse anesthetists, and operating room nurses and technicians are subject to increased risks of hepatic disease and congenital abnormalities in their children. Women who work in operating rooms also are subject to elevated risk of spontaneous abortion and cancer (American Society of Anesthesiologists 1974).

Diseases caused by medical treatment, called *iatrogenic* diseases, are becoming a major category in modern society as well. The side effects of drugs and diagnostic procedures and unnecessary or incompetent surgery account for a large share of modern iatrogenic disease. Iatrogenic disease is not unique to industrial society, however. The Yano-mamö, for instance, blow a hallucinogenic snuff into each others' nostrils through a hollow tube to attain visions and contact *hekura* demons (Chagnon 1977:24). This drug, which is also used by shamans when they perform curing ceremonies, may cause chromosome damage (Neel 1971). The possibility of iatrogenic damage exists wherever disease is treated, but as medical intervention has become more extensive, the risks have become correspondingly complex.

METHODS FOR STUDYING THE EVOLUTION OF DISEASE PATTERNS

Rich evidence for inferring disease patterns in ancient populations comes from contemporary populations living in similar circumstances. This kind of evidence built up the understanding of disease evolution discussed in the preceding sections of this chapter. However, simply projecting the current health conditions of hunting or agricultural populations into the past is a risky strategy. An important check on these inferences about evolution is provided by direct methods for assessing the health of ancient populations. Archaeologists' studies of environment and material culture can be linked to evidence of disease in skeletal remains to give time depth to the study of the ecology of disease. The study of disease in prehistoric populations is called **paleopathology.** Paleopathologists usually must depend on bones and teeth, but under unusual conditions where a corpse has remained frozen or covered by a peat bog, soft parts may be preserved. In ancient Egypt and Peru, mummies give evidence of a wider range of diseases than would be known from the bones alone. Mummies have shown evidence of arteriosclerosis, the eggs of parasitic schistosomes in the kidneys, and smallpox.

Skeletal remains alone show abnormalities of many kinds. Anomalies of the spine, clubfoot, dwarfism, and other congenital defects show up. There is evidence of trauma, both as fresh injuries or weapon wounds that caused the death and as old, healed fractures or arthritic inflammation of the joints. A consistent pattern of such injury or inflammation in a population indicates culturally specific stresses. For example, the Anglo-Saxons frequently fractured their legs in a way that suggests that they wore clumsy footwear while farming rough ground. In contrast, Egyptians had fewer leg fractures, probably because they farmed smoother ground and went barefoot. However, this same Egyptian series of skeletons includes many females with broken arms, a particular kind of break that occurs when an arm is raised to guard the head from a blow (Wells 1964). In interpreting skeletal data such as these, the paleopathologist uses the same methods that are used in legal cases to get information about a victim of foul play.

Arthritis can also be studied in skeletal populations. Degenerative knee disease has been compared in skeletons of Eskimos, Pueblo Indians, and black and white Americans (Jurmain 1977). Of these populations, Alaskan Eskimo hunters showed the most degenerative knee disease and agricultural Pueblo Indians the least. The stresses of walking on ice and snow may contribute, but the impulse stresses produced by jarring rides on dog sleds were probably most important in Eskimo knee problems.

Old bones can also give evidence of infectious diseases such as syphilis and tuberculosis. The vertebrae shown in figure 4.9a were weakened and destroyed by a disease that filled and surrounded them with pus. The spine, found in New York state, was from an adult female Native American who lived between the thirteenth and fifteenth centuries. Although the disease is most likely to have been tuberculosis, other kinds of infection cannot be ruled out (Wells 1964:272).

One skeleton may tell us something about the presence of a disease or a type of injury, but a whole population of skeletons yields epidemiological and demographic information. By estimating the age and sex of individuals buried in a cemetery, judgments can be made about average life span. Another technique for comparing populations is to

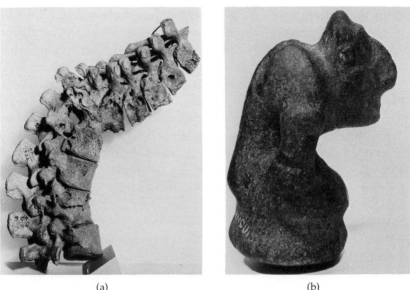

(a)   (b)

FIGURE 4.9   The presence of spinal tuberculosis among pre-Columbian Native
Americans is inferred from the evidence of skeletal materials and art
(Wells 1969: 272).
(a) The thoracic and lumbar vertabrae of a Seneca woman who lived in
what is now New York state sometime between the thirteenth and
fifteenth centuries. The destruction of bone is the result of an infectious
disease, probably tuberculosis.
(b) A pre-Columbian stone grainpounder from Middle America, which
shows the hunched back typical of spinal tuberculosis.

SOURCE: (a) From the collection of the Rochester Museum and Science Center,
Rochester, New York. (b) Department of Ethnography, the British Museum;
reproduced by Courtesy of the Trustees of the British Museum.

make X-ray studies of long bones that show Harris's lines, the scars of
a period of arrested growth in the child. A count of these lines gives an
indication of the number of episodes of malnutrition and infection the
individual experienced while growing up (Wells 1964:155). Comparing
these figures gives a comparison of the health status of populations.

Another source of information about prehistoric health is dried
feces, called *coprolites*, which have sometimes been found in or near
prehistoric camps or shelters when excavated by archaeologists. A
chemical test helps the researcher decide whether the specimen is of

human origin (Bryant and Williams-Dean 1975:100). If so, inspecting it under a microscope gives a great deal of information about disease, diet, and the environment hundreds of thousands of years ago. Ancient coprolites have yielded the eggs of tapeworms and pinworms as well as the remains of ticks, mites, and lice. Diet is indicated by parts of food that pass through the digestive tract unchanged, such as the scales of fish and reptiles and bits of animal hair adhering to meat. The undigested outer coats of seeds show whether a person had been eating blackberries or chili peppers. In some cases they even show how the food had been prepared, as when crushed grains indicate pounding and split grains give evidence of grinding on stone *metates* (Bryant and Williams-Dean 1975). Windborne and insectborne pollen, accidentally ingested with food or drinking water, give evidence of the season of year and the plants and trees in the environment, which fills out the ecological study of a prehistoric population.

Cultural artifacts supplement the paleopathological data from bones and coprolites. Art is difficult to interpret: an oddly shaped human figure may not realistically represent a deformity that the artist observed. But taken in conjunction with skeletal evidence of the same disease, stone or pottery figurines and paintings are ancient witness to the crippling effects of diseases such as polio in ancient Egypt or tuberculosis of the spine in Central America (figure 4.9b).

CONCLUSIONS

As culture has evolved, its relationships with the physical and biological environment have altered. In this chapter, we have seen how the risks of accidental injury or exposure to harmful substances and interactions with pathogenic organisms differ among nomadic hunters and gatherers, settled agricultural peoples, and preindustrial and industrial city dwellers. While medical anthropologists have derived most of their understanding of the evolution of disease patterns from the study of contemporary peoples with different lifestyles, some of that understanding comes from historical studies, such as the study of plague, as well as from increasingly sophisticated paleopathological methods for studying ancient populations.

One of the key factors in cultural evolution is population growth. Technological evolution itself is a creative response to a burgeoning population's demands for new sources of food, shelter, and new social institutions capable of coordinating larger groups. Culture, as the characteristic human adaptation to ecosystemic change, has alternately speeded and checked the rate of population growth in ways that range from infanticide to birth control pills, from smallpox vaccinations to cultural values placed on motherhood or virginity.

In this chapter, the focus has been mostly on accident and disease, the uncomfortable or uneasy relationships humans have with their environments at times. In chapter 5, the emphasis will be more positive, and the environment will be seen as a resource. For example, the plant and animal species of concern will be food plants and domesticated animals rather than the pathogens and vectors of infectious disease. But these two emphases cannot really be separated for two broad reasons: (1) the synergism between disease and malnutrition, and (2) the close relationship between the evolution of food-getting technology and patterns of disease.

The *synergism* of disease and malnutrition refers to the interaction that multiplies their impact on the organism. In chapter 6, we will look at toddlers whose weaning diet is insufficient for their own needs, at the same time having to cope with heavy loads of intestinal parasites. Combating an infection increases the body's need for nutrients, precisely when the nutrients become less available.

The oldest subsistence technology, hunting and gathering, carries with it characteristic patterns of disease, influenced by climate and other local specifics, but everywhere constrained by life in small nomadic groups. For a hunting and gathering system to function without destroying its resource base, population size must be limited, and cultural practices of family limitation such as the postpartum taboo and infanticide help do this. The shift to agriculture brings with it opportunities for population growth—both families and villages are larger than in hunting societies, but agriculture also brings a new vulnerability. Agricultural groups are vulnerable to new patterns of infectious disease, famine, and economic exploitation that hunter-gatherers are able to avoid. Given evolutionary time, humans have adapted to many of the risks of farming, as chapter 3's health profile dealing with malaria and the sickle cell indicated. The growth of preindustrial cities steps up some of these processes: the massive mortality from epidemic disease in the fourteenth century, for example, must have left a population much altered by natural selection in ways we cannot readily reconstruct. The shift to an industrial system of harnessing energy has been accompanied by further population growth, pollution, and stress-related diseases. These major changes in disease patterns offer new adaptive challenges.

RESOURCES

Readings

Cockburn, T. Aidan
    1971   Infectious Disease in Ancient Populations. Current Anthropology 12:45–72.
    This article reviews the evidence for the evolution of disease patterns, beginning with the primates.
Dubos, René
    1965   Man Adapting. New Haven, Connecticut: Yale University Press.
    Dubos, a microbiologist, makes a masterful attempt to apply an ecosystemic approach to all of human health and disease.
McNeill, William H.
    1976   Plagues and Peoples. Garden City, New York: Anchor Press/ Doubleday.
    This account of the place of disease in history is anything but stuffy. McNeill discusses disastrous encounters across the boundaries of disease and immunity such as Cortes and smallpox in Mexico.
May, Jacques M.
    1958   The Ecology of Human Disease. New York: MD Publication.
    This book is a disease-by-disease study of the geography and ecology of the major infectious diseases throughout the world.
Polgar, Steven
    1964   Evolution and the Ills of Mankind. In Horizons of Anthropology. Sol Tax, ed. Pp. 200–211. Chicago: Aldine.
    Polgar's short essay is the prototype for this chapter. He was concerned

with the evolution of human disease that accompanied the evolution of human communities.

Swedlund, Alan, and George J. Armelagos

1976   Demographic Anthropology. Dubuque, Iowa: Wm. C. Brown. This is a nontechnical introduction to demography for the anthropology student. It especially emphasizes paleodemography, the study of population processes in prehistoric populations.

Film

Song of the Canary. 58 minutes. By Josh Hanig and David Davis. Produced by the Film Fund, San Francisco, California. Available for rental from P. O. Box 315, Franklin Lakes, New Jersey 07417.

This film documents two cases of industrial disease in the United States: "brown lung" among cotton mill workers in North and South Carolina, and sterility among workers in a pesticide plant in California.

The Ecology and Economics of Nutrition

CHAPTER 5

PREVIEW

Rural nutrition is primarily determined by ecology and urban nutrition by economics (Whyte 1974). This chapter will develop that theme on a worldwide scale, beginning with studies of subsistence ecology among hunter-gatherers, tropical farmers, and peasant agriculturalists. In these rural settings, the dietary pattern is prescribed by the biophysical and cultural environment. The specific nutritional diseases that occur are related to weaknesses of the staple foods of each cultural region. People who are able to maintain a highly diversified diet tend to have good nutritional health, a finding supported by the health profile of Kalahari Desert hunter-gatherers.

Malnutrition in urban areas is more closely tied to economic inequality. Poverty and population growth contribute to protein-calorie malnutrition among the urban disadvantaged. However, rural areas come to resemble urban areas when cash-cropping ties the rural economy into the world economy and agribusiness replaces subsistence farming. In these areas, a family's nutritional state depends on the food they can afford to buy rather than on what they grow. In most cultures, people consume a great many non-nutritive substances that have some effect on nutrition. These include traditionally used drugs, such as the coca leaves chewed by South American peoples described in the chapter's second health profile.

Malnutrition means a disorder of nutrition, which can be too much food or the wrong kinds of food, as well as not enough food. Thus it includes the malnutrition of affluence. One aspect of this is obesity resulting from a combination of overnutrition and underactivity. In addition to obesity, other patterns of disease result from modern food processing and consumption.

HUMAN FOODWAYS AND NUTRITIONAL NEEDS

Central to every culture is its way of obtaining food. Kalahari Desert hunters track game and shoot it with bow and poisoned arrows. Later they tell the story of the hunt while munching nuts and fruits collected by the women of the band. New Guinea women toil in sweet potato gardens cleared from tropical forests by their husbands, who wield axes made of stone or imported steel. Peasant farmers in the Andes at an altitude of 11,000 feet (3400 meters) above sea level plant potatoes, one of the few crops that can endure the chilly nights. Americans go to the supermarket to choose among thousands of products marketed mostly by large corporations. Increasingly, these corporations control every step of the process of food production and preparation from the farmer's field to the fast-food restaurant.

Nutritional anthropologists remind us that people do not eat protein and carbohydrates, but rather *food*, whether it is hamburgers and french fries or rice with fish sauce. In this chapter, the focus will be on food: the way it is produced in different ecosystems, the way it is prepared in different cultures, and the way it is distributed in different economies. Each of these factors has certain implications for human nutrition. It will become clear that there are certain characteristic nutritional problems in a population of tropical farmers that are different from those in a U.S. suburb.

Generally speaking, what are the nutritional needs for which societies must provide? People need *energy,* for maintenance and growth as well as for the internal and external work their bodies do. Carbohydrates, fats, and proteins are all sources of energy, which is measured in kilocalories. They need *protein,* comprised of chains of nitrogen-containing organic compounds called **amino acids.** Most of the amino acids needed for growth and metabolism can be synthesized by the body, but the eight **essential amino acids** are ones that cannot be synthesized by the human body and therefore must be present in the diet. People need *fats,* not simply to provide a concentrated source of energy, but to supply certain essential fatty acids, which are necessary for building nerve tissue. People need *water.* They also need *vitamins,* some sixteen organic compounds found in very small concentrations in the body. The body cannot synthesize these substances, and if one is missing from the diet or poorly absorbed, its absence leads to deficiency disease. And people need *minerals,* inorganic elements present either in fairly large amounts in the body such as calcium and phosphorous or as trace elements such as iron, fluorine, copper, and zinc. Fortunately, these needs can be met in a wide variety of ways, so that human beings have been able to thrive in environments offering very different food resources.

SUBSISTENCE BY HUNTING AND GATHERING

Less than 1 percent of the world's population earns its living by hunting and gathering today, yet studies of hunter-gatherer subsistence have a special importance to medical anthropologists. After all, taking the long-range evolutionary view, humans are basically hunter-gatherers with a brief, recent history of farming and industry.

Homo sapiens may have existed in essentially modern form at least 50,000 years before people started to farm.

The most striking fact about hunting and gathering peoples is that they are so fit and well nourished. Their traditional diets are well balanced and generally adequate despite seasonal shortages and occasional bad years. Although twentieth-century hunter-gatherers are limited to the most inhospitable of environments, their life seems not to be full of toil, hardship, and insecurity. They live in small communities in which there is no occupational specialization, except that certain tasks—especially hunting—are considered men's work and others are considered women's work. Food is shared within these communities. As a result, marked inequalities of consumption are unlikely, despite variations in luck and skill among individual hunters.

The particular balance between animal and vegetable foods depends on the resources of the environment. The highest proportion of animal foods is found in the traditional diet of the northernmost Inuit, described in chapter 1. Few Inuit eat anything like a traditional diet today, however, as the health profile in chapter 8 will show. The Native Americans of the subarctic interior of northern Canada also traditionally had a predominantly meat diet, which has been modified by the flour, sugar, and canned goods available at the trading post. Except in the Far North, hunting tends to provide a smaller proportion than gathering and fishing. Data from the !Kung San, the people discussed in the following health profile, have made an important contribution to the re-evaluation of hunter-gatherer subsistence and health.

PROFILE: SUBSISTENCE ECOLOGY OF THE !KUNG SAN

A wily, fearless hunter stalks big game with bow and arrow to bring home meat to his waiting wife and children—or a skinny starving band digs for shriveled, bitter roots and fat, white grubs. Which of these stereotypes of hunting-gathering peoples do you think is more accurate? Recent research by Richard B. Lee and his colleagues of the Harvard Kalahari Research Group suggests that neither the heroic hunter nor the starving gatherer is an accurate picture of the hunting-gathering way of life. Their studies of the !Kung San depict a people whose subsistence is quite secure, resting on a well-balanced combination of wild plants and animals.

The San, also called the Bushmen, live in and near the Kalahari Desert of southern Africa (see map, figure 5.1), in the countries of Botswana, Namibia, and Angola. The !Kung are one cultural and linguistic subgroup of the San, whose languages include click consonants such as the one symbolized by the exclamation point in the word !Kung itself.

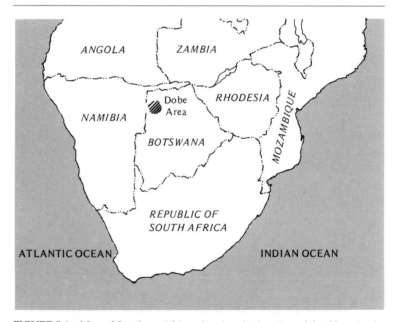

FIGURE 5.1   Map of Southern Africa, showing the location of the !Kung in the Dobe area.

SOURCE: Modified from Lee, in *Kalahari Hunter-Gatherers*, eds. R. B. Lee and I. DeVore (Cambridge, Massachusetts: Harvard University Press, 1976), p. 11.

The group of !Kung that Richard Lee began studying in 1963 were camped in the area of the Dobe waterhole in the northern Kalahari Desert. The plateau is high, about 3400 feet (1100 meters) above sea level, which means that winter nights are cold. The area is dry for most of the year, but variable amounts of rain fall in the hot summer season, between 6 and 24 inches (150 and 600 mm) per year (Lee 1973:307). During the wet season, the !Kung can disperse to small camps of one or two families at seasonal waterholes to take advantage of hunting and gathering throughout a wide area. During the dry season, they must congregate into larger camps of thirty to fifty people, building their grass huts near one of the eight permanent waterholes in the Dobe area. Food resources are less abundant when the people are this closely settled.

The !Kung habitat is a semidesert, in which areas of thorny shrubs alternate with open woodlands. Grasslands cover most of the Kalahari but are rare in the Dobe area. The varied vegetation includes some 110 species of edible plants: roots and bulbs, berries and fruits, melons, nuts, edible gums, and leafy greens (Yellen and Lee 1976:43). For most of the year, the vegetable foods are so plentiful that the !Kung can bypass those that are less tasty or more difficult to collect, concentrating on the most attractive ones. At the end of the dry season, when food is scarce, people must either walk longer distances to get these foods or eat less desirable foods such as bitter melons, roots, and edible gum.

The major, year-round food resource of the !Kung is the mongongo nut. The mongongo tree grows in groves on sand dunes and rocky outcrops. At the end of the rainy season, the fruits fall to the ground, where they are easily gathered. The soft flesh of mongongo fruit can be eaten after peeling. Beneath the flesh is a thick, heavy shell, which is very difficult to crack and protects the nut, making it usable even after it has lain on the ground for months. Beneath the outer shell is a thin inner shell and the kernel itself, about the size and shape of a hazelnut. The hard shell is one thing that has preserved the mongongo nut as a food resource for the San, since the nut is too difficult to shell to make it attractive to large animals or commercial exploitation.

After the nuts are gathered from the ground, they are carried back to camp in a *kaross*, a leather cloak that is knotted up to make a carrying bag. There the nuts are roasted. Roasting makes them easier to shell, which is done by hammering them with a stone (figure 5.2). The nuts may be eaten whole or pounded in a

FIGURE 5.2   Three generations of !Kung roasting, cracking, and eating mongongo nuts.
Photo by R. Lee, Anthro-Photo.

mortar with a pestle and combined with other foods. The mongongo nuts are rich in protein and polyunsaturated fats and are a high-energy food, containing 600 calories per 100 grams. The protein content is comparable to that of soybeans or peanuts. Other vegetable foods gathered by the !Kung, such as the tsin bean and the baobab nut, are equally nutritious (Yellen and Lee 1976:38). About two-thirds of the !Kung diet comes from the vegetable foods gathered by the women.

The !Kung prize meat highly. It contributed about one-third of the caloric value of their diet and a little more than one-third of the protein during one four-week period when Lee weighed all the food that came into camp (1968:39). The proportion of meat in the diet probably varies from about 20 to 50 percent in different camps at different times. In contrast to the abundance and reliability of vegetable foods, game animals are scarce and unpredictable, making meat more of a luxury food. Lee found that hunters made an average of one kill per four man-days of hunting (Lee 1968:40) while gatherers got some food every time they went out of camp. One way in which !Kung hunters adapt to the risks of hunting is to concentrate on the game animals that give the highest return for their effort. The big antelopes and giraffes are difficult to stalk and likely to escape even when wounded. Success is greater with smaller mammals, especially the warthog, the small antelopes, the spring hare, and the porcupine.

Another way to express the difference between hunting and gathering is in terms of the amount of time necessary to bring home a given amount of food. Lee observed that to produce 100 calories of food energy by hunting took more than twice as long as by gathering. In fact, !Kung men do not work that much longer than the women; instead, they eat more of the easily obtained vegetable foods than they eat meat. For the !Kung, getting food is not a full-time task. Lee found that the average adult devoted a $1\frac{1}{2}$- to $3\frac{1}{2}$-day work week to the food quest. Additional time was spent in manufacturing tools and processing food (Lee 1968).

The work load of the !Kung is closely related to the demographic structure of the group. Families are of moderate size. If a woman lives to menopause, she will give birth to five children, of whom one will die before the age of one year (Howell 1976). If families were larger, the ratio of productive adults to dependent children would be higher than it is and each adult would have to work longer. In the camp where Lee did his input–output study of subsistence, adults outnumbered children almost two to one.

Family size relates to work output in an even more direct way. A !Kung woman carries her baby with her as she gathers food. The burden of carrying a child, who cannot keep up with the group on his or her own until age 3 or 4, is added to her load of gathered food. The four-year birth spacing observed under nomadic conditions is an adaptation to these circumstances (Lee 1972; Howell 1976:145). The !Kung do not practice contraception, and abortion and infanticide are not significant means of family limitation for them. The postpartum sex taboo of about one year could not by itself account for four-year spacing of births. How then is the long spacing maintained? Prolonged lactation plays some role in supressing ovulation, and !Kung women breast-feed their infants for four to six years. Recent research in !Kung endocrinology (van der Walt, Wilmsen, and Jenkins 1977) shows seasonally low levels of the hormones estradiol and testosterone in women. The researchers interpreted this as a sign that these women were not ovulating at certain times of the year. The anthropologist Wilmsen (1978) found that the frequency of births was sharply seasonal, peaking in May, nine months after the wet-season maximum of food resources and body weight.

The seasonal shortage of calories seems to be the only nutritional problem the !Kung have. This energy shortage accounts, in part, for why they are rather short and thin and slow to mature. This quantitative deficiency is not matched by any qualitative deficiency in their diet. Clinical and biochemical examinations of the !Kung San found no evidence of deficiencies of any essential nutrients and no obesity, coronary disease, or hypertension (Truswell and Hansen 1976). The mixed diet of these hunter-gatherers protects them against specific deficiencies just as their wide knowledge of the diverse food resources of their environment helps buffer them against hard times.

The subsistence of hunter-gatherers has perhaps been studied with greatest detail in desert and semidesert regions. The !Kung San are only one of the subgroups of San, or Bushmen, who have been studied by anthropologists. Their subsistence ecology varies somewhat from that of the San of the central Kalahari studied by Tanaka (1976) and Silberbauer (1972). Lacking the rich nut resources of the !Kung, these people depend more on melons and tubers. The high water content of the melons and tubers is important, too, because of the absence of permanent waterholes. Most of their drinking water is obtained from plants. Compared with the Dobe area !Kung, their environment forces them to rely more heavily on larger migratory game animals.

The subsistence ecology of the San of southern Africa invites comparison with hunting and gathering in other arid regions such as the Great Basin of Nevada and Utah and the Western Desert of Australia. In the Great Basin, foraging for food is no longer an ongoing way of life, but Julian Steward's studies of the Shoshoneans in the 1930s reconstructed their subsistence pattern. Communal hunts for jack rabbits and antelope could be held only every few years in any one area, which indicates the scarcity of game. Smaller mammals, rodents, lizards, and insects were probably more important than larger species. The seeds of wild grasses were gathered in baskets. The richest resource was the annual fall harvest of piñon nuts in the pine forests of the mountains (Steward 1955:104). Like the !Kung, the Shoshoneans lived and gathered food in small bands that varied in size depending on the seasonal availability of resources.

A similarly arid region is the Central and Western Desert of Australia. The foraging way of life there has now given way to wage work on cattle stations and dependence on welfare rations for most Aborigines, but studies of traditional subsistence have been made. The Aborigines hunted with a throwing stick or a spear. Their largest game was the kangaroo and the emu, a large, flightless bird. Lizards and other small game were important. But again the vegetable food resources were critical. Grass seeds were collected in wooden bowls, ground on a flat stone, and baked into bread (Gould 1969).

Some Aboriginal Australian groups had additional food resources from coastal and inland waters. Nutritional anthropologist Margaret McArthur studied four camps of Aborigines in Arnhem Land who had abundant supplies of fish, more than one pound per person per day (McArthur 1960:127). Each of the four camps had different vegetable foods. At one camp, the women gathered water lily rhizomes by diving in the lagoon. At two other camps, wild yams and other roots were abundant. At the fourth camp, Fish Creek, fishing was good and the hunters brought in huge quantities of kangaroo meat as well, but vegetable foods were very scarce because it was near the end of the dry season. Finally, the scarcity of wild vegetable foods led the Aborigines to go to the mission station for rice and flour, indicating that these groups are really part-time hunter-gatherers.

McArthur's study of the Australian Aborigines, like Lee's study of the !Kung, provides data that allow us to evaluate the amount of time that hunter-gatherers spend in the food quest. She found that women gathered food nearly every day for three hours or more. The men, whose activities were observed by anthropologist F. D. McCarthy, hunted about every other day, but typically for about six hours

(McCarthy and McArthur 1960). This subsistence effort is somewhat greater than that of the !Kung, as observed by Lee, though still allowing for leisure.

One way in which such subsistence economies can be compared was devised by the anthropologist Robert Carneiro (1968b). He suggested that subsistence efficiency could be measured by the number of hours of labor time required to produce 1 million kilocalories of food energy, a figure he selected as a round number approximating what it would take to feed a person for one year. Carneiro's own field work was with Amazonian peoples. He estimated very roughly that the Amahuaca of Peru required 795 hours of hunting to produce 1 million kilocalories. Expressed in these terms, McCarthy and McArthur's figures on work time (1960) indicate that the Australian Aborigines were working somewhat more than that, between 1300 and 1460 hours at fishing, gathering, and hunting to produce 1 million kilocalories. Looking at Lee's data on the !Kung in this way indicates that !Kung hunters need to work 1000 hours to produce 1 million kilocalories, while !Kung women need to work at gathering only 400 hours to collect food with an energy value of 1 million kilocalories. Some subsistence farmers have to work this long to produce equivalent amounts of food (Townsend 1974:229).

Partly because of this favorable input:output ratio of gathering, vegetable foods often constitute more than half of a typical hunter-gatherer dietary. They are usually quite varied, which means that specific nutritional deficiencies are unlikely to occur. A leafy fern may be rich in vitamin A and iron, a fruit in vitamin C, a nut in protein, and a root in carbohydrates. The diversity leads to a well-balanced diet.

Typically, the more serious nutritional problem of hunter-gatherers is one of *seasonal* variation in the foods available. In the !Kung profile, the seasonal shortage of water in their semidesert environment constricted the people's movements and their access to vegetable resources even though some of these were available to be gathered year-round. Even in a tropical rain forest, where drought is not a factor, tiny variations in rainfall, from the wet season to the slightly less wet season, trigger flowering and fruiting and create seasonal variation in the availability of different vegetable foods. The rivers rise and fall, causing changes in hunting and fishing conditions. Seasonal hunger can be a problem for hunter-gatherers in any environment.

Tropical forest hunter-gatherers are perhaps the most misunder-stood groups in terms of subsistence. We tend to think of their environment as rich because it is lush with vegetation; the problem is that very little of all that green vegetation is edible. The heat and high rainfall create acid soils that are leached of minerals, and the tropical plants adapted to these conditions are consequently high in bulk and low in nutrients. They tend to reproduce vegetatively (by sending out suckers) rather than producing nutrient-rich seeds and fruits. This scarcity of nutrients means that animals are generally few and small, in contrast to the large herbivores of grasslands or temperate forests. Many of the tropical animals, like the monkeys and birds, live high in the trees and are difficult to hunt. Despite all these difficulties, small bands of hunter-gatherers are found in tropical forests around the globe, including the pygmies of Africa, the Negritos of Southeast Asia, and South American Indian groups in Amazonia. The expansion of tropical farmers has often cut away at their control of their lands. Where this has occurred, they have sometimes taken on a symbiotic relationship with the farmers, trading forest products for crops and tools.

SUBSISTENCE BY FARMING

Tropical Farmers

The transition from gathering wild plants to protecting and encour-aging natural stands of useful plants and then to cultivating plants actively is subtle and gradual. By depending on cultivated plants rather than wild ones, people intervene in the natural process of ecological succession in an area to produce more of the plants that they are interested in eating. Tropical farmers do this, just as any Kansas wheat farmer does, but the kind of intervention is somewhat different. In their technique, called *slash-and-burn cultivation*, they cut the tropical forest with axes and bushknives and then dry and burn the debris.

FIGURE 5.3   New Guinea women prepare sago, a starch obtained from the trunk of
palms that grow in tropical swamps. In some areas of New Guinea and
Southeast Asia, the palms grow wild, and in other areas they are
cultivated.
Photo by William H. Townsend.

They interplant the crop plants of many species in the mineral-rich
ashes of the burned-over field, planting and cultivating with the aid of
digging sticks or hoes. After a farmer harvests one or more crops, he
allows the forest to grow back and moves on to a new clearing.

In his study of Indonesian agriculture, Clifford Geertz (1963) contrasted slash-and-burn fields, called *swiddens,* with terraced and
irrigated rice fields. The swidden mimics the tropical forest and

maintains its structure, while the wet-rice field radically reshapes the landscape. The swidden is extensive, using large amounts of land; the wet-rice field is intensive, putting tremendous amounts of labor into a small area to increase production. The demographic implications are clear: irrigation agriculture can absorb tremendous amounts of labor, and population growth is stimulated. In contrast, the slash-and-burn system can work only if population density remains low; otherwise, there is a tendency to shorten periods when the land lies idle until irreversible deterioration takes place and grassland takes over.

The major food crops of tropical slash-and-burn cultivation, like the nondomesticated plants of the forest, are high in bulk and low in nutrients and mostly propagated by cuttings rather than by seeds. The edible parts are most often not seeds but other parts of the plants where starch is stored: usually underground tubers. Some of these plants are shown in figure 5.4. They include manioc or cassava, sweet potatoes, yams, and many others. In other tropical crops, the edible

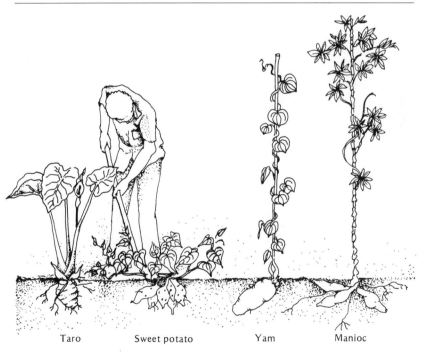

Taro   Sweet potato   Yam   Manioc

FIGURE 5.4   Major tropical root crops.

starch is found in other parts of the plant, for example, bananas and plantains and the stem of the sago palm (Ruddle et al. 1978). Some cereal crops are grown in slash-and-burn cultivation, too, especially rice in Southeast Asia and maize in Central and South America.

The starchy tropical crops have this in common: all are effective sources of food energy but all are poor sources of protein. (Table 5.1 shows the protein-to-kilocalorie ratio of several of these foods, along with some cereals and legumes and foods of animal origin.) What are

TABLE 5.1   Grams of protein per 100 kilocalories in certain foods.

Sago	<1
Cassava	<1
Plantain	1
Sweet potato	1
Yam	2
Taro	2
Irish potato	3
Rice, highly milled	2
Maize	3
Wheat	3
Lentils	7
Soybeans	9
Milk, human	2
Milk, cow's, whole	5
Milk, cow's, skim	10
Eggs	8
Beef, lean	9
Poultry	14
Fish, freshwater	19

Application: If one were to eat enough sweet potatoes to provide 2000 kilocalories per day, one would get 20 grams of protein in the sweet potatoes. If one were to eat enough wheat to provide 2000 kilocalories per day, one would get 60 grams of protein in the wheat.

SOURCE: Data recalculated from B. S. Platt, "Table of Representative Values of Foods Commonly Used in Tropical Countries." (London: Medical Research Council, Special Report Series, No. 302., 1962).

the nutritional implications of these low protein-to-kilocalorie ratios for tropical farmers? First of all, as long as they have such abundant, reliable sources of carbohydrates, they can easily meet their requirements for food energy. In a world where many people cannot meet their basic energy requirements, this is not to be taken lightly. Second, they cannot satisfy their requirements for protein and many vitamins and minerals simply by eating larger amounts of their staple foods. The sheer bulk of these starchy foods and the kilocalories taken in would have to be excessive before the protein would be sufficient. This is especially true for a small child, whose need for protein is proportionally even higher than an adult's.

Growing a wide variety of green leafy vegetables, fruit trees, and other crops in kitchen gardens or interplanted with the staple foods in the swiddens helps meet the need for vitamins and minerals, as well as liven up monotonous meals. Gathering wild foods can help out as well. Protein is more of a problem, one most often met by adding some concentrated source of animal protein from meat or fish.

The critical protein component of the tropical diet is often provided by fish. In his comparative study of Amazonian tribes, Robert Carneiro (1968) found that large, settled villages of manioc farmers were found only along major rivers where fishing was good. The vast areas lacking access to fish as a resource were peopled by smaller, less permanent farming communities that relied on hunting as their main source of protein. When the areas around a village site became hunted out, they moved on. The new settlers along the Trans-Amazonian highway face the same problem (Moran 1975). As long as rivers were the main avenues of transport and settlement, fish were available. But with the highway opening up the interior and urban centers growing, new sources of protein will be needed. Moran recommends that manioc flour be enriched by the addition of yeast to meet this need.

Many tropical farmers also keep domesticated animals. For example, pigs are raised in New Guinea by cultivators of sweet potatoes, taro, and yams. Roy Rappaport's 1968 study of the Tsembaga Maring, a milestone in the development of ecological anthropology, was titled *Pigs for the Ancestors.* The title underscores the fact that pigs are butchered only on ritual occasions as sacrifices to the ancestors. These rituals, Rappaport argued, serve to regulate the production and consumption of this scarce animal protein. Although, as his dietary studies showed, most of the Marings' protein comes from vegetables, the pigs they raise can effectively convert waste food such as sweet potato peelings into needed protein and fat.

Fishing, hunting, and raising animals are the usual ways starchy diets are supplemented with animal proteins, but some cultures have met this need in unusual ways. Peoples who use sago palm starch also eat the larvae of beetles that tunnel their way through the pith of the sago palm. The plump white grubs are a source of fat and protein. Since small amounts of animal protein are so critical in the diet of tropical farmers, some anthropologists have argued that even cannibalism should be understood as having nutritional value. It is true that most peoples who practiced cannibalism were tropical farmers of the kind we have been discussing. Cannibalism in these cultures was customary, expected behavior, quite a different thing from the desperate act of starving people in times of famine or disaster. Cannibalism had very different meanings in different cultures: to honor a dead relative, to insult a despised enemy by implying that you killed him just as you might kill an animal, to gain the powers of a respected enemy. Regardless of the cultural meaning, could the food value have been significant? Garn and Block (1970) claimed that the amounts of protein would have been insignificant unless a group were in a position to consume its own number each year. However, Morren and Dornstreich (1974) argued that in marginally nourished New Guinea groups, such as those they studied in their field work, a much less intense practice of cannibalism would have made the critical difference of a few grams of protein per person per day. The sacrifice of war captives by the Aztecs in the Valley of Mexico has even been interpreted as large-scale cannibalism with nutritional value (Harner 1977). While accepting that small amounts of protein may be critical in certain ecosystems, most anthropologists regard the nutritional aspect of cannibalism to be trivial in comparison with its social and psychological effects (Price 1978; Ortiz de Montellano 1978). Even ecological anthropologists are more likely to emphasize the *indirect* effects of cannibalism and warfare in spacing out tribal populations in relation to resources, rather than the direct effect on nutrition. While protein is generally the limiting factor in the food supply of tropical slash-and-burn cultivators, it is also possible to go too far and overemphasize what is, after all, only one of the requirements for sustaining human life.

Peasant Farmers

Most of the food energy and protein for most of the world's people comes from cereal crops such as wheat, rice, and corn (figure 5.5). Modern farmers use heavy machinery, petroleum, and fertilizers to grow these crops, but in much of the world peasant farmers still grow them using technologies much like those in use thousands of years ago. These agricultural techniques are typically more intensive than the slash-and-burn root-crop farming discussed in the preceding

FIGURE 5.5   Major cereal grains.

section; that is, higher amounts of labor are expended per acre of land. This more intensive use of land may take the form of irrigation works, terracing, use of natural fertilizers, or other methods of increasing productivity. Peasant cultivators typically harness the energy of domesticated animals to pull a plow, though sometimes they depend on the digging stick or hoe. Those domesticated animals also provide dairy products and meat as an addition to the diet.

The peasant agriculturalists tend to have a diet dominated very heavily by a single cereal staple: rice throughout much of South and Southeast Asia, wheat in temperate Asia and Europe, maize in the New World, millet or sorghum in Africa. These are sometimes called *superfoods,* not because they are superior but because a population is culturally and economically focused on a single staple. Where a single food dominates in this way, its nutritional limitations become the critical nutritional problem for the population (Haas and Harrison 1977). Lack of diversity in the diet leaves poor peasants vulnerable to deficiencies, just as the very diversity of the hunter-gatherers' diet protected them from deficiencies. Specific deficiency diseases tend to have a distribution that reflects the ecology of food plants, except where people are protected from deficiency in some way through cultural or biological adaptation.

Maize (corn) was the principal cereal to be domesticated in the New World. Populations that heavily depend on maize may have two related nutritional problems: (1) pellagra, a disease caused by a deficiency of niacin, and (2) protein deficiency, because the protein in maize has relatively small amounts of the amino acids lysine and tryptophan.

Pellagra is a disease characterized by a distinctive rash, diarrhea, and mental disturbances (Roe 1973). It was a disease of poor share-croppers who lived on cornmeal mush and corn bread in the southern United States and in southern Europe. Yet the corn-eating peoples of Central and South America rarely developed pellagra because they traditionally prepared maize by treating it with alkali (lye, lime, or wood ashes). They did this in order to soften the hull, not knowing that they were also improving the availability of niacin (Katz, Hediger, and Valleroy 1974). The practice is thus an excellent example of a cultural adaptation that offers a selective advantage to the people who practice it.

The balance among the amino acids found in maize is another nutritional problem for which there was a cultural solution. For protein synthesis to take place in the body, all eight essential amino acids must be present simultaneously in appropriate amounts. If one or more of them is lacking, the amount of protein that can be synthesized will be limited. Most protein from single plant sources does not match up to the proportions of the different amino acids that the body needs as closely as protein from meat. By combining the protein from different plant sources, however, a better match can be made. The traditional American Indian diet of maize and beans, or the Mexican equivalent of *tortillas* and *frijoles*, exemplifies this **protein complementarity.** Maize is relatively low in the amino acids lysine and tryptophan, while beans are relatively lacking in the sulfur-containing amino acids. Although either food eaten separately is an incomplete protein source, if eaten together at the same meal they provide fully adequate protein even without milk, eggs, fish, or meat. Protein complementarity is achieved by people who get most of their protein from vegetable sources by eating many different combinations of cereals with legumes, seeds, and dairy products. Figure 5.6 shows how the protein in beans complements the protein in maize, each supplying amino acids that are relatively lacking in the other. Familiar food combinations that

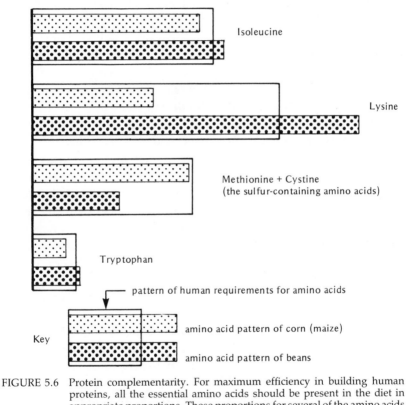

FIGURE 5.6 Protein complementarity. For maximum efficiency in building human proteins, all the essential amino acids should be present in the diet in appropriate proportions. These proportions for several of the amino acids are shown in the above graph. Corn is relatively lacking in lysine, for example, but can be complemented by beans, which supply additional lysine.

SOURCE: Data from FAO/WHO *Energy Requirements and Protein Requirements*, WHO Technical Report Series No. 522 (1973), p. 63, and FAO *Amino-acid Content of Foods and Biological Data on Proteins* (Rome, 1970), pp. 38 and 50.

work on the same principle are the peanut butter sandwich or hominy grits with black-eyed peas.

Rice was originally domesticated in western Asia and is still the staple for the dense populations of that area. Rice as a staple cereal has its distinctive pattern of limitations. Even brown (unmilled) rice has a rather low ratio of protein to carbohydrates and bulk, so that children can seldom eat enough of it to meet their protein needs. Fortunately, most rice-eating people also have fish to help fill the protein gap. In most cultures, white rice is preferred, and the milling and washing process removes the water-soluble vitamins. The resulting deficiency of thiamine can lead to beriberi, a vitamin-deficiency disease that involves inflammation of the nerves. Rice that is parboiled or steamed before milling retains more of its vitamins because the water-soluble vitamins become diffused through the whole grain and are not lost in milling. In cultures such as India where parboiling is the practice, beriberi is less prevalent than it would otherwise be.

Wheat has spread far from its original homeland in the Middle East. It does not seem to be strongly associated with a particular vitamin deficiency as is rice with thiamine deficiency and corn with niacin deficiency. In parts of the Middle East, however, poor rural people living on wheat bread show signs of mineral deficiencies. A deficiency of the trace element zinc shows up as retardation of growth and sexual development in young men (Sever 1975). The deficiency stems from the coarse unleavened whole wheat bread eaten in the area, a bread high in fiber and phytate, a substance that seems to interfere with mineral absorption. The deficiencies are most common in the poorest rural people who eat the coarsest bread and have few other food sources available.

Protein complementarity is characteristic of traditional wheat-based diets. Most wheat-farming areas also have dairy animals, and the combination of bread and cheese is frequently eaten. The limiting amino acids in wheat (that is, those that are present in minimal quantities and thus limit the body's use of the other amino acids) are isoleucine and lysine, and these are present in proportionately greater amounts in dairy products.

The nutritional status of peasant agriculturalists thus differs in several ways from the subsistence economies that we have discussed previously. Dependence on a single staple food increases vulnerability to specific deficiencies of vitamins or minerals. For example, a deficiency of vitamin A can produce xerophthalmia, a leading cause of blindness in the world today. Adequate consumption of dark green vegetables can prevent it. Overdependence on cereals alone would also lead to protein deficiency, but if legumes and dairy products are available in sufficient amounts to complement the protein from cereals, this can be avoided.

Scarcity of some of the components of a balanced diet does occur in rural areas among peasants who grow their own food. Why is this so? One reason is that peasants do not produce for themselves alone but are parts of a larger society in which they support—through taxes, rent, and trade—landowners and town dwellers who produce no food.

Additional pressure on food resources comes from population growth. In chapter 4 we discussed the fact that larger families are more associated with agriculture than with any other type of economy. Recently, researchers have begun exploring a possible nutritional basis for higher fertility in cereal-eating populations as well.

THE ANTHROPOLOGY OF FOOD HABITS

A peoples' diet is a product of environment and tradition. We have been emphasizing the *ecological* factors in diet, for example, the predominance of fish or game as a source of protein in different parts of the Amazon Basin. Environmental factors are responsible for the choice to grow oats and barley in cold, damp Scotland rather than the wheat and rye that are prominent in the rest of Europe. In New Guinea, sweet potatoes thrive in the highest mountain valleys while yams and taro are limited to lower altitudes.

Tradition is also important in determining diet. Traditional foods become symbols of ethnic identity, and diet can be highly resistant to change. This dietary conservatism can itself be viewed as adaptive.

After all, traditional cuisines have been subject to cultural and natural selection over a long period, and any change is more likely to be deleterious than helpful. We have seen several examples of recipes and menus that are highly adaptive. Among these are the lime treatment of corn and the use of curdled milk by lactase-deficient populations. In the menus of India, a largely vegetarian country, protein complementarity is achieved by traditional menus combining legumes and cereals.

Traditional diets are a product of the process of adaptation. Therefore, in any situation of rapid change in environment or diet, nutritional diseases can be expected. When maize was introduced into Spain and Italy and spread into the rest of southern Europe, for example, the deficiency disease pellagra followed. The traditional American Indian customs of lime processing and eating beans had not accompanied the maize. In chapter 8 we will look at the multiple health problems of Inuit who have moved into towns and changed from a meat diet to a diet high in sugar and flour, another example of the deleterious nutritional change accompanying other cultural changes. One of the earliest comparative studies of nutritional change was done by a dentist, Weston A. Price, who traveled for many years to peoples all around the world. He looked at the teeth of Eskimos, Swiss, Gælics, Africans, peoples of the South Pacific, and Native Americans. Everywhere he found that the change from traditional to modern diets produced dental caries and a narrow dental arch with crowded, crooked teeth (Price 1939).

Even a seemingly trivial change may disrupt a nutritional balance. Noniodized trade salt was introduced by Europeans into Papua New Guinea. By 1962 it had completely displaced locally made salt formerly obtained from salt springs by the Maring people. When the Maring population was surveyed by an epidemiologist and an anthropologist in 1968, they found that goiter was endemic (Buchbinder 1977). Enlarged thyroid glands were especially apparent among adolescents and women of reproductive age, although heavy chokers of beads came into fashion and effectively hid the goiters. At the same time, several children were discovered to be cretins with multiple neurological defects, another condition attributed to iodine deficiency. Endemic goiter and endemic cretinism are fairly common in other highland areas that are geologically similar to the Maring area, but the Maring had traditionally been protected from iodine deficiency by the use of the iodine-rich traditional salt. After the problem was discovered, women were given injections of iodized oil; somewhat later, all commercial salt in Papua New Guinea was iodized. By 1974, there were no visible goiters in the Maring population and no more cretins had been born to the women who were treated.

Because traditional diets are the outcome of adaptive processes, when planning to introduce a change, it is safest to work with the assumption that the traditional diet is beneficial, or at least neutral, until it is proved otherwise. Traditional dietary practices do sometimes prove dysfunctional, however. In Thailand, for example, beriberi is a widespread problem although the dietary intake of thiamine is sufficient. It has been found that the raw fermented fish eaten there contains thiaminase, an enzyme that destroys thiamine. In addition, the betel nut and tea that Thai consume contain tannic acid, which reacts with thiamine. This reaction can cause thiamine deficiency even when the diet contains adequate amounts (Vimokesant et al. 1975). Thus the whole pattern of diet and other activities such as chewing betel nut need to be taken into account in interpreting the nutritional situation.

Although resistance to change in food habits is usual, when ecological and economic conditions change it is amazing how rapidly people change even their staple foods. In nineteenth-century England, bread was largely replaced by potatoes, a New World domesticate. In Africa, many populations shifted from sorghum to maize and then to cassava, attracted by higher yields. Cassava (manioc) has spread from South America throughout Africa, Asia, and the Pacific even though it is nutritionally inferior to the crops it is replacing. It is likely to be used even more in the future, because it is a crop that yields well on poor, depleted soils and is quite resistant to pests.

Traditional menus and recipes are so much a part of culture that anthropologists rarely avoid altogether discussing food preparation, but studies of food habits have never really been given high priority or status in the discipline. Anthropologists have joked about Franz Boas's painfully detailed collection of Kwakiutl salmon recipes (1921). Even so, in ethnographies they have at least given lists of foods and descriptions of the major techniques of food preparation before going on to subjects they found more interesting. Although until the past few years few anthropologists explored the nutritional significance of the food habits they described, there are exceptions, such as Audrey Richards, who wrote *Land, Labour, and Diet in Northern Rhodesia* (1939), and Margaret Mead, who was involved in a multidisciplinary study of U.S. food habits during World War II (1943).

Nutritional anthropology moves beyond simple description of food preparation techniques to consider their implications for health. Cooking may alter the chemical composition of food as well as making it more digestible. Soya beans, for example, are a good source of protein but are not very digestible. Chinese and Japanese cooking use fermentation to make soya beans more digestible; the action of molds and microorganisms makes the beans more accessible to digestive juices (Robson 1972:145).

Anthropologists are also concerned with the symbolic meaning of foods in different cultures and with the ways in which foods are combined to form culturally acceptable meals. French anthropologist Claude Lévi-Strauss is especially well known for his analysis of South American Indian myths that elaborate on the themes of food and cooking. His book *The Raw and the Cooked* has more to do with symbolism and the structure of thought than with nutrition. Yet Lévi-Strauss (1969:164) indicates that "the gustatory code," the cultural message communicated by eating habits, occupies an essential and central place in human thought.

Building on the work of Lévi-Strauss, British anthropologist Mary Douglas, in her article "Deciphering a Meal" (1971), puzzled over why soup and pudding do not add up to supper for her family and worked out the symbolic structure of British meals. Nutritional anthropologist Norge Jerome (1975) used interviews and participant observation to study cultural food patterns in black and white households in the Kansas City area. In a study of the decline in the use of the sweet potato in North Carolina, Fitzgerald (1976) found that sweet potatoes were seen as low-status "country food," despite their nutritional value, especially as a source of vitamin A. These studies are just a sampling of contemporary anthropologists' interest in studying the food habits, or *gastronomy*, of our own culture (Arnott 1975).

ALL THAT GOES INTO
THE MOUTH IS NOT
FOOD

Cultural values and symbols influence the foods we eat, but culture also prescribes that we put many non-nutritive substances into our mouths. What have you downed today? Aspirin? Birth control pills? Coffee? Diet soda? Even when a substance is not consumed for its nutritional value, it may have important effects on nutrition.

One of the effects that these nonfood substances may have on nutrition is simply to replace a food that might otherwise be consumed and thereby reduce the intake of essential nutrients. Alcoholics, for example, may meet some of their energy needs by drinking, for alcoholic beverages are high in sugars. At the same time, their diet patterns are usually poor and protein intake is frequently low. This deficit can lead to the degeneration of the liver, which progresses to cirrhosis (Robson 1972:67). Nor are all alcoholic beverages alike in this respect. An African millet beer, thick and unclarified, is a rich source of calcium, iron, and vitamins B and C. The change to a prestigious imported beer will deprive the drinker of an important and inexpensive source of nutrients (Robson 1972:151). The situation is parallel to that of a child who substitutes soda pop, with its "empty" calories, or even diet pop, which is even more empty of nutrients, for fruit juice or milk.

Geophagy, the eating of earth or clay, is probably the most dramatic instance of eating a substance that is not food but has an effect on nutrition (Hochstein 1968). While geophagy has been reported sporadically in cultures around the world, it occurs more frequently in certain groups, for example, until recently among black women in the southern United States, who now eat laundry starch more often than clay. The practice is most common during pregnancy. It has been suggested that eating these substances quiets uneasy sensations in the abdomen and helps the user cope with other physiological changes that may accompany pregnancy, as well as meeting psychological needs. In parts of the world where intestinal parasitism is common, the clay eater may become infected by eating clay, but it also may make the person feel better if it quiets intestinal spasms. Other researchers have suggested that the clay eater may unconsciously seek some mineral for which nutritional deficiency exists, as in West Africa, where the clay from termite nests may be a source of minerals such as copper, calcium, and zinc (Hunter 1973). However, the minerals in clay are ordinarily in a form that is chemically unavailable for the body's use. Worse yet, the clay may bind minerals from other foods into an unusable form. Prolonged clay eating can result in potassium-deficiency disease. While eating laundry starch does not have exactly the same effects, it is filling enough to displace necessary foods from the diet.

Instead of displacing a food, a nonfood item may exercise its effect by changing the way nutrients are used by the body or the requirement for them. Taking birth control pills (Hodges 1971) and other drugs may increase certain vitamin requirements, for example. Smoking cigarettes seems to affect the way in which vitamin C is used or to make less of it available for use (Pelletier 1970).

Drugs also have implications for nutrition and health that go far beyond their intended effects. This is so whether the drug is a popular stimulant or a medically prescribed drug. For example, while an antibiotic is bringing a disease-causing microorganism under control, it may disrupt the relationships among the normal, nonpathogenic organisms inhabiting the gastrointestinal tract. The resulting imbalance in the ecology of mouth or intestine may lead to inflammation or diarrhea, which influences the individual's nutritional state.

PROFILE: COCA CHEWING AND HEALTH IN THE HIGH ANDES

Anthropologists have recently been taking a closer look at coca chewing by the people of the High Andes in Ecuador, Peru, and Bolivia to see how a traditionally used drug affects nutrition. The leaves of the coca bush contain a complicated mixture of many alkaloids, one of which is cocaine. Unprocessed coca leaves have been used by South American Indians for centuries (see figure 5.7). In the nineteenth century, European pharmacologists learned how to isolate the most powerful component, cocaine, from the leaves. Cocaine was used as a local anesthetic by physicians, but the euphoria-producing drug quickly came to be a major form of illicit drug abuse.

(a)   (b)

FIGURE 5.7   Ancient Peruvian pottery showing coca use.
(a) Nasca jar depicting a wounded warrior with a quid of coca in the left side of his mouth.
(b) Moche vase showing the materials for coca use, including a lime container and a stick for removing the lime and a bag for carrying coca leaves.

SOURCE: E. Yacovleff and F. L. Herrera, "El Mundo Vegetal de los antiguos Peruanos," *Revista del Museo Nacional,* vol. 3, no. 3, (1934). Reproduced by permission.

This abuse of cocaine in Europe and the United States has created confusion about the real implications of chewing coca leaves, which with their complex mix of chemicals have quite different effects than refined cocaine. As far as is known, the use of coca leaves is not addictive; coca users who cannot obtain supplies of coca do not show withdrawal symptoms. The leaves are chewed into a wad, or quid, that is held in the cheek. Lime, which is included to sweeten the quid, has the chemical effect of releasing the alkaloids. The lime and juices trickle into the stomach, but the leaves are not actually chewed up and swallowed. Coca can be abused, as visitors to the Andes have proved by chewing large amounts to get stoned. In the traditional Andean cultures, however, coca chewing is integrated into a cultural context, which makes its unrestrained abuse less likely.

In Inca times, coca was a sacred plant. Its use may have been restricted to the nobility and priests, though there is some controversy over this. After the Spanish conquest in the sixteenth century, coca came to be widely used by common people. Both men and women use it, though men use it somewhat more. Chewing coca together has an important dimension of sociability. Coca has also continued to have religious significance as an offering to the gods and a means of divination. It has economic significance as well: high-altitude farmers trade their potatoes or sell the wool of sheep and alpacas for coca grown on plantations in the foothills, and thus trade in coca helps maintain inter-regional trade networks.

When asked why they use coca leaves, Quechua and Aymara-speaking highlanders reply that coca alleviates feelings of fatigue, helps them keep warm, and satisfies feelings of hunger. All these effects help them keep working longer at the chilly, tedious tasks of high-altitude farming and herding. Anthropologists who have worked in the Andes have attempted to identify the physiological basis of each of these reported effects.

Experimental research by physical anthropologist Joel M. Hanna (1974) tested residents of Nuñoa, Peru, living at altitudes over 13,000 feet (4000 meters). He found that coca use aided in body heat conservation by its effect as a vasoconstrictor. With the blood supply thus restricted, fingers and toes become cooler and less heat is lost from the extremities. This conservation of body heat in coca chewers results in higher rectal temperatures after prolonged cold exposure than in non-coca-users.

The effects of coca chewing on the physiology of work are less clear cut. If a high-altitude Indian is set to work pedaling on a

FIGURE 5.8   A man at work in a high-altitude potato field in the Bolivian Andes.
Photo courtesy of Wheelock Educational Resources.

bicycle ergometer, work output, oxygen intake, heart rate, and blood pressure can be recorded. Hanna found no statistically significant differences between habitual users and nonusers in their physiological responses while working or resting.

Anthropologists Ralph Bolton (1976) and Roderick Burchard (1975) downplay the effects of coca on cold resistance and work capacity, and instead emphasize its effects on metabolism. Coca chewing elevates blood glucose levels and seems to be helpful in regulating glucose levels for the individual with mild hypoglycemia (low blood sugar). Bolton's research in a village of Quechua-speaking Qolla in southern Peru (1973) indicated the importance in that society of aggressive behavior induced by hypoglycemia. The hypoglycemia is aggravated by a low-protein diet, which is a result of poverty. Bolton found that the hypoglycemic individuals in his sample chewed significantly more coca than did subjects of the same age with normal blood sugar patterns. (It is necessary to specify that subjects are paired for age because older men chew significantly more coca than do younger men.)

In addition to the suggested function of coca in regulating glucose metabolism, coca may contribute small amounts of vitamins and minerals to the diet. Folk medical beliefs of the coca-using cultures attribute to it various curative properties, including the ability to aid digestion (Martin 1970). All this suggests that coca plays a positive role in the nutritional adaptation of Andean highland peoples.

In contrast to these positive findings, other researchers have claimed that coca chewing has a negative impact on nutritional status. According to them, the coca user is more likely to become malnourished because of reduced feelings of hunger and fatigue. Many such claims show little sensitivity to the poverty—lack of food and lack of fuel and other protection from the cold—that further increases food-energy needs. Blaming the victim is an all-too-familiar pattern of explanation.

There is some supporting research that does indicate that coca use may adversely affect health, however. In the Peruvian village of Cachicoto, a team of researchers from Johns Hopkins University (Buck et al. 1968) compared coca chewers with nonusers matched with them for age, sex, and ethnic status. They found that the coca users were more poorly nourished and had more illness. Their most striking observation was the interaction between hookworm infections, anemia, and coca use. Probably because their poorer nutrition makes them less able to tolerate blood loss to the intestinal parasites, users show more anemia at a similar level of hookworm infestation than do nonusers. But even this carefully designed study cannot tell us whether people are malnourished because they chew coca or whether they chew coca because they are poor, sick, and malnourished. Also, as the researchers indicate, the village studied was at a low altitude (2400 feet, or 750 meters) in a tropical climate where parasitic infections are much more prevalent than in the High Andes. Population pressure has been pushing highland peoples to resettle at lower altitudes, exposing them to the risk of new diseases, such as hookworm. The major conclusion to be drawn from this study, then, is that a cultural practice that is adaptive in one environmental setting may become maladaptive when it is transplanted to another environment.

Since the sixteenth century, there have been intermittent attempts to suppress the use of coca leaves. The prejudice against coca has in part been simply a prejudice against the Quechua-speaker and the poor. Negative attitudes have been reinforced by inappropriate comparisons with cocaine use and with some laboratory findings based on the ingestion of larger amounts of coca than are traditionally used. It now appears that the moderate, culturally patterned use of this mild narcotic may play a part in physiological adaptations to the stresses of high-altitude cold and a low-protein diet. Its users credit it with enabling them to work harder and longer. If this is so, their increased productivity may help them work to feed their families better. The issue is complex, and the studies that attempt to resolve it must deal with a wide range of factors, including climate, physiology, psychology, and culture.

A HUNGRY WORLD

The Andeans described in the health profile are representative of the traditional rural peoples of the less developed countries of the world. Because they live on the land and produce their own food, they are not as vulnerable as the poorest slum dwellers, who must buy, beg, or steal their food. But if they are sharecroppers, owning no land or not enough land for the family, their food supplies may be inadequate. The family may have to market some needed food in order to get cash for clothing and other expenses. Even a farm family raising food can go hungry.

More serious nutritional problems are faced by the rural family that does not grow food for its own consumption but instead grows a cash crop for the world market. Every year an increasing proportion of land is planted in cash crops. Often the land devoted to these export crops is the best land. During the African drought and famine of the early 1970s (to be discussed in more detail in chapter 6), it was noted that the cash crops of cotton and peanuts were least affected because they were planted on the best-watered lands (Messiant 1975:67). When land is diverted from producing local foods to producing an export crop, there are often severe nutritional repercussions.

One example of the impact of cash cropping is northeastern Brazil, where traditional subsistence farming provided a precarious living because droughts were frequent. The dry conditions were well suited to growing an export crop, sisal, which is used to make twine. An anthropologist and a nutritionist (Gross and Underwood 1971) have documented the deleterious effects of the shift to growing sisal on the nutritional status of the population. The energy requirements of the workers are very high because of their heavy physical labor. Almost all their wages are spent on food, but few families earn enough money to buy sufficient food to prevent their children from being malnourished.

Even low-paid wage workers on export crops may be able to maintain an adequate diet if they have access to some land to raise food. For example, the workers on sugar plantations in Jamaica studied by Ehrlich (1974) were able to grow their own rice on wet lands unused for sugar cultivation. When the landowners drained the wet lands to increase the area under sugar cultivation, the workers suffered because they were no longer able to supplement their diet of store-bought foods.

Economic development through the export of food has often been ecologically as well as nutritionally detrimental to local populations. For example, the green turtle was traditionally a major food resource of the coastal dwelling Miskito of Nicaragua. Involvement in the market economy increased in 1969 when the Miskito began to sell turtle meat to companies that freeze and export it. Less meat was available as a protein source within the Miskito villages, and at the same time tremendous pressure was placed on the green turtle population to the point that the species was threatened with extinction (Nietschmann 1973).

As economic conditions worsen in rural areas, increasing numbers of rural people migrate to the cities in search of a better life. With this move, the dependence on purchased food becomes much greater. Traditional foods may not be available in the cities, even to those with sufficient income, so that dietary change is inevitable. For example, Malays moving to the city of Kuala Lumpur cannot obtain the vegetables they are familiar with and disdain the Chinese vegetables that are available in the market (Anderson 1976). Although their economic conditions may improve, their nutritional conditions may worsen as a result of the move to the city.

The new migrants to the cities must adapt to the money economy. Budgeting food purchases is often difficult. In towns and cities, there are fewer relatives to help out when food or money is scarce. Less help from relatives also means poorer child care, so that child nutrition especially suffers. "Malnutrition is emerging as a significant force in the rapidly growing towns of Africa," according to Hughes and Hunter (1970:471) in their survey of the relationship of disease and economic development in Africa. Even in a more stable town of about 3000 people in rural Mexico, the best predictor of adequate nutrition is economic status (Dewalt and Pelto 1977). Household composition is also relevant; households in this Mexican town that included dependent elderly people had less adequate diets, and those that included children old enough to earn wages were better off.

At least in the short term, the dietary changes that accompany urbanization are generally for the worse. Black families migrating to Milwaukee from the South, for example, seem to be nutritionally better off either if they maintain their traditional rural Southern diet or if they completely switch to a varied Midwestern diet. They are worst off nutritionally when they are in transition, caught halfway between the two patterns of eating (Jerome 1968).

HUNGER IN THE UNITED STATES

Americans have been slow to recognize that hunger and malnutrition exist in their own country. It has widely been assumed that the wealth and high food production of the nation, combined with social welfare programs, assured that virtually everyone had an adequate diet. Scientific research did little to challenge these assumptions because there has been remarkably little research into the eating habits or nutritional status of Americans. The emphasis on nutrition in medical practice tended to be limited to pregnant women, infants, and pre-school children. This is so partly because these groups were known to be nutritionally vulnerable, but also partly because these are the groups who tend to get checkups. The rest of the population tends to see a doctor only for some specific illness.

Hunger, U.S.A., a report by the Citizens' Board of Inquiry into Hunger and Malnutrition in the U.S.A. (1968), and the Ten-State Nutrition Survey by the Center for Disease Control of the U.S. Department of Health, Education, and Welfare (1972) assessed the nutritional conditions in America in the late 1960s. These studies also stimulated new programs, which, it was hoped, would help change the conditions that were found.

Where is hunger in the United States? Figure 5.9 shows something of the geographical dimensions of the problem in 1973. The "hunger counties" designated on the map are counties that had high percentages of poor families and low participation in federal hunger programs such as food stamps. The map is not based directly on dietary or clinical studies of nutrition, but on the social and economic conditions associated with poor nutrition in the United States. One difficulty with a map that shows data by counties is that it tends to exaggerate the extent of poor nutrition in the rural areas of the South and Southwest while failing to show equal numbers of poor people who are hidden in the averages for the more populous counties of the northern states and California (U.S. Senate Select Committee on Nutrition 1973:9).

Who are the hungry people in these areas? They are both the urban poor and the rural poor, often displaced by mechanization from their work in the fields. They include migrant workers and Native Americans; some of the most severely malnourished are children on Indian reservations. They include the aged, whether in hunger counties or not, whose poverty is compounded by difficulties in shopping for and preparing food.

The specific nutritional problems of the poor in the United States are somewhat different from those in the poorer countries of the world.

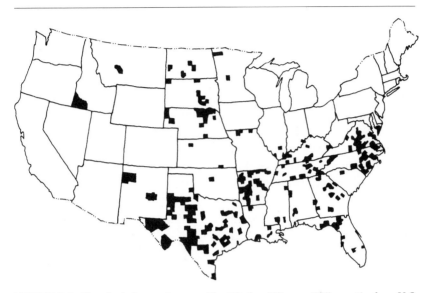

FIGURE 5.9   The shaded counties were identified as "Hunger '73" counties by a U.S. Senate committee report. In 1973, more than 25 percent of the population of those counties had incomes below the poverty level, but less than 33 percent of the poor were being reached by federal food programs.

SOURCE: United States Senate Select Committee on Nutrition, " 'Hunger 1973' and Press Reaction," (Washington, D.C.: U.S. Government Printing Office, 1973), p. 9.

Outright protein-calorie deficiency disease is seldom observed, although severely malnourished children are found in many parts of the country. The Ten-State Nutrition Survey attempted to pinpoint the more serious and widespread nutritional problems by clinical examination of a sample of the population. Iron-deficiency anemia is the most widespread problem involving all ethnic groups (black, white, and Spanish-American) in both high- and low-income states. Of these groups, the problem of iron deficiency is greatest for low-income blacks. Mild anemia leads to fatigue and lassitude. It can be avoided by eating adequate amounts of foods like liver, meat, egg yolk, dark green vegetables, peas, beans, molasses, prunes, and raisins. Certain low-income population groups in the United States are getting marginal amounts of specific vitamins, according to the Ten-State Survey. Vitamin A was especially lacking among Spanish-Americans, and riboflavin among blacks. These marginal vitamin intakes are not low enough to produce outright deficiency diseases, which are rare in the United States. These vitamins are available in a wide variety of foods such as milk, eggs, and vegetables.

There are not only ethnic differences but also sex differences in nutritional problems. Adult males, whether black or white, tend to lack vitamin C, which is available from citrus fruits, tomatoes, and other fruits and vegetables. Low-income black women, who are generally speaking the most nutritionally disadvantaged group in U.S. society, are also the most likely to be obese, according to the Ten-State Nutrition Survey, 1968–1970 (Center for Disease Control 1972). This observation underscores the fact that it is generally the *quality* rather

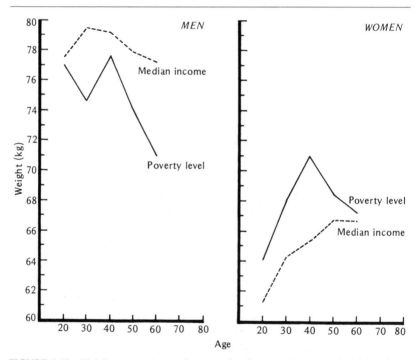

FIGURE 5.10   Weight comparisons of poverty level men and women (solid lines) and weights of men and women of median U.S. income (dashed lines) show the opposite effects of income on weight in the two sexes.

SOURCE: Reprinted from Stanley M. Garn and Diane C. Clark, "Economics and Fatness," in *Ecology of Food and Nutrition,* vol. 3 (London: Gordon and Breach Science Publishers, 1973), p. 20.

than the *quantity* of food that is critical for poorer Americans. In addition, cultural ideals seem to affect weight differently for rich and poor, male and female. The "cult of leanness" presented in the mass media has its greatest impact on higher-income women, suggest Garn and Clark (1974). In blacks, whites, and Chicanos alike, higher income means higher fatness in men and lower fatness in women (figure 5.10).

One index of the abundance of food in America is the amount of food that goes into the garbage can. University of Arizona archaeology students sorted through the garbage of randomly chosen households in Tucson in 1973 and 1974. They found that the average household throws out between $80 and $100 worth of edible food each year. About 9 percent, by weight, of the food they purchase goes into the garbage can, in addition to the waste that goes down garbage disposals (Harrison, Rathje, and Hughes 1975).

OVERNUTRITION AND OTHER PROBLEMS OF AFFLUENCE

Although nutritional deficits exist in the United States in pockets of poverty, the most common form of malnutrition is nutritional excess. Malnutrition simply means bad nutrition. With all nutrients, too much can be as serious as too little. The most common manifestation of overnutrition is obesity, increased storage of excess food energy as fat. The basic problem may be stated simply:

Energy in $>$ Energy out $=$ Obesity

The reasons for the imbalance are not so simple, however (Robson 1972:21). It is difficult to untangle the complex of influences, which include genetics, sex, climate, underactivity, culture, and early experience.

An important factor in overnutrition in modern society is underactivity. A level of food consumption appropriate for pioneer farmers or athletes accompanied by a typical sedentary lifestyle is bound to lead to a surplus of food energy to be stored as body fat. The pattern of inactivity begins early in childhood, as does the pattern of overfeeding.

FIGURE 5.11   The pattern of overeating and inactivity that leads to obesity begins in childhood and is more prevalent in lower-income groups in the United States.
Photo: World Health Organization.

A simple availability of abundant food year-round in modern society is not sufficient to explain why people eat too much. One factor is the type of food available. Highly refined foods are more concentrated sources of calories than foods that contain large amounts of bulky indigestible fiber. Consumption of sugar and fats, which are very concentrated sources of food energy, is high in the United States. The most distinctive fact about American diet when compared with the diet of a country like India is the high intake of sugar and fat, and the sources of protein, rather than the total amount of protein. Because protein in the United States and other wealthy nations comes more from animal than plant sources, it is almost inevitably accompanied by a high intake of animal fats.

The modern Western diet, high in refined starch, sugar, and fat, has been implicated in certain diseases of cholesterol metabolism. Atherosclerosis, coronary heart disease, and gall bladder disease are such diseases. The use of these highly refined foods also implies a diet lacking in fiber. Such a low-residue diet passes through the intestine slowly and makes a small, firm stool. Constipation is a common complaint, and the raised pressures in the abdomen as well as in the large intestine itself have been blamed for many modern diseases, diseases seldom reported from hunter-gatherers or agricultural peoples (Burkitt 1973). They include noninfective diseases of the large bowel such as diverticular disease, appendicitis, cancer of the colon and polyps, and ulcerative colitis. They also include vein problems, such as varicose veins in the legs and hemorrhoids, which may be caused by the pressures transmitted while straining to pass hard stools.

While obesity is an obvious and common sign of overnutrition in modern society, excessive consumption of certain specific nutrients also can occur when vitamin- or mineral-enriched foods or pills are used in excess. When eating normal foods, it is almost impossible to consume a toxic level of vitamins accidentally. The rare exceptions to this rule have been arctic explorers who ate too much polar bear liver and fishermen who ate too much fish liver and showed the toxic effects of excessive vitamins A and D. Vitamins A and D are fat-soluble vitamins and are not excreted in the urine so toxicity can build up. In contrast, the water-soluble B and C vitamins are excreted in the urine. This means that toxicity is less likely to build up but also that deficiencies can develop more rapidly. Excessive vitamin pills and vitamin-fortified foods hold the risk of toxic effects from the fat-soluble vitamins.

When excessive amounts of minerals are consumed, many of them can be excreted in the urine and feces also, but disposal problems are created in other cases. Special concern has been expressed about the overload of sodium, which comes from the addition of salt to many prepared foods and which may be implicated in the prevalence of hypertension.

Another problem of mineral nutrition in the United States is that chronic dietary deficiency of calcium and excess of phosphorus are prevalent and increasing. The consumption of soft drinks, which are high in phosphorus, has been increasing, while the consumption of milk, which is high in calcium, is declining. Meat is also high in phosphorus. Calcium/phosphorus imbalance leads to the demineralization of bones, which serve as the body's calcium store. The classic picture of the result is an elderly lady with a broken hip, her calcium stores depleted over a lifetime of mineral imbalance. Another manifestation of the calcium/phosphorus problem is periodontal disease, in which the tissues supporting the teeth are weakened and the teeth may be lost.

The nutrition-related ills of modern society thus range from dental problems to obesity to cancer of the colon. The pattern of eating that is implicated has been emerging over the last century in the Western countries, more recently in Japan, and only in elite sectors of much of the rest of the world. The rapid speed of these dietary changes is remarkable. For example, in the United States per capita beef consumption *doubled* between 1950 and 1970 from about 60 pounds (27 kg) per person per year to nearly 120 pounds (54 kg). The consumption of soft drinks doubled in 15 years from 109 pints (50 liters) per person in 1960 to 221 pints (100 liters) per person in 1975 (U.S. Senate Select Committee on Nutrition 1971).

The pace and direction of dietary change is accelerated by the food industry, whose profits largely depend on processing and packaging and not on producing the raw food. Advertising and marketing techniques influence people to buy the foods that offer companies the highest profits. A major factor in the shift to more highly refined and processed foods has been their longer shelf life and ease in shipping, which increase profitability. Many of the chemical additives serve the same purpose, adding color and flavor to increase sales. The addition of sugar, salt, and fat increases consumer prices much more steeply than it increases manufacturing costs. One important effect of the extensive processing of food is that flavor and appearance are no longer a reliable guide to the nutritional value, or even the identity, of foods. The combination of many ingredients in unknown proportions before they reach the consumer in a package or a restaurant meal means that people no longer know what they are eating as they did when they purchased staples and combined them at home.

American society is no exception to the generalization that urban nutrition is basically a matter of economics. (Actually, in the United States even farm families buy most of their food in the supermarket, so almost everyone, rural and urban, is eating the urban diet.) The American diet is mostly a product of an industrial system in which food processing and distribution are controlled by large companies. Through advertising and marketing their brand-name foods, they change food habits, staying within the cultural tradition but shaping it in ways that increase profitability. Increasingly, the food-processing companies are investing in farms and fast-food restaurants, so that they dominate the entire process from field to table.

Whether controlled by a large firm or owned by a family, American farms are involved in a very different kind of food production than the subsistence farms described in earlier sections. They are larger and involve a much smaller percentage of the population, only 5 percent of the work force in contrast to 90 percent or more of the work force in traditional societies. This decrease in the input of human energy is accompanied by a much greater increase in the input from other energy sources, mostly petroleum. These energy sources power farm machinery and produce fertilizers and pesticides.

Most of what has been said about the American diet and its implications for health and disease would apply with equal force to other industrialized nations, despite cultural differences. The rise in beef consumption in Japan since World War II has the same health implications there that it does here. Yet there are differences in diet among the industrialized nations, and some of these differences reflect ecological differences. Jacques May (1957) points out the ecological basis on which the fame of French cuisine rests. Unlike any other nation in Europe, the French had ready access to both the temperate-climate products of northern Europe, such as wheat and dairy products, and the Mediterranean products of southern Europe, such as olive oil and wine. This combination made possible the emergence of a rich culinary tradition. The Scandinavians have for environmental reasons traditionally eaten more dairy products than other countries, and their high rates of arterial disease reflect this.

CONCLUSIONS

On a snowy January day, you may eat a fruit salad of fresh strawberries, tropical bananas, and pineapple. Your culture includes a system of food production and distribution that may provide you with a nutritious diet, if you can afford it and if you choose well. The very diversity of your supermarket diet helps ensure that you are likely to meet your body's needs for vitamins, minerals, and other nutrients.

In other ecosystems, diversity in the human diet is attained in other ways. Hunter-gatherers seek many species of edible plants and animals. Subsistence farmers who grow a cereal or root crop in their fields also plant small kitchen gardens with vegetables, fruits, and herbs that add interest, and varied nutrients, to otherwise monotonous fare.

With rural or urban poverty comes the loss of diversity in diet. People narrow their focus to obtaining in barely sufficient quantities just those few foods that they can afford. This leads to the prevalence of deficiency diseases. The most important of these diseases in the world population today (WHO 1977) are:

> *anemia*—insufficient hemoglobin in the blood, causing fatigue and weakness and resulting from lack of iron or vitamin B$_{12}$ or folic acid in the diet
> *endemic goiter*—enlargement of the thyroid gland, resulting from lack of iodine
> *xerophthalmia*—eye symptoms leading eventually to blindness, resulting from lack of vitamin A
> *kwashiorkor and marasmus*—severe protein-calorie malnutrition in infants and children (to be described in chapter 6)

In the following chapter, we will look more closely at the nutritional status of individuals, young and old, male and female, malnourished and healthy. We will attempt to assess the personal and social significance of the nutritional patterns we have begun to explore in this chapter. While in this chapter we have been concerned with societies as *producers* of food, in chapter 6 we will be more concerned with individuals as *consumers* of food.

RESOURCES

Readings

Fitzgerald, Thomas K., ed.
1977 Nutrition and Anthropology in Action. Assen: Van Gorcum.
This is a collection of varied papers—theoretical, methodological, and ethnographic—in the emerging field of nutritional anthropology.
Haas, Jere D., and Gail G. Harrison
1977 Nutritional Anthropology and Biological Adaptation. In Annual Reviews in Anthropology. B. Siegel, ed. Pp. 69–101. Palo Alto, California: Annual Reviews.
This review of the current literature includes an extensive bibliography.
Lappé, Frances Moore, and Joseph Collins
1977 Food First: Beyond the Myth of Scarcity. Boston: Houghton Mifflin.
Lappe and Collins explore the problem of world hunger in a lively question-and-answer format, emphasizing the socioeconomic factors that prevent hungry people from producing enough to feed themselves. They stress positive action for change rather than the gloom and guilt that characterize many discussions of this problem.
Lee, Richard B., and Irven DeVore, eds.
1976 Kalahari Hunter-Gatherers: Studies of the !Kung San and Their Neighbors. Cambridge, Massachusetts: Harvard University Press.
This book brings together recent work on the !Kung by many researchers.
Rappaport, Roy A.
1967 Ritual Regulation of Environmental Relations among a New Guinea People. Ethnology 6:17–30.
Rappaport demonstrates how ritual regulates ecosystemic variables, including the population of pigs and the frequency of warfare among tropical root-crop cultivators. This is one of the best-known studies in the field of ecological anthropology.
Robson, John R. K.
1972 Malnutrition: Its Causation and Control. 2 vols. New York: Gordon and Breach.
This is a basic textbook on normal nutrition as well as malnutrition. Unlike ordinary nutrition textbooks, it is worldwide in its scope and ecological in emphasis, making it an especially useful reference work for anthropologists and public health personnel.

Journals

The journals Ecology of Food and Nutrition, which began publication in 1971, and Human Ecology, which began publication in 1972, include many articles of interest in nutritional anthropology.

Films

The Hunters. 1956.   73 minutes, color. Made by John Marshall. Distributed by
   McGraw-Hill Contemporary Films, Hightstown, New Jersey.
   This film shows four San hunters of the Kalahari Desert region track a
   giraffe. The techniques of hunting with poisoned arrows and the sharing
   of food back in camp are shown.
Potato Planters. 1974.   17 minutes, color. From the *Faces of Change* series,
   produced by the American Universities Field Staff. Distributed by
   Wheelock Educational Resources, Hanover, New Hampshire.
   The Aymara, an Andean people of Bolivia, are shown planting potatoes,
   which are their main crop. Coca leaves are used in the associated ritual.
   For this film and the one below, essays have been published that can be
   ordered from the films' distributor. Each essay provides background
   information useful in viewing and discussing the film.
The Spirit Possession of Alejandro Mamani. 1974.   27 minutes, color. From the
   Faces of Change series, produced by the American Universities Field Staff.
   Distributed by Wheelock Educational Resources, Hanover, New Hampshire.
   This film deals with an anguished, old Bolivian man who has outlived all
   his contemporaries. Believing himself to be possessed by evil spirits, he
   prepares for death. Although the film is included here because it deals
   with the Andean cultures described in the health profile, it could as well
   be viewed in connection with the topics of stress and suicide, ethnomedicine, or old age.
The Turtle People. 1973.   26 minutes, color. Photographed by Brian Weiss and
   edited by James Ward. Distributed by B & C Films, Los Angeles.
   Like the cash-croppers described in this chapter, the Miskito Indians of
   Nicaragua are impoverished by boom-and-bust economic cycles. By
   selling green turtles to outsiders, they are endangering their own food
   supply.

Nutrition Throughout the Life Cycle

CHAPTER 6

🝝

PREVIEW

This chapter traces human nutrition from the critical periods of prenatal life and infancy through old age. At each stage of life, the individual's nutritional needs vary; the ways that people meet those needs are distinctive. Prenatally, nourishment reaches the fetus by way of the placenta, and in early infancy, by way of the mother's breast. In late infancy and early childhood, there is a critical transition from this physiological dependence to dependence on the food resources of a particular cultural environment. In an impoverished setting, that transition is especially challenging; the weaning period is the time of highest rates of disease and death from malnutrition. The older child is less vulnerable to malnutrition but grows at a rate that reflects nutritional circumstances.

In this chapter we will look at nutrition throughout the entire life cycle. Although this chapter begins with a discussion of the prenatal period, we need constantly to keep in mind the concept of a life cycle in order not to ignore long-term effects, even ones that span more than one generation. For example, the nutritional health of a newborn baby may be influenced not only by the mother's diet during pregnancy but also by her nutrition during her own infancy and adolescence.

The divergent roles of men and women in production and reproduction are recognized in culturally distinctive patterns of food consumption. Women have special nutritional needs during pregnancy and lactation, which are often inadequately met. The lifetime patterns of nutrition in a society contribute to the health and longevity of older adults, as the health profile dealing with some very long-living people indicates.

It is important to be able to assess the nutritional status of a population when planning public health programs. Some methods for assessment discussed here are dietary surveys and clinical examination. Rapid assessment may be especially crucial in times of famine such as the Sahel famine, discussed in the second health profile in this chapter. The chapter concludes with a study of the social impact of hunger and malnutrition. Whether nutritional stress is severe and short term or chronic, its human costs are incalculable.   𝒬

PRENATAL NUTRITION

A pregnant woman is bombarded with contradictory advice. Her mother-in-law urges her, "Have another helping; remember you're eating for two!" Her obstetrician may be insisting that she gain no more than fifteen pounds, while a magazine article says twenty-five is "best for baby." Jokes about pickles and ice cream point to another cultural expectation about diet during pregnancy. No other period in life is so loaded with food taboos; Thus our culture is not exceptional in placing emphasis on the diet of pregnant women. The Mbum Kpau women of Chad in equatorial Africa eat no chicken, goat, eggs, or game birds even when they are not pregnant, for fear of pain or death in childbirth, the birth of abnormal children, or sterility. During pregnancy, they avoid still more foods, such as the meat of antelope with twisted horns and bony-headed fish, to avoid bearing a deformed child (O'Laughlin 1974). Many cultures place special emphasis on beliefs that the eating habits of pregnant women affect child health.

During the first few months of fetal development, the tiny but rapidly growing embryo does not make great demands on its mother's nutritional stores. The nourishment of the embryo is not directly a matter of the woman's diet at that time. Rather, it is critically important for the nutrition of the fetus that the placenta is well established. Poor placental development is often found if the mother is poorly nourished or immature. An undersized placenta, and a subsequently low-birth-weight baby, is also characteristic of a woman who smokes cigarettes. Fetal malnutrition can result from poor circulation in the mother or from poor placental transport of nutrients as well as from inadequate nutrients in the mother's circulation.

The placenta serves as an organ to transport nutrients from mother to fetus and wastes in the opposite direction. Other substances can cross the placenta as well. When alcohol crosses the placenta in large amounts, it creates the pattern of birth defects characteristic of the fetal alcoholism syndrome (Jones and Smith 1975). These malformations include defects of the limbs and head and delays in growth and development. When heroin crosses the placenta, it causes drug addiction in newborn infants; such addiction is increasingly seen in big-city hospitals. Certain infectious agents such as viruses and the syphilis microorganism can cross the placenta. Heavy metals can do so also, as the discussion of Minimata disease in chapter 4 showed. Mothers who ate fish contaminated with mercury compounds from polluted Minimata Bay gave birth to brain-damaged infants. Thus even before birth, an individual is subject to environmental influences that differ from one cultural setting to the next.

The nutrients that reach the fetus through the placenta and umbilicus are those circulating in the maternal blood stream. The diet during pregnancy is the source of most of these, but prepregnancy stores are also tapped. For example, if the mother's current diet is deficient in calcium, the calcium stores of her teeth and bones may be depleted. This process led to the popular concept of the fetus as the perfect parasite, taking what it needs even at the cost of the mother's health. This concept has some validity, but it is also misleading. Although poorly nourished mothers often do give birth to healthy infants, their infants tend to have low birth weights and subnormal stores of nutrients (Jelliffe 1968:86). The mother's nutritional state during the last few months of pregnancy seems to be especially critical for the fetal storage of nutrients. Inadequate stores of nutrients may not be at all apparent at birth but may show up later, during a period of rapid growth. For example, tropical infants with subnormal iron reserves commonly develop anemia in their second six months of life, after showing normal hemoglobin values in earlier months (Jelliffe 1968: 161).

The importance of fetal nutrition is underscored by the concept of *critical periods of growth*. An organ system that is growing especially rapidly by cell division is especially vulnerable to malnutrition. The critical period for brain development is the prenatal period and the first year of life (Winick 1976). Thus, the child most at risk of brain impairment from malnutrition may be the one who is nutritionally deprived in the few months just before and after birth.

INFANT FEEDING

For the first four to six months after birth, breast-feeding alone is normally sufficient to provide for infant nutrition. After six months, breast milk continues to be an important protein supplement to the infant's diet of semisolid foods; therefore in most societies it is continued beyond the first year. Breast-feeding also meets important non-nutritional needs, including psychological needs and some protection from infection (Jelliffe 1968:22–25).

The decline of breast-feeding in Europe and America began three centuries ago. Well-to-do women hired wet nurses to breast-feed their infants, and the women of the poorer classes who worked as wet nurses gave up their own infants to foundling hospitals. There they were fed a poor diet of flour or cereal cooked in water, and many of them died. The regular use of cow's milk as infant formula has become prevalent only in the last century since dried and canned milk have been available and have been promoted by medical personnel and by industry. Where hygienic conditions are good, cow's milk does not lead to diarrhea as it did in the early days of artificial feeding, although it has some important disadvantages. Allergies to cow's milk are common among infants in the United States. Obesity in infants is raising increased concern, and bottle-feeding contributes to this problem because it encourages overfeeding. Cow's milk is higher in protein than human milk and has a different balance among the various amino acids and fatty acids that milk contains. Human milk is presumably best adapted to the nutritional requirements of human infants, who grow more slowly than calves.

In the United States in 1946, 38 percent of infants were being breast-fed on leaving the hospital, but by 1966 only 18 percent were being breast-fed (Meyer 1968). The decline was sharpest in the poorest states, and the recent resurgence of interest in breast-feeding has been mostly limited to upper-income groups. The poorest families are those who can least afford to give up breast-feeding, for even if the nursing mother consumes the added calories recommended during lactation, the cost is lower than the cost of artificial feeding for the infant. Although the lactating woman must have extra food and fluids if her own nutritional stores are not to be depleted, these are normally cheaper and more easily available than milk. Regardless of whether the mother is well or poorly nourished, the protein, fat, and sugar content of human milk varies little. However, the quantity of milk and the content of vitamins and minerals does vary with the maternal diet (Jelliffe 1968:164–169).

The decline of breast-feeding, which began in the Western countries, has spread to the less developed countries, beginning with urban areas. In some countries, the pace of change has been phenomenal. For example, in 1960, 95 percent of Chilean mothers breast-fed their children beyond the first year; by 1969, only 6 percent did so, and only 20 percent were being nursed as long as two months (Monckeberg 1970). The message that bottle-feeding is the modern, high-status way to feed an infant has been transmitted by advertising and by health personnel. Leisure activities and work outside the home are organized in ways that inconvenience lactating mothers. Only a small percentage of these Third World mothers have outside employment, however, so that is not the most important factor in the decline.

The spread of bottle-feeding has many important effects on the health of children of poor families, whether in affluent or poor countries. The bottle formula may be diluted with water, sugar, and other less costly substitutes for milk. Bottle-feeding increases the risk of infection while at the same time reducing resistance (Jelliffe 1968:23). Gastroenteritis, an inflammation of the stomach and intestines, is the most significant cause of illness and death in infants and young children in many countries. With diarrhea, nutrients are poorly absorbed and the infant's nutritional state worsens.

Infants who suffer from severe calorie and protein deficiency develop *marasmus*. The main symptoms of marasmus are growth retardation and severe emaciation. Subcutaneous fat is virtually absent, and muscles atrophy (figure 6.1). The infant is apathetic and becomes irritable when handled. Marasmus has become an increasingly serious problem of world health with the decline in breast-feeding.

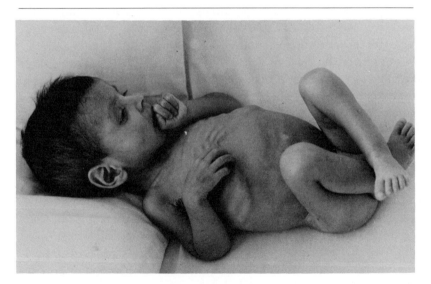

FIGURE 6.1   Infant with the severe wasting characteristic of marasmus.
Photo: World Health Organization/World Food Programme.

Bottle-feeding has a further indirect effect on family health, in that it can lead to shorter birth intervals and larger families, since the contraceptive effects of lactation are lost. In women who breast-feed successfully, ovulation is suppressed and menstruation is delayed for several months. The contraceptive effect is weakened if the child is also fed cow's milk or cereals, thereby reducing the sucking stimulus (Jelliffe and Jelliffe 1972). Unless another form of contraception is used, the mother soon will have another mouth to feed.

Cultures differ in the age at which other foods are added to the baby's diet of milk. In a cross-cultural study including eighty-three societies from around the world, Nerlove (1974) found that supplementary feeding began very early, before one month of age, in thirty of the societies. A closer look at one of the thirty societies, the Alorese of Indonesia, shows one of the factors behind this early supplementation: the mother's work load. Alorese women have heavy responsibilities for farm work, especially during the wet season. A mother returns to regular field work ten days to two weeks after giving birth if she is needed there (DuBois 1944:34). In most farming societies, the infant is taken along to the fields, but the Alorese mother leaves her child with a relative. The babysitter feeds the infant premasticated banana and vegetable gruel until the mother returns to breast-feed the child. Weaning from the breast is gradual and does not take place until after the child is walking and then only soon enough to ensure that the child will be weaned before the next baby is born (DuBois 1944:40). Early supplementary feeding such as that practiced by the Alorese reduces the contraceptive effect of breast-feeding so that weaning in preparation for another birth may come sooner than it would without the supplementary feeding.

The best time to introduce supplementary foods, according to nutritionist Jelliffe (1968), is when the infant is six to twelve months old. Some societies delay the introduction of semisolid foods until after the child is a year old, and doing so can cause nutritional problems. In rural West Bengal, the introduction of semisolid foods is marked by a rice-feeding ceremony when the infant is six or seven months old. The ceremony is an important social occasion, and relatives give presents and bless the infant. If the ceremony is postponed because the family cannot afford to pay for it, the infant is sick, relatives are absent, or the day is not astrologically auspicious, the baby will not receive any food other than milk and barley. Even after the ceremony, some Bengali mothers avoid giving ritually unclean foods such as rice, eggs, meat, and fish because the infant's bowel movements are also believed to be ritually unclean, and the mother must wash all the bedding and her own sari. Ritually clean foods (primarily milk and barley) create less work for the mother because the baby's stools are also considered clean and only the child need be washed (Jelliffe 1957).

The first semisolid foods added in most cultures are soft, starchy foods, cooked into a porridge or prechewed. Food taboos often severely restrict the fruits, vegetables, and protein foods that might otherwise make a valuable contribution to the diet at this time. Eggs are a good example of a food widely avoided for infant feeding. The cultural rationale varies: eggs will make the child bald or dumb, they will make the child a thief, or they will interfere with fertility. Even the milk of dairy animals is not everywhere regarded as appropriate food for children. In India, for instance, milk is regarded as a danger to infant health because it is classified as a hot food. It is diluted with water when fed to children, and it is withdrawn completely when the child develops diarrhea.

WEANING AND THE CRITICAL SECOND YEAR

In traditional cultures adapted to the protein-poor diets that are especially common in tropical and subtropical areas, weaning from the breast takes place at two to three years, occasionally even four years. As indicated earlier, a postpartum taboo on sexual intercourse, as well as lactation-suppressed ovulation, helps maintain the birth spacing that allows this long nursing period. A classic cross-cultural study by psychological anthropologist John Whiting (1964) demonstrated relationships between this nutritional situation and other social and psychological variables. Societies in tropical climates, where protein-deficient diets are common, tend to have sleeping arrangements in which the mother and child sleep together and the father sleeps separately. They also tend to have a long postpartum taboo. Since the households are often polygynous—that is, since a man may have more than one wife — the long postpartum taboo is less onerous for the husband, unless both his wives happen to give birth at about the same time. These customs also create a close relationship of dependence on the mother. Since these societies emphasize the male line in kinship and residential groupings, dependence is especially a problem for boys. The cultural solution to this problem, Whiting found, was the practice of fairly severe male initiation rites involving circumcision. Thus a whole chain of social and cultural facts is tied to the weaning of children in these populations.

Protein sources are especially critical during the weaning period, when breast milk is no longer available as a protein source, because infants and children need relatively more protein per unit of body weight than do adults. If children eat the normal adult diet, they may reach their capacity for bulk and their need for calories before their protein needs are met. This is even more likely to happen when children are fed generous amounts of bulky carbohydrate foods such as cassava or bananas.

Kwashiorkor is the nutritional disease most often seen in children being weaned to a protein-scarce diet. "Kwashiorkor" is a West African term that literally refers to a child displaced from his mother by a subsequent pregnancy (Jelliffe 1968:115). The disease was first described in West Africa and is especially significant there because of the prominence of starchy cassava, plantains, and yams in subsistence. The disease is not limited to the tropics, however; alert physicians have even diagnosed it in New York City infants. The key symptom of kwashiorkor is edema, or fluid retention, which begins with the feet and lower legs and progresses until the child looks blubbery (figure 6.2). The body's biochemical self-regulation breaks down in kwashiorkor, unlike marasmus, and metabolic imbalances occur. Laboratory tests of the blood show lowered protein levels and other abnormalities. The child with kwashiorkor is withdrawn, apathetic, and miserable. The mother may desperately try to cram down more food, but the child loses appetite. The child takes on a distinctive "moon-face" appearance, and his or her hair looks limp and pale. Skin may be light colored, too, and a skin rash that looks like flaking paint may develop.

Although the symptoms of kwashiorkor seem radically different from those of marasmus, both types of childhood malnutrition basically involve the failure to grow, and the distinction between them

FIGURE 6.2   A South Indian child suffering from kwashiorkor. The symptoms are edema, muscle wasting, enlarged liver, and ascites, which is the accumulation of fluid in the abdomen.
Photo by Derrick Jelliffe.

should not be overemphasized. Kwashiorkor and marasmus are simply the extremes of a continuum; many malnourished infants and children show intermediate conditions and combinations of symptoms. The whole continuum can be termed **Protein-Calorie Malnutrition** (PCM) or **Protein-Energy Malnutrition** (PEM): if energy needs are not met, protein will be metabolized as an energy source and will not be available for growth and repair. Recently it has been suggested that the term should be inverted to "calorie-protein malnutrition" since protein shortage alone is less common among the malnourished children of the world than is a shortage of nutrients in general. This suggestion comes especially from those who have worked in countries like India, where the predominantly grain diet would provide sufficient protein if a child could only get enough food to eat (Gopalan 1975). For every child in such a malnourished community who shows clinical symptoms of nutritional disease, many more are marginally nourished, showing slow growth and lack of vitality.

Weaning is a critical time for child health because inadequate nutrition, infection, and psychological stress interact synergistically, magnifying the effects of each. The toddler displaced from a mother's breast by the birth of a sibling is no less under stress than a pressured executive or harried commuter. Infections increase the need for certain nutrients, such as protein. At the same time, gastrointestinal infections reduce the body's capacity to absorb these nutrients, and appetite may be reduced. When a child is marginally nourished, an episode of infectious disease may push her or him over the line into outright malnutrition. Caught in a vicious circle, the poorly nourished child is less resistant to infection because antibody production is impaired. Figure 6.3 shows the weight record of a female child in India who developed kwashiorkor. As is typical even in the poorest communities, she did well on breast milk for the first four months. The development of kwashiorkor symptoms was precipitated by dysentery at

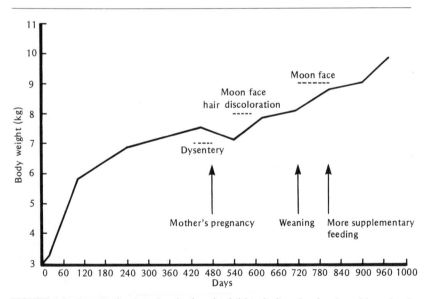

FIGURE 6.3   Longitudinal study of a female child in India who developed kwashiorkor.

SOURCE: Reprinted from C. Gopalan, "Protein vs. Calories in the Treatment of PCM," in Robert Olson, ed., *Protein Calorie Malnutrition* (New York: Academic Press, 1975), p. 333, by permission.

twelve months and by weaning at twenty-four months. After medical intervention with supplementary feeding, she began growing again.

Gastroenteritis is the most important of the infections that interact with malnutrition in young children, so much so that it is even called "weanling diarrhea." Diseases such as measles and chicken pox, which are usually trivial in a well-nourished child, may be fatal to a poorly nourished child. This fact leads to the suggestion that the mortality rate in the second year of life (see table 6.1) or even in the entire preschool period (ages 1 through 4), is the most accurate, though indirect, measure of the nutritional status of a country (Gordon, Wyon, and Ascoli 1967). As breast-feeding declines and the mortality from infant malnutrition is pushed to earlier ages, the second-year mortality rate will no longer be as accurate a measure.

TABLE 6.1   Second-year age-specific death rates for selected countries.

Country, region	Date	Death rate per 1000 children age 1 year but less than 2 years
Sweden	1963	0.9
USA	1963	1.6
Canada	1961	1.7
Japan	1963	2.5
Fiji	1963	5.4
Thailand	1960	16.4
India, urban Bombay	1961	25.9
Mexico	1960	30.9
Senegal	1957	61.0
Guatemala	1963	62.1
India, rural Khanna	1957–1959	72.2
Egypt	1961	107.0
St. Vincent (Caribbean Is.)	1960–1962	147.6

SOURCE: Selected from John E. Gordon et al., The Am. J. Medical Sciences 254:365, 1967.

Children in poorly nourished communities are not equally at risk of death in the second year of life. Even within poor families, some children are more at risk than others, probably reflecting the food available to them. A study in the Punjab, India, found that the second-year death rate climbed stepwise with the number of living children in a family, with the seventh child in a family more than twice as likely to die in the second year of life as the first or second child (Gordon, Wyon, and Ascoli 1967:375). In agricultural societies like India, where sons are especially important to a family, girls are far more likely to die than boys at this age. But in families from India who have migrated to Fiji in the South Pacific, where food is abundant, the second-year death rate is much lower, close to that of developed nations. The difference between the death rates for girls and boys disappears as well, indicating that cultural biases can respond quickly to changed environmental pressures.

In populations where the death rate is very high during the weaning period, there must be great selective pressure favoring children who can make the best use of the food they get. Physical anthropologists have suggested that natural selection under these circumstances would favor children who are genetically programmed to be smaller and slower-growing because their nutritional needs are more easily satisfied. Children with a genetic predisposition to be larger would be more likely to develop marasmus or kwashiorkor during a period of rapid growth.

NUTRITION IN CHILDHOOD AND ADOLESCENCE

After the vulnerable years of early childhood, disease and death from malnutrition become infrequent, even in populations where malnutrition is common at younger ages. Children aged 5 and older are growing more slowly. They can compete better for their share of the family diet and can chew and digest whatever is available. They have developed immunities against many of the prevalent infections that interact with nutrition to affect health.

Children in many settings learn to forage for tidbits of food. In a city they may do their foraging in the cupboard or in the garbage can, but in a rural setting they may forage for significant amounts of wild fruits, berries, nuts, small animals, and insects. Among the Sanio-Hiowe of Papua New Guinea, children are even more likely than adults to eat beetles and their larvae, spiders, mayflies, and other insects. Insects should not be ignored as a potential source of both protein and fat; the percentage of protein in many of them is as great or greater than it is in beef (Taylor 1975:55 and Appendix I). Gathering fruits and berries while at play can supply vitamin needs effectively for children in an agricultural society with an otherwise monotonous diet. In times of famine from crop failure, when even adults turn to wild food sources, their nutritional status has at times actually improved with respect to vitamins and minerals.

In many societies, children make a significant contribution to the household economy. Many tasks, such as herding sheep and goats, can be performed as effectively by children as by adults. Because children are smaller than adults and their food requirements are scaled to their size, they can perform these tasks at less cost (measured in food energy) than an adult can. It is advantageous for the tight food economy of a poor farming or herding family to have children do as many of these tasks as possible. Even in an urban society, children can perform many tasks at a lower energy cost than adults can, such as running errands and caring for smaller children. In addition, children may become an indirect source of income and food for the entire household under programs such as free milk distributions and child welfare payments.

The marginal intake of calories, protein, and other nutrients among children in poorly nourished populations is reflected in slower growth rates than in better-nourished populations. Figure 6.4 compares the growth in height of some well-to-do children in urban Nigeria with the slower growth of poorer village children.

In poorly nourished populations, skeletal maturation is delayed, that is, a delay in closure of the epiphyseal plates permits the long bones to continue growing. In a study of poorly nourished people in the village of Heliconia, Colombia, physical anthropologist William A. Stini (1971) found that males continued to grow slowly until about age 26. Only a century ago, this was also true in Europe. But now it is unusual for an American or European to get much taller after age 19.

In the last hundred years in Europe, the United States, Canada, and certain other countries, people have been getting taller. The early anthropologist Franz Boas measured European immigrants to the United States and their American-born children and found the off-

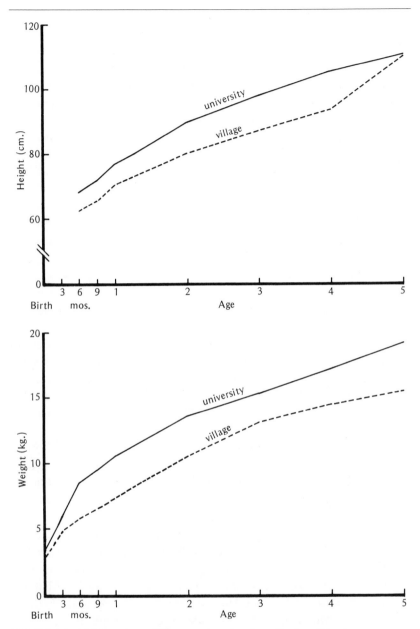

FIGURE 6.4   Children in a village twenty miles from Ibadan, Nigeria, grow more slowly than the control groups of well-fed preschool children of Nigerian faculty members at the University of Ibadan. In communities throughout the world where protein-calorie malnutrition is found in a significant number of children, even the rest of the children, who are not severely malnourished, show growth retardation when compared with children in a well-fed community (Edozien 1970).

spring in some ethnic groups to be taller than their parents (Boas 1940, 1st ed. 1910). This pattern has continued, and even stay-at-homes experienced the change: in most Western European countries, fully grown adults are from $2\frac{1}{2}$ to $3\frac{1}{4}$ inches (6 to 9 cm) taller than in 1870 (Tanner 1968). Even more striking than the increase in adult stature is the fact that children are getting taller *earlier*.

Another index of the trend to earlier maturation is the age of girls at menarche, their first menstrual period. In Sweden, Denmark, Finland, Germany, Britain, and the United States, the age at menarche has been declining for the last hundred years, dropping from an average age of 16 to 13. Under markedly better economic conditions, menarche occurs earlier. The latest ages at menarche yet reported are from Papua New Guinea, where Bundi, Chimbu, and Lumi women first menstruate at an average age of 18 (Malcolm 1970). Malcolm also found that the populations with the latest average age for menarche also showed the shortest adult statures, despite growth that continued into the twenties. In contrast to these rural populations, the children of migrants to towns are growing more rapidly and are headed toward taller adult stature.

Variations in human growth are responses to a complex of genetic and ecological factors. "Small is beautiful" under conditions of nutritional stress like that now experienced by many of the people of the world. A 132-lb. (60-kg) South American man requires about 2300 kilocalories per day to perform the same round of activities for which a 154-lb. (70-kg) man in the United States requires about 3200 kilocalories (Stini 1975a). For very few of those activities is larger size of any real advantage, yet the larger man is burning more kilocalories even while at rest.

The sharp trend to greater height and earlier maturity that has been conspicuous in the last century in many populations indicates that people had a potential for growth that was not previously being realized. What has changed? One important change in the environment in which growth takes place has been the decline of infectious disease, as discussed in chapter 4. Children whose growth is not interrupted by bouts of severe infections will grow more rapidly. Food also has become more abundant in populations experiencing the trend to earlier maturity, and new modes of preserving and distributing food have decreased seasonal variation in diet. The effects of these changes in infectious disease and nutrition interact synergistically to promote growth.

In addition to these environmental factors, there is probably a significant genetic component in the trend to taller stature. While the genetics of stature are not clearly understood, outbreeding seems to result in an increase in stature. For example, the physical anthropologist Frederick Hulse (1957) found that adult sons of Swiss parents who emigrated to California from different villages in Switzerland were an inch taller than the sons of Swiss parents who came from the same village. In the last century, urbanization, transportation, and communication have decreased the amount of inbreeding in many areas of the world, and this may have contributed to the increase in stature.

NUTRITION
THROUGHOUT
ADULT LIFE

Sexual differences in nutrition begin early and continue throughout life. Girls do seem to have some inherent, physiological protection against growth retardation under conditions of poor nutrition (Stini 1971:1025). Nonetheless, malnutrition is much more prevalent among girls than among boys in many cultural groups where boys are favored and better fed. Especially strong sexual biases in nutrition were found in the Mexican community studied by Muñoz de Chavez and her associates (1974), in the Punjab in northern India (Levinson 1974), and in Bangladesh (Lindenbaum 1977).

In adult life, the sexual division of labor influences some of the dietary differences between men and women. Among East African cattle-herding and farming peoples, the young men in the seasonal cattle camps have a diet almost exclusively of animal products, mainly milk and blood, while the women back in the villages have mostly a cereal-based diet of millet. The Hadza, a hunter-gatherer group of East

Africa, eat much of their food as soon as they obtain it. Men eat small game animals and carrion in the bush, carrying larger game back to camp to share. Women snack on wild fruits and berries as they gather them, so that the diet of the two sexes differs markedly (Jelliffe et al. 1962). This phenomenon is not entirely unfamiliar to certain segments of the American population, where the businessman's expense account lunch contrasts with the homemaker's snacking as she works. Even when families are together for a meal, in many cultures males and females are customarily served separately, the adult men being served first.

In addition to social patterns that direct different proportions of food to different age and sex groups, cultural symbolism may be attached to specific food items. Contrast the foods that would be considered appropriate for a ladies' bridge luncheon with the foods associated with the male athlete's training table or business lunch:

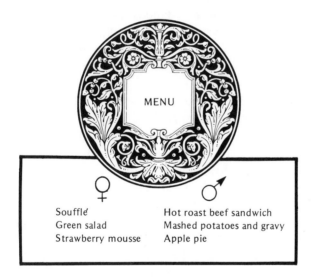

♀	♂
Soufflé	Hot roast beef sandwich
Green salad	Mashed potatoes and gravy
Strawberry mousse	Apple pie

In other cultures, such gender distinctions may be formalized into a series of male/female *food taboos*. The Sanio-Hiowe of Papua New Guinea assign many small game animals to either men or women. Of nineteen kinds of furred animals (marsupials and rats), four may be eaten by men only, six may be eaten by women only, and nine may be eaten by either sex. A Sanio-Hiowe man who breaks a food taboo risks only the teasing of his colleagues for his lack of manliness. A widow, however, risks more severe punishment if she has broken one of the numerous additional food taboos imposed on her. An infraction shows a lack of respect and submissiveness and may cost her life at the hands of her husband's grieving kinsmen.

The imposition of especially severe food taboos on women is a widespread cultural phenomenon. They may be imposed on all women or concentrated in certain physiologically and socially critical stages of life: widowhood, adolescence, or, most often, pregnancy and lactation. The term "taboo" covers prohibitions with a wide range of sanctions. At one extreme are those that carry the threat of physical punishment or the expectation of supernatural retribution. At the opposite extreme are simple food avoidances, enforced by no one, but more or less adhered to by a woman in order not to take chances with her or her child's health. Whether imposed on women, children, the sick, or any social category, food taboos are most often concerned with foods of animal origin, including meat, milk, and eggs. Animal foods are the subject of much symbolic elaboration based on cultural perceptions of animal behavior. A sexual division of labor that assigns hunting or herding to men is often a further basis for symbolism, women's fertility being viewed as threatening the success of the hunt or the reproduction of the herds.

Although it is easy to find ethnographic lists of food taboos in hundreds of cultures, it is much harder to evaluate the real impact of these taboos on the nutrition of the people who are supposed to obey them. If the forbidden food is rarely available anyway or if alternatives are abundant, the taboo will have little dietary impact. But if many of the major sources of protein are forbidden, the dietary impact may be severe. In each case, the investigator needs to know whether the taboos are really obeyed or if they are ignored when food is too scarce to afford the luxury of dietary substitutions. Sometimes the permissible foods are reserved for people who are subject to many food taboos. Such was the case for Sanio-Hiowe widows. Their relatives made special efforts to provide them with bitter wild yams and rats, which were among the few foods allowed them early in the mourning period; nonetheless, they were severely enough deprived to lose weight during this time.

Taboos on certain foods may have a helpful biological function for the person who observes them. Salt was taboo to pregnant women among the Cherokee and other Native Americans of the Southeast. This sodium restriction may have been physiologically beneficial in preventing fluid retention, Neumann argued (1977). Anthropologists who were critical of Neumann's hypothesis argued that more often than not, food taboos are biologically dysfunctional for the individual, although they serve a social function in marking statuses.

To evaluate the impact of food taboos on maternal and child health in a Malayan village, the nutritional anthropologist Christine Wilson (1973) observed the food intake of a few women on sample days. The women had not been subject to food taboos during pregnancy, but taboos were stringent in the forty days following childbirth. During this period, the women also spent some time each day lying on a platform bed over warm coals, a practice believed to "dry up the blood." They avoided foods that they regarded to have a cooling effect on the body, according to the ancient hot/cold classification of foods. They feared that the harmful effects of cold foods would be transmitted to the infant through the breast milk. The prohibition includes many fruits, vegetables, and seasonings. The remaining permissible foods are mostly rice, roasted fish, and coffee, adequate for their energy and protein needs but less than adequate in terms of vitamins and minerals.

Nutritionists have been of the opinion that food taboos for mothers and children are irrational and harmful, unnecessarily restricting the foods available to these nutritionally vulnerable groups. Building on this view, public health programs must take these taboos into account by providing acceptable alternative protein sources while working to change the beliefs through education. Anthropologists share the assumption that not every aspect of culture works to the advantage of individual health and well-being, but they have been more concerned to discover why food taboos are so widespread and persistent.

Restrictions on the food consumed by pregnant and lactating women are unlikely to have easily observable effects on their babies' health. Hence traditional cultures are unlikely to be confronted with clear-cut evidence that women who disobey the taboos have healthier babies than those who obey. This helps explain why established beliefs are resistant to change. When a woman breaks a taboo and her child happens to become sick soon afterward, feelings of guilt or shame reinforce the belief. The long accumulation of contrary evidence that would be necessary to test and question the belief is unlikely to be attained.

What positive function might the food taboos have? Ecological anthropologists suggest a latent function of population control. In times of food scarcity, women are less likely to ovulate, to conceive, and to carry infants to term (Frisch 1978). Any cultural practices diverting food from women to men would magnify the effect of food scarcity on fertility. The scattered evidence that food deprivation reduces fertility comes from very different social settings: the seasonal pattern of births among the !Kung (Wilmsen 1978) and among the women of Bangladesh (Lindenbaum 1977) seems to be related to seasonal changes in nutrition. Fertility was depressed in European women during the famines of World War II, such as that in Holland.

Although the long-term ecological effects of taboos are subtle, the sociopolitical effects are immediate and obvious. Food consumption involves sexual politics. Bridget O'Laughlin's study "Why Mbum Women Do Not Eat Chicken" (1974) deals with a society in Chad that is typical of equatorial Africa in regard to food taboos. O'Laughlin suggests that the food taboos express a metaphorical equivalence of women and livestock and support the dominance of senior males. The subordination of Mbum Kpau women does not stem from the technological division of labor, for the women fully participate with men in production. Instead, it stems from the patrilineal organization of labor and bridewealth. The Mbum women, like the women of many other cultures, are systematically deprived nutritionally by a cultural symbol system in which food symbolizes the social hierarchy.

Men are bound by food prohibitions in many cultures also, though not usually as severely as women. Hunters may be denied the meat of animals they have killed, though they may share in gifts of meat from other hunters. Initiation to manhood or to ritual office may require abstinence from sex and food.

Ritual practice in many religions requires that men and women of the congregation fast. Moslems are obligated to fast daily during the month of Ramadan, abstaining from all food and drink until after sunset. The normal foods continue to be available for children and, in the evenings, for everyone else, so that the nutritional impact is blunted.

More severe effects may be felt by members of the Ethiopian Orthodox Church, who practice partial fasting on Wednesdays and Fridays year-round and for longer periods surrounding several Christian holidays, even though the fast is not total. Common people fast about 110 to 150 days per year, but priests and monks may fast 220 days per year. No meat, eggs, milk, and butter are allowed during the fast. Protein is available to the well-to-do in the form of fish, legumes, and pulses, but poor families cannot usually afford these, since prices go up during fasting periods. Exemptions from fasting are allowed for children, pregnant and lactating women, and the sick, but since animal foods are not available in the markets during fasting periods, the exemption does not help them very much. Through suffering the hardships of the fast, these Ethiopian Christians affirm their ethnic identity and attempt to build inner strength and to increase the flow of divine power into the world (Knutsson and Selinus 1970).

NUTRITION AND OLD AGE

Fasting in particular and food deprivation in general tend to be closely associated in our thinking with malnutrition and ill health. While it is true that a shortage of certain nutrients (especially at critical periods of growth) is harmful, the corollary that more is necessarily better is not true. Several lines of research are converging to indicate that a diet that is restricted in total food intake is more compatible with a long, healthy life.

Research with white rats is one line of evidence of the relationship between diet and aging. Pioneering research by Clive McCay at Cornell University in the 1930s showed that severe underfeeding early in life, beginning immediately after weaning, increases the white rat's normal life span of two or three years to five years. With a calorie-restricted diet that is otherwise well balanced, the animals mature slowly. They are undersized and underdeveloped sexually but otherwise healthy and protected against degenerative diseases (Kent 1976).

No one has yet discovered an equivalent feeding program to double the *human* life span, but laboratory researchers are hard at work trying to understand the biochemistry of aging and the way it is influenced by early nutrition. One kind of anthropological contribution to the study of diet and aging is the ethnographic description of cultures in which a healthy old age is fostered, such as the Abkhasian culture in the Caucasus region, discussed in the following health profile.

PROFILE: LIVING PAST 100 IN THE CAUCASUS

Among the Abkhasians and other peoples of the Caucasus, a rugged mountain area in the southern part of the Soviet Union (figure 6.5), there is an exceptional concentration of people who claim to be over 100 years old. Even more impressive than their sheer survival to an advanced age is their health and vigor. Many of them work regularly, tending the courtyards and orchards of their homesteads. Some walk over rough terrain to bathe in mountain streams. Substantial percentages enjoy good hearing and vision and still have their own teeth. Medical and anthropological research into the lifestyle of these people has been directed toward understanding the factors that contribute to a long and healthy life.

Russian gerontologists have done most of the medical research among the peoples of the Caucasus, but an American anthropologist, Sula Benet, has also made several field trips to study these people. The first research problem has been to establish whether the people are really as old as they say. Claims of extreme longevity, especially by people who are so healthy and active, are generally received with skepticism. Certificates of baptism and marriage are available for some, but careful field work to record family trees and biographies is necessary as well. Even so, many scholars remain unconvinced that the claims to extremely old ages have been validated.

FIGURE 6.5   Map of the Caucasus, a region in the southern part of the Soviet Union.

SOURCE: Modified from S. Benet, frontispiece, *How to Live to be 100: The Life-Style of the People of the Caucasus* (New York: Dial Press, 1976).

Soviet demographers have established some striking patterns in the distribution of longevity within the Caucasus. The area can be divided into three ecological zones: the mountains, the foothills, and the plains. The proportion of people over ninety years old is largest in the mountains, lowest in the plains, and intermediate in the foothills. A study of health in a smaller sample of the aged found the same distribution by altitude. Among people over ninety, the largest percentage of active people with an interest in life and good disposition was found in the mountains. The percentage dropped in the foothills and was lowest in the plains. The mountain people's success seems to be due to their employment in animal herding, which is a physically active but unpressured lifestyle. Demographers also report that rural people in the area live longer than urban people, and a greater number of women than men live to old age in the Caucasus, just as in the rest of the world.

In other parts of the world, long-living people tend to report that close relatives have also lived long. This is not as often the case in the Caucasus, suggesting that long life has a less clear-cut genetic component there. A genetic explanation also seems unlikely when we note that long-living people are found in many different ethnic groups in the Caucasus, which is an area of substantial ethnic diversity. Religion is also diverse; the long-living population includes Muslims, Christians, and Jews. Researchers have sought shared environmental factors among these diverse peoples and made comparisons within the area to try to identify features of the lifestyle that lead to active good health in old age.

Although studies have tended to focus on the old people themselves, looking at the whole life cycle suggests that what is happening is not a prolongation of old age but rather a slowing down of the whole aging process. Menopause seems to be delayed, the birth of children to women said to be over fifty is not unusual, and men claiming to be over ninety have fathered children. The extremely long-lived show few clinical signs of aging such as hypertension and arteriosclerosis.

Diet is regarded as an especially important factor in longevity. The traditional diet of the Caucasus, despite ethnic variation, has certain stable features. There is an emphasis on eating in moderation; meals are regular and leisurely. Despite the emphasis on feasting and hospitality, overeating is frowned on and obesity is regarded as illness. Caloric intake is low from an American or European perspective. The everyday diet emphasizes milk products, cereals, an abundance of fresh vegetables, fruits, and nuts. Meat is eaten only a few times a week, but it plays an important part on special occasions. When a guest arrives, freshly slaughtered mutton or chicken is roasted or boiled. *Matzoni* (a cultured milk product like yogurt) and cheese are eaten in large amounts. Nuts are used in many ways; for example, ground walnuts are used in spicy sauces for beef or mutton.

Freshness of food is regarded as very important and thus contributes further to an already high intake of vitamins. According to Benet (1974:26), it is common for Abkhasians to pick a fresh breakfast salad of watercress, green onion, and radishes or to-matoes and cucumber, which is followed by a glass of *matzoni* and a dish of warm cornmeal mash and goat cheese. Grapes and other fruits are eaten in abundance. Wine is used in modera-tion—toasts with wine are an essential part of a social occasion.

There are regional and ethnic differences in diet that have an effect on longevity. Benet reports (1976:107) the work of Soviet researchers on diet differences between the eastern and western parts of one of the Caucasus republics. In the west, where longevity and good health are more marked, people eat less meat than they do in the east, while they eat twice as much milk and cheese. The animal fat used in the east tends to be replaced by nuts in the healthier west. Vegetables and fruits are used extensively in both areas. Both use potatoes and wheat products as the main carbohydrate sources, but people in the eastern area consume somewhat more of these. The less healthy population of the eastern area uses sugar as a sweet while the western population uses honey as well as sugar.

Diet has drawn much attention as a factor in longevity. How-ever, many other factors in the lifestyle of the long-lived peoples of the Caucasus are significant. Exercise is one. Life in the rug-

FIGURE 6.6   At the venerable age of 100, vigorous Abkhasian men greet each other.

Photo: Tass from Sovfoto.

ged mountain areas assures that climbing and walking will be built into the daily schedule. The concept of retirement is unknown, and the extremely long-lived report that they did not reduce their work load until into the eighties or nineties, and even then they continued to work at lighter tasks. The elderly retain leadership within the extended family and the villages, where "councils of elders" are composed of people over age 90. There is clearly little basis for a feeling of powerlessness, uselessness, or social isolation. Sula Benet lays emphasis on continuity in the regular routines of daily life, tradition, noncompetitiveness, and training from childhood in moderation and self-control. Benet noted an especially striking contrast to our own culture: people *expect* to live long and deterioration is not regarded as inevitable.

Some of these patterns recur in other places where there are long-lived people. The physician Alexander Leaf visited allegedly long-living people in three areas: the Caucasus, the village

FIGURE 6.7   Khfar Tarkukovna Lasuria, the woman in the center, celebrated her 140th birthday in 1974 at this dinner. Her 100-year-old son is at her side.

Photo: Tass from Sovfoto.

of Vilcabamba in the Andes Mountains in Ecuador, and the state of Hunza in West Pakistan (Leaf 1973). These last two areas are so isolated that he concluded that chance genetic factors may play a more significant part in longevity there than in the Caucasus. The people of Vilcabamba and Hunza do share certain features with the long-lived Caucasus peoples: a mountainous setting where physical activities keep people fit, the continued active participation of older people in social and economic activities, and an increase in social status with age. In all three areas, caloric intake is low and consumption of animal fats is low, but the diets are different in other respects. There does not seem to be a single group of foods that people can eat to assure a healthier old age.

Although the diet and lifestyles prevalent in the United States do not foster extreme longevity, there is a large and increasing proportion of old people in this country. As population growth has slowed, the proportion of older people increased even though life expectancy has increased only slowly. The 1970 U.S. census listed 20 million people over age 65, or 9.3 percent of the population. The diverse nutritional problems in this age group are a serious concern. People in this age group are living with the results of lifetime eating habits in the form of the diet-related diseases discussed in chapter 5, such as cardiovascular disease, osteoporosis, and diabetes. Here our concern is with their present diet, the way they are eating in old age. Low intakes of specific nutrients are related to poor health in the elderly (Schlenker et al. 1973). Because their energy requirements are less than those of an active young adult, they must eat wisely in order to get adequate amounts of nutrients without too many calories.

Many factors make it difficult for old people to eat well. One frequently mentioned factor is dental problems: more than half of the U.S. population over age 55 have lost all their teeth. Another factor is the problem of loneliness; people who live alone are reluctant to prepare and eat a well-balanced meal. It is often difficult for older people to get out to shop for food. However, the single most powerful factor that dominates nutrition in the elderly is economic. In one

study, 529 people whose average age was 73.6 were asked to recall
what they had eaten in the last twenty-four hours. Analysis of the
responses showed that the best predictor of inadequate diet was
economic status (Todhunter 1976).

ASSESSING DIET
AND NUTRITION

In the last two chapters, we have mentioned "inadequate intake of
nutrients," but we have avoided specifying just what an adequate
intake might be or how it might be determined. How can the diet of a
population be evaluated? In the study of elderly Americans just
discussed, subjects were asked what they had eaten in the past
twenty-four hours, and these foods were compared with tables of food
composition to determine their probable food value. These values
were then compared with the Recommended Dietary Allowances
(RDA). This *twenty-four-hour recall method* is used in many research
settings. However, even such a common, seemingly straightforward
method involves many assumptions that must be examined.

The first assumption is that the method adequately reflects actual
food consumption. The twenty-four-hour recall depends on the
informant's memory and frankness. It is especially difficult to judge
retrospectively the size of servings. The twenty-four-hour period
chosen will not reflect the whole range of the diet, so the sample needs
to be large enough to include days of feasting and fasting and seasonal
variation as well as differences among individuals. Some of the
problems of inaccurate recall may be solved, though at great cost of
time and effort, by following an individual through the day and
weighing all food before he or she eats it. This was done in the study of
Malay women after childbirth, discussed earlier in this chapter (Wilson
1973). Often this type of study is expanded into a seven-day *household
food consumption survey*. In such a study, it is challenging to establish
and maintain rapport despite the invasion of privacy, to ensure that

the household does not modify its eating habits because of the study, to keep track of food eaten away from home, and to judge the extent to which the findings are representative of some larger population.

After the researchers record the types and quantities of food eaten, they must calculate their nutritive values. Although the results of laboratory analysis of many foods are available, the use of the tables requires the assumption that they correspond to the foods actually eaten. In fact, foods may vary considerably in nutritional value depending on the conditions under which they were grown, marketed, stored, and cooked. Unexpected factors may turn out to be important. Among the !Kung, for example, iron from cooking pots obtained in trade with the Bantu raises !Kung hemoglobin levels much higher than would be predicted from the foods alone.

The nutritive value of the diet is finally compared with some standard recommended allowance for each nutrient, and the comparison is expressed as a percentage. This comparison can be only as meaningful as the standard chosen and its appropriateness for people of the body build, activity level, and climate in question. The standards recommended by the Food and Agriculture Organization and World Health Organization (WHO 1973) and by the United States National Research Council (National Research Council 1968) are widely recognized. They do not represent the final, definitive word, however; they are constantly subject to revision as further research calls them into question.

Regardless of how their diet measures up against established standards, the evaluation of a people's diet requires assessing the nutritional health of individuals. This can be done by clinical examination, recording symptoms such as those associated with kwashiorkor or the eye changes associated with vitamin A deficiency and the thyroid enlargement of iodine deficiency. Because many symptoms are ambiguous, clinical examination is best supplemented by other measures such as biochemical tests of blood and urine and anthropometric measurements (Jelliffe 1966). Some common measurements are height, weight, head circumference, skinfold thickness (to indicate the amount of subcutaneous fat), and upper arm circumference (to indicate muscle development or wasting).

The assessment of a population's nutritional status requires a broad interdisciplinary approach to evaluating many types of data: dietary, economic, ecological, clinical, and cultural. There is still much to learn about the state of nutritional health in every country of the world, including our own. This does not make it any less important to study the nutritional anthropology of the small, exotic populations that have traditionally been the laboratory of anthropology. Studying the mystery of *kuru* (chapter 2) illuminated a wide range of other phenomena of importance for health; similarly, certain nutritional enigmas in exotic societies remain to challenge comfortable assumptions. One such enigma is presented by New Guinea peoples who eat much less than current standards for protein and calories without showing signs of deficiency. By careful studies, they are found to expend more energy than they consume (Norgan, Ferro-Luzzi, and Durnin 1974) and to excrete more nitrogen in their urine and feces than they consume in their food (Oomen 1970). Are the measurements of food intake flawed? Is the methodology for measuring daily energy output inappropriate? Or do these people have special nutritional adaptations that are not yet understood? Perhaps bacteria in their intestines fix atmospheric nitrogen, making them "walking legumes," as Oomen suggests. Whatever the answer, continuing to work on this puzzle will advance the understanding of nutritional health.

FAMINE

The methods for assessing the nutritional status of a population become of urgent importance in times of famine. How serious is the famine in each region? Which groups are hardest hit? What kinds of emergency medical care are needed? What foods should relief agencies send in? Decisions like these call for rapid evaluation under difficult field conditions.

In times of famine, the central themes of the last two chapters are brought into sharp focus. One of these is the synergism of nutritional stress, infectious disease stress, and social stress. Earlier in this chapter, we viewed this interaction on the level of the individual organism—depicting a weanling child struggling with inadequate diet, infectious diarrhea or chicken pox, and the painful separation from mother following the birth of a younger sibling. In times of famine, these stresses are seen in entire populations, as widespread food shortages, epidemic disease, and social dislocation almost inevitably occur together.

The need to look at food in its ecosystemic context was emphasized in chapter 5. This principle is confirmed by the analysis of famine. Whether the famine is directly attributed to a so-called natural disaster such as drought or to a social disaster such as war, the causes lie in the interaction of sociopolitical and biological systems. The following health profile of the famine resulting from the Sahel drought makes this clear.

PROFILE: THE SAHEL DROUGHT AND FAMINE

The southern edge of the Sahara Desert is called the Sahel, from the Arabic word for "border." These desert-edge lands of West Africa were devastated by drought and famine from 1968 through 1973. Although drought, famine, and other so-called natural disasters are as old as human history, the Sahel case is a prototype for the kind of ecosystemic catastrophe that many people fear may become more common in the future.

The vegetation of the Sahel consists of thorny shrubs and trees and drought-resistant grasses. This desert-edge vegetation forms a band that cuts across six West African nations: Senegal, Mauritania, Mali, Upper Volta, Niger, and Chad (figure 6.8). The last four of the six countries are landlocked and are among the very poorest nations in the world, with per capita gross national products of less than $100. Mauritania, with deposits of iron ore, and Senegal, with cash crops like peanuts to export, are only slightly better off than the other four countries. Throughout the six countries, the main cash crops in better-watered areas are cotton and peanuts, often displacing vegetables and cereals

FIGURE 6.8   Map of the Sahel countries showing climate zones. The term
"Sahel" refers to the border between desert and grassland.

needed for subsistence. Cattle raising provides cash income to the drier Sahel zone itself.

The present-day poverty of the Sahel is a stark contrast to the prosperity of past centuries, when the nomads of the area were involved in a trade network that stretched from North Africa across the Sahara to the south. When they became colonies of France, the center of trade shifted to the coast and the Sahel was bypassed. Although the six countries became politically independent in the 1960s, France retains strong economic involvement.

The six Sahel countries have a combined population of about 25 million. Only about 5 million live in the dry Sahel zone itself, where the drought and famine had their greatest impact, and half of these people are nomads. In the better-watered parts of the Sahel, as well as in the Sudan area, sedentary farmers raise subsistence crops of sorghum and millet. The drier areas are exploited by pastoralists of several ethnic groups including the Tuareg, the Moors (Bedouin Arabs), and the Fulani. Cereals and legumes are traded for livestock continually, linking the ecologically specialized farmers and pastoralists and providing each with a more diversified diet.

Pastoralists in the Sahel have to contend with extremely variable rainfall from year to year, even in normal, nondrought times. In the best years, green grass is more abundant than the herds can effectively use, livestock reproduces rapidly, and milk is abundant. In a bad year, vegetation is sparse and the animals do not reproduce or produce much milk. The pastoralist cultures have adapted in several ways to provide some insurance against these year-to-year fluctuations. The diversification of their herds to include cattle, sheep, goats, and camels is one such protection. Cattle and sheep require grass, while goats browse on shrubs and trees. Goats are hardier animals and breed quickly to yield milk and replenish the herds after a dry spell, so they serve as a reserve in hard times, though they are less desired in the outside market.

Other traditional forms of protection against loss in hard times included a system of loans and gifts, which spread around the animals so that a herd decimated by some localized disaster could be rebuilt. Raiding other pastoral groups also helped rebuild a herd. Movement from vegetation-poor areas into areas more favored with rain in a given year was another important feature of nomadism. These movements were hindered by the establishment of international boundaries in the colonial period. Although traditional Sahel cultures had these and other means of responding flexibly to annual variation, from time to time a series of dry years led to severe famine. Previous to the 1970s, famines were recorded in 1913–1914, 1930–1932, and the early 1940s (Swift 1977:475).

There have been continuing efforts to develop pastoral production as a source of cash income for the countries, making it more than a means of subsistence for the pastoralists. To improve production, cattle diseases were controlled, and deep bore-wells were dug to provide water for the animals. This allowed herd sizes to be increased, since the limiting factors of disease and drinking water were removed. Vegetation for grazing now became the limiting factor. This overgrazing exposed land to irreversible damage, but not only the pastoralists were at fault. Cutting wood for timber and fuel and extending cultivation into marginal land was denuding lands of natural vegetation, initiating the process of "desertification," or desert encroachment into the Sahel. Population growth and the colonial demand for taxes and export crops intensified these pressures on the land.

After average to high rainfall in the 1950s and early 1960s, five successive years of low rainfall reduced vegetation severely. Livestock mortality was very high, especially among cattle. At least half of the cattle were lost in 1972 in every area, and some areas, such as the entire country of Chad, lost all their cattle. The farmers' crops were cut in half, but the nomads suffered most. Many migrated to the towns and to refugee camps that were set up. Although reliable figures are lacking, it has been estimated that 100,000 to 250,000 of the total nomad population of 2,500,000 may have died of famine-related causes. Measles was a major cause of death in people weakened by malnutrition, although an earlier immunization program prevented even more serious outbreaks. Medical surveys showed higher percentages of malnourished people among nomads than among sedentary peoples (Seaman et al. 1973; Imperato 1976). Young children and old people were most vulnerable.

By spring 1973, the outside world began hearing of the famine, and efforts were made to get emergency food aid to these countries. Relief came from other African countries, Europe, the Soviet Union, and China. The United States was the largest contributor, giving one-third of the total. The relief program was plagued with unprecedented delay and inadequacy. Considering that in many other disasters the humanitarian response has been quick, generous, and effective, why was it so poor this time?

Communication was part of the problem. It was difficult to get an accurate assessment of conditions, especially among the nomadic groups where the problems were most severe. Some responsibility rests with politicians in the Sahel countries, who

FIGURE 6.9   A cow that has died from starvation makes a macabre foreground
for a family meal in the Sahel. The loss of their herds made it
difficult for families to rebuild their subsistence economy after the
drought and famine.
Photo: United Nations/Food and Agriculture Organization.

were slow to request aid and squabbled over it when it came,
discriminating against the nomads and seeking to use the situation to their political advantage. The location and isolation of the
countries was another factor. Food sitting on the docks was
ruined by rain and rats for lack of an adequate network of road
and rail transport to get it to the interior.

The U.S. response was ineffective partly because of bureaucratic
bungling (Sheets and Morris 1976). The Sahel area was poorly

known and did not have the powerful advocates in Washington that other countries have, though the U.S. black community was supportive. The first year's shipments of grain to the starving people were of a coarse variety of sorghum used in the United States as animal feed. It caused stomach cramps and diarrhea in the nomads, who are accustomed to a diet that consists mostly of dairy products. This famine, unlike the famines in the previous decades, came at a time when the United States no longer had large food surpluses it was eager to dump. Further tarnishing the humanitarian image, critics have noted that in these years over half of U.S. food aid was going to less needy countries that were militarily strategic, such as the countries of Southeast Asia and the Middle East (Wiesberg 1976:115). The United States was not the only country with these problems, however. Bureaucratic red tape and ignorance of the Sahel situation also impeded other countries and international agencies such as the Food and Agriculture Organization (FAO). Even France, long the dominant power in this area, responded very weakly.

Everyone involved in the Sahel situation had an opportunity to learn something. Some of the rural peoples had their first positive introduction to what modern health care can accomplish (Imperato 1976). The Sahel countries and the donor agencies had a vivid illustration of the need for long-term planning for rural development based on sound ecological analysis. The only sure impact of the drought is that a temporary ecological balance on the desert edge has been restored by the reduction of the herds and by the migration of many nomads to the cities.

    Looking at the Sahel famine may cause us to become disillusioned about the effectiveness of food relief alone, without basic social and economic reforms and attainment of ecological balance. Still, such humanitarian efforts can be made more effective as short-term aid if they are based on better knowledge of the existing food distribution networks, the food habits of the people, and their nutritional needs. Each situation needs to be assessed in its own terms, or the response may be inappropriate. For example, in the Ethiopian drought of 1973, relief agencies provided expensive, high-protein items like milk, protein biscuits, and protein tonics, which were not locally acceptable. In retrospect, it appears that the best response would have been to send wheat, legumes, and vegetable oil. The oil would have helped meet the need for energy in an efficient and locally acceptable manner, and in this case it was energy that was the critical problem (Mason et al. 1974).

The famines in Africa and Bangladesh in the last decade are more severe because the period of critical food shortage is superimposed on already marginal nutrition. This is in contrast to the famines about which we have the most detailed medical information, those that occurred as a result of World War II and affected people such as the Dutch, who had been well nourished until their "hunger winter."

THE SOCIAL COST OF MALNUTRITION

In purely economic terms, malnutrition is costly. In his study *The Nutrition Factor*, Alan Berg (1973) examines the economic aspects of malnutrition in developing countries. Some of these costs are in medical care for those most seriously affected and lowered productivity for those less seriously malnourished. High birth rates despite unnecessarily high mortality are a costly combination for a developing country, because the number of dependent children is inordinately high. Solving a country's nutritional problems is costly too, and development planners weigh the cost-effectiveness of alternative solutions.

There are highly cost-effective solutions for some nutritional problems. Vitamin A deficiency, the leading cause of blindness, which is prevalent in Bangladesh, India and Indonesia, can be prevented by inexpensive, long-lasting injections (Van Veen and Van Veen 1974). Endemic goiter can be prevented by inexpensive iodine supplements such as iodized salt. The social cost of endemic goiter and endemic cretinism is extremely high. Mentally retarded, deaf-mute cretins are a social burden. In addition, many of the normal-appearing individuals in these populations are neurologically handicapped as well, though to a lesser degree, making the society even less able to bear the burden of supporting dependents (Greene 1973). The regions affected are usually mountainous areas, where soils are deficient in iodine and where seafood (with its high iodine content) is unavailable (Gillie 1971). The people affected are generally the poor, whose less varied diets offer less protection from deficiency. Not all nutritional problems have such simple technological solutions as vitamin A and iodine. Solving the basic problem of protein-calorie malnutrition would require far-reaching changes in the way income and food are distributed throughout the world.

The nutritional problems of affluent countries are costly, too. The economic cost is measured in expensive health care, lost work days, and lowered productivity from diseases such as heart disease, diabetes, and many others that have a dietary component.

If the economic costs of poor nutrition are large and measurable, the total human costs are incalculable. One controversial aspect is the effect of malnutrition on cognitive functioning. Severely malnourished children, those with kwashiorkor, are apathetic and their mental development is slowed. As might be expected, they perform poorly on IQ tests, though it is hard to say whether this is a measure of their mental abilities or their poor level of motivation. Even chronically undernourished children who do not show symptoms of kwashiorkor perform poorly on IQ tests, compared with well-nourished children. Again, it is difficult to know how much this performance reflects nutritional deprivation since these impoverished children have generally also been deprived in other ways (Frisch 1971). Experiments with rats have shown that permanent, irreversible brain damage can occur as a result of malnutrition during the critical period of brain growth. However, lack of environmental stimulation early in life in well-fed rats produces the same effects as malnutrition. These include biochemical changes in the brain as well as psychological changes such as decreases in exploratory behavior (Winick 1976:131). If experimenters with rats cannot easily sort out the meaning of behavioral changes and isolate nutrition as a variable, the difficulty of deciding these questions in research with humans is apparent.

One of the most careful efforts to date to study the relationship of early malnutrition to intelligence in a socioeconomically deprived population is the series of studies in a rural Mexican village by Cravioto and his associates (1966). They tested children's performance on tasks requiring intersensory integration, for example, matching an object they could *see* with one they could *feel* behind a screen. In these tests of neurointegrative development, Cravioto and his colleagues found significant differences in the rural village between short and tall children. The shorter children, who are assumed to be stunted by poor nutrition, performed poorly in the younger age groups, but the differences in performance tended to disappear later in childhood. Among well-nourished urban children, in whom differences in height reflect genetic potentials rather than nutrition, short children performed just as well as tall children. Much attention has been focused on the question of *irreversibility*—the extent to which subsequent improvements in nutrition allow a child to make up for the damage done by early malnutrition. The current answer seems to be that some but not all of the damage can be made up.

Chronic malnutrition affects other aspects of human personality, although these effects are as difficult to measure as the effects on intelligence. Brazilian Josué de Castro claimed in his powerful book *Geography of Hunger* (1952) that a low-protein diet had a biochemical effect that increased sexual drive and that this physiological factor was responsible for high birth rates in poor countries. Although this specific finding has not found much acceptance, and it is now conceded that poor nutrition restricts fertility (Frisch 1978), de Castro's work as a whole has continued to be regarded as a classic work in the politics of hunger. Hunger is a taboo subject, claimed de Castro; although we may have escaped Victorian hush-hush attitudes toward the public discussion of sex, we still cannot discuss hunger without embarrassment and guilt. Perhaps this discomfort has contributed to the controversy over two anthropologists' studies of societies that, they claimed, were entirely dominated by the hunger drive: the Siriono of South America (Holmberg 1969) and the Ik of Africa (Turnbull 1972).

Holmberg refers to the Siriono as "nomads of the long bow" because their seven- to nine-foot bows are probably the longest in the world. They wander the tropical forests of eastern Bolivia as hunter-gatherers, but they also plant small fields of maize and other crops. They hunt monkeys, birds, peccaries, deer, tapir, and crocodiles, and they collect palm cabbage, wild fruits, and the honey from wild bee hives. Holmberg was unable to keep accurate records of the food consumed, though he did estimate the meat consumption at something under one pound per person per day. Although that figure includes bone and waste, it seems adequate.

Holmberg's impression was that hunger frustration and insecurity about food were the dominant concern of the Siriono. Yet there cannot have been significant malnutrition because vegetable foods continued to be available even when there was no meat available for a few days. Instead, it was more a question of anxiety about food, which manifested itself in hasty preparation and wolfing of food, stealing off into the forest to eat alone and avoid sharing, quarreling and dreaming about food, and many other such behaviors. Magic, the attainment of prestige, and other spheres of culture were focused on producing food, which was regarded as a painful, unpleasant quest. Holmberg concluded from observing the interactions between men and women that the sex drive was subordinated to the hunger drive.

Is Holmberg's picture of the Siriono exaggerated? Probably not, although the personal hardships and illness Holmberg suffered during his field work may have colored his outlook. The poverty of Siriono culture and the social breakdown that Holmberg noted are not simply the result of hunger in an otherwise stable aboriginal culture, as Holmberg infers. From his own data, as well as from other sources, it is apparent that the Siriono have suffered ecological dislocation from a savannah to a forest environment to which they were not adapted, depopulation from epidemics of smallpox and influenza, and destructive contacts with Bolivian settlers (Isaac 1977).

A similar but even more frightening account of social collapse under suffering and hunger is Colin Turnbull's study of the Ik, *The Mountain People* (1972), a controversial book that has been heavily criticized by some of Turnbull's anthropological colleagues (Barth 1974; Wilson et al. 1975). Once living as nomadic hunter-gatherers in the mountain stronghold on the border between Uganda and Kenya, the Ik were settled as farmers in this inhospitable land when their traditional hunting territory was turned into a national park.

Turnbull's field work was done during two years of drought and famine. First the old people and then the children succumbed to starvation. Turnbull reports his own struggle with disgust and hatred toward the Ik as he watched the breakdown of the human values of love and goodness. Family life and morality broke down as individual survival took precedence over all else. Unlike the Siriono, the Ik were suffering severe malnutrition in addition to anxiety about food. Like the Siriono, they had undergone severe ecological dislocation and stress resulting from acculturation.

CONCLUSIONS

The Ik and the Siriono are extreme examples of whole populations undergoing stress so intense that it exceeds the capacity to adapt. In the following chapter, we will be examining more closely the phenomenon of stress and human adaptation. Nutritional stress interacts synergistically with other kinds of stress, such as the stress that originates in rapidly changing cultural and personal circumstances.

The last two chapters have identified some points in the individual life cycle and in the history and evolution of societies at which nutritional stress is especially critical. Human life at the juncture where some of these circumstances coincide is exceedingly fragile—picture a young child displaced from mother's breast in a family displaced, in turn, from its lands by the expansion of mechanized farming of a cash crop.

The dominant finding of these chapters has not been that severe malnutrition exists in the world; you knew that, and you are perhaps committed to working for change. What is more striking is that so little positive, glowing nutritional health exists anywhere. Marginal nutrition among the poor and overnutrition among the affluent are so widespread as contributing factors to poor health that we have given them extensive treatment in this text.

RESOURCES

Readings

Berg, Alan
1973   The Nutrition Factor: Its Role in National Development. Washington, D.C.: Brookings Institution.
Berg examines malnutrition as an obstacle to economic development from the point of view of economic planning and government policy.
Jelliffe, Derrick
1968   Infant Nutrition in the Subtropics and Tropics. Geneva: World Health Organization.
Jelliffe describes present infant feeding practices in the less technically developed countries and suggests how they might be improved to prevent nutritional disease.
Leaf, Alexander, and John Launois
1973   Every Day is a Gift When You Are Over 100. National Geographic 143(1):93–119.
This article includes photographs and descriptions of the lifestyles of three very long-living peoples: the Abkhasians, the Hunza, and the residents of Vilcabamba, Ecuador.
Newman, Marshall T.
1975   Nutritional Adaptation in Man. In Physiological Anthropology. Albert Damon, ed. Pp. 210–259. New York: Oxford University Press.
This chapter covers much the same ground as chapter 7 in this textbook, but it was written by a physical anthropologist who is especially noted for his work on growth and body build.
Schneour, Elie
1974   The Malnourished Mind. Garden City, New York: Anchor Press.
This book is a popularly written discussion of the effects of nutrition on mental development.

Films

Kwashiorkor. 1968.   32 minutes, color. Produced by R. G. Whitehead for the Medical Research Council, United Kingdom. Available from Audiovisual Services, Pennsylvania State University, University Park, Pennsylvania. This film examines practices of the people of Uganda that lead to the development of kwashiorkor in young children. The production and preparation of the staple food, bananas, are shown. In addition, the clinical signs of protein-calorie malnutrition are shown clearly.

Stress and Disease

PREVIEW

Stress is a process that occurs when an organism must cope with environmental demands that require functioning significantly above or below its habitual level of activity. The stress process is a normal part of life and usually defends the body against pathogens, injury, threat, and difficult climatic conditions.

In some cases, the body responds inappropriately to environmental demands, or the pressures may be so excessive and so prolonged that the body's defenses are exhausted. The body may develop symptoms that are evidence of strain—ulcers, hypertension, lowered resistance to viruses, emotional disorder. The effort to survive in the face of physical or symbolic danger can contribute to maladaptive physiological changes, as the health profile of magical death illustrates.

Stress and adaptation are closely related concepts in medical anthropology, for stressful conditions in the environment are often a stimulus for adaptive responses. Stress may arise when ecosystems are disrupted by natural disasters such as famines and earthquakes. Stress also is present in ecosystems that steadily exert pressures on human adaptive capacities, for example, high altitude regions or extremely hot climates. Stress comes from deprivation as well; the health profile of arctic hysteria examines the role of calcium and vitamin D deficiency and biorhythm desynchronization in a form of mental illness found in northern regions.

Medical anthropologists are especially interested in how ethnomedical systems manage stress processes. Familiar rituals and family support help reduce the emotional stress of illness, death, and grief. In other contexts, ethnomedical rituals may induce stress as part of the healing process, as in blood-letting, fasting, prolonged dancing, trance, and use of stimulants.

Anthropologists have also used the concept of stress to explain social pathologies such as suicide, violence, drug abuse, and inter-ethnic tensions. These problems are thought to be the results of social stress. While this approach to explaining social problems remains controversial, epidemiological data indicate that psychological and social pressures do affect the health of populations because the body does not differentiate between physical and nonphysical threats. The hormonal response to verbal insult, conflict, and rejection is very similar to the response to injury, loss of blood, and pain. The infant deprived of love and emotional stimulation suffers as much as the one who is starving, as the profile of deprivation dwarfism shows. The person who believes in the power of magic to kill, the old person who is moved involuntarily into an institution, and the prisoner of war all cope with emotional threat and social deprivation through physiological mechanisms of defense that pose some risk of bodily strain. 🖾

THE CONCEPT OF STRESS

That first week is really going to be rough; big parties with relatives and all that. Makes me feel funny because I know I don't deserve it . . . . I sure hope they don't make a lot of fuss over me. I'd rather be just left alone, maybe take a fishing trip for a few days.
—Released prisoner of war, on coming home from Korea, in Spaulding and Ford (1976:311)

Psychologists have found that coming home is a time of mixed emotions for Americans who have been prisoners of war. To survive during years of physical and emotional abuse, the POW has learned to guard against all feelings of self-pity, in fact, against any strong emotions. In addition to treatment for malnutrition and infection, the repatriated POW often needs help in communicating his feelings. For years, the POW's efforts to survive have been motivated by the desire to be released and return home, and yet paradoxically coming home proves stressful in many ways. For men whose sense of worth is very low after years of denigration and dehumanization, the "hero's welcome" produces emotional conflict. Communication is blocked; the POW feels that no one except fellow prisoners could possibly comprehend what he has experienced. Guilt, high self-expectations, and continuing anxiety about punishment and criticism are bottled up under an appearance of calm apathy. The bland behavior, shallow and vague statements, and a seeming lack of hurry to get home have been seen in many Americans released from camps in Japan, in Korea, and in Vietnam; these are all defenses that proved adaptive in prison camps, and the POWs continue to use them in coping with the pressures of homecoming.

We are gradually beginning to understand that experiences that threaten the survival of the body and mind continue to affect the individual long after the actual danger is past. For some men who have returned from North Vietnamese prisons, the effects include insomnia, depression, guilt, and nightmares. Some are afraid of crowds, find it difficult to concentrate at work, hoard food, and have flashbacks of prison experiences (Hall and Malone 1976). Abnormal levels of guilt, suggestibility, rates of speech, and need achievement are especially characteristic of men who have experienced prolonged solitary confinement (Hunter 1976).

American servicemen held in Asian camps in other wars have had similar delayed responses to the stress of capture, imprisonment, and then readjustment to civilian life. Not only is there evidence of similar long-term emotional damage, but mortality rates document the impact of this stress on physical health. During the first two years after release from Japanese camps in World War II, the mortality rate among returnees was twice as high as that of other veterans and three times as high as that of POWs who had been in European prisons. The cause of death in many cases could be shown to be only indirectly related to health problems that began during imprisonment. The death rate from heart disease, cancer, fatal accidents, and suicide was twice the expected incidence (Cohen and Cooper 1954).

Studies of U.S. prisoners of war in Korea give similar statistics. Over a period of twelve years after release, the risk of death for these POWs was 40 percent higher than it was for other white Americans of the same age. The major causes of death were accidents, tuberculosis, and cirrhosis of the liver. The returned POW was twice as likely to die in an accident as were young men in the general population, and the rate of suicide was 30 percent higher (Segal, Hunter, and Segal 1976:597–598).

Survival of mind and body under conditions of excessive and abnormal pressures and deprivations required optimal adaptive responses from these POWs. Many could not attain the level of response needed: 35 percent died in prison camps in Japan, and 38 percent in Korea (Moos 1976:305). But those who did survive often seemed to have lowered resistance to new demands in the postwar environment, as if their adaptive capacity had diminished in the years of confinement, malnutrition, and emotional suffering.

When an individual experiences situations that push him or her to the outer limits of a particular adaptive capacity, no matter how wide or narrow that capacity is, we think of that individual as being under stress. Although few of us encounter conditions as stressful as those inflicted on war prisoners, we all experience stress in our lives. The death of someone close to us brings on a stressful sense of loss. Examinations can be very stressful; so can adjusting to a new job. Each of us has emotional and biochemical defenses for coping with these circumstances. These defenses use energy, both the chemical energy of blood sugar and the psychic energy of ego functioning. If this energy becomes drained by excessive or prolonged demand for defense, there is always a risk of lowered resistance to new demands. Further, the very process of defending the body and mind may bring about damage. To understand this paradox, we need to define stress and then examine the physiology of stress.

A Model of Stress

One of the first barriers to understanding stress is that it is tempting to think of it as a thing that causes poor health. With this kind of mind set, one might erroneously think of stress as being analogous to a virus, a bacterium, an injury—just another cause of disability. But stress is not a thing. It is a *process,* involving a complicated series of changes and adjustments in the relationship between the body and the environment. The body works to defend itself against pressures from the environment; it also works to provide energy for self-induced pressures, for example, in strenuous exercise. The stages of this process are shown in figure 7.1.

A **stressor** is a condition or stimulus that elicits a response from an

THE PROCESS OF STRESS

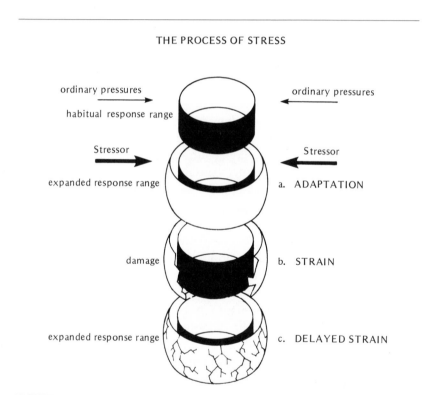

FIGURE 7.1   A model of the stress process. *Stressors,* or nonordinary pressures on the individual, evoke three types of responses: *(a)* the individual's response range expands and *adaptation* occurs; *(b)* the individual does not respond adequately or appropriately and *strain* occurs as physical or emotional damage; *(c)* the individual adapts to the stressor but at the risk of *delayed strain*—for example, increased susceptibility to infection, cardiovascular problems in middle age, or emotional vulnerability.

organism. It involves a level of stimulation that varies from the ordinary, and thus it requires an adjustment by the organism. The variation may be either above *or* below the usual level to which the individual is habituated or the species adapted. Too much heat is a stressor; so is too much cold. Being bored can be as stressful as being too busy. The low-oxygen tension in high altitudes is a stressor because it is a climatic variation requiring physiological adjustments. A virus is a stressor because it is a threat to the body, although its impact clearly depends on the individual's level of resistance. Stressors always have the potential to elicit response, but the nature of the response varies from individual to individual.

In the cultural environment as well, the demands that humans place on one another are stressors. An earthquake or blizzard are natural disasters; a prison camp is a man-made disaster, with as devastating an effect on health as any climatic disturbance. As members of societies, individuals must defend themselves not only against problems coming from the physical and biotic components of their environment, but also against problems arising from imperfect social arrangements. Being fired from a job, failing an important examination, or getting a divorce can have immediate or delayed effects on an individual's emotional and physical health.

Stress is a process in which a relationship between a person and the environment changes as the body attempts to cope with a stressor. There are at least four stages in this process:

1. The stressor is perceived as a threat.
2. The body mobilizes energy for defense.
3. The body attempts to resist or adjust to the stressor.
4. There is either adaptation or strain (maladaptation) in the organism.

In this model, **adaptation** means that the body is able to respond appropriately and adequately to the stressor. This does not imply total success, however. In contrast, **strain** is a sign of inappropriate or inadequate response to a stressor. Following the definition given by the anthropologist John Honigmann (1967:84–85), strain is evidence of struggle, damage, and exhaustion. Ulcers, high blood pressure, and rheumatoid arthritis are believed to be direct signs of strain, the result of a negative outcome of the body's response to a stressor. Many other diseases are believed to be intensified by the stress process: diabetes, hyperthyroidism, hay fever, asthma, tuberculosis, pancreatitis, glaucoma, eczema, and especially a range of cardiovascular problems. These problems usually do not start simply because people respond inappropriately to stressors. Genetic factors and diet often play an important role, but stressors can exacerbate and intensify such problems.

Since stressors vary in their intensity and degree of threat, we should separate environmental pressures into several categories. Changes that disrupt the order of a person's life or physiological functioning altogether can induce *acute stress*. Whether acute stress is short-term or prolonged depends partly on individual response and partly on external circumstances. Environmental pressures that impinge on an individual every day or at frequent intervals without excessive disruption induce *chronic stress*. Categorization here depends on individual response capacity. The person who travels to high-altitude regions for the first time will experience short-term acute stress. The native experiences everyday chronic stress under the same environmental circumstances. Springtime may induce the acute stress of hay fever in some individuals, while others have chronic, mild allergies, and others are not affected at all. The differences lie in variation in physiological responses to pollen, dust, and pollution.

Individual and
Cultural Variation in
Tolerance of Stress

Tolerance of stress varies individually and culturally, and it is probable that we learn to enjoy or cope with certain levels of stimulation depending on our particular childhood environments. For example, from the time of birth, Inuit infants are rarely alone, and they manage to sleep through constant noise of conversation, radios and record players, dogs barking, snowmobiles sputtering, children yelling. When they grow up, Inuit fall asleep easily no matter how noisy it is, but they complain that they feel nervous and cannot sleep when it is too quiet. In contrast, the anthropologist living with an Inuit family may find it very difficult to fall asleep when there is noise but will welcome silence as relaxing and comforting. For the Inuk, silence represents sensory deprivation and is not easily tolerated; for the American, excessive household noise creates sensory overload and problems in sleeping.

Whether noise is comforting or distressing, then, depends on individual background and expectations. What is defined as noise also varies. Inuit enjoy the comfortable clamor of a crowded dwelling, but they often feel uncomfortable in heavy city traffic in Montreal. In contrast, the anthropologist may ignore the noise of the city but find the howling dogs, shouting children, and wailing wind of the arctic village alien and overstimulating. We must be careful about categorizing conditions as stressful. We cannot say that the city induces stress to an equal extent for all people. It depends on what they are used to, what they expect, and whether they have been able in the past to expand their capacity to respond adequately to the stressors of the city.

We tend to think of stress as negative, perhaps because the term most frequently refers to crisis, disaster, and unpleasant life circumstances. Yet changes culturally defined as positive also require *coping* responses—that is, behavior that departs from ordinary or automatic responses to circumstances. Receiving a job promotion, moving to a new city, or getting married are all positive life events. Yet each is a major life change requiring special coping techniques during a period of adjustment. Most of us have the capacity to adjust; it is only when too many life changes occur at once that positive changes can lead to strain.

The stress process is a normal part of life. The person who drives to work in heavy city traffic experiences stress; so does the person who jogs or cycles to work. The Inuit hunter in his kayak, the Persian farmer threshing wheat, the Peruvian working in a mine at 19,000 feet—all experience stress as their bodies expend energy to cope with problems that arise unexpectedly and problems that are a constant part of environmental pressures. Whether the body functions normally or abnormally in the stress process depends on the intensity of the challenge or threat to the body, the duration of the threat, and most important, the adaptation capacity of the mind and body. This capacity derives from the person's heredity, nutrition, health history, and general psychological makeup.

Seeking out Stress

We usually think of stress as something that happens *to* us—a difficult work assignment, a death in the family, adjusting to a new climate. Yet there are also stress experiences that the individual seeks out, such as a vigorous tennis game. As the competition intensifies, the heart beats faster, adrenaline is released and increases energy, and the body's alertness and endurance increase. After the game, the person feels either exhausted or invigorated, sore or very fit, depending on the induced intensity and the body's capacity to provide the needed energy.

Hans Selye, the biochemist who pioneered in studies of disease and stress, reminds us that stress is a part of what makes life challenging and interesting: "a game of tennis or even a passionate kiss can produce considerable stress without causing conspicuous damage" (Selye 1956:53). As joggers well know, it is beneficial to push one's body to the limits of one's present capacity, to the point of mixed pleasure and pain. The afterglow of jogging indicates the high level of biochemical response to self-induced stress. Athletes often push to the limits, not merely to win but also to test their own capacity and to expand their ability to tolerate stress.

Some societies seek stress for therapeutic or religious purposes, deliberately pushing the body and the mind past normal limits in order to experience visions, a sense of unusual power and life-energy, and restoration of balance within the body. The trance dance of the !Kung Bushmen illustrates this ritual use of the stress process. The dancing is done, the !Kung believe, to heat up the medicine that is in their bodies and that can be transferred from dancers to patients. The dancing usually goes on for at least twelve hours through the night. The dancers go into a trance twice during the night, around midnight and just after dawn. Sometimes the dances continue for thirty-six hours, with individuals participating in four- to six-hour shifts.

Through the stimulation of the constant rhythm of the music, through hyperventilation in breathing, and through autosuggestion, the dancers easily enter a state of trance. The stress of excessive stimulation, called *sensory overload,* will induce an altered state of consciousness in most human beings. Without using any drugs, the !Kung experience dizziness, disorientation, hallucinations, and muscle spasms. In some contexts, we would view such symptoms as alarming evidence of illness; in this context, we see that the dancers strive to reach a trance state in order to transmit healing power and protection to patients (Lee 1967).

Both sensory overload and sensory deprivation are used in the rituals of many ethnomedical systems to induce altered states of consciousness. Trance can be induced either through rhythmic over-stimulation or through extremely low stimulation, as in meditation techniques. In meditation, the rate of metabolism drops sharply, and there are changes in brain wave functioning. The level of anxiety goes down, as indicated by increased resistance of the skin to electric current and lowered levels of lactate concentration in the blood (Wallace and Benson 1972). This information suggests that self-inducement of physiological responses that clinically resemble part of the stress process may in fact have some health benefits in coping with

(a) (b)

FIGURE 7.2 After hours of dancing, this !Kung San of southern Africa has entered a self-induced trance without use of drugs or other stimulants (a). He transmits "medicine," or healing power, through his hands to a woman and child (b) to give them protection against forces that bring illness.
Photos by Irven DeVore, Anthro-Photo.

other stressors such as anxiety or physical tension. This is an example of how inducing stress can be a defense against other stressors. This may seem a contradiction, but only if you fail to remember that the stress process has several possible outcomes. Some kinds of stressors can damage the body, while others stimulate the body and expand its overall adaptive capacity. Some stressors come from the external environment, while others are self-induced. Stress cannot be avoided, but how we use stress and respond to external stressors affects our overall health. Hans Selye (1976) reminds that stress ". . . cannot be avoided, since just staying alive creates some demand for life-maintaining energy. . . . Complete freedom from stress can be expected only after death" (p. 15). Selye came to this conclusion after forty years of research on the subject; in the next section we consider the fundamental findings of that research.

UNDERSTANDING THE PHYSIOLOGY OF STRESS

Selye's General Adaptation Syndrome

Hans Selye developed the concept of stress through many years of research in endocrinology at McGill University and the University of Montreal. As Selye tells his story in *The Stress of Life* (1956), he first became aware of the signs of stress while he was a medical student at the University of Prague in 1925. Patients exhibited to the class displayed a cluster of symptoms: diffuse aches and pains in the joints, loss of appetite, intestinal disturbances, fever, an enlarged spleen or liver, inflamed tonsils, and skin rash. Since the patients had been chosen to demonstrate the early stages of different infectious diseases, Selye found it impressive that the patients had such similar symptoms. Because the characteristic signs of each specific illness were absent, no one could be certain of the diagnosis or course of treatment. The signs that *were* obvious to everyone were disregarded because they were nonspecific. Fever, aches, loss of appetite, and so on were dismissed as the syndrome of "just being sick."

Although the professor and other students considered such early symptoms to be of no importance diagnostically, Selye was curious. He was just eighteen years old at the time (having done his premedical studies with a private tutor), and perhaps because of his youth and inexperience he was able to see and question a pattern that his older, more conventional classmates missed.

Ten years later, Selye encountered another puzzle while doing research on sex hormones. When he injected extracts prepared from animal ovaries and placenta into rats, the test animals showed tissue changes. These changes were (1) enlargement of the adrenal cortex and increase in discharge of hormones into the blood; (2) shrinking of the thymus, spleen, and lymph nodes, all made up of white blood cells that give resistance in disease and injury; (3) almost complete disappearance of eosinophil cells, a type of white blood cell; and (4) the appearance of bleeding, deep ulcers in the stomach and duodenum.

Selye thought he had discovered a new ovarian hormone and continued injecting substances into rats in an attempt to isolate the hormone in pure form. Many kinds of extracts produced the same kinds of tissue changes. The more impure the extract, the more severe the symptoms. Selye suddenly realized that it was not a hormone, but rather some toxic factor, that produced these effects. When injections of formalin produced the same effects, he was certain that he had simply been producing damage by injecting a variety of impure and irritating substances.

At first, Selye was convinced that his experiments had been a total failure. He had not discovered a new hormone, and he had wasted time and money. But he continued to brood about the meaning of the rats' response to the various extracts. He remembered his curiosity as a medical student about the syndrome of "just being sick," and it occurred to him that he might have accidentally elicited a similar nonspecific and stereotyped response in his rats. Possibly the same pattern might occur in many types of diseases. He decided to study this question systematically despite the criticism and discouragement that his proposal received from senior colleagues. One of them even protested: "You have now decided to spend your entire life studying the pharmacology of dirt!" (1956:28). One of the few scientists who did support his plans was Sir Frederick Banting, the discoverer of insulin. Selye writes: "I often wonder whether I could have stuck to my guns without his encouragement" (1956:29).

As he continued experiments, Selye found that many substances stimulate the typical response syndrome to irritation. Stimulation of the adrenal cortex, shrinking of thymicolymphatic structures, and intestinal ulcers are predictable responses to injections of adrenaline or insulin, to excessive cold or heat, to X rays, to forced and prolonged exercise, and a variety of other noxious conditions and agents. In addition, the test animal loses weight, its blood volume goes down, and the white blood cell count is low. In effect, the body is using energy and mobilizing resistance to cope with irritation or harsh conditions. Selye called this response an *alarm reaction*. In the second phase, the *stage of resistance*, body weight returns to normal. The blood becomes more diluted, the adrenal cortex builds up a reserve of

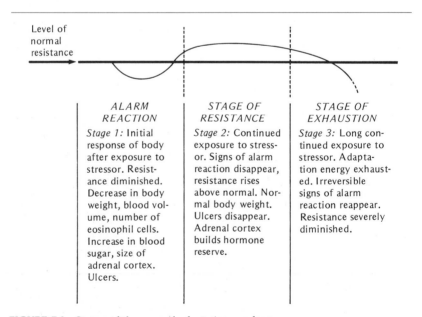

ALARM REACTION	STAGE OF RESISTANCE	STAGE OF EXHAUSTION
Stage 1: Initial response of body after exposure to stressor. Resistance diminished. Decrease in body weight, blood volume, number of eosinophil cells. Increase in blood sugar, size of adrenal cortex. Ulcers.	*Stage 2:* Continued exposure to stressor. Signs of alarm reaction disappear, resistance rises above normal. Normal body weight. Ulcers disappear. Adrenal cortex builds hormone reserve.	*Stage 3:* Long continued exposure to stressor. Adaptation energy exhausted. Irreversible signs of alarm reaction reappear. Resistance severely diminished.

FIGURE 7.3   Stages of the general adaptation syndrome.

SOURCE: As adapted from the book *Stress without Distress.* Copyright © 1974 by Hans Selye, M.D. Reproduced by permission of J. B. Lippincott Company.

hormones, and the ulcers begin to heal. If the animal continues to experience stress, a third phase develops in which resistance goes down and the animal may die. This is the *stage of exhaustion*. Body weight drops, blood volume goes down, and blood sugar levels are low. Ulcers return, and the animal has little resistance to microbes.

Selye called the entire response pattern the **general adaptation syndrome.** The animal is experiencing stress throughout the three stages (figure 7.3), but the body's response differs in each stage. The third stage is not inevitable; only the most severe or prolonged kinds of conditions lead to exhaustion and death.

The Role of Hormones in Stress and Disease

The body defends itself during the stress process by producing *inflammatory hormones,* which provide defense against various stressors such as pathogens and injury, and by producing *anti-inflammatory hormones,* which limit the extent of inflammation against stressors. In many cases, it is the balance and interaction of these two types of defense that affect the relative resistance of the body during the stress process. These hormones are released from the adrenal cortex. Inflammatory hormones are stimulated by a substance from the pituitary gland, STH (somatrophic, or "growth," hormone). Anti-inflammatory hormones are stimulated by ACTH (adrenocorticotrophic hormone). ACTH also induces the secretion of hormones, which in turn induce the formation of glycogen, which can be converted into sugar and provide energy (Selye 1976).

Inflammation is a normal response to injury. When the tissue around an injured area swells, reddens, and becomes warm, this indicates dilation of blood vessels and proliferation of connective tissue in the affected area. The number of white blood cells in the area increases, and the lymphatic system works to destroy bacteria and dead tissue, and to allow repair of tissue. Inflammation is not the same thing as infection, although symptoms are similar. Infection is invasion by a pathogenic agent; inflammation is tissue response to injury. The suffix *-itis* denotes inflammation, as in appendicitis, colitis, hepatitis, arthritis, dermatitis, cervicitis, and dozens of other terms.

Inflammation defends tissues around wounds, and it helps to contain noxious microbes (as in appendicitis) and irritating foods (as in gastritis). But inflammation can occur in response to relatively harmless stressors. In hay fever, arthritis, rheumatic fever, and even extreme swelling after a bee sting, the body's defense is exaggerated. Under normal circumstances, the action of anti-inflammatory hormones will prevent excessive and self-damaging inflammation, but this safeguard can become derailed. The overall maintenance of health depends in part on a balance between inflammatory and anti-inflammatory reactions, depending on the specific effects of stressors. Inappropriate regulation of the body's biochemical defenses can contribute to disease as much as do genetic factors, external pathogens, and nutritional deficiencies.

How specifically does imbalance between inflammatory and anti-inflammatory hormones contribute to disease? A demonstration of the process is provided by an experiment Selye developed called the inflammatory-pouch test, illustrated in figure 7.4. The method is to

A

Airsack on the back of a rat

B

C

D

Normal tissue is digested by gastric juice.

Inflamed tissue of pouch is normally not digested by gastric juice.

Stress of frustrating forced immobilization causes perforating peptic ulcer on the pouch. Inflammatory fluid escapes.

FIGURE 7.4   Illustration of Selye's inflammatory-pouch test.

SOURCE: Modified from Hans Selye, *The Stress of Life* (New York: McGraw-Hill, 1956), pp. 152, 181, by permission.

produce a pocket of air under the skin of a rat. If gastric juice is injected into the sack, the skin is normally damaged by the digestive action of the gastric juice, and an ulcer forms. But if an irritant such as oil is first injected into the cavity, the normal response of the animal involves changes in the connective tissue surrounding the pocket. Inflammation produces a kind of barricade, and when gastric juice is injected after the inflammatory layer is present, the digestion of tissue does not occur (figure 7.4c). When an animal with an inflammatory layer is held down and not allowed to move, however, there is digestion of tissue by gastric juice and the rat develops a perforating ulcer on its back. Being held down is frustrating for a rat—it struggles, shows signs of anger, and presumably experiences stress. Because of the body's struggle against this frustration, there is increased secretion of anti-inflammatory hormones, and the inflammatory barrier is weakened. Similarly, in human beings the discharge of anti-inflammatory hormones may break down the barriers that normally keep ulcers from developing or that keep chronic ulcers in check.

Stress does not always evoke a pathological response, and it may in fact provide what is called *cross-resistance*. Pretreatment with one stressor may increase the body's resistance to other stressors. Selye demonstrated this through a similar inflammatory-pouch experiment (figure 7.5). He used two groups—one with a weak irritant of diluted oil in the air sack, the second with a strong irritant of concentrated oil. Both groups were subjected to the frustration of immobilization. In rats with the weak irritant (a), the response to stress cured the local irritation by inhibiting inflammation (c). In animals treated with the strong irritant (b), a strong inflammatory barricade was formed but did not hold up under stress, and the surrounding tissues were destroyed (d).

The concept of cross-resistance has been put to use in treating human beings. Normally, people suffering from rheumatoid arthritis can be treated with drugs that reduce inflammation, but in severe cases, this treatment may not work. Insulin shock treatments, however, which stimulate the patient's stress response and production of anti-inflammatory hormones, can bring relief.

Thus far we have considered the role of hormones in stress and the research findings of Hans Selye. But stress involves other physiological variables that we must consider in order to understand fully how stress is related to environmental adaptation. The research of Walter B.

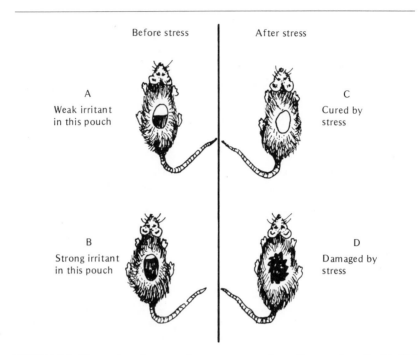

FIGURE 7.5   Illustration of cross-resistance to stress depending on strength of initial
irritant.

SOURCE: Modified from Hans Selye, *The Stress of Life* (New York: McGraw-Hill,
1956), p. 155, by permission.

Cannon helps us understand how our mammalian heritage is related
to our capacity to respond to stressors and the reasons our natural
responses may prove maladaptive when environments change.

Cannon's Concept of the Fight-or-Flight Response

Human beings have survived as hunters and gatherers for more than
99 percent of the last 3 to 4 million years, and human physiology is still
geared to the special demands of a hunting way of life. When the
hunter encounters a dangerous situation—say, a lion or a snake in his
path—his body responds automatically in preparation for action. His
blood pressure increases, his heart and breathing rates rise, blood

flows to his muscles, and he is ready to run away or to fight the predator.

What creates the quick burst of energy and alertness of the muscles and brain? Certain hormones, epinephrine (adrenalin) and norepinephrine, raise the blood pressure and stimulate the release of glycogen from the liver to raise the blood sugar levels. Other hormones act to mobilize fat reserves and release them into the blood stream in the form of free fatty acids that the muscles can use as fuel. These automatic **fight-or-flight responses** are found in most species of mammals. The ability to respond quickly to danger and to use biochemical reserves for mobilization of energy has been selected in the evolution of mammals, as has been the ability to form mental associations between past experiences of pain and new situations of danger. These associations combine memory with expectation. They are experienced physiologically as emotions, particularly fear, excitement, and anxiety.

The evolutionary basis of fear and its counterpart, anger, was of particular interest to the physiologist Walter Cannon, who called fear "the premonition of pain" and studied emotion in laboratory animals during the early part of this century (Cannon 1929, 1932). Cannon was generally interested in how the body protects itself, and he is well known for developing the concept of homeostasis, an idea that influenced Selye's early investigations.

We experience fear and rage subjectively as two different kinds of emotions, but physiologically there is little difference in the body's response, except that the adrenal gland secretes epinephrine during fear and norepinephrine during anger. The hormones are chemically very similar; epinephrine raises blood pressure by increasing cardiac output while norepinephrine does the same by constricting the blood vessels. Whether the emotion is intense fear or anger, it is the *sympathetic* nervous system that initially goes into action during the alarm reaction. The nerve fibers transmit impulses that widen the pupils of the eyes, direct more blood to the muscles and brain, accelerate the heartbeat, raise the blood sugar, inhibit intestinal activity, and in general prepare the body for an emergency. This is basically what happens during the fight-or-flight response, and it will occur whether the person is really being chased by a lion or is simply experiencing intense fear as if his or her life were in danger.

After the real or symbolic danger is over, during the stage of resistance, the *parasympathetic* system begins to operate. This system, generally opposite to the sympathetic system, acts to conserve body resources and energy levels. It constricts the pupils, protecting the eyes from light; it lowers blood pressure and heart rate; it encourages digestion by increasing salivary secretion and digestive juice secretion in the stomach; and it causes the bladder and colon to empty waste products. These two nervous systems almost always work together in sequence or in a complementary manner, and the organism's response during long-term danger, emotion, or stress oscillates between the two patterns—mobilization of energy versus conservation of energy.

The Body's Response to Symbolic Danger

Most humans today do not subsist as hunters or live in danger from predators. The technological relationship between human groups and their environment has changed radically and far more rapidly than has the body's physiological capacity to respond to perceived danger. The body continues to respond to *any* kind of threat according to the pattern selected for in evolution up to the present. Despite the protest of the cerebral cortex, which rationally reminds one that the airplane is certainly not likely to crash, or that criticism from one's boss is not really life-endangering, or that one will surely survive an examination, the body responds to threatening situations as if it were in danger. The amount of glucose and lipids (fats) available as energy to the body increases. The blood coagulability increases to prepare for possible injury, and blood pressure increases as if to prepare for combat. Probably all of us have experienced the subjective sensations that accompany this mobilization of energy—the hot, tingly flash, the unusual alertness of the senses, the feeling of physical strength and exceptional coordination, the sudden dryness of the mouth and constriction of the breath.

But what happens when action does not take place, when the person neither fights nor flees but simply endures the plane ride, the criticism, or the examination? What happens when the fats released are not metabolized, or when the rise in blood pressure does not lead to high stroke volume and decreased vascular resistance as it would during physical action? Energy has been released in the body in response to a stressor, but if physical action in the immediate situation is inappropriate or impossible, the biochemical constituents of that energy are not used. Lipid mobilization will occur whether the threat requires physical action or not. When the immediate situation precludes full use of this energy (and even more important, when the individual does not use the energy at all, even in sports), excess fat may be deposited in the internal lining of the arteries. Over time, this pattern may contribute to atherosclerosis, a form of arteriosclerosis in which fatty deposits serve to narrow and obstruct the arteries.

Atherosclerosis is one of several stress-related conditions that contribute to cardiovascular diseases. Half the deaths of American men, 40–60, are due to cardiovascular disease, and the United States ranks 40th in the world for male longevity. One researcher comments, "We have returned unwittingly to the days of the great pandemics where one quarter or a half of the population died of one disease. This time, the pandemic is a degenerative rather than an epidemic disease" (Jean Mayer, as quoted in M. T. Newman 1975:246–247).

People whose work involves little physical exertion but considerable emotional pressure particularly run the risk of developing cardiovascular disease, and personality factors may increase this risk. For example, two groups of men who worked in similar occupations were compared in terms of three variables: their attitudes toward work, how much fatty acid in the form of cholesterol they had in their blood serum, and their history of cardiovascular problems. Men who were very competitive and also showed a sense of urgency about time had a greater increase in norepinephrine secretion, higher serum cholesterol levels, and faster blood clotting time during working hours than did men who were not as competitive or as concerned about time. This first group of men responded to work conditions as if they were in an emergency situation, and it is not particularly surprising that this group had a higher incidence of clinical coronary disease (Dubos 1965:32).

The ability to release glucose and lipids for use in situations requiring quick energy was selected for in evolution by differential mortality. The ability is also advantageous in ordinary physical work and chronic stress situations. But this mobilization capacity can be maladaptive for individuals who do not use the energy released. Over the years, serum cholesterol can build up, particularly in individuals who are high-achievers, independent, and continually striving against what they perceive to be barriers and opposition (Wolff 1968).

Cardiovascular diseases are the major cause of death in the United States, more than twice as high in incidence as cancer for both men and women. Many stress factors contribute to this high rate of heart disease. Sedentary work is often considered more prestigious than physical labor, and many urbanites have either little opportunity or little inclination for regular exercise. We have many small, self-induced stressors in our culture, for example, the daily stimulants of nicotine, caffeine, and sugar. We tend to value the personality traits of the high-achiever and to reward people who are ambitious and work very hard. Exercise patterns, diet, values, and general stress levels contribute toward inappropriate or inadequate use of the physiological resources intended to help the body cope with the physical and symbolic threats of the environment.

We do not mean to give the impression that hunting peoples are completely free from stress-related diseases simply because they are more physically active than people in an industrialized society tend to be. All cultures can at times create fears and anxieties, and these anxieties may spark the physiological stages of the stress process, with definite health consequences for the individual. The next health profile deals with a dramatic example of how stress can lead to illness and death.

PROFILE: MAGICAL DEATH

Physicians in almost every part of the world from West Africa to California have from time to time encountered a very special kind of patient, the sorcery victim. A person who comes to believe that he or she has been attacked by a sorcerer or has broken an absolute taboo may believe that death is inevitable. No matter how the Western physician tries to treat the terrified patient, the patient becomes weaker each day and may actually die within a relatively short period. Magical death is a fact, but how it happens is still a mystery. Can fear kill?

One account, written by a physician working with Australian aborigines in the 1920s, gives a sense of the acute terror of the victim:

> The man who discovers that he is being boned by any enemy is, indeed, a pitiable sight. He stands aghast, with his eyes staring at the treacherous pointer, and with his hands lifted as though to ward off the lethal medium, which he imagines is pouring into his body. His cheeks blanch and his eyes become glassy and the expression of his face becomes horribly distorted . . . . He attempts to shriek but usually the sound chokes in his throat, and all that one might see is froth at his mouth. His body begins to tremble and the muscles twist involuntarily. He sways backwards and falls to the ground, and after a short time appears to be in a swoon; but soon after he writhes as if in mortal agony, and covering his face with his hands, begins to moan. After a while he becomes very composed and crawls to his wurley. From this time onwards he sickens and frets, refusing to eat and keeping aloof from the daily affairs of the tribe. Unless help is forthcoming in the shape of a countercharm administered by the hands of the Nangarri, or medicine-man, his death is only a matter of a comparatively short time. If the coming of the medicine-man is opportune he might be saved. *Cited in Cannon (1942:181)*

Skeptics may ask whether such an individual has been poisoned or whether he is shamming. In some situations, either of these suggestions may be correct. But usually the idea of poisoning is ruled out because a surprisingly rapid recovery will occur if the medicine man uses a countercharm. And too many cases of death are verified by physicians to consider all examples hoaxes. Still, the detailed physiological observations to interpret the deaths are missing. One physician did keep clinical records on a victim hospitalized in a military clinic in Papua New Guinea, and the details of the case are as follows (Wolff 1968:199–200).

When the patient was admitted to the hospital, he explained that he was a victim of magic because he had broken a taboo. He had been treated as if excommunicated by the tribe, and his relatives totally avoided and neglected him. Upon admission, he did not appear to be severely ill, but he was clearly depressed and apathetic. He refused to eat and would drink no fluids, remaining inert on his bed. His pulse rate was 65, and his blood pressure was only slightly elevated. The doctors were able to get a potion from the tribe, which they assured would bring back his health. He tried some of the mixture but then rejected it.

Over a few days he became increasingly apathetic and seemed detached, barely moving. His skin and mouth were dry, his urine had a high specific gravity, and he stopped defecating altogether.

FIGURE 7.6 In many cultures, successfully surviving to an old age is by itself sufficient evidence of supernatural power. Even without any malicious behavior on his part, an old man may be presumed to be capable of sorcery or witchcraft.

Photo by William H. Townsend.

He received penicillin, arsenicals, and digitalis. No one came to see him, and he showed no interest in other patients. He was found dead on the ninth day after admission. The autopsy showed cirrhosis of the liver, enlargement of the spleen, and widespread arteriosclerosis. The spleen, kidneys, pancreas, and liver showed damage, but no immediate cause of death was apparent. The doctors decided that his death was suicide through voluntary rejection of fluids. His tribe, however, believed he died because he had broken a taboo.

In 1942, Walter Cannon attempted to explain magical death in terms of the response of the autonomic nervous system to extreme emotion. He suggested that the victim enters a state of shock. The mobilization of the sympathetic nervous system through the discharge of epinephrine induced by intense fear would prepare the individual for defense. But if cultural belief suggested that resistance was futile, the continuous production of epinephrine without action might lead to a state of shock. The lack of food and water would be contributing physical factors.

Cannon suggested that his hypothesis could be tested by observing the symptoms of sorcery victims. He predicted that the observer would see a rapid and "thready" pulse, cool and moist skin, low blood pressure, high blood sugar, and other signs of shock. And he urged that any observer with the opportunity to witness magical death "conduct the simpler tests before the victim's last gasp" (Cannon 1942:181).

Another physiologist who became interested in the sudden death phenomenon, Curt Richter, admitted that although he had never observed a voodoo victim, he had seen sudden and mysterious death among laboratory animals. In the course of carrying out experiments on stress, he found that some rats could swim for as long as eighty-one hours, while others died within five to ten minutes (Richter 1957). Some swam on the surface for a short time, less than a minute, and then they dove to the bottom of the tank and drowned without coming to the surface once. Wild rats, who are much fiercer and more aggressive than the domesticated or hybrid species, always died within fifteen minutes, while three-fourths of the domesticated rats managed to swim between forty and sixty hours. The wild rats especially showed a negative reaction to having their whiskers clipped and being immersed suddenly in the water.

Why did the wild rats die so suddenly without any struggle? The physiological reactions of these rats could be measured by attaching electrodes to the animals and taking electrocardiograms. The various diagnostic tests showed that their hearts slowed down, respiration and body temperature dropped radically, and the heart quickly stopped in a dilated state, the cavities filled with blood. Richter concluded that the rats died from overstimulation of the parasympathetic system. It seemed as if the rats simply gave up and were reacting physiologically to the hopelessness of the situation. It was possible, however, to condition the wild rats to the situation by taking them out of the water after immersion. After a few trials, the animals learned that the situation was not hopeless and they were able to swim for a long time.

On the basis of this research, Richter suggested that voodoo victims do not die in shock through overstimulation of the sympathetic system, but rather that they die because their feelings of hopelessness lead to excessive responses of the parasympathetic nervous system.

A third explanation of voodoo death has been given by the anthropologist Barbara Lex (1977), who has suggested that so-called voodoo death is caused by dysfunction of the autonomic nervous system. She develops her idea around the concept of **tuning,** the sensitization of centers in the nervous system through stimulation of the sympathetic or parasympathetic divisions. This stimulation can be produced by certain types of mental activity, by the use of drugs, or through direct experimental stimulation.

Tuning has three stages. In the first stage, the usual pattern of sympathetic–parasympathetic interaction occurs—response in one system increases, while response in the other decreases. In the second stage, the sympathetic responses reverse, and extreme parasympathetic responses set in. The muscles become relaxed and brain rhythms synchronize. But if stimulation continues, a third phase can develop with simultaneous excitations of *both* systems. Evidence of simultaneous excitations, also called *mixed discharges,* is seen in neuroses or psychoses and sometimes in the brain wave patterns of people practicing Zen, yoga, and transcendental meditation. The individual moves beyond an analytic, logical state into an altered state of consciousness in which suggestibility is higher than usual. This suggestibility may lead to a mystical experience or deep relaxation, but it may also lead to intense anxiety and altered perception. Lex suggests that a tuned individual "is by definition uncritical and therefore ripe for the suggestion that he or she will die by magical means" (1977:330).

We may presume that a person's first reaction upon hearing his or her "death sentence" is an acute sympathetic response, as Cannon suggested, with normal inhibition of the parasympathetic system. But the intensity of this phase moves the individual into stage-two tuning. Perceiving the situation as hopeless increases the depression and the intensity of the parasympathetic response, as in the rats whose hearts slowed down. Continued stimulation will elicit the third stage of mixed discharges. In the victim of magical death, intense fear may be adequate stimulation to evoke this phase of tuning. The behavior of others reinforces the sense of helplessness; some societies actually carry out funeral rituals for the person while she or he is still alive. If the victim is already in poor health, fear may simply reduce the body's resistance to pathogens even further. Loss of appetite and difficulty in ingesting food and water contribute to weakness and dehydration.

Critics of these explanations suggest that we do not have much of a sample of magical death cases, nor can we be fully certain of the reliability of reports. Some critics suspect poisoning or prior infectious disease (with sorcery being an after-the-fact explanation). *Kuru,* for example, is now known to be caused by a slow virus that affects the central nervous system. But from the victim's perspective, the cause of *kuru* is sorcery.

The question remains: Can stress kill, or does it simply increase the risk of death from other causes? The custom of sorcery is absent in mainstream U.S. society, but our culture creates situations that produce feelings of helplessness in individuals. Old-age homes are one setting in which people feel helpless, and it might be worthwhile to examine cases of sudden death in old people as instances of the stress response.

STRESS AND HEALING

The magical death profile is an example of how magic and medicine intersect in a non-Western society. Ethnomedical practices often prove effective when the patient strongly believes in the magical power of the healer, as shown in the Australian healer's ability to reverse his patient's acute stress.

Ethnomedical practices often attempt to reduce emotional stress in the sick person through the reassurance of familiar rituals and the support of family members and the community, but sometimes curers deliberately attempt to induce stress as part of the healing process. The principle here is that the body is able to heal itself. This idea is certainly not new in medicine; more than 2000 years ago Hippocrates taught his students in Greece that disease is the toil of the body to restore itself to normal and that there is a "healing force of nature, which cures from within" (Selye 1956:11). Old medical practices such as inducing fever with herbs or irritating potions, deliberately exposing mentally disturbed people to infectious disease, flogging and throwing patients into cold water, and bloodletting may have activated the body's response to stress as a way of alleviating chronic disease. Such techniques were not always successful. Bloodletting, for example, contributed to George Washington's death (Landy 1977:130). Bloodletting is still used in treating hematomas and embolisms by European physicians, evidence of its empirical value in dealing with certain clinical problems (Crapanzano, personal communication).

Many of the therapeutic practices of non-Western societies may also be of more empirical value than we have realized, because they use the principle of cross-resistance. For example, a modern Comanche medicine woman in Oklahoma treats victims of witchcraft by sucking blood out of small incisions (Jones 1972:96). The symptoms of an illness believed to be caused by witchcraft include spasms and contractions of the arms and hands. The illness is probably due to a deficiency of calcium and vitamin D, and bloodletting may induce an alarm reaction by the body that leads into the stage of resistance and reduction of the symptoms.

Bloodletting is part of many healing rituals. Members of the

Hamadsha, a ritual healing cult in Morocco, slash their own foreheads during ceremonies with pocketknives, axes, iron balls, clubs embedded with nails, and water jugs. They draw blood, but the wounds are normally superficial and do not require treatment. During ceremonies, the participants also go into self-induced trances. Drumming, chanting, hand clapping, inhalation of incense, hyperventilation, and exhaustion brought on by long periods of dancing all add up to massive sensory overload (Crapanzano 1973:195–210, 231–234).

The Hamadsha rituals help relieve many illnesses, especially those related to anxiety, physical tension, and emotional stress. For example, cult members may be bothered by paresthetic pains, which are feelings of numbness, prickling, and tingling. After dancing and going into trance, the members wake with a feeling of revitalization and relief from these pains (Crapanzano 1973:210). A more serious illness is attack by a *jinn*, a spirit, indicated by paralysis of the face, convulsions, and sudden (hysterical) blindness or deafness, or other forms of paralysis. Excessive anxiety and hyperventilation can cause these symptoms by raising the pH level of the blood higher than normal (respiratory alkalosis). People attacked by a *jinn* often recover from these symptoms overnight if they dance; they may experience aftereffects of stiffness, depression, and a lack of energy, however. Using our knowledge of the stages of alarm, resistance, and exhaustion (see figure 7.2), we can see that respiratory alkalosis and paralysis are an alarm reaction to the stressor of anxiety, a recurrent psychological feature of the Moroccans who belong to the Hamadsha. Through a variety of sensory overload techniques, the dancers induce stress, which brings on a stage of resistance to the initial psychosomatic illness of paralysis. The depression and temporary fatigue experienced after trance are analogous to the strain evidenced in the stage of exhaustion; since the initial stressor is removed, however, there is little serious danger that this strain will lead to permanent damage.

Ethnomedical systems employ the stress principle in many ways. Fasting and abstinence from water, salt, or other specific substances; seclusion and meditation; and long periods without sleep involve the stress of deprivation. Prolonged dancing, drumming, and singing in synchronization with the heart beat or alpha waves of the brain, feasting, and using stimulants, hallucinogens, or alcohol are all sources of sensory overload that many societies use as therapeutic

(a)

(b)

FIGURE 7.7   (a) A performance of the *hadra* ritual by a Hamadsha group in Morocco. The man with his head exposed is slashing it with a knife. (b) The men of this Hamadsha group are in *hal* or trance, while the woman in the striped *jallaba* has joined the line to "come down" from trance.

SOURCE: Vincent Crapanzano, *The Hamadsha* (Berkeley: University of California Press, 1973). Photos: Vincent Crapanzano. Reproduced by permission of the University of California Press and the author.

practices. Emetics, purgatives, and sweat baths are regularly pre-scribed by Native American healers. The Sanio of New Guinea rub irritating nettles on the body of a sick person.

An example from Western society of how stress can induce healing comes from the case of Amsterdam Jews imprisoned in Nazi concen-tration camps (Wolf and Goodell 1968:145–146). A physician who treated these individuals both before and after the war kept careful medical records and could document that a number of these successful and competitive merchants and professional people suffered from peptic ulcers before the war. After the shock of capture and incarcera-tion, the symptoms disappeared. But after these individuals were released and resumed as normal a life as possible in postwar condi-tions, the ulcers returned.

Why should the ulcers essentially disappear during the terrible stress of trying to survive in a concentration camp? We know that the acute stress of air raids, extensive skin burns, wounds, surgery, and other crises can bring on ulcers (Selye 1976). Why would concentration camps not be equally stressful? One answer might lie in the survivors' coping responses, which varied widely. Some individuals became apathetic, submissive, and even identified their guards as father figures, to be obeyed and admired (Moos 1976:334). Others limited their expectations to narrow goals consistent with the camp environ-ment; just acquiring a little extra food was a triumph (Wolf and Goodell 1968:145). Another coping strategy was psychological removal, insu-lating oneself from an awareness of stress. One survivor recalled: "We talked together as friends about concrete things, not about feelings. I think all of the feelings were blocked; if you felt too much, you felt bad. To feel was to feel unpleasant, better not to feel at all, don't think about it" (Dimsdale 1976:354).

The one key aspect of these various coping strategies is that the individual stopped struggling against hopeless circumstances or generalized frustrations. Struggle was rarely possible in concentration camps; the prisoner who openly defied guards had little chance of surviving. Too great a passivity and withdrawal however, would bring on the "musselmann" syndrome, a total cessation of feeling or awareness that proved a form of suicide since the individual would be killed or would die rapidly from infection (Dimsdale 1976:355). But an appropriate degree of fatalism reduced the level of stress to a barely tolerable point, and this reduction may have indirectly facilitated the healing of ulcers or the remission of symptoms. After the war, those who survived had to cope with many of the same emotional conflicts and delayed physical effects as did American POWs, and in their struggle to cope, the ulcers returned.

STRESS IN THE PHYSICAL AND BIOTIC ENVIRONMENT

Nutritional Stress

Children deprived of adequate calories and needed vitamins, minerals, and protein are often retarded in physical and cognitive development, as chapters 5 and 6 have documented. Malnutrition can also be seen as a form of stress. One of the ways that the body responds to malnutrition is that the adrenal cortex produces anti-inflammatory glucocorticoids. This typical stress response helps in the adaptation to poor nourishment, but it hinders the production of antibodies, the defense against infection (Stini 1975b:66–67). Both chronic and acute stress of malnutrition contribute to "wear and tear" on the body, to use Selye's term, so that adaptability to other stressors is reduced. The child shown in the opening photograph of this chapter, for example, managed to survive the extreme malnutrition of the Sahel drought, but not without considerable risk of continued vulnerability to infection and emotional strain.

An *over*nourished, obese child is also under stress. Being overweight puts a burden on the circulatory system especially, and the physiological compensations made by the body are costly. An overnourished infant adapts to dietary excess by developing excess fat cells. These fat cells remain throughout life; even later dieting shrinks rather than eliminates them (M. T. Newman 1975:245).

The psychological adjustments to obesity are also costly. In a society where obesity is stigmatized, an obese child is under emotional stress.

Behavioral response to the stigma of obesity often involves a curious circularity. The child feels ostracized and rejected by peers, and so he or she seeks out food as a source of comfort and nurturance. In some cases, eating may be a way to release anger as well. The response pattern may ease emotional stress temporarily, but the child continues to damage the body by overeating and to perpetuate the stigmatizing condition. In this example, defense of the ego takes priority over defense of the body in the individual's adaptive responses.

Climatic Stress

In earlier chapters, we considered how humans cope with the stressors of unusual cold and the low-oxygen tension of high altitude. Climatic extremes are a special kind of stressor. Like malnutrition, they usually induce chronic stress, to which most individuals can adequately respond without evidence of strain, provided additional stressors do not accumulate and impinge simultaneously or in rapid succession on the individual.

The responses of populations to extreme heat have been less well documented than responses to cold and high altitude, but desert environments do involve a number of stressors. In a review of studies on populations in the Sahara Desert, Briggs (1975) notes that climatic stressors include high solar and ground radiation, extreme variation in temperature, high aridity, dry winds, and small amounts of poor-quality water. The most critical problem is to avoid dehydration.

The body responds to heat through sweating, a reduced flow of urine, and regulation of the rate of salt elimination in balance with salt consumption. During exposure to heat, the blood is diverted to the skin and muscles of the limbs, and cardiac output increases. As the individual becomes acclimatized to the desert, the symptoms of increased heart rate and rise in body temperature gradually decrease, although the person may develop chronic low blood pressure.

As in the Arctic, clothing provides an important cultural buffer against environmental stress in hot, dry climates. A nude person attains maximum sweat rate when the air temperature is 109°F (43°C), while a properly clothed person reaches a maximum sweat rate at 125°F (52°C). Appropriate clothing gives insulation, shielding the body from heat while allowing sweat to evaporate. Loose-fitting, loosely woven clothing that covers the body completely allows for a layer of air between the cloth and the skin and allows passage of evaporation. Saharan peoples traditionally have worn hooded robes and body-length veils, loose trousers, and full-sleeved shirts. Turbans are usually loose and made of lightweight, absorbent material (Briggs 1975:112, 115–116, 122).

The very young, especially newborn infants, are under special stress in the Sahara. Newborns have difficulty in adjusting to heat because their ratio of surface area to volume is far less than that of adults, and their rate of vasodilation, sweating, and blood flow is inadequate. The highest infant and child mortality rate is in summer. Mortality in general increases in summer, but heat stress in adults is usually just an additive factor imposed on diseases such as dysentery and the risk of dehydration.

Extremely hot climates cause a very high incidence of menstrual disorders in European women who have come from temperate regions, even those who have had time to become acclimatized to the desert. Native women may have delayed onset of menarche, but this is as likely to be related to nutritional patterns as to heat stress. Males living in the desert, either natives or non-natives, show fewer physiological responses to stress, although newcomers show a disturbed sleep rhythm and resulting fatigue, irritability, and depression (Briggs 1975).

Cumulative Stressors

When people living in areas of extreme climate suffer additional stressors—say, drought and famine—they experience what researchers have called *gross stress:* reactions to an accumulation of acute stressors. Gross stress was first used as a psychiatric category in World War II to describe reactions of soldiers to combat, of concentration camp survivors, of the people of Hiroshima and Nagasaki, and similar cases of disaster or intense stress. The category has proved useful in understanding the health repercussions of long-term drought in small populations such as the Kaiadilt of Bentinck Island off the coast of Australia, who suffered drought in one- to five-year periods throughout the first part of this century. Heat stress combined with dehydration, a high work load needed to gather greatly diminished food resources, and continuing infections all produced a severe cumulative effect. Surprisingly, during this period a major factor in the high death rate was warfare, adding a man-made stressor to the severe ecological situation. Finally, in 1948 a tidal wave or unusually high tide inundated the island, leaving the people without fresh water, and they had to be evacuated by missionaries (Cawte 1978).

Anthropologists and physicians working to rehabilitate the Kaiadilt perceived the physical and emotional strain of these people as due to the gross stress of a disrupted ecological situation. The Kaiadilt defined their situation differently, however, explaining to psychiatrists that they felt highly stressed by the persistent fighting over women that they had experienced. Hunger and sickness were far less important stressors in their minds than were warfare and revenge (Cawte 1978:103). A single man set off a sequence of killing and feuding by other men who were competing for women. The initial factor may have been ecological disturbance, leading to a high death rate in women or possibly higher-than-usual female infanticide rates. But the human response of competition and conflict increased the degree of stress on this population, and from the perspective of these Australians, internal strife was far more threatening to their survival than was external deprivation of food and water.

Biological Rhythms

Human beings as well as other animals have regular physiological patterns that oscillate in relation to seasonal and lunar variations and daily light–dark cycles. *Circadian* rhythms follow an approximate twenty-four-hour cycle, while *circannual* rhythms are on a twelve-month cycle. Among the physiological processes that oscillate in relation to external stimuli are body temperature, blood pressure, pulse, respiration, blood sugar, hemoglobin levels, and corticoid levels. Normal functioning depends on the various biological rhythms being in synchrony according to a pattern that is at least partly phylogenetic, that is, characteristic of the human species. Desynchronization of these rhythms can result from jet travel, from prolonged isolation from normal light–dark cycles (as in submarines, space vehicles, or polar regions), and from working night shifts on an irregular basis.

Our most common experience of desynchronization is that of "jet lag." The traveler who crosses four or five time zones may be tired and disoriented for several days. Even though it is possible to catch up on sleep within a short time, the body takes longer to adjust its metabolic cycles. For example, diurnal temperature rhythm takes about four days to adjust when one has traveled from Canada to England, and the timing of the excretion of sodium, potassium, and adrenal hormones requires about nine days for readjustment after a trip from the United States to Japan (Dubos 1965:52–53).

The problem in traveling, or in moving to a high-latitude area with irregular light–dark cycles, is that the body's physiological cycles adjust to the change at different rates. Body temperature oscillations change much more rapidly than do pulse rate or hormone secretion patterns. Even individuals who have lived all their lives in arctic regions, in which winter days may have up to twenty hours of full darkness and summer days as many hours of full sunshine, experience biorhythm desynchronization. This is the kind of stressor, like high altitude or poor nutrition, that rarely leads directly to disease, but it does affect the neurological functioning of the body and makes it less resistant to other stressors.

Europeans who have lived in the Arctic have particular difficulty adjusting to the long hours of winter darkness, but Inuit report that they also experience a lack of energy, mild depression, and disorientation during the darkest winter days. Summer is disorienting in a different way: people sleep at irregular intervals, often only a few hours at a time, and have a hyperactive, agitated sense of energy and alertness. This sleep disturbance affects natives as well as non-natives.

For many years, anthropologists have attributed the characteristic forms of mental illness among arctic peoples to the stress of living in such a harsh climate. Several studies have contrasted a folk illness of the Far North, arctic hysteria, with an illness found among subarctic Ojibwa Indians called *wiitiiko* (or *windigo*) psychosis. While arctic hysteria involves a frenzied and dissociated state, *wiitiiko* is a morbid depression, the victim obsessed with cannibalistic fantasies.

Wiitiiko cases have not been studied clinically, and we can only guess from historical reports and informants' accounts whether the bio-chemical precipitant of this illness is low blood sugar, general malnu-trition, anxiety about food deprivation, or actual schizophrenia, all hypotheses suggested by medical anthropologists. Arctic hysteria is better documented through the research of Edward Foulks, a psychi-atrist with advanced training in anthropology who has done clinical evaluations of ten cases in Alaska. Foulks's study, discussed in the following health profile, suggests that desynchronization of biological rhythms is one of several factors contributing to arctic hysteria.

PROFILE: ARCTIC HYSTERIA

Around the turn of the century, explorers traveling through Greenland noted cases of an illness that the Polar Eskimo called *pibloktoq*. Observers thought it to be a kind of mental illness, and it became known as arctic hysteria. The following report by Robert Peary in 1910 is typical of descriptions of the illness:

> Aside from rheumatism and bronchial troubles, the Eskimos are fairly healthy; but the adults are subject to a peculiar affliction which they call pibloktoq, a form of hysteria. The patient, usually a woman, begins to scream and tear off and destroy her clothing. If on the ship, she will walk up and down the deck, screaming and gestic-ulating, and generally in a state of nudity, though the temperature may be in the minus forties. As the intensity of the attack increases, she will sometimes leap over the rail upon the ice, running perhaps half a mile. The attack may last a few minutes, an hour, or even more; and some sufferers become so wild that they would continue running about on the ice perfectly naked until they froze to death if they were not forcibly brought back. *Foulks (1972:13)*

Pibloktoq occurs at any season of the year, but it is more frequent in winter. Women are more frequently affected than men, and at times the illness reaches almost an epidemic level. At least one incident of Europeans being affected in Greenland has been reported, and dogs are subject to seizures similar to the convulsions of the *pibloktoq* syndrome (Wallace 1972:372).

The person experiencing an attack of *pibloktoq* may show any or all of the following symptoms: tearing off clothes, speaking meaningless syllables and making animal sounds, running away, rolling in the snow or jumping in the water, throwing things, and imitating others. Photographs of a woman having a seizure indicate that spasms of the hands and feet occur, and some case histories mention periods of irritability, confusion, and depression before an actual attack. Sometimes the attack lasts only a few minutes, sometimes several hours. The person is in a daze or semiconscious and will not respond to others. After the attack, he or she will fall into a deep sleep and will wake up later feeling normal and having no memory of the attack. The attacks occur irregularly with little social or physical disability in the person's everyday functioning (Foulks 1972:18–19).

The Inuit consider *pibloktoq* a physical illness like a cold or a broken leg rather than a psychosis. It is not explained in terms of supernatural causation, and both dogs and humans are believed to be susceptible to it (Wallace 1972:374). There is less consensus among social scientists as to how this syndrome is to be classified. Is it a folk illness, exclusive to arctic cultures only and best understood in terms of Inuit personality development and social stresses? Or is it a biochemical disorder, due perhaps to neurological dysfunction or nutritional deficiency? Scientists with a psychoanalytic orientation have suggested that *pibloktoq* is a form of learned hysteria that allows people to express acute feelings of helplessness and insecurity in a dramatic way that evokes group support rather than stigma or censure.

Scientists with a more biological orientation have considered a variety of diagnoses: epilepsy, encephalitis, food poisoning, low blood sugar, a slow virus. The most strongly supported hypothesis, proposed by the anthropologist Anthony F. C. Wallace, is that *pibloktoq* is due to calcium deficiency. Hypocalcemia can produce tetany, with symptoms of muscle spasms, convulsive seizures, and mental confusion. The irregular and transient nature of *pibloktoq* attacks may be explained through the mechanism of hyperventilation (prolonged deep breathing), which depletes the blood of carbon dioxide, altering the acid balance and reducing the proportion of calcium ions in the blood. Wallace suggests that hyperventilation during emotional stress may induce short-term tetany in persons who already have low calcium levels (Wallace 1972:376).

While it is not certain that victims of *pibloktoq* have clinical tetany, various early reports on Inuit health suggest that calcium deficiency was a problem. Observers noted convulsions in infants in East Greenland and a high frequency of cramps in the legs and general muscle pains in adults. Nevertheless, rickets was very rare in infants, and a condition called osteomalacia (a softening of the bones found in pregnant or nursing women) was rarely reported. Wallace has suggested that there was environmental selection against individuals with a predisposition toward rickets or osteomalacia, simply because these physically crippling conditions would not allow survival through adulthood in an environment requiring mobility. Wallace also reminds us that the medieval Norsemen who attempted to settle in Greenland and eventually died out did in fact suffer from rickets and osteomalacia (Wallace 1972:377).

In testing Wallace's calcium deficiency hypothesis, Foulks found that about 75 percent of the diet records of nine Alaskan Eskimo villages surveyed from 1956 through 1961 showed calcium intake below the levels recommended by the National Research Council. All age groups and both sexes had deficient calcium intake, but with wide variation in each group. Ascorbic acid (vitamin C) intake was also deficient, while iron was more than adequate due to high animal protein in the diet.

Foulks analyzed the blood of the ten Alaskan Inuit with a history of *pibloktoq* and found that all but one of the subjects had normal levels of serum calcium throughout the year, with no decreases during the winter months. Half the patients were in the low normal range, however, and Foulks suggests that hyperventilation might precipitate hypocalcemia in these subjects (1972:76–78).

Foulks also tested the possibility that arctic hysteria might be related to the effect of unusual light–dark cycles on circadian rhythms in the Arctic. Physiological functions are normally in synchrony over a twenty-four-hour cycle, varying according to social and environmental cues. When certain rhythms begin to "free run" out of phase, the body may be under stress. One investigation of seasonal variation in the biological rhythms of Alaskan Eskimos showed that while body temperature and excretion of potassium remained in phase throughout the year, the urinary excretion of calcium became free-running in winter. It was believed that this desynchronization was related to the irritability and depression of Inuit in winter and might lower the threshold of some individuals to epileptic seizures (Foulks 1972:83–84). Foulks did analyze the rhythms of one of the *pibloktoq* patients and of two controls and found the same pattern of calcium desynchrony.

A final major focus of Foulks's study was the psychological components of arctic hysteria. It was possible that individuals might precipitate attacks unconsciously by hyperventilating when experiencing emotional conflict, anxiety, or shame. Foulks studied the history and personality patterns of each of the ten subjects and found that each was indeed insecure about his or her identity and felt inadequate, not because of the irregular seizures but rather because of general failure to fit into the native communities. A number of the subjects experienced role conflict or incongruence between what they would like to achieve and what they had actually accomplished socially or economically. Foulks suggests that this incongruence and feeling of inadequacy produce emotional stress.

The approach used by Wallace and Foulks to investigate the etiology of *pibloktoq* exemplifies the multideterminant model used in medical ecology. A wide variety of stressors impinge on the Inuit of the High Arctic regions—cold and lack of sunlight in winter, variation in light–dark cycles, nutritional deficiency and infectious disease, an uncertain food supply, and absolute social interdependence. Physiological and social response to these stressors is normally adequate. But in certain individuals, the cumulative effect of this total stress load leads to the behavior known as *pibloktoq*.

Whether desynchronization of circadian rhythms is a critical factor in arctic hysteria is still not certain. A larger sample of cases must be tested before definite conclusions can be drawn, but this is difficult, for as arctic peoples modernize, their patterns of mental illness change. Depression and alcoholism are more prevalent today than is *pibloktoq*. It is probably not possible to find a single cause of arctic hysteria. Like all stress diseases, whether

primarily organic or mental in symptomatology, *pibloktoq* involves a complex response of the body to multiple stressors. Most
mental illnesses are probably equally complex in their etiology
and are best studied with a variety of theoretical models and
analytical techniques.

STRESSORS IN THE SOCIOCULTURAL ENVIRONMENT

Since Hans Selye introduced the concept of physiological stress
processes in the 1950s, psychologists and other social scientists have
speculated whether Selye's model can be applied to social processes.
For example, can behavioral disorders such as alcoholism and drug
abuse be regarded as maladaptive attempts to cope with emotional
stress? Are other forms of deviance "symptoms" of strain in our
society? Are mental illness, suicide, homicide, and high divorce rates
indications that modern urban culture is stressful for individuals?

The cultural environment creates many of the stressors with which
individuals must try to cope. Noise and pollution are by-products of
human activities; they also act as stressors on some individuals.
Competition, crowding, unemployment, poverty—all these problems
of our society can create conflict and disruption in people's lives.
When these problems are linked to physiological strain, then our
analysis remains within the parameters of the Selye and Cannon
models. For example, we can see that unemployment makes some
people frustrated and angry, and these emotional responses may
contribute to hypertension. Whether frustration also leads to drug
abuse, or looting during blackouts, or juvenile gangs, or suicide—and
whether these behaviors are indeed evidence of strain—is a question
that goes beyond the conventional stress model. When one is looking
at social problems, it is particularly important to ask *who* has defined
the behavior as a problem. What is the evidence that the behavior is

"sick?" Is the behavior actually a way of coping with culturally induced stress? These questions need to be answered before one blames social problems on stress or takes it for granted that certain environments—for example, urban centers—are inherently stressful for people.

Urban Environments

Many social scientists believe that cities are stressful places to live, pushing many people beyond normal limits of crowding, noise, stimulation, and rapid change. Studies of many different societies have shown that people in small, cohesive, traditional communities tend to have low blood pressure, while people who leave these communities often experience changes in levels of blood pressure, especially if they go to cities. In chapter 2 we discussed Scotch's study (1963) of two Zulu groups, one living on a rural reserve and the other in an urban area. High blood pressure was more prevalent in the urban group, especially among those who had recently migrated and who maintained traditional beliefs and customs. Migrants who were relatively inflexible in adapting to city ways and changing their beliefs showed more symptoms of strain than did those who did change. One question that remains unanswered is whether lack of success in the city reinforced hypertension, or perhaps whether hypertension contributed to difficulty in adapting.

Rapid change is often stressful for the body, sometimes because of nutritional change or exposure to new pathogens, and sometimes because the body is defending against symbolic threats and anxieties. The person experiencing rapid change may feel somewhat helpless and overwhelmed by a barrage of new information to process. Failure to focus on a manageable level of stimulation and to filter out the "noise"—that is, irrelevant or unmanageable details of the situation—can create a sense of emotional and sensory overload. The cognitive processes of learning new things, dealing with fears, trying not to fail, avoiding dangers, and striving for control in an unpredictable situation, are accompanied by physiological defense processes. The mind and body work together in the coping process, and as we have seen throughout this chapter, the body's attempt to defend itself may lead to strain. In addition, the cumulative impact of a series of stressors impinging on the person, some emotional and some physical, can easily lower a person's resistance to disease and ability to cope with crisis.

Among the stressors that affect urban populations, noise, crowding, and social alienation are of major concern to medical anthropologists. Thus far the approach to assessing the health impact of these stressors has been primarily epidemiological, correlating the intensity of these stressors and disease rates. Noise is the most controversial of these stressors, because other than the obvious hazards to auditory nerves of certain occupations or wartime activities (or, as some parents claim, of rock concerts), it is not certain that ordinary urban noise is a noxious stimulus. A laboratory study by Glass and Singer (1975) showed that subjects adjust to steady or predictable noise, but it was unpredictable and uncontrollable noise that affected performance on tests. In routine work, noise does not impair efficiency, but work requiring skill and concentration suffers when there is prolonged noise.

It is difficult to separate noise from other kinds of stressors in an urban environment, but a few studies have managed to isolate noise as an independent variable. One field study carried out in New York City investigated the relationship between noise intensity and children's auditory discrimination and reading ability. All the children lived in one apartment complex, and there were no significant class differences in the sample. Those living on the lower floors closer to expressway traffic had greater auditory and reading impairment than those living on the upper levels of the thirty-two-story complex (Glass and Singer 1975:355). Research conducted by Damon in Boston has shown correlations between noise level, the size of families, and the rate of arrests and school dropouts, but this study is less conclusive about the role of noise as a stressor (Damon 1977:238). Similarly, it has been shown that persons living in a maximum noise area near a London airport have a higher rate of admission to mental hospitals than those living in quieter areas (Damon 1977). This kind of information is intriguing, but the rate of mental illness is generally higher for lower socioeconomic classes in urban areas. The relationship between mental illness and noise may be accidental or nonsignificant, or it may be that excessive noise over which one has no control can in fact be "the straw that breaks the camel's back"—a minor stressor in itself that proves significant when combined with a series of other pressures.

Crowding is considered another urban stressor. The New York City subway at rush hour allows two square feet per person, although this is temporary crowding. The density of Manhattan is about 100,000 per square mile, (36,000 per square km) and the density of New York City on the whole is 25,000 per square mile (9000 per square km). Tokyo is similar, with about 20,000 per square mile (7200 per square km) (Damon 1977:240). These densities are considered unusual for human beings, yet people manage to tolerate such physical closeness. Humans generally manage to survive and reproduce even in crowded cities, unlike laboratory rats who, when experimentally crowded, become sterile, have high rates of spontaneous abortions and still-births, or kill their young.

Symptoms of emotional stress and mental disorder are often prevalent in crowded cities. The Midtown Manhattan study in the mid-1950s (Srole et al. 1975) showed that at least 23 percent of 2000 persons studied seriously needed psychiatric help, and that only 5 percent were receiving care at the time. Of the 1600 persons interviewed, only 18 percent were judged by psychiatrists to be free of emotional problems (Honigmann 1967:359–363).

Social alienation is a stressor that is difficult to measure, but epidemiological studies have shown that marginal persons who do not have positive social bonds have a higher risk not only of mental illness, alcoholism, and suicide, but also of infectious disease. Holmes's studies of tuberculosis in Seattle have shown higher rates among people who lived alone in one room, in those who were single or divorced, and in those who were of minority status in their neighborhoods (Cassel 1970:195). Tuberculosis rates are also higher among those who experienced the death of a parent, or divorce or separation of the parents, before age 18 (Holmes 1956:68).

Social alienation may not always be a matter of clear-cut status marginality. In some cases, it involves ambiguous status or incongruence between status indicators such as education level and occupation. For example, rheumatoid arthritis is especially frequent among people who have a discrepancy between income and education (the income being lower than might be expected from the level of education). Women who experience a sense of discrepancy between their family role requirements and their sense of identity are more likely to have arthritis. Moreover, their daughters are likely to have arthritis particularly if the mothers are "overeducated" (in other words, if the mothers' education levels are incongruent with the status of their husbands' occupations). Clearly, these social factors do not cause the arthritis, but they may be conducive to the muscular tension and the chronic sense of resentment that induce the symptoms of rheumatoid arthritis (Kahn and French 1970:246–247).

Role Conflict

The stress model has been used in a number of studies on the effects of blocked aspirations on physical and mental health. Just as the body strives to defend itself and to maintain homeostasis, social psychiatrists believe that the mind also seeks equilibrium. Human beings normally strive after certain vital ends—security, love, creativity and spontaneity, a sense of identity and worth, and the feeling of belonging to a moral order. When this striving is blocked, the individual experiences disequilibrium in the form of anxiety, disappointment, depression, or other negative emotions. The person usually copes by finding other goals or by changing her or his expectations. But when too many goals are blocked or when basic needs (such as a child's need for stimulation) are not met, emotional or physical strain may result (Honigmann 1967:332–334).

Blockage of goals can be symbolic, for example, when one receives negative feedback about one's competence in carrying out a certain role. Expectations are partly internal, so that a person has certain standards of how he or she should behave as a parent, an employee, a spouse. Simultaneously, situational factors may make it difficult to meet those standards or may provide contradictory expectations. Whether feelings of inadequacy and frustration in carrying out one's expected social role are due to internal conflict or to external problems, these feelings are believed to be stressful for most people. Role conflict is usually a contributing stressor rather than a primary factor in illness. As in the case of urbanization and high blood pressure, sometimes it is difficult to decide whether role inadequacy is the cause or the effect of stress processes.

Role conflict is a hypothesis often used to interpret cases of mental illness with no discernible biochemical basis. For example, one interpretation of a form of hysteria called *amok* in New Guinea, Indonesia, and Malaya is that the victims are under excessive financial pressure and cannot meet others' expectations. The illness allows people who cannot live up to their expected role a chance to be free of obligations without being total outcasts. The hypothesis is supported by the fact that in a New Guinea community studied by Phillip Newman, the only cases reported are of young men, who expected to enter in a series of financial transactions (Honigmann 1967:406). If *amok* had a biochemical cause, presumably people in other age groups and women would also be affected. This does not rule out the influence of physical stressors, of course. There may be some special aspect of the diet, use of stimulants, or ritual behavior of these men that interacts with the emotional pressures incurred by financial responsibilities.

Another example of role conflict leading to disability is in the folk illness *susto* ("fright") found in a number of Spanish-speaking societies in the New World. It is believed that a frightening experience causes the illness. Some groups also believe that the soul of the patient has been captured by spirits and taken from the body. The symptoms include loss of appetite, listlessness, loss of weight, apathy, depression, and withdrawal (Rubel 1964).

Most cases of *susto* show a sense of helplessness in carrying out one's role. Rubel (1964) observes that "*susto* appears to communicate an individual's inability to fulfill adequately the expectations of the society in which he has been socialized" (p. 278). In one case, a woman experienced an attack of *susto* after she got into a fight with her unfaithful husband and he hit her with a rock. In another case, a man had an attack after an embarrassing accident at work that evoked laughter from onlookers. A third case involved a five-year-old boy who became ill while his seven-year-old sister and family went swimming in a pond. Each of these examples is thought to illustrate a response to feelings of inadequacy and helplessness. The cultural explanation of soul loss and the usual forms of ethnomedical treatment serve to relieve the victim from embarrassment and blame and to provide the attention and support that will help ease feelings of insecurity.

The role conflict model is not necessarily in conflict with a biochemical approach to stress disorders. Before anthropologists became aware of the importance of nutrition for normal emotional and cognitive functioning, interpretations of hysterical behavior were understandably confined to concepts of role dissonance, psychological coping mechanisms, and symbolic communication. Within the sociocultural framework, these concepts remain valid. Biochemical data simply complement and expand our theory of illness. A disorder found traditionally among the Greenland Inuit, kayak phobia, is a case in point. About 15 percent of all native hunters in Greenland experienced this illness periodically. While sitting in their kayaks in still water, the hunters would become paralyzed and disoriented. Noise or wind would pull the hunter out of the trance, but excessive anxiety after this experience was likely to prevent the man from going out in his kayak again (Foulks 1972:21).

FIGURE 7.8   Inuit man preparing to depart for open-water hunting in his kayak. The absence of stimulation and the glare of sun on water can move the hunter into an altered state of consciousness, one explanation of the traditional illness of kayak phobia.

Photo by D. Wilkinson, N.F.B. Photothèque.

Psychological interpretations have focused on the emotional conflicts of the hunter who must suppress fears of drowning, of failure as
a hunter, of being alone and helpless. Kayak phobia, like *pibloktoq* and
amok, was believed to be a way for a person to communicate helplessness and elicit group support without being labeled as a failure. Recent
research on the effects of sensory deprivation, however, suggests an
alternative interpretation. While waiting for seals to appear and staring
at the still, glaring surface of the water, the Inuit hunter could easily
move into an altered stage of consciousness. He was not actually
paralyzed, but he did experience the same kind of physical and mental
disorientation that persons feel when experimentally isolated. Later he
had the severe headaches, nausea, startled response to noises, and
general anxiety that often follow extreme sensory deprivation. The
continuing disorientation made him realistically fearful to go out in the
kayak again.

Sensory deprivation as a stressor is of concern regarding institutionalized people. Among the elderly, lack of stimulation and contact
increases the onset of senility and the risk of apathetic withdrawal,
lowered resistance to infection, and other indications of strain. Sensory and emotional deprivation also affect the health of infants and
small children in institutions, as the following health profile discusses.

PROFILE: DEPRIVATION DWARFISM

*His second folly was that he wanted to find out what
kind of speech and what manner of speech children
would have when they grew up, if they spoke to no
one beforehand. So he bade foster mothers and nurses
to suckle the children, to bathe and to wash them, but
in no way to prattle with them or to speak to them,
for he wanted to learn whether they would speak the
Hebrew language, which was the oldest, or Greek, or
Latin, or Arabic, or perhaps the language of their
parents, of whom they had been born. But he la-
boured in vain, because the children all died. For they
could not live without the petting and the joyful faces
and loving words of their foster mothers.*
                            —Patton and Gardner (1963:14)

What happens when infants are not loved and are deprived of contact and communication? This famous story about Emperor Frederick II of thirteenth-century Sicily shows that infants who receive no stimulation will not thrive. It is not enough to be fed adequately and to be kept clean and dry. The infant death rate in institutions is high even when the physical care is adequate. In 1915, the mortality rate of infants within one year after admission to Baltimore orphanages and foundling homes was 90 percent (Gardner 1972). A study done by Spitz (1954) in the 1940s showed that thirty-four out of ninety-one institutionalized infants died within the first year of life. The infants who were not returned to their mothers and remained in the foundling home for longer than two years were retarded in mental development and were found to be well below the normal height and weight for their age (Patton and Gardner 1963:35).

Spitz called the condition of the infants an "anaclitic depression" or "emotional deficiency disease." The symptoms were loss of appetite and weight, insomnia, slow movements and general listlessness, and withdrawal. Spitz suggested that these were stress symptoms due to emotional deprivation. Although hygiene was excellent, each nurse had ten infants to care for and thus each infant had only "one-tenth of a mother" (1954:122). Other studies in the 1940s of infants in institutions, including those in regular hospitals, gave evidence of a general syndrome caused by emotional deprivation: failure to gain weight despite adequate nutritional intake, regurgitation and diarrhea, respiratory irregularity and susceptibility to infection, depression, and lack of response. These infants developed bald spots from lying so long in one position without moving, and some were so thin that they seemed to be suffering from marasmus. Such symptoms quickly disappeared when the infants returned to their mothers or were provided full-time mother substitutes in the hospital.

In the 1950s, Robert Patton and Lytt Gardner did long-term studies of six children who had to be hospitalized because they were so thin. The children were losing weight at home in spite of normal appetites. One fifteen-month-old girl, for example, weighed only 10 pounds (4.6 kg). At a height of slightly under 2 feet (58 cm), the child's height age was only three months. A three-year-old boy was even smaller for his age, weighing only

15 pounds (7.9 kg) and having a height equivalent to that of a normal twelve-month-old child.

Each of the six children was severely retarded in height, weight, and bone growth. Most of them could not talk or walk upon admission to the hospital, and they were very apathetic and lay for long periods with little motion other than periodic head-banging and self-rocking movements. Patton and Gardner found that each of the children had been adequately fed at home but otherwise given little attention. The fifteen-month-old girl, for example, was kept isolated in a dark room and had contact with adults only when she was fed. Another child was fed only with a propped-up bottle and was never held. In most of the cases, the mother was hostile and resentful toward the child and had herself been rejected and mistreated as a child in a "broken home" or conflicted marriage situation.

All six children gained weight after hospitalization and gradually began to respond to the personal stimulation that nurses provided. Even the most serious case, a tiny, anxious girl who seemed to be in shock and who kept her hands constantly cupped over her nose and mouth, began to improve after three weeks when a nurse was assigned to "mother" her by picking her up and carrying her about whenever possible. Within two months, this fourteen-month-old child was finally able to sit up without support, to roll over, and to creep, and she began to smile and say "mama" to her substitute mother (figure 7.9) (Patton and Gardner 1963:64–65). By age 8, she was living with foster parents and measured within the low normal range for height, weight, and intelligence.

Another case studied in 1964 by Gardner and Hollowell demonstrated even more strongly the effect of emotional deprivation on growth. A child hospitalized for growth failure was one of a pair of twins growing up in a broken home. The mother had become pregnant unexpectedly only four months after the twins were born, and the father had lost his job and abandoned the family. Up to this time, the twins—a boy and a girl—had been growing at a normal rate, but during these conflicts the boy began to lose weight. It was believed that the mother's hostility toward her husband was also directed toward her son but not toward the daughter; this differential hostility affected the boy's growth rate. Later the husband returned to the family, and after

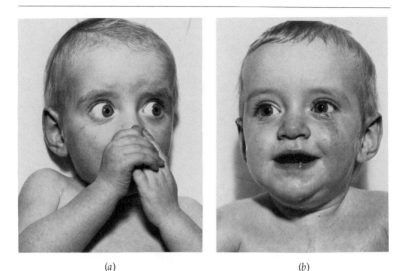

(a)   (b)

FIGURE 7.9   (a) A fourteen-month-old girl who had been isolated at home in a dark room with little contact or stimulation. When admitted to the hospital, she kept her hands cupped over her face and her legs drawn up whenever left alone. (b) The same child after four months of care in the hospital by a mother-surrogate nurse—with considerable improvement in weight gain, responsiveness, and motor ability.

SOURCE: Photos from Robert G. Patton and Lytt I. Gardner, *Growth Failure in Maternal Deprivation*, 1963. Courtesy of Charles C Thomas, Publisher, Springfield, Illinois.

release from the hospital the child returned to a normal growth rate and eventually caught up with his sister (Gardner 1972). The history of another child, whose growth resumed after his mother remarried, is shown in figure 7.10.

These examples suggest that emotional deprivation is as much of a stressor for an infant as an actual lack of food would be. But what is the actual physiological mechanism that inhibits growth under the condition of inadequate stimulation? Research on this problem is still going on. It is probable that deprivation dwarfism is a type of stress disease involving dysfunction of the hypothalamus and, secondarily, the pituitary gland. Under experimental conditions, secretion of growth hormone (somatotrophin) by the pituitary normally increases in response to an injection of insulin, which induces low blood-sugar levels. Chil-

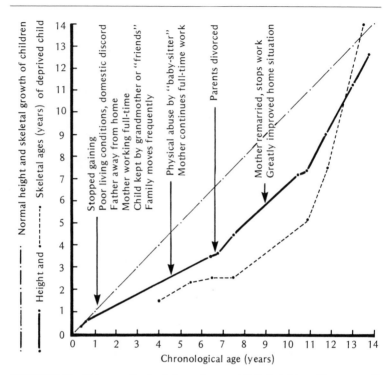

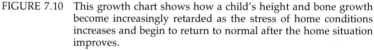

FIGURE 7.10   This growth chart shows how a child's height and bone growth
become increasingly retarded as the stress of home conditions
increases and begin to return to normal after the home situation
improves.

SOURCE: From Robert G. Patton and Lytt I. Gardner, *Growth Failure in
Maternal Deprivation*, 1963. Courtesy of Charles C Thomas, Publisher,
Springfield, Illinois.

dren being treated for deprivation dwarfism, however, have a
subnormal response to insulin, with an inadequate secretion of
growth hormone. After such children are placed in a normal
home environment, levels of somatotrophin increase.

The low level of somatotrophin may also be related to abnormal
sleep patterns. Growth hormone is normally secreted at night
during the first few hours of sleep. One of the symptoms related
to deprivation dwarfism is insomnia alternating with long periods of a stupor-like sleep. Gardner and Patton noted that some
of their patients slept eighteen hours a day while others stayed

awake all night. If sleep patterns are disturbed and irregular, the production and secretion of somatotrophin are likely to be affected (Gardner 1972).

Children who live in a conflicted home environment may experience mixed or inconsistent messages from their parents, and this kind of stress may contribute to disturbance in sleep patterns. In institutionalized infants such as those studied by René Spitz, the sensory deprivation of the quiet, efficient, joyless atmosphere may be the reason for abnormal sleep patterns. The experimental production of extreme sensory deprivation has shown that subjects experience hallucinations and delusions, unusual sleep and dream cycles, and general feelings of confusion. Apparently, the human brain requires certain levels of sensory input, and the infant's brain particularly needs information and stimulation.

Harlow's work with rhesus monkeys (1971) has given us certain clues toward understanding the critical importance of love to the infant. In this research, the development of monkeys, raised without their mothers, was followed to show which factor is more important, tactile stimulation or food. Infants growing up in isolation become insane, while those caged only with a hard, cold wire "mother" to cling to are fearful, asocial, and abnormally aggressive as adults. The best of surrogate mothers is a terry cloth–covered form that provides a rocking motion, but even better for infant rhesus monkey development is the chance to play a few hours a day with other infants. Contact comfort, minimally having a soft surface to cling to but optimally sensing another heartbeat, feeling warmth and motion, being held and stimulated, is what love means for a monkey baby. It is possible that the first experience of love for the human being is also based on such stimulation.

Stress is not only the response of the body to external stimuli. In a significant number of life situations, stress can result from a *lack* of stimulation from the environment. Boredom and monotonous activity can be just as stressful as excessive noise and too busy a schedule. The human infant has certain needs for stimulation, and a lack of input will lead to the hormonal changes and attempts at physiological adjustment typical of many types of stress responses.

Alcoholism

The final example of stress and disease to be discussed in this chapter deals with the consumption of addicting and self-damaging substances, using alcohol as an example. The abuse of mood-altering substances such as alcohol is assumed to be related to stress, but social scientists disagree about whether people consume these substances as a way of reducing stress. The "folk model" of alcohol use in our society is that it relaxes the person; the same explanation is often given for the use of tobacco and other addicting substances. Thus other stressors, such as pressures in one's job or feelings of inadequacy, are thought to induce alcohol use as a coping mechanism. When use turns into abuse, however, the mechanism has become "derailed," and addiction itself becomes a stressor.

Some models of alcoholism dismiss stress theory altogether and suggest that certain people become addicted to alcohol easily for genetic reasons. This approach emphasizes that such persons are allergic to alcohol; the symptoms of the allergy include rapid loss of inhibitions while drinking, total inability to drink in a controlled manner, and an intense compulsion to drink. A very effective self-help organization, Alcoholics Anonymous (AA), has developed a therapeutic approach around this explanatory model. The AA program attempts to convince the addicted person that he or she is not to blame, is helpless in the face of an incurable but manageable illness, and must accept the necessity of life-long abstinence from alcohol.

It had been assumed that men in the United States had a much higher rate of alcoholism than women until recently, since far more men than women were arrested for public intoxication, were treated in public facilities, and suffered from cirrhosis of the liver, a condition induced by chronic alcoholism. Women who drank in public were quite stigmatized in the past, and women alcoholics were more likely to be "closet drinkers."

The number of women seeking treatment for alcoholism is increasing dramatically, but we are not certain whether this is due to increasing use of and addiction to alcohol among women or due to decreasing stigmatization. And if use of alcohol is indeed increasing, is it because women are experiencing greater role conflicts and frustration than they did in the past, or because they are asserting their right to enjoy the same privileges that men have traditionally exercised in using alcohol and tobacco?

The more frequent explanation of the increasing female alcoholism is that it is precipitated by social stress, particularly life crises. The average age range of onset of alcohol abuse for a woman is 28 to 33 (Fraser 1974:13). In men, the addictive illness progresses gradually over a period of fifteen years or more, but addiction occurs within only a few years among many women, often in response to a particularly stressful situation such as a marriage breakdown. About two-thirds of alcoholic women are divorced, a much higher rate than among male alcoholics.

The social stress explanation has also been used to account for the high rate of alcohol consumption among many Native American groups. The stressors include poverty, political powerlessness, high infectious disease rates, poor nutrition, unemployment, and generalized anxious and angry responses to these socioeconomic conditions. The general model is this: Because Native Americans are disadvantaged, anxious, and live in conflict with the dominant society, they drink alcohol to cope. In other words, drinking reduces stress. It gives a chance to release anger, to enjoy camaraderie among peers, and to reject the norms of the most conventional segment of the dominant society. This is the approach that most anthropologists have favored. One notable exception is a study of Navaho drinking by Levy and Kunitz (1974), who suggest that drinking among these southwestern Indians is not a response to stress at all but rather a style of behavior that fits into the traditional culture. Relatively few Navahos have liver disease, nor do they usually experience delirium tremens (DTs) or withdrawal symptoms when abstaining from alcohol. Levy and Kunitz believe that most Navahos are not alcoholics at all, even though consumption is high.

What Levy and Kunitz have done in their study of drinking styles is to focus on the *functions* of alcohol use among Navahos, that is, the role of drinking patterns in maintaining social relations. Drinking together allows people to share and reciprocate, to develop group identity, and to participate in certain degrees of "ritual license" or "time out" from ordinary routines and conventions. MacAndrew and Edgerton (1969) have shown in a study called *Drunken Comportment* that alcohol use has little to do with social stress in many societies.

Rather, alcohol allows people an alternative pattern of behavior, usually one that is learned from others and is actually fairly predictable.

Interpretations of the stress model tend to confuse the strain of a maladaptive response (for example, the strain of alcohol addiction) with possible antecedent stressors (such as assuming that American Indians drink because of rapid change). It is possible that one of the functions of group or individual use of alcohol is to reduce sociopsychological stress. But there are many other functions of this behavior that are intrinsically interesting to the medical anthropologist. Stress is a broad concept, but it should be applied properly and not used as an explanation of every type of behavior that might conceivably have negative effects on health.

CONCLUSIONS

This chapter has discussed the relationship between stress and disease. When the body responds to a problem posed by the physical or social environment, it is under stress. It both produces and uses adaptation energy in the form of hormones, glucose, lipids, and other biochemical substances. The mobilization of energy in response to a stressor, or external stimulus-evoking response, is facilitated by the sympathetic nervous system, which prepares the body for defense, a mechanism that Walter B. Cannon calls the fight-or-flight response. Continued defense will involve the action of the parasympathetic nervous system, which conserves energy and rests the body in complementary sequence with the sympathetic system. Hans Selye's research has shown that the stress response also involves the release of hormones that act to produce or inhibit local inflammatory defense against injury.

Our discussion of stress has emphasized three rather controversial points of view: (1) that stress is normal and can in fact induce healing processes; (2) that human beings require a certain level of stress in the form of stimulation and challenges from the environment; and (3) that the category of "social stress" may involve unwarranted assumptions that subcultural behavior patterns are pathological and caused by stress.

Studies of social stress must take into account the intermediate biochemical factors that always link perceived environmental demand and physiological strain. For example, the concept of role conflict in studies of arctic hysteria and kayak phobia is facilitated and complemented by information on the effects of seasonal variation, nutritional deficiency, and sensory deprivation on human neurophysiological functioning. Without these biochemical data, anthropologists are unable to develop an evolutionary and ecosystemic perspective on stress-related diseases, especially forms of mental illness. Similarly, without consideration of the sociocultural matrix of health and disease, the biochemical perspective fails to account for the role of emotion and cognition in stress processes.

Students often ask whether stress is greater in the contemporary world than it was in the past, or whether the city dweller in America suffers more from stress than the present-day non-Western hunter or horticulturalist. These are difficult questions to answer. Many different kinds of stressors evoke the standard stress responses in the body, and the body does not discriminate between them. There are dangers in every environment. The city person needs the jolt of epinephrine to respond properly when trying to cross the street in heavy traffic; the hunter in the Arctic needs it when the melting spring ice he has been standing on while sealing suddenly breaks beneath him. It is true that the incidence of stress diseases is higher in industrial societies, however, and there are several reasons for this. One is that infectious and parasitic disease rates are lower, and thus individuals tend to live longer and to accumulate gradual wear and tear after years of coping with stress. A second factor is that hunters, fishers, and farmers have physically active lives and metabolize serum cholesterol and glucose more efficiently than those who are sedentary. Thus they are more likely to avoid build-up of cholesterol in the arteries or the development of diabetes. When hunters and farmers change their lifestyles and move into cities or towns, they show predictable and striking relationships between decline in physical activity, increase in the amount of sugar, fat, and general carbohydrate intake, and the rate of stress-related diseases, as we consider in the next chapter on culture change.

The answer to who experiences more stress, the hunter or the office worker, is difficult to find because the question is misleading. The total amount of stress is not the issue. Rather, one should ask: What are the differences in how the hunter and the office worker experience stress, in how their bodies respond, and in their general level of energy utilization? It is more productive to compare lifestyles and response capacity than it is to compare levels of stress. Stress itself is not abnormal; rather, it is inadequate coping with stress that can contribute to disease.

RESOURCES

Readings

Brown, Barbara B.
    1977   Stress and the Art of Biofeedback. New York: Harper & Row. This book reports on the use of biofeedback techniques to reduce strain and induce relaxation for medical purposes, including control of hypertension and reduction of pain during childbirth. It also gives information on the benefits of transcendental meditation. The bibliography is thorough and current.

Foulks, Edward F.
    1972   The Arctic Hysterias of the North Alaskan Eskimo. Anthropological Studies no. 10. Washington, D.C.: American Anthropological Association.
    Foulks examines several hypotheses about the causes of arctic hysteria, including the calcium-deficiency theory, calcium rhythm desynchronization, and social stress models. The volume includes additional information on patterns of mental illness among Alaskan natives.

Laughlin, Charles D., Jr., and Ivan A. Brady, eds.
    1978   Extinction and Survival in Human Populations. New York: Columbia University Press.
    This collection of readings documents how populations have adapted to the stressors of drought, famine, warfare, slavery, and other crises. It is one of the best sources available on how physiological stress interacts with cultural and individual coping processes.

Lee, Richard B.
    1967   Trance Cure of the !Kung Bushmen. Natural History 76:31–37. Lee's article dramatically describes and illustrates through photographs the healing rituals of the !Kung San. Details on observed physiological changes illustrate how people can induce stress for therapeutic purposes.

Moos, Rudolf H., ed.
1976 Human Adaptation. Lexington, Massachusetts: D. C. Heath.
This book deals with human coping processes, especially in life transition crises such as divorce and bereavement, marriage and entering college, and migration. There are also chapters about prisoners of war, concentration camps, and coping with disasters, including being captured in a skyjacked plane.
Seligman, Martin E. P.
1974 Submissive Death: Giving Up On Life. Psychology Today 7 (12):80–85.
Seligman's article discusses how prisoners of war, voodoo victims, hospitalized infants, rejected old people, and experimental animals respond physiologically to situations of helplessness. It suggests that all these categories involve "submissive death," in which vulnerability and loss of control increase the risk of disease and possible death.
Selye, Hans
1956 The Stress of Life. New York: McGraw-Hill.
Selye's classic introduction to the theory of stress traces the history of his research in a nontechnical style. The book illustrates how strongly the background and personality of the scientist influence how a theory is developed.
Selye, Hans
1976 Stress in Health and Disease. Boston: Butterworths.
This massive, 1256-page volume presents an indexed and cross-indexed series of annotated references and brief summaries of research findings on hundreds of topics related to stress. This reference is essential for any student planning a term paper or project about stress.

Films

The Holy Ghost People. 1968. 53 minutes. Produced by Peter Adair. McGraw-Hill Films #407920-4.
This film is a study of a Pentecostal congregation in West Virginia. Interviews with church members and footage of a church service help the viewer understand how this ritual organization helps members deal with the social stressors of Appalachian poverty. During the service, participants become possessed and go into a trancelike state as they handle poisonous snakes.
N/um T'Chai: The Ceremonial Dance of the !Kung Bushmen. 1966. 20 minutes. Audiovisual Services, Pennsylvania State University, University Park, Pennsylvania, #21594.
The film portrays segments of the night-long trance dance of the !Kung San of the Kalahari Desert, which heats up healing power manifested as the sweat of the dancer. The rhythmic singing, prolonged dancing, and power of group suggestion create the sensory overload typical of group ceremonials.

Health Repercussions
of Culture Contact

CHAPTER 8

PREVIEW

Of all the stressors affecting a population's health, one of the most devastating is rapid and irrevocable change in a people's way of life. Over the course of history, such change has often come from floods, earthquakes, droughts, and other natural disasters. But contact between populations also has an impact on health and ecological stability. The type of contact emphasized in this chapter is that of colonialism and territorial intrusion for purposes of exploration, migration and settlement, trade and alliance.

Whatever the business of contact agents, whether to find a home, to preach the gospel, or to make a profit, they often disrupt the lives of the native peoples whose lands they enter. Sometimes this disruption is deliberate, but often the ecological and economic repercussions are unintended. Outsiders may introduce disease organisms to which native people have little immunity. They may cut off access to traditional foods and provide imported foods instead, and consequent shifts in diet can create nutritional imbalances. Colonial governments often encourage or force native people to settle in permanent villages or reservation communities, leading to demographic and epidemiological effects that continue for generations after contact.

The study of culture contact illustrates the ecosystemic approach to health and disease. As contact induces changes in one aspect of health—for example, nutritional status—the population's relationship to its habitat becomes altered, with feedback to a number of other health variables. Four variables especially emphasized in the health profile of modern Inuit health are changes in epidemiological patterns, reproduction, nutrition, and health care resources.

Changes in these four variables are further illustrated through three extended examples of culture contact. A discussion of a malaria epidemic that decimated California and Oregon Indians in the 1830s illustrates epidemiological factors. Reproductive—and thus demographic—changes due to pacification and acculturation of the head-hunting Asmat of New Guinea include higher birth rates, shorter intervals between births, and general population growth despite high infant mortality. The Zulu of South Africa, confined to reserves after conquest with an inadequate subsistence base, benefited from health care programs in the 1940s, but their high-carbohydrate diets continued to create health problems. These and other examples illustrate the concept that health is a reflection of ecosystemic equilibrium, and that contact between populations usually changes the equilibrium of one or both groups. This principle holds in the case of involuntary and voluntary migration as well, as shown in examples from Native American history, the island of Bikini, and Japanese in Hawaii. ⦿

> *With the death of each of these individuals*
> *There disappeared from the face of the earth*
> *The last living representative of*
> *A people*
> *A language*
> *An independent tribelet-state*
> *A particular way of interpreting life and its mysteries*
> *The last survivor confronts*
> *An absolute loneliness*
> *He possesses total identity only to himself*
> —Kroeber and Heizer (1968:20)*

* Reprinted by permission from "Last Survivors" by Theodora Kroeber and Robert Heizer, *Almost Ancestors* (New York: Sierra Club–Ballantine, 1968), p. 20.

THE STORY OF ISHI

The Yahi Indians of northern California were a tribe of 300 to 400 people who lived in the foothills of Mount Lassen near the Sacramento River. The Yahi came into conflict with the white settlers in the area, and by the end of the nineteenth century it was believed that all the Yahi had been killed by vigilantes and ranchers. But in 1911 one survivor, a wild-looking, terrified man of about fifty years of age, was found near the town of Oroville. Starving and exhausted, he had come down from the hills and given himself up, expecting to be killed by the whites. He had burned his hair off close to his head, a sign of mourning.

This man was taken to San Francisco and lived in the anthropology museum building at the University of California. Since he would not tell anyone his name, he came to be known as Ishi, "man" in his language. He worked with the anthropologists at the museum until his death in 1916 from tuberculosis. The anthropologists, especially the distinguished A. L. Kroeber, were fascinated with Ishi's account of how he and a few other Yahi had lived in isolation for forty years.

To explain why the Yahi survivors were forced to live in hiding so long, we need to trace briefly the history of contact in northern California. The Yahi were one of many tribes in the Mount Lassen foothills and Sacramento River valley who subsisted mostly through hunting, fishing, and gathering nuts and seeds. During the gold rush of the 1840s and after, white ranchers, farmers, and miners moved into the region. The settlers' livestock spread into the hills and overgrazed the vegetation, and the natives were cut off by hostile ranchers from the areas where they seasonally gathered acorns. The miners polluted the streams and cut off the salmon runs. Their usual food sources diminished, the Yahi began raiding the farms, taking cattle and horses, flour and other supplies. In retaliation, the whites organized posses to raid Yahi villages, shooting and hanging as many Indians as possible (Kroeber 1961:49, 58 ff.).

The hill tribes continued raiding and sometimes in revenge killed settlers and kidnaped their children. Vigilantes increased retaliatory attacks, not only on Yahi but also on other, more peaceful native tribes in the region. Indians were kidnaped and enslaved during the 1850s, and many died from venereal diseases, malaria, flu, smallpox, and other diseases (Kroeber 1961:60).

The Yahi suffered greatly, and by 1870 only twelve were left. More than sixty people had been killed in massacres that year, and the loss of almost all the young women, small children, and infants had been critical. Ishi was about eight or nine years old at the time, one of the few children not to be massacred. The blow to the reproductive potential of the community was irreparable, and the tiny band of twelve who went into hiding in the hills failed to thrive or to reproduce (Kroeber 1961:84–85, 90). By 1894, only five persons remained alive, subsisting by fishing, hunting, and occasional raiding of cabins. Only Ishi and his sister provided food to the group; the others were too old, and one of them died at some point during the long hiding.

In 1909, settlers tracked and discovered the camp of the four Yahi. In the rush to escape, Ishi's sister and the old man disappeared, probably drowning. The raiders took as souvenirs the group's total means of livelihood—all their stores of food, their tools and weapons, and their utensils and clothing.

Ishi's mother died soon after this attack by settlers. Ishi then lived alone in the hills for two years, hungry and grieving, and finally in desperation surrendering to the feared world of the white men.

STRESSORS OF CONTACT

The Yahi case provides a sense of the kinds of physical and social stressors created when two populations encounter each other, especially when they are ecologically in competition and are technologically unequal. There are many types of contact situations, but in the type emphasized here, one indigenous group in relative ecosystemic equi-

FIGURE 8.1   *(a)* Ishi at Oroville, California, August 29, 1911. *(b)* Ishi showing anthropologists how to make a bow from juniper wood.

Photos: Lowie Museum of Anthropology, University of California, Berkeley.

librium encounters people coming from a system undergoing ecological change. The best documented examples of this contact come from
the colonial expansion and imperialism of European and North
American societies since the late fifteenth century, but examples can be
found in any historical period or geographic region. Societies have
been in contact with one another in relations of conquest, trade, and
alliance for thousands of years.

This text has emphasized that human populations are constantly
changing as they adapt biologically and culturally to environmental
problems. Change is not inherently damaging to a population, just as
stress does not necessarily make a person sick. But when ecological or

cultural change leads to imbalance in the relationships that make up an ecosystem, the usual adaptive mechanisms do not work well. The entire population experiences stress in many ways, and actual survival may be at stake if a balanced nutritional, reproductive, and epidemiological system is not restored. Most societies do survive contact, although not without considerable debilitation of individual health and psychological well-being. Groups that do not survive, like the Yahi, suggest the types of change and degrees of stress that are outside the limits of a population's tolerance.

Destruction or depletion of food resources, epidemics, enslavement and confinement on reserves, genocide—these are among the stressors of contact. Human populations are resilient, and in most cases it is more profitable to focus on this capacity for resilience rather than on the negative effects of contact. Still, examples of populations becoming extinct, or no longer existing as culturally distinct units, demonstrate that it is not so much contact itself that threatens a group as it is the cumulative effect of multiple stressors over a short period.

For example, the aborigines who lived on the island of Tasmania near southeastern Australia became extinct by 1876. The 1200 or so nomadic hunters and shellfish collectors were contacted by British soldiers, settlers, and convicts in 1804. Relations between the Tasmanians and the newcomers were much like those between the Yahi and the settlers in California. The rate of decimation was rapid, and only 82 Tasmanians remained alive by 1838. Massacres, capital punishment for even minor offenses, and torture and murder of servants contributed to the death rate, but the major factor was the transmission of diseases to which the natives had no resistance—mostly influenza, tuberculosis, and pneumonia. The poor diet of potatoes, rice, and tea at the mission stations where the people settled added to the population's health problems (Travers 1968).

Extinction after contact is certainly not inevitable. (If it were, cultural anthropology might never have developed.) Most groups initially decline in population and then eventually recover and sometimes even exceed precontact numbers. There is a fairly predictable set of epidemiological, demographic, and nutritional trends in the various stages of contact relations, depending on the intensity of contact. In the next section, we consider types of change processes that occur.

TYPES AND DEGREES
OF CONTACT

Diffusion

When the Polar Eskimos of northwestern Greenland first encountered European explorers, they were astonished to discover that they were not the only people in the world. They believed they alone were Inuit, "human beings." And yet the explorers found that these isolated people of the High Arctic, where there is no wood and little meteoritic iron, already used metal and wood extensively in their tools, boats, and sledges. They had acquired these materials through trade with other Inuit groups to the west and south, who in turn regularly traded with Europeans. Because they recognized the utility of Western goods, the Polar Eskimos readily accepted guns, needles, thimbles, knives, steel traps, tea, flour, and many other items from these explorers (Van Stone 1972). Incorporating foreign tools and foods into their way of life did not bring rapid change, but each new item, especially those used in hunting, had ecological and health repercussions over the long run.

The process of a people "borrowing" an idea, a piece of equipment, or a type of food from another people and incorporating it into their way of life is called **diffusion.** Diffusion involves selective borrowing on the basis of the perceived usefulness and acceptability of the idea or item borrowed. It is the least intense contact process because the borrowers decide whether to accept or to reject the innovation, depending on their own needs and the advantages they hope to gain.

An example of the health repercussions of diffusion comes from the wide acceptance of tobacco all over the world since its introduction into Spain from the New World in 1558. The relative health risks posed by tobacco depend in part on the selective borrowing of smoking patterns. The style, frequency, and context of smoking vary from society to society, and these differences in use patterns correlate with epidemiological patterns. Lung cancer has been much higher in males than in females in the United States partly because it has been more socially acceptable for males to smoke. As tobacco use diffused into Inuit society across the Arctic, women as well as men took up pipe smoking, a less risky form of tobacco use than cigarette smoking. Now that Inuit women have become aware that pipe smoking is not considered "feminine" by southern Canadian and U.S. standards, they are switching to cigarettes, while native males consider either option acceptable. In the future, Inuit women may have higher rates of lung cancer than Inuit men, although at present the risk of tuberculosis is more serious for both sexes than is the risk of lung cancer.

Health problems also arise because of partial diffusion and cultural lag. People often borrow attractive or prestigious traits without acquiring the resources to minimize the health risks. For example, the New Guinea peoples adopted blankets and fitted clothing from Westerners, but only later were they able to incorporate the practice of washing them with soap. In the meantime, the mites that cause scabies thrived in these garments and the problem of skin irritations increased.

Acculturation

A second type of change, **acculturation,** involves continuous and intense contact between two previously autonomous cultural traditions, usually leading to extensive changes in one or both systems (Woods 1975:28–29). Acculturation is more than just the borrowing of material goods or the acceptance of certain ideas: it entails large-scale reorganization of a society to accommodate to the presence of another cultural group. The health problems of acculturation are many, ranging from poor nutrition because of changes in diet to the emotional stress of political or economic subordination, and to exposure to new hazards in the environment.

Not all individuals or families in a population undergo acculturation at the same rate. Some accommodate easily and quickly to the pressures and opportunities created by institutions of the contact society, whereas others resist accommodation. Health status plays a part in such differences. People who are disabled and thus marginal as hunters or farmers are often the first to take advantage of jobs offered by missionaries or traders early in the contact period. Some people have more opportunities than others to acculturate to the new system. Again, health can affect this process of differential opportunity. The first Canadian and Alaskan Eskimos to learn about the modern world were those sent south to hospitals for treatment of tuberculosis and other illnesses brought on by contact.

When they study culture change, anthropologists often find it useful to compare groups at different levels of acculturation within a population. The health problems and practices of each group are often related to its level of acculturation. Hobart (1975) found that Inuit infant mortality rates differed according to the parents' acculturative levels. We might expect that the most acculturated (that is, the most modern) group would have lower infant death rates because the parents can provide better food and medical care for their children. This is in fact true in small settlements of about 200 to 600 people who are still fairly traditional. But in the larger towns where more than 1000 Inuit live, the more acculturated families have *higher* infant death rates. There the more modern parents provide poorer nutrition and hygiene for their children than do the more traditional parents. Modern parents are more apt to spend money on alcohol, and the mother is more likely to be employed and to wean her baby early.

Assimilation

Assimilation occurs when one group changes so completely that it becomes fully integrated into the dominant society or when two groups merge into a new cultural system. Assimilation is a long-range process and is more easily accomplished by individuals motivated to change than by total groups. Generally speaking, assimilating people face health problems similar to those of the dominant group. The new lifestyle they take on poses new disease risks as well as occupational and recreational hazards.

Studies by Cassel and his associates of the social epidemiology of U.S. groups have shown how changes in lifestyle affect health. People who have moved from rural to urban areas suffer higher rates of lung cancer than do lifelong city dwellers. Those who have moved farthest away from their childhood class level and place of residence have the highest rate of heart disease (Cassel 1970:196–198). To be successful in a society that values upward social mobility and encourages geographic mobility entails certain health costs.

The assimilation of ethnic groups into urban settings involves special effects on health, especially in the developing nations of Africa, South America, and the Middle East. If the urban migrant woman becomes a wage laborer, for example, she is likely to breast-feed infants only a few months and to rely on bottle-feeding by caretakers. The middle-class woman also may find it desirable to work as a teacher, as a health worker, or on an office staff, and she too will prefer to wean her babies early. Whether lower- or middle-class, the assimilating individual usually has less choice and fewer options in health alternatives than does the individual at earlier stages of culture contact. Selectivity about what is useful or not, healthy or not becomes difficult because the individual has become completely involved in a new lifestyle.

Ethnic Revitalization

When racial or class barriers to assimilation deter total changes in lifestyle, or when people become disillusioned and frustrated in accommodating to a powerful foreign culture, attempts to revitalize the old system may emerge. Actually, at each stage of contact and acculturation, some individuals do look to ritual or political mechanisms to regain a sense of control, to revitalize their culture, and to attempt to restore equilibrium. In reaffirming ethnic identity, these movements reduce the psychological stress of rapid change. They may also encourage people to reject unhealthy behaviors, foods, and stimulants that have diffused from the intrusive society. A classic case is the religion introduced by Handsome Lake, a Seneca prophet of the Iroquois Confederacy of the early nineteenth century. This religion provided a new code for the Iroquois, who had become physically and socially demoralized during contact (Wallace 1969). Handsome Lake, himself severely weakened by alcoholism, preached that the Seneca were to abstain from drinking whiskey and other disruptive practices. The new code helped to revitalize the traditional identity of the Seneca and to reduce the stress and disorganization of too rapid change.

In the last few years, the Inuit too have showed alarm about the high rate of alcoholism, infant mortality, and the risks of pollution in northern towns. One of the major demands of activist organizations like Inuit Tapirisat (Eskimo Brotherhood) of Canada is for progress in alleviating these health problems. These organizations are also encouraging people to cut down on alcohol and tobacco consumption. Very recently, they have raised the issue of the moral and political implications of government-employed doctors sterilizing Inuit women as a birth control method.

Although for some purposes it is useful to think of diffusion, acculturation, assimilation, and ethnic revitalization as stages of culture change, whole societies do not pass through one stage at a time. In reality, there is much intracultural diversity in how people respond to contact. Some families modernize easily, and others resist change. Some people try out modern practices but later reject them. It is difficult for groups to reverse the direction of change, however. One diffused practice may allow for other desired changes, as when bottle-feeding allows a woman to hold a job. It is difficult for acculturating people to regain the equilibrium of precontact periods. Each new adjustment simply creates new problems requiring further adjustments, as the following profile of Inuit health shows.

PROFILE: CULTURE CHANGE AND INUIT HEALTH

After the Kobuk family* had moved away from Frobisher Bay in 1968 and word came back that their oldest daughter had committed suicide after the move, the neighbors were not particularly surprised. The family was more unlucky than most, but their troubles were familiar to the Eskimo community.

In 1967, Sam Kobuk returned to the Arctic after more than a year of treatment in a southern hospital for tuberculosis. He got his old job back, but he found driving a school bus tiring. His boss complained too much about his being hung over in the mornings.

---

* The names and certain identifying details have been changed in this description, but all other details are true and as accurate as the ethnographer could ascertain. The individuals and house shown in accompanying photographs are *not* those of the "Kobuk" family.

Sam admitted that two or three six-packs of beer a night was a lot, and that all that smoking wasn't helping his lungs. But he needed something to help him forget how his little boy had died while Sam was hospitalized. The toddler had been strangled by the ropes of a child's harness chair suspended from the ceiling. Sam felt somehow responsible for the child's death, and he couldn't get over his anger that such a dangerous apparatus would be sold in the stores.

Sam's wife was pregnant again, and he hoped the baby would be a boy. Mary didn't really care. This was her ninth pregnancy and she was twenty-seven years old. She planned to ask about birth control after the baby was born. She was surprised that the nurses hadn't suggested it earlier. It was too hard to hold down a part-time job, take care of three preschool children, and be pregnant every year and a half.

When four-year-old Tommy was hospitalized in Ontario for tuberculosis, things had been easier, but now he was on chemotherapy at home and constantly complaining about stomach aches from the medicine. It seemed that all seven children got sick too much with ear infections and bronchitis. The littlest one wasn't adjusting well to the mixture of canned evaporated milk, tea, and sugar that Mary prepared for his bottle, and it seemed that he was actually losing weight from diarrhea.

By the winter of 1967, Sam's drinking had increased, and he was coughing up blood. Mary stopped working, so there wasn't much cash in the house. There were fights about Sam's drinking up his pay check. With Sam in no shape to go out ice fishing or seal hunting to bring in a little extra meat, the meals were mostly potatoes, canned beans, and a lot of *bannock,* a pan bread made with flour, lard, baking powder, and water. Even eggs were expensive at the store, $1.60 per dozen, and the price of meat was double the prices in Toronto.

When the oldest daughter, Evie, tested positive for gonorrhea at the nursing station, Sam became furious. She was not yet fourteen, and he was afraid she would get pregnant like so many other teen-age girls in town. The argument escalated, and when Mary tried to intervene, Sam beat her so badly that she miscarried and almost died. Friends urged her to press charges against Sam, or at least to leave him, but she would not. With government assistance, the family relocated the following year to another northern settlement. Shortly after the move, Evie fatally shot herself during a family argument.

When Ann McElroy first heard about the Kobuk family during field research in 1967, their health problems seemed unusually severe. By 1974, after four field trips and a total of fourteen months spent in this Baffin Island community and in another nearby settlement, it was clear to her that the Kobuks were not particularly unusual.

Almost every Inuk had been treated for tuberculosis at some point, and the rate of active cases among children remained around 25 percent. The highest cause of death in the region was injuries due to accidents and violence, 27 percent of all deaths, and a quarter of those were associated with use of alcohol at the time. The second highest cause of death was pneumonia, at 20 percent. Medical personnel considered the rate of venereal disease to be at epidemic proportions.

The birth rate was 64 per 1000, far higher than the figures of 46.8 per 1000 for the Northwest Territories and 24.6 for Canada as a whole in 1965. The mortality rate among infants less than one year old was 124.4 per 1000 in Frobisher Bay, twice as high as the overall rate for the Northwest Territories and six times as high as the rate for all of Canada. In the smaller settlement of Pangnirtung, with about 600 Inuit, the infant mortality rate was 87.4 per 1000, still more than four times the Canadian average. The large town of Frobisher Bay, with 1200 Inuit and 900 Eurocanadians, was more modern and had better medical facilities than Pangnirtung, and yet the infant mortality rate was even higher there (Hobart 1975).

The native adults in these small arctic communities had lived in nomadic hunting-gathering bands in their childhood. Following encounters with whalers and traders, they suffered epidemics of measles, diphtheria, and influenza, and in the 1950s a polio epidemic left many crippled. When hunting was bad and people went hungry, the death rates soared. The opportunity to settle near military bases and construction sites was attractive; not only was there a chance to have jobs and warm houses, but medical help was available. Settling in towns did prevent famine and limit epidemics, but it brought new health problems.

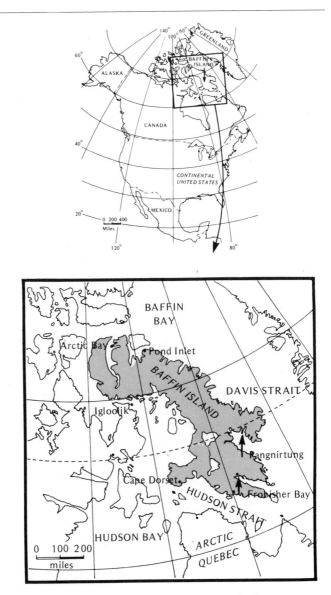

FIGURE 8.2 The Eastern Canadian Arctic and Baffin Island. The two communities of Frobisher Bay and Pangnirtung, sites of McElroy's research, are marked with arrows.

McElroy's study was not initially designed to investigate health problems. The purpose of the research was to discover the impact of culture change on child rearing and family life, but it was important to consider changes in health status in order to understand how children and their parents deal with the pressures of town life (McElroy 1975, 1977). Poor health and inadequate nutrition affect children's energy level and cognitive functioning in the classroom. Adult performance on the job is affected by fatigue, depression, and low resistance to illness. There are also important psychological factors in acculturation, especially political subordination and conflict with white teachers, employers, and supervisors. To comprehend the full weight of these psychological factors, it is important to consider the physical stressors impinging on the people. High absenteeism from work or

FIGURE 8.3   An important part of any anthropological field work is participant-observation—in this case, babysitting. Ann McElroy joins two pre-teen friends in their daily task of carrying toddlers in the *amaut*, or mother's parka. The women are then free for hunting-camp work, principally preparing seal and caribou skins for clothing and export.

Photo by Ann McElroy.

FIGURE 8.4   A prefabricated Inuit house equipped with electricity, telephone
service, and oil spaceheater, but no indoor plumbing. The small
picket fence encloses huskie puppies. In summer, Inuit children
ride their bicycles on the gravel roads of the town.
Photo by Ann McElroy.

school cannot be explained solely as due to ambivalence or
repressed hostility toward the dominant Eurocanadian system,
an explanation favored by psychologically oriented anthropologists.

As noted in the health profile in chapter 1, the Inuit of northern
Canada had remarkably good health in the centuries before
contact with Europeans, just as do most hunter-gatherers living
in isolation. They had relatively few parasites or infectious
diseases, and accidents were the most frequent cause of death.
The food supply was generally abundant, although its seasonal
dispersal did not allow large permanent groups to form. Famine
did occur occasionally, but chronic malnutrition was rare.

How and why did the health of native peoples change so significantly in the Arctic? The change did not come only within a few
years. Rather, the poor health status of the Inuit reflects many

generations affected by epidemics, inadequate nutrition, and
diffusion of inappropriate styles of housing, clothing, and footwear. Their health reflects a long history of contact with explorers, fur traders, whaling crews, and missionaries, who all
brought new disease organisms to a population with little resistance. It reflects the ways the Inuit have accommodated to the
original contact agents as well as to more recent ones—the
military, administrators, teachers, and northern development
companies searching for oil and natural gas.

The Inuit do not have a written history of this century and a half
of contact and change, but they remember more recent times of
sickness and have saved old, yellowed photographs taken by
missionaries in the 1920s and 1930s. These photographs vividly
illustrate the hunger and confusion that epidemics brought.
Earlier periods of sickness are documented by the first anthropologist to study the people of Pangnirtung, Franz Boas. In 1883,
Boas wrote about an epidemic of diphtheria during which a
number of Inuit children died. He also documented frequent
cases of pneumonia and syphilis. When whalers first came to
Baffin Island in 1840, about 1600 Inuit hunted around the Cumberland Sound area. By 1857, a Moravian missionary could count
only 300 people in all the camps, and Boas himself found ten
bands ranging in size from 11 to 82 people, giving a total of only
328 (Boas 1964:17–18). This reduction is considerably more than
the average decimation rate in the Arctic, estimated by Guemple
to be 30 percent (1972:95), but the people of Cumberland Sound
had more intensive contact with whalers and traders than did
many groups. By 1850, the natives were working for the whalers
every winter, hunting the whales, repairing sails, making clothing, and supplying them food. They were also drinking the
whalers' whiskey, enjoying their tobacco, tea, and molasses, and
in some cases setting up housekeeping with them. Economically,
the Inuit profited, but their health suffered greatly. Relations
with the Europeans also altered the ecosystem. Firearms were
indiscriminately used, trapping for furs predominated over
hunting for meat, and the whales were overhunted and depleted.

Epidemics did not stop with the turn of the century and the
arrival of medical personnel. In 1902, the entire population of
Saglermiut of Southampton Island died from a disease resem-
bling typhus, introduced by Scottish whalers (Ross 1977:4). In all

populations, tuberculosis became the leading cause of death, and the flu epidemic of 1918–1919 hit just as hard as it did all over the world. Between 1951 and 1955, measles and flu epidemics in Ft. Chimo, on the western shore of Hudson Bay, killed 130 people out of a total of 600 (Hughes 1965:14). Throughout the 1950s, polio killed and crippled many people. The still uncontrolled diseases today include venereal diseases, bronchitis, and otitis media (middle ear infection). Tuberculosis is essentially under control, although most of the population is still not as resistant as Eurocanadians and many still require chemotherapy.

Rates of injury and death from the hazards of modern life remain at critical levels, especially for children and young people. Between 1967 and 1970, McElroy noted the following accidents in Pangnirtung and Frobisher Bay, and this is in no way an exhaustive list: six children drowned when their canoe overturned and two drowned by falling off a bridge into rapids. Two children died in a house fire, one was hit fatally by a schoolbus, and one was killed by a ricocheting bullet during a quarrel between two men. Two youths died in a snowmobile accident, and two young women committed suicide, one by shooting herself through the abdomen and thus also killing her unborn child. Two children were attacked by dogs. One boy caught his arm in the propeller of an airplane and had to have it amputated. A child swallowed a safety pin, and several toddlers were scalded. Several young girls almost died from exposure to cold when they passed out from intoxication outdoors in subzero weather.

Changes in nutrition are having especially important effects on children's growth. Otto Schaefer, a physician, has found that the present generation of Inuit children on Baffin Island are growing taller and faster than was the generation tested in 1938. Modern children also reach puberty earlier than their parents did. Schaefer attributes these changes to an increase in the consumption of carbohydrates, especially sugar, rather than to better nutrition in general.

Not only were young adults one to two inches taller than their parents, but in the 1950s and 1960s average birth weights had increased by more than a pound. This trend stopped in the 1970s, however, and birth weights are now going down. Schaefer believes (1977:33) that this is due to heavy smoking by women during pregnancy and the fact that birth rates are highest among

ᐱᐊᖃᐄ ᐃᐊᐧᖕ ᐊᓗᑕᘇᐱ?

Should you breast-feed your baby?

ᑲᐅᐱᖪᐃᔅ ᐊᑕᐃᖪᐧᑯ ᐃᐊ
ᐱᐧᖢ, ᐧᐅᖢᐅᘇᐧ ᐅᐊᔅ ᐧᐧ ᑲ
ᑕᓚ ᐃᐧᐃᕍᐃᖪᖪ, ᐅ
ᔅ ᐧᘇᐧᔅ ᓇᖪᘇᐅᔅ. ᐃᕍᐅᔅ
54

Some important information about brea-st-feeding, prepared by Dr. Connelly of Northern Health Services, recently arrived on our desks. We think that all expectant mothers, as well as young mothers

FIGURE 8.5 Two pages from an article on breast-feeding in the bilingual magazine *Inuit Today*. The magazine's publishers, Inuit Tapirisat (Eskimo Brotherhood) of Canada, attempt to inform Inuit families about health risks of modernization through articles like this. Most Eastern Arctic Inuit can read

ᒥᓂ, ᓱᐅᑎᒥᓂ, ᐊᒪᓗ ᐊᓱᒥᓂ ᑎᒥᒥᓂ,
ᓴᓚᑲᕈᓇᑎᐊᒃ ᒃᑯᐱᒃᕈᕋᓛᕈᓗᓂᒃ ᐊᓂᒪᐃᒪ
ᒥᒃ ᐊᓇᓇᒪᑕ ᐃᓗᐊᓂᒃ ᒃᑯᐱᕈᑲᒥᑐᒥᒃ.
ᐊᓇᓇᐃᑦ ᑐᓂᓱᐸᐳᑦ ᐃᓚᒪᓂᒃ ᓴᒥᓂᒃᒥᓂᒃ
ᐊᒪᓗ ᒃᑯᐱᕈᑲᓇᒥᑐᒥᒃ ᐃᒧᒥᒃ ᐊᒪᒪᑎᓱᓕ
ᕋᐃᒪᒥᒃ ᐃᐱᐊᒥᒃᒥᓂᒃ ᒃᑭᑐᒪᒥᓂᒃ.

Here we found, for example, that bottlefed Inuit babies have in different areas three to ten times more running ears than breastfed ones. We found also that practically all Inuit and Indian infants and children with recurrent and chronic chest trouble were bottlefed, and that breastfed infants, by contrast, had chest infections very rarely. We found also that bottlefed Inuit and Indian babies had a much poorer chance to survive infancy than breastfed ones.

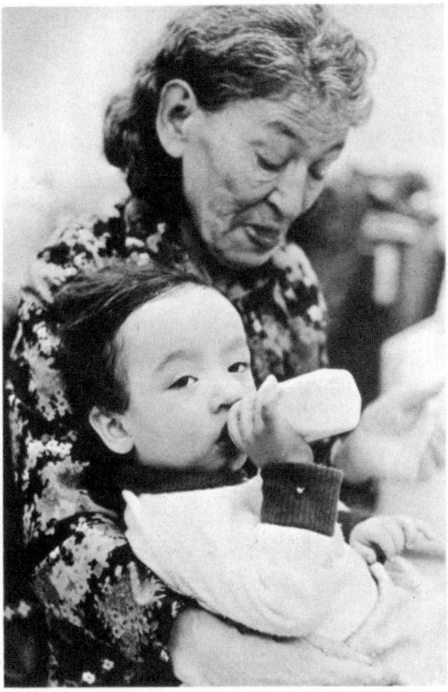

Photo - Layng, Ottawa

ᐃᓅᕈᕋᑕᒃᑐᑦ ᐱᐊᕋᐃᑦ ᓂᑎᒍᓇᒥᒪᑕ
ᓂᑭᓂᒃ ᑎᓱᐹᓂᒃ ᐊᑲᐅᐹᒥᒃ. ᐊᒃᑭᐊᕈᒥᑦ
ᐱᑎᑕᐅᐸᑕ ᐃᒧᒥᒃ ᐃᒧᓱᐅᒪᐅᑉ ᐃᒧᒪᓂᒃ
ᐱᓴᕋᐃᓗᐊᒃᓗᓂ, ᐃᒪᑲ ᐊᑭᐊᕈᒪ ᐃᓇᓗᐊ
ᒥᓗ ᐊᑲᐅᒥᓕᕋᔭᐸᓛᐃᒪᑕ. ᐊᓯᐃᓚᒃ ᐊᒪᒃ
ᑎᒃᓂᒃ ᐱᑕᑲᓱᒪᔭᒃᒪᑦ ᐊᒪᓗ ᐊᒪᒃᑎᓕᒃᑐᑦ

Therefore, if you want to do the best you can to help your baby to survive and grow up healthy, you should do all you can to breastfeed him or her. The first step to be a successful nursing mother

56

either English or the syllabic script shown here, originally introduced by Anglican missionaries and now taught in many schools.

SOURCE: Reprinted with the permission of *Inuit Today* (Ottawa, Ontario).

adolescents, who tend to have a higher rate of premature or low-birth-weight babies than do older women.

In 1959, the per capita annual consumption of sugar in all forms was 26 pounds (12 kg) in Pangnirtung. By 1967, each person consumed on the average 104 pounds (46 kg) each year, a fourfold increase in less than ten years (Schaefer 1971). With this change, the protein–carbohydrate ratio approached the typical urban North American pattern, estimated in 1955 in the United States to be 103 grams of protein per day and 275 grams of carbohydrates per day, of which 51 percent were sugars. By 1964, the consumption ratio in Frobisher Bay was similar, with a daily average of 128 grams of protein and 254 grams of carbohydrates per day. In Pangnirtung, protein intake remained higher, 318 grams to 254 grams of carbohydrates, 30 percent sugars.

What are the effects of this shift toward carbohydrates? In addition to growth acceleration, the rate of dental caries is very high. Among adults, Schaefer found increasing prevalence of diabetes mellitus, obesity, excessive lipids in the blood, and gall bladder disease. He found in a series of tests that the Inuit have difficulty keeping blood sugar levels stable after ingesting sugar. The body's response includes overstimulation of insulin production, growth hormones, and glucocorticoids. In other words, the high sugar intake is unusually stressful for them. Schaefer is particularly concerned about the children, "considering the way the Eskimos eat candies and other sweets and gulp sweet drinks frequently at all times of the day" (1971:11).

Another change is that Inuit women are breast-feeding their infants for shorter periods. Formerly, two to three years of nursing was typical, but today many mothers prefer to wean their babies at around twelve to sixteen months, and canned or powdered milk and commercial baby foods have made this possible. Schaefer found that bottle-fed Inuit children had a higher incidence of gastrointestinal diseases, middle-ear infections, anemia, and respiratory infections than did breast-fed infants.

For the Kobuks and many other Inuit families, culture contact has brought far-reaching changes, some of which the people perceive negatively. For example, they believe that caribou and seal are much healthier than store food, and they are concerned about alcohol use. Other changes are considered to be positive, though, especially the availability of doctors and medicines. The Inuit are realists, and so they see both advantages and disadvantages in town living. Most important, though, they see no good alternative to living in permanent settlements. The risks of living out on the land are too great and the security of town is too attractive. As one Inuk told Ann McElroy during a conversation about land claims:

> We don't want to be rich, you know. We just want enough food in the house to feed the kids, so the family doesn't go hungry. A lot of kids used to die because there wasn't enough food. It's important to us to keep the kids healthy. You know, some people say that the government should leave us alone, just pull out and let us keep the old way of life. But my wife says who would run the hospital? What if the kids get sick? I don't know, what I figure is that the government is pretty good for us right now. The only thing is I can't always understand what the government wants, what those people are trying to tell us.

MODELS FOR THE STUDY OF CONTACT PROCESSES

The profile of the Kobuk family illustrates many of the stressors of contact: low immunity to infectious disease, malnutrition, inappropriate use of alcohol, high birth rates, and high infant mortality rates are all problems that plague many Native American groups today. The changes that the Inuit experienced can be analyzed as changes in four major categories of variables that determine health status: epidemiological variables, demographic variables, nutritional variables, and health care variables. We will be looking at these variables separately to see how they are affected by contact, but remember that they are linked to one another and work together in maintaining a population's adaptation to the environment.

Figure 8.6 shows changes in these four variables through the stages of contact between Inuit and Europeans. Inuit had no immunities to

	STAGE I Pre-contact	STAGE II Early contact and diffusion	STAGE III Settlement and acculturation	STAGE IV Modernization and assimilation
Epidemiological subsystem	Few pathogens in ecosystem; low immunities to infections	Epidemics of infectious diseases	Hyper-endemic infectious & nutritional diseases	Endemic infectious, nutritional, and stress-related diseases
Demographic subsystem	Births $\simeq$ deaths, population stable	Births $<$ deaths, population decline	Births $>$ deaths, population growth	Births $\geq$ deaths, slow population growth
Nutritional subsystem	High protein, low carbohy-drate; fluctu-ating supply	Carbohydrate supplements; famine inter-acting with epidemics	High carbohy-drate, low protein; food supply steady but nutrition-ally poor	High carbohydrate, low protein; supply and quality varies by socio-economic status
Health resources subsystem	Shamans and midwives fulfill limited medical & psychothera-peutic needs	Shamans dis-credited in epidemics; missions pro-vide relief	Government & missions pro-vide modern medical care; health needs greatly in-creased	Modern medicine continues; birth control increases; health care and ethnic politics interconnected

FIGURE 8.6   Changes in health subsystems of Canadian Inuit during stages of culture contact.

most of the diseases transmitted by Europeans, and the result was a series of epidemics and a declining population, as shown in stage II of the epidemiological and demographic subsystems. Weakened by illness and by loss of productive group members, the hunting bands faced famine and had to depend increasingly on high-carbohydrate rations from the missions and trading posts, as shown in the nutritional subsystem. The poor nutritive value of imported foods perpetuated low disease resistance and demographic imbalance for several generations. Shamans who had proved successful in the past in treating primarily psychogenic illnesses were discredited both by missionaries and by Inuit because they could not cure diphtheria, tuberculosis, or other diseases. They lost power and credibility during the early contact and diffusion stage, and the health resources subsystem was open to change.

Health Risks of Acculturation

In some ways, the data in figure 8.6 are typical of most contact situations; population decline followed by rebound population growth is predictable, as long as the population does not dip below a critical threshold and become extinct. In other ways, the Inuit are not typical because the Europeans did not want their land or their food resources, but rather their furs, ivory, whale oil, and religious conversion. In return, the Europeans offered new means of livelihood and settlement patterns, and the weakened population found such opportunities advantageous, although not free of health risks.

The following paragraphs provide specific examples of Stages III and IV in the Inuit case.

EPIDEMIOLOGICAL RISKS   The concentration in new settlements of relatively large numbers of Inuit intensified the transmission network of communicable diseases. Every summer when new ships from Scotland, Nova Scotia, or New England arrived, various illnesses termed "ship's fever" would break out, and newcomers to the settlements were prone to contract chronic illnesses from other natives. Changes in housing, clothing, and food also lowered disease resistance. The wooden or prefabricated houses were either too drafty or too hot, difficult to keep clean, and lacking plumbing and sewage disposal. Imported clothing required frequent washing, yet fresh water is always in short supply in arctic villages.

DEMOGRAPHIC CHANGES   Birth rates rose following settlement, despite continuing high rates of disease and death. This rise was an adaptive response to the severe decimation of the early contact period, but it persisted into the next phase of acculturation and resulted in rapid population growth and births that were too closely spaced. Traditional population regulators such as infanticide had fallen into disuse during the period of population decline and are no longer acceptable or legal. Men are less frequently away for hunting and more often at home, increasing the frequency of sexual intercourse and the chance of conception.

Inuit also have painful memories of having lost many children and siblings during the time of epidemics. They enjoy children and value large families even though they acknowledge the financial strain and overcrowding of houses. So there is not yet strong support for the idea of birth control, at least not until a woman has had four or five children.

NUTRITIONAL SHIFTS Diet is yet another of the factors that affect fertility. Binford and Chasko (1976) found that most of the increase in Alaskan Inuit birth rates is due to the shift toward consuming more carbohydrates. They suggest that deficiencies in vitamin E in the traditional diet inhibited sperm production and that a modern diet increases spermatogenesis and the chances of conception.

The shift from a diet mostly of animal protein to dependence on high-carbohydrate imported foods lowered disease resistance. It also contributed directly to certain diseases such as diabetes and affected growth patterns in children and dental health. It is also possible that the special energy needs of the body in such a cold climate are best met by large amounts of animal protein and fats; at any rate, Inuit complain of less tolerance to cold than in previous decades.

CHANGES IN HEALTH CARE The health resources subsystem has changed from a fairly simple ethnomedicine to a small-scale replica of the Western medical system. The change has been necessary because the very culture-contact process providing modern health resources has also created severe epidemiological and nutritional problems. And modern medicine has created new problems while solving others. Birth control is one example: contraceptives are now available to all married Inuit women, but information about the long-term health risks of the most popular form, oral contraceptives, is not well communicated. Women who smoke are especially at risk of complications from the pill, and Inuit women generally smoke heavily.

A second example of problems created by medical care is that serious medical problems are usually handled in southern cities. The patient is typically flown by twin-engine plane to Frobisher Bay and then by jet to Montreal or Toronto. The hospital stay is likely to last several months and sometimes much longer, which is stressful both for the patient and for his or her family. Not only are cities strange and fearful, but often no one in the hospital speaks the Inuttitut language. The stress of separation is difficult for all family members, but small children who have recently been weaned are particularly traumatized when their mothers must be away.

The variable of health resources includes not only hospitals and medicines, but also access to medical care. As in all societies, in Inuit communities age, status, and power affect one's access to information about health resources. For example, unmarried Inuit girls are not counseled about contraception, and they have no legal access to contraceptives or abortions. The doctors, nurses, and conservative native elders are opposed to providing teen-agers with contraceptives for moral rather than medical reasons. But their moral stance does not prevent teen-agers from having sexual freedom and becoming pregnant.

In the following three sections, we examine specific examples of how each of the subsystems (epidemiology, demography, nutrition, and health care) has been affected by culture contact. Each historical case illustrates basic principles of change. Our purpose here is to work toward understanding how relationships within a human ecosystem change under varying kinds of contact and degrees of impact. Because these health variables form a system, when there is change in one part of the system—for example, in nutrition—we expect change in disease patterns, demography, and health care.

In discussing historical cases, we usually focus on only one of the societies in contact, the one whose home territory is involved. This approach helps simplify our model. But if we wished, we could emphasize that the intrusive population also faces disease risks. The Spaniards suffered as much from yellow fever as did the Indians during an epidemic in Yucatán in 1648 (Ashburn 1947:134), and some disease historians claim that Christopher Columbus and his crew brought syphilis back to Europe from the New World, although this has been debated (Crosby 1969; Wood 1978). Although the health effects of contact are usually not drastic enough to threaten the survival of the intrusive population, the fact that settlers and explorers are often in a poor state of health themselves helps us understand the way they respond to the natives they encounter. Theodora Kroeber (1961) gives us some insight into the inhumane behavior of the settlers responsible for the extermination of the Yahi. Searching for an answer to why "people of principle, many of them, and of good upbringing and antecedents, some of them, could act toward their Indian predecessors on the land with such ferocious inhumanity and brutality," Kroeber found in reading historical accounts and journals that "between frustrated cupidity, cholera, scurvy, dysentery, starvation, filth, exhaustion, and disillusionment, they arrived in California already dehumanized and brutalized in their behavior to one another and to strangers alike" (pp. 52–53).

EPIDEMIOLOGICAL CHANGE

Malaria in the New World

Between 1830 and 1833, a disease thought to be malaria swept through Oregon and north central California. The epidemic debilitated settlers and decimated between 50 and 75 percent of the populations of all native groups affected (Cook 1972:192). Its effect on the history of the West Coast was significant, for native survivors had little strength in numbers or in morale to resist the continuing waves of gold prospectors and settlers.

We noted in chapter 3 that malaria is an insectborne protozoal disease. Direct contact between persons is not necessary for transmission of the disease. What is necessary is the presence of a vector species of *Anopheles*, stagnant water and sunlit pools for their breeding, and a large, concentrated, and at least partially nonimmune population whose habitat overlaps with that of the mosquitoes. These conditions were met along the Columbia, Willamette, and Sacramento and San Joaquin rivers (see figure 8.7), areas where the mosquito species *A. maculipennis freeborni* thrived and where thousands of native

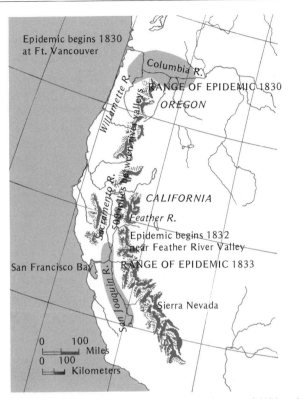

FIGURE 8.7   Origin and boundaries of the malaria epidemics of 1830 and 1833 that decimated Native Americans along the Columbia–Willamette and Sacramento–San Joaquin river system.

people lived. The course of the disease was directly related to mosquito habitats; villages around San Francisco Bay were not affected at all because that area was exclusively occupied by a nonvector anopheline (Cook 1972:177). The same is true of the 500-mile region between the Columbia–Willamette and the Sacramento river systems. With no vector mosquitoes in the region, the epidemic could not take hold although infected persons might be in contact with nonimmunes. Two important factors are operating, then:

1. There is a suitable vector for the infection in the ecosystem.
2. There is a nonimmune reservoir population in the ecosystem.

These two factors are sufficient conditions for transmission of the disease, but malaria was not endemic to the region and had to be introduced by a **carrier**—that is, an infected person who suffers chronically and intermittently from malaria—coming into the region. Thus we need to consider the intrusion and mobility of carriers.

In this case, the epidemic began at Fort Vancouver (see figure 8.7) in 1830. The parasite was probably transmitted when a mosquito bit a sailor infected with malaria he had contracted when he went ashore in malarial parts of the Pacific or even Africa, and thus the cycle of transmission began. Both whites and Indians around Fort Vancouver came down with the disease in late summer 1830.

If the whites had been immune, the epidemic in California might not have occurred three years later. But infected frontiersmen and settlers traveled from Oregon into California where large numbers of natives lived along the San Joaquin and Sacramento rivers. Up to this point, the mosquitoes of the rivers had been annoying but not harmful, but now their bites transmitted the newly introduced pathogen. The large and semisedentary populations depended on the river systems for subsistence and could not easily move to other regions as did many of the pioneers who were on their way to the coast and were exposed to the mosquitoes only temporarily. Thus we can list three additional factors:

3. Carriers of the parasite migrated from the site of the original epidemic to a new area.
4. Large numbers of nonimmunes were living in close contact with one another, allowing an extensive transmission chain between a thriving vector population and new victims.
5. The human population was sedentary and adapted to a habitat shared with the vector, without suitable alternatives for subsistence in other regions.

Malaria is more often endemic than epidemic. Where the disease persists, populations are continually exposed to infection in childhood. Those who survive build up a degree of immunity or tolerance over time. Rarely is malaria as virulent as it was in nineteenth-century California. One of the worst malaria epidemics on record in recent years affected 3 million people, half the population, in Sri Lanka in

1934–35, but only 3 percent of these (80,000 people) died (Burnet and White 1972:235–236). Cook's estimate was a 75 percent fatality rate for most California groups affected. What factors contributed to such a high death rate?

First, remembering the kinds of stressors that Ishi's people experienced, all native Californians were under considerable strain throughout the 1800s. Malaria was only one of the many diseases introduced. Tens of thousands died from venereal disease, influenza, smallpox, typhoid, and other illnesses (Kroeber 1961:47). Three thousand to 4000 children were kidnaped and sold as slaves or forced into prostitution. All these physical and emotional stressors contributed to lowered disease resistance, as did the breakdown of social organization and of health care resources. So many people were sick at any given time that the provisioning system broke down, depleting supplies of food and adding poor nutrition to the weight of infection.

In studying changes in epidemiological systems, then, it is important to consider the range of stressors and the group's ability to mobilize health care in the face of massive sickness and social disequilibrium. Thus two more conditions lead to epidemiological change:

6. The reservoir population was under considerable social and physical stress before the epidemic began.
7. There was a general breakdown of care facilities and provisioning activities in the population, increasing nutritional and emotional stress.

Figure 8.8 is a schematic representation of the example we just covered. If we were to analyze other historical cases, we might add or delete certain factors depending on the pathogen's requirements for survival, the population's vulnerability, and the particular ecosystemic relationships between humans and other organisms. The change model will vary according to each of these factors.

The history of conquest of the New World by Europeans becomes clarified when we understand how significant a role disease played in lowering the resistance of Native Americans. Fifty years after the arrival of Cortez, the population of central Mexico had been reduced to only a tenth of its previous size. The ravages of smallpox gave Cortez an easy victory over the Aztecs in 1520, and the disease spread to

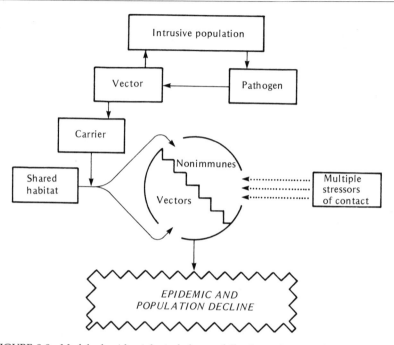

FIGURE 8.8   Model of epidemiological change following culture contact.

Guatemala and then to the Incan Empire of the Peruvian Andes by 1525. The disruption of the smallpox epidemic led to civil war, and the Incas were unable to resist Pizarro and his soldiers. Smallpox was only the first of several epidemics in Central and South America. Measles spread through Mexico and Peru in 1530 and 1531, typhus fifteen years later, and influenza twelve years after that (McNeill 1976:180–185).

In this section, we have analyzed a case of epidemiological change, isolating a few factors that influenced the process of change. If the data were available, we might also focus on the reproductive changes and nutritional problems that resulted from the high death rates and collapse of social organization. In the next section, we consider an example from New Guinea that illustrates the rise in fertility and birth rates that follows acculturation.

DEMOGRAPHIC CHANGE

The Asmat of New Guinea

The 40,000 Asmat of Indonesian New Guinea, now called Irian Jaya, remained isolated from permanent contact with the modern world until 1953. The Asmat traditionally engaged in tribal warfare and headhunting, and the dislocations of populations resulting from initial contact doubtless intensified these conflicts. The Dutch and subsequent Indonesian government personnel, whose main goal was pacification, tried to suppress warfare by jailing and fining the warriors. Infanticide was also suppressed. Medical teams participated in contact relations and worked to eradicate yaws, to reduce the severity of malaria and elephantiasis, and to screen all people coming into the region to limit the transmission of measles, tuberculosis, and cholera.

Despite these medical efforts, the crude death rate was high after contact, between 21 and 45 deaths per 1000 population per year in communities surveyed between 1955 and 1961 (van Amelsvoort 1964:196). As late as 1973, the rate was 37 per 1000 in the region studied by Van Arsdale (1975:7). To get a sense of how high this is, the crude death rate of Canadian Eskimos in 1968 was 10.6 per 1000, while the rate for all Canada was 7.5. The causes of death are not well documented. The Asmat did suffer epidemics of whooping cough and chicken pox, and infant mortality from pneumonia and other infectious diseases was especially high.

In some communities, there were almost as many infant deaths during certain years of the 1950s as there were births. The rate ranged from 125 to 900 per 1000 infants per year. Slightly less than half of all children born to adults in Van Arsdale's sample survey had died either in infancy or in childhood.

After the extent of infant mortality became known, one of the first medical steps taken was to encourage women to give birth in hospitals. Well-baby clinics were also established in the communities. But after four years, the infant mortality rate was *higher* in villages with these services than in communities lacking clinics. Hospital delivery made no difference in the rates, and it was found that mortality from natural causes right after a normal delivery was generally low in any event (van Amelsvoort 1964:113–115).

Two demographic characteristics of this situation of early acculturation, then, are the following:

1. While traditional causes of death (warfare, headhunting raids, infanticide, malaria) were reduced by contact, new causes of death were induced by contact, primarily infectious diseases.
2. The rate of infant mortality was very high despite modern medical facilities; hospital delivery did not reduce mortality, which was primarily due to postnatal factors.

The crude live birth rate was also high among the Asmat, ranging from 28 to 86 per 1000 between 1955 and 1961 (van Amelsvoort 1964:196) and 56 per 1000 in 1973 (Van Arsdale 1975:4). This rate is very similar to that of most developing countries as well as most acculturating tribal societies. The rate of natural population increase is 1.5 percent (Van Arsdale 1978:457). The general birth rate pattern is as follows:

3. Birth rates varied annually and by community from low to unusually high levels during early contact; in the 1970s birth rates continued to be high, with a growth rate of about 1.5 percent.
4. The overall pattern of high death rates and high birth rates is characteristic of acculturating societies and developing nations; high infant mortality accounts for much of the inflated death rates.

What factors account for the high birth rates? It is possible that all women are having more children and thus fertility has increased in the acculturation process. Or, as seems to be the case, spacing between pregnancies may be decreasing among younger women. Women over age 50 had given birth to an average of 7.6 children. The group of Asmat women aged 25 to 29 had already had an average of 3.1 children when surveyed in 1973, and it is projected by Van Arsdale that their completed fertility may be even higher than that of women of the older generation with 7.6 children.

Shortened birth intervals may be the reason for increase in birth rates, and several factors contribute to decreased intervals, though the relative contribution of each factor is unknown. Shorter birth spacing may be a way of compensating for high infant mortality and deaths in epidemics. Nutritional change and a more sedentary life may contribute in some way.

Changes in birth rates, then, involve the following two factors:

5. Women in their mid-twenties had a larger number of completed pregnancies than expected in comparison with birth rates of other age groups.
6. Shorter birth spacing acted to compensate for high infant mortality rates.

Another factor in demographic change is the decline in female infanticide, which is related to the suppression of tribal warfare. Like many tribal peoples with population pressure and limited territory, the Asmat emphasized ritual warfare, headhunting, and male supremacy (cf. Divale and Harris 1976). With a premium on male infants, selective female infanticide had provided some degree of population control. Also, when men participated in ritual and warfare in the days before pacification, their wives were not as frequently exposed to the risk of conception because of restrictions on intercourse.

With infanticide far less frequent, the ratio of male to female surviving children was more equal than before contact. Not only did this increase the general population size, with a disproportionately large number of children and young people (the average age being 22.1 years), but it also made it possible to continue high rates of population growth because of the increased number of females available for reproduction in the next generation.

The final factor in demographic change among the Asmat, then, is the following:

7. With the suppression of warfare and female infanticide, there were larger numbers of surviving female infants, a potentially larger pool of reproducers in the next generation, and less restriction on sexual intercourse due to male warfare-connected rituals and taboos.

Figure 8.9 gives a schematic summary of the demographic changes in the Asmat case.

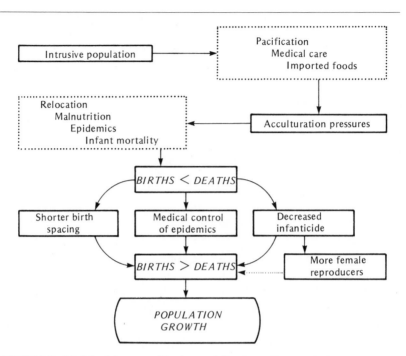

FIGURE 8.9   Model of demographic change following culture contact.

NUTRITIONAL AND HEALTH CARE CHANGE

A Rural Health Center in South Africa

Our third extended example of effects of culture contact on health emphasizes nutrition and health care variables in assessing the impact of a rural health center on the food habits of a Zulu community in South Africa. The information is drawn from the research of John Cassel, a social epidemiologist (1955, 1977).

The type of culture contact described here is characteristic of post-colonial government attempts to change health behavior and beliefs. There is often a critical need for health education programs to remedy nutritional problems created by acculturation and economic change. This was the case in 1940 with the Zulu, a Bantu people who had been a powerful Southeast African state in the nineteenth century. Internal conflict, famine, and war with Europeans had broken their unity, and the policy of confinement to reserves brought ecological imbalance.

The Zulu raised cattle and farmed. Nutrition had been good, with plentiful supplies of milk products, meat, wild greens, and millet, a high-protein grain. But by the 1940s, there was evidence of severe nutritional deficiencies among the 16,000 Zulu of southwestern Natal. Cases of pellagra and kwashiorkor were frequent, as were epidemics of typhoid, typhus, and smallpox. The people also suffered from tuberculosis, syphilis, and dysentery. The infant mortality rate was 276 per 1000 and the crude death rate was 38 per 1000.

The reasons for malnutrition were partly diffusion from Western diets and acculturation pressures and partly traditional taboos and food preferences. The main staple was maize, introduced by settlers to South Africa and gradually accepted by the Bantu, who found it preferable to millet because of its higher yield. Commercially refined carbohydrates, especially sugars, had also diffused from urban centers. The Zulu supplemented their diet with dried beans, potatoes, pumpkin, beer brewed from millet, and small amounts of milk curds. They bought sugar, white bread, and refined maize meal with whatever cash was available. The soil was so poor and eroded that most families could not grow enough maize to support themselves and had to buy it with wage income.

Most important among the many acculturation pressures was the introduction of wage labor in mines and factories. The poor quality of reserve lands for farming and grazing meant that urban migration of male laborers was essential. Women, children, and elderly men were left behind to farm and herd with inadequate techniques and insufficient energy. They did not carry out crop rotation or mulching, and soil cover was destroyed by deforestation for fuel and by burning pasture land each spring. These practices led to severe soil erosion.

The third factor involved traditional food restrictions. Most families raised chickens, but few people ate eggs. It was believed that eating eggs was a sign of greed and would make females promiscuous. In addition, girls and women were not allowed to consume milk because it was believed that menstruating or pregnant women were dangerous to cattle.

The nutritional problems of the Zulu were due to three major factors:

1. Foods of poorer nutritional quality than those consumed traditionally had diffused and become preferred by most people because of convenience and economic benefits.
2. Reserve lands were inadequate for farming, and the people, accustomed to migrating whenever necessary to new grazing and farming areas, had not learned intensive agriculture techniques. Inadequate yield required wage labor by men in the cities, thus increasing dependence on commercial foodstuffs.
3. Traditional beliefs prevented the full use of available eggs and milk products, especially by girls and women.

Culture contact involves not only change in health-related personnel and practices, but also change in information and beliefs related to health behavior. The health resources of a people always include important cognitive and symbolic dimensions. Food is symbolically important to all societies, and it is very difficult to persuade a people to accept nutritional change unless their beliefs about food also change. The health workers of the Polela Health Centre knew that pregnant and lactating women critically needed the calcium and protein from milk products, but they could also understand and respect the emotional strength of Zulu beliefs. Health personnel sometimes dismiss such beliefs as "superstitions," failing to recognize that cattle represent the wealth and pride of each family. Women who are menstruating, pregnant, or have just given birth are in a special physiological state that to the Zulu denotes power and danger. A woman's contact with milk products symbolizes contact with cattle. Such beliefs are resistant to change because they are important defenses against anxieties. Such deeply felt beliefs are unlikely to change because of logical arguments.

The medical personnel recognized that their program could not become an acceptable or effective resource for nutritional change unless they began with an issue that was less sensitive than milk consumption. Thus they chose to begin with gardening. First, they had to convince the Zulu of the need for dietary change. The people knew they were in poor health, but they believed their diet was identical to their ancestors' traditional diet and therefore could not be to blame for their problems.

The first step was to get older tribesmen to confirm that the traditional diet had indeed been different. The prestige of these elders strengthened the credibility of the health team. Then health education about digestion and nutrition began, with emphasis on prenatal development. Model gardens, seed-buying cooperatives, and eventually small markets for sale of surplus vegetables from home gardens were successfully established. Similar techniques were used to increase egg consumption. Success was slower, but eggs were being fed to children on a regular basis within twelve years.

Increasing milk consumption was anticipated to be the most difficult problem, but it turned out that no one objected to allowing women to drink powdered milk. As long as it was clear that the powder was not processed from the milk of Zulu cows, consumption by women was acceptable. This nutritional change barrier turned out to be easily surmountable. Moreover, the health workers did not attempt to discredit the traditional belief system, often one of the reasons for conflict between a native community and Western contact agents.

The factors that brought about change in health resources, then, included the following:

4. Barriers to the credibility and effectiveness of the health team were probed by surveying beliefs about food, reasons for food taboos, and the emotional significance of cattle and milk products.
5. Health educators used respected elders to verify information about nutritional change; their efforts included concrete examples such as model gardens. In general, health workers attempted to demonstrate positive benefits to be derived from changes in food consumption.
6. Health workers attempted to work with neutral issues such as gardens and egg consumption during the early years of the project; in dealing with the sensitive area of milk-product consumption, workers avoided discrediting native beliefs and discovered culturally acceptable substitutes in powdered milk products.

After fourteen years, the health program was judged successful in most respects. The infant mortality rate was reduced from 276 to 96 per 1000, and the incidence of kwashiorkor reduced from more than 600 cases per year to fewer than 12 cases. Infant and childhood diets improved greatly with increased amounts of eggs, powdered milk, vegetables, and millet. Nevertheless, there was no change in the problem of soil erosion. Attempts to improve agriculture and to prevent overgrazing were not successful. People resisted reducing the size of their herds, and consequently the cattle faced starvation because of inadequate forage.

While the program of the Polela Health Centre met many of its short-range goals, new ecological problems were created. With reduction in mortality rates and increase in live births and infant survival, population growth has resulted. But the land cannot support larger numbers of people, and so there has been increased dependence on imported foods and a cash economy, maintaining the need for men to work in the city ten months out of the year.

The diet of men in the cities is extremely high in refined carbohydrates, and it was found in the 1960s that the incidence of diabetes mellitus among urban Zulu was forty times that found in the rural population (Eaton 1977:50). Throughout Africa, the shift to higher intake of sugar and white bread has been correlated with increasing rates of diabetes. Even though the maize eaten by Zulu on reserves is inferior to millet, it is an unrefined carbohydrate, not rapidly absorbed and thus less likely to put heavy demands on the body for insulin production and less likely to contribute to diabetes. The Zulu who live in the city also suffer from higher rates of hypertension than those on reserves (Scotch 1963), and we have seen in chapter 2 that diet contributes to high blood pressure.

We can list three additional factors, then, resulting from a change in nutrition and health resources:

7. Infant mortality and protein-deficiency diseases were reduced through successful health education efforts.
8. Population growth was an outcome of lowered mortality rates. Under conditions of restricted reserve lands and continued low agricultural yield, dependence on imported foods and cash economy increased migration of males to cities for wage labor.

9. The diet of laborers in the city was high in refined carbohydrates, increasing the chances of diabetes and other
nutrition-related health problems.

To sum up, this example has shown that changes in nutrition can
lead to short-term improvements in general health, but there are
far-reaching implications affecting demographic patterns and, ultimately, new epidemiological developments such as the rise in incidence of diabetes. Changes in health resources designed to remedy
critical health problems may in turn create new problems in the future.
Figure 8.10 depicts the main variables of the Zulu situation.

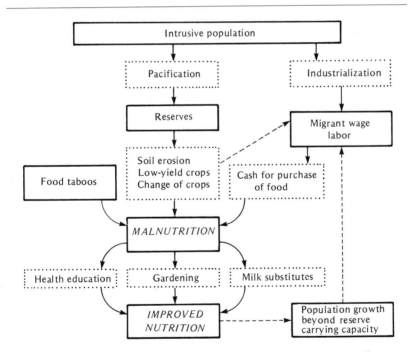

FIGURE 8.10 Model of changes in nutritional and health resources subsystems
following culture contact.

MIGRATION AND
CHANGES IN
HEALTH STATUS

This chapter has emphasized the ways in which habitat intrusion disturbs the ecological equilibrium and health of a native population. Because few tribal peoples have remained unaffected by technologically dominant societies in the last few centuries, anthropologists are most concerned with this kind of contact. But the reader will recognize that other kinds of culture contact have influenced the course of history, for example, when a migrating population must adjust to the pathogens, diet, and health resources of a new environment. We have been considering various models of health changes following contact between a minority, indigenous group and an intrusive, dominant group. Our question here is whether these models apply equally well to the case of migrating peoples. We will try to answer this by looking briefly at some examples of the health repercussions of migration.

Involuntary Migration

Migration is potentially stressful for any population, but especially in cases of involuntary moves. One of the more dramatic examples in U.S. history is the Indian removals of the 1830s. Altogether about 70,000 people were forced to leave their homes in the eastern states and to travel under armed guard to Oklahoma and other areas west of the Mississippi. The reason for removals was to gain access to Indian lands, although the official rationales spoke of protecting Indians from whites and giving them time to become assimilated. But the Cherokee of North Carolina were already being assimilated. Although they had their own churches, schools, legislature and supreme court, and newspaper, they were not exempt from the forced march, which the Cherokee call the "trail of tears." Without medical care, lacking adequate food, and experiencing the shock of having to abandon their farms and homes to white looters, many did not survive the journey. At least 4000 Cherokee and probably more died enroute (Farb 1968:304). Many more died in Oklahoma, and the subsistence and technological resources provided in the new territory were so meager that it was impossible for the Cherokee to regain their power and strength. The major effect of these removals was severe population decline due to starvation and epidemics. The stress of upheaval and inadequate subsistence affected many generations to follow. Although they were under government supervision, the tribes had almost no health care until the 1920s, and until quite recently Native American average life expectancy was the lowest and infant mortality rates were the highest of any ethnic group in North America.

A more recent example of forced migration involves the islanders of Bikini, located in Micronesia about 2000 miles (1200 km) southwest of Hawaii. Bikini and the other Marshall Islands were taken by the United States from Japan in 1944, and in 1946 the government decided that Bikini was climatically and geographically suitable for testing

FIGURE 8.11   Bikinians loading their possessions aboard a U.S. ship for the move to Rongerik in 1946.

Photo by Carl Mydans, *Life Magazine.* © 1946 Time Inc.

nuclear weapons. The 161 people who lived on the Bikini atoll (a group of twenty-six islands) were quickly relocated to another island. The people agreed to the move because they assumed the relocation would be temporary. With hasty planning, a small atoll of only ten islands and a very small lagoon was chosen. The planning showed little understanding of the subsistence technology and dietary needs of the people. The new atoll, Rongerik, proved totally inadequate. In a little more than a year, a visiting medical officer reported symptoms of malnutrition in the population (Kiste 1974).

The nutritional problems were mostly due to ecological differences between Rongerik and Bikini. The coconuts were smaller and the palms less productive. Some species of fish that had been edible on Bikini turned out to be toxic here, causing diarrhea, partial paralysis, and stomach disorders (Kiste 1974:78–79). Coconut husk fiber was so poor that roofs could not be thatched or canoe repairs made. Within a short time, the people had exhausted the crops and the palms stopped bearing. They assumed that they would be returning to Bikini shortly, not understanding the problem of radioactive fallout.

By 1948, the food shortage was critical. The canoes could not be repaired for fishing and for travel to other atolls for food, and in desperation some people were even consuming small quantities of the toxic fish. The Bikinians were finally relocated on another island, having to adjust to still another ecosystem. It was more than twenty years before new vegetation could be planted on Bikini; some of the islanders finally returned to the home atoll in 1969.

Ten years later, in 1978, radiologic tests showed high radioactivity in well water, vegetables, and fruit on the island of Bikini. There were alarming levels of strontium, cesium, and plutonium in the people tested: the level of radioactive cesium was twice the accepted U.S. standard for the population. The government decided that Bikini would be unsuitable for inhabitation for at least thirty years, and that the islanders would have to be evacuated and relocated again (Pincus 1978; *Time,* April 3, 1978, p. 25).

Voluntary Migration

Some people choose to migrate, though their choice may be constrained because only a few alternatives are available. Persons in good health are probably more likely to risk emigration and are better able to accommodate to a new environment, and so voluntary migration may be less stressful than in the preceding examples. But many factors push people to leave their homeland and pull them toward new continents or frontiers, and the complexity of these factors does not allow a simple dichotomy of voluntary versus involuntary migration.

Hawaii has grown through the voluntary immigration of many ethnic groups. Japanese now make up about 30 percent of Hawaii's population, and their disease patterns differ from those in Japan and those of Japanese living in the mainland United States. At least in part, changing diets are responsible for epidemiological differences. The prevalence of stomach cancer is high in Japan, intermediate in Hawaii, and lower among Japanese on the U.S. mainland (Stemmermann 1970:266–267). Among immigrant Japanese, the prevalence of intra-cerebral hemorrhage decreases, while glucose intolerance, diabetic responses, and breast cancer increase. Japan has an extremely low mortality rate from breast cancer, which may be due to preferences for breast-feeding. Acculturating Japanese women who wean their children to the bottle earlier may have a higher risk of cancer, though they still do not approach the rates found in U.S. Caucasian women.

The final migrant population to be discussed are the Puerto Ricans who have moved to New York City, whose critical health problems range from hundreds of cases of rat bites annually to tuberculosis, parasites, and malnutrition. One study showed that 20 percent of a sample of 216 migrant Puerto Ricans had to be hospitalized during the first year of living in New York (Bullough and Bullough 1972:78). Rates of emotional disturbance have been judged high. Since psychiatric services for these people have been neither adequate nor culturally appropriate, they rely on folk psychotherapists. Through establishing liaisons between conventional health professionals and these folk healers, a recent project in South Bronx has sought to improve the mental health resources available to Puerto Ricans (Garrison 1977; Fields 1976). In neighborhood-based storefront clinics, psychiatric residents learn from Puerto Rican spiritist healers about community life and cultural beliefs, methods of therapy likely to be effective such as role-playing, and information about patients' backgrounds.

The examples covered in this section suggest that the models we have developed in this chapter are general enough to be applied to any group that has experienced rapid and extensive change in ecosystemic relationships. Minority groups that must accommodate to the diet, pathogens, and health resources of a new geographical region or cultural system may be under as much stress as populations who have stayed in their home territory and experienced intrusion. Migration, as in the case of Japanese in Hawaii, may simply change epidemiological patterns without necessarily increasing the amount and severity of disease.

CONCLUSIONS

We have used an evolutionary framework in this book to study relationships between ecological adaptation and health. How does culture contact fit into the evolutionary framework? The specific historical events of culture contact and change have not been traditionally considered by anthropologists to be a part of evolution. In this book, we deal with change mostly in terms of large-scale evolutionary transitions in subsistence and settlement patterns. We have considered the new health problems created as populations move from hunting-gathering to agriculture, from preindustrial to industrial systems, but we have not considered the kinds of historical events that brought about these large transformations. In many cases, the major factors were indeed evolutionary in a strict sense—that is, they involved increases in complexity, in the accumulation of surplus, in population pressure, and in the efficient use of energy. But this chapter has shown the extent to which external contacts have transformed ecosystems just in the last few centuries. We would argue that contact between societies and the resulting health repercussions have played a significant role in cultural evolution.

Culture contact affects ecosystemic relations, changes health patterns, and initiates demographic cycles of decline, rebound, and growth. Groups that survive the first shocks of disease and dislocation undergo multiple internal shifts that attempt to restore equilibrium. Rarely does equilibrium mean a return to the original ecosystem and epidemiological pattern. As diets and reproductive patterns change, as people try to make health decisions based on the immediate problems and pressures, a series of strategies gradually emerges. Each of these strategies—the option of migration, of wage labor, of change in subsistence crops, or of cash-cropping and purchase of food—poses certain risks not only to health but also to ecosystemic independence. These groups are no longer isolated but rather have been pulled into the regional or international economy, which is the subject of the following chapter.

RESOURCES

Readings

Cassel, John
 1955 A Comprehensive Health Program among South African Zulus. *In* Health, Culture, and Community. Benjamin D. Paul, ed. Pp. 15–41. New York: Russell Sage Foundation.
 Cassel's article describes the history of the Polela Health Centre's nutritional change program. Especially useful to health workers is the analysis of factors that determined the relative successes and failures of strategies to motivate Zulu to change food habits.
Chinweizu
 1975 The West and the Rest of Us. New York: Vintage Books.
 A powerful study of colonialism and imperialism, Chinweizu's book documents the history of African encounters with Westerners.
Graburn, Nelson H. H.
 1969 Eskimos without Igloos. Boston: Little, Brown.
 This is a history of contact between Ungava Peninsula Inuit and Europeans. The pattern of ecological changes and the influence of disease in this history are traced from earliest encounters in the 1600s to the mid-twentieth century. The book includes ethnographic accounts of traditional and modern life.
Kiste, Robert C.
 1974 The Bikinians: A Study in Forced Migration. Menlo Park, California: Cummings.
 Kiste's study is a unique blend of ethnographic analysis and historical details of the displacement of these Marshall Islanders by military priorities and international politics.

Kroeber, Theodora
    1961   Ishi in Two Worlds. Berkeley: University of California Press.
    This is a beautifully written account of Ishi's last few years as a public
    figure, "the last wild Indian in North America," with a historical recon-
    struction of the reasons for Yahi population decline and extinction.
Woods, Clyde M.
    1975   Culture Change. Dubuque, Iowa: Wm. C. Brown.
    This introductory text explains anthropological approaches to the study
    of culture change and provides numerous ethnographic examples.

Film

Ishi in Two Worlds. 1960. 19 minutes. Produced by Richard C. Tomkins.
    McGraw-Hill Films #406755-9.
    This film, based on Theodora Kroeber's account of the discovery of Ishi
    and his story of survival in the hills of northern California, combines still
    photographs of Ishi in San Francisco with footage of the Yahi territory.

Health Costs of
Modernization

CHAPTER 9

PREVIEW

This chapter deals with the health problems of populations linked to the world economy through a history of colonialism, cultural and technological diffusion, and international trade and alliance. These include nation-states, many recently liberated from colonial dependence, territorial acquisitions of industrialized, developed nations, and ethnic enclaves within developed nations. We will consider the impact of modernization on these populations, focusing especially on how economic development affects ecosystems, health, and health care resources.

Modernization is directed change in which people extensively modify their lifestyles, technology, and value systems. When the modifications are planned and financed by governments, the process is called development. The usual developmental goal is to achieve economic self-sufficiency through industrialization, increased food production, and extraction of natural resources for export as well as national needs. Through these development activities, nations make a new "ecological contract" with the environment (Hughes and Hunter 1970:479). Individuals who are modernizing have additional goals: to improve the quality and pleasures of life, to acquire material goods, to achieve some mastery over the environment. To achieve these goals, they too create new "contracts" among themselves that depart from traditional sociocultural patterns.

Modernization, like any other fundamental change in human ecology, has both benefits and costs. The costs include population growth that exceeds economic growth and agricultural productivity. Developing nations often have more hungry people and higher infant mortality rates than do isolated, *un*developed communities. Attempts to increase food supply through irrigation projects often have epidemiological repercussions because they create new habitats for disease vectors, as the health profile on the disease schistosomiasis shows. Mechanization and land reform put farm laborers and small landowners out of work and push them into cities to look for wage labor, where they live in overcrowded and unsanitary conditions.

Economic development does create health problems, but it also attempts to solve these problems through chemical control of disease vectors, immunization programs, clinics and hospitals, and health education. Applied anthropologists have attempted to assist health delivery programs by explaining how change efforts may conflict with community values and may threaten the local political and social organization.

While the populations of developed nations generally have high average life expectancies and good health care delivery, there are rural and urban pockets of impoverished and malnourished ethnic groups whose health status resembles people in underdeveloped nations. Anthropologists have studied ethnic differences in perceptions of health and illness and recommended ways to overcome linguistic and cultural barriers to providing adequate health care. The final health profile discusses a study of the health of two minority groups, blacks and Arab immigrants, in an industrial American city.

> It is bad enough that a man should be ignorant, for this cuts him off from the commerce of other men's minds. It is perhaps worse that a man should be poor, for this condemns him to a life of stint and scheming, in which there is no time for dreams and no respite from weariness. But what surely is worst is that a man should be unwell, for this prevents his doing anything much about either his poverty or his ignorance.
> —Kimble (1960:151), quoted in Hughes and Hunter (1970:449)

NEW ROADS
AND
OLD DISEASES

If you were to map the distribution of diseases today in the West African nations of Liberia, Ghana, and Nigeria, you would notice a curious fact: the highest incidence of sleeping sickness, trypanosomiasis, follows the major highways. Sometimes the most effective tool for predicting the direction of disease transmission is a road map!

Trypanosomiasis is transmitted by the tsetse fly, an insect vector found mostly in swampy river valleys and lowland thickets. Many African communities traditionally settled on hillsides and plateaus for defense against invaders, and this limited their contact with tsetse flies. For groups in lowland habitats, sleeping sickness was an endemic disease, but Western medical programs sharply reduced the incidence by the 1940s. Sleeping sickness is now being reintroduced into many areas in western and central Africa, where it had practically been eradicated. The population is far more mobile than in the past. As large numbers of migrant laborers and travelers move from one region to another via newly constructed highways and railroads, humans and tsetse flies come into contact. Travelers are bitten by flies when they stop at river crossings to rest and get water. The flies are also attracted by moving vehicles. They may in fact be carried inside a truck for miles! Another reason for the increase in trypanosomiasis is that farmers displaced by dam construction or soil erosion are moving from highland areas to river valleys (Hughes and Hunter 1970:452–455).

Highways and railroads, dams for hydroelectric power, laborers migrating to plantations, mines, and factories—each important aspect of economic development creates unanticipated health problems. These problems add up to the "hidden costs" of development, a series of detrimental consequences not found in the blueprints and budgets of economic planners nor calculated in decisions to modernize.

In the last chapter, we considered the impact of change on small and self-sufficient populations. With the exception of voluntary migrants, most groups described did not seek out the change process. Rather, they were victims and beneficiaries of changes initiated by intruders. Over time, these populations became inextricably linked to larger economic systems, transforming them into peasant or reservation communities, ethnic minorities, or colonies.

In this chapter, we move to a type of culture change in which people extensively modify and reorganize their individual lifestyles and group techniques of adaptation. Depending on context, this type of change is called economic development, industrialization, or urbanization, but in this chapter we will call the overall process **modernization.**

Modernization is change in technology, social organization, and communication that is directed toward certain goals. For the individual, these goals may simply be improvements in the quality, ease, or pleasures of one's life. For a nation, the goals may be autonomy, wealth, and power. Why people modernize is a complex, fascinating question, but our major concern here is how modernization affects health. Even a small change such as building a road can affect a region's epidemiology. As whole nations attempt to reorganize their methods of extracting resources from the environment, of developing an export trade, and of manufacturing goods, the effects on health are immense. In the long run, the effects may be positive as the standard of living rises and population growth stabilizes, but many negative and unexpected effects are produced during development. Too often, health factors are not considered in planning roads, factories, power plants, and dams, and the social and psychological disruption of rapid change is particularly ignored.

This chapter begins with a "repercussions" model similar to the basic approach taken in chapter 8. The central idea in this approach is that one change sparks a series of other changes. Later in the chapter, a second perspective is introduced, which views modernization as a two-edged sword; although it creates health problems, it also provides the resources and knowledge to deal with those problems. We will consider how various nations have organized the delivery of health care, especially to rural areas, and how applied anthropologists have assisted in change programs. We will also consider ecological and economic criteria for evaluating whether development is beneficial or not. The final section deals with special health problems of ethnic minorities in developed nations.

WHAT MODERNIZATION
MEANS

When Ann McElroy first traveled with an Inuit family to a hunting camp on Baffin Island, she noticed that a clock was part of the gear. She was curious: Why was a clock needed in camp, where there was no need to be anywhere on time? The reason, she discovered, was that everyone wanted to catch the 8 o'clock news broadcast on the international-band portable radio. Reception was so good that favorite broadcasts came from Greenland, London, Moscow, and Chicago.

Curiosity about the outside world and access to mass communication are part of being or becoming modern. Through the transistor radio, found in the most isolated villages and hunting camps, new ideas, knowledge, and aspirations can diffuse from urban centers. And because Inuit hear the same broadcasts as do farmers in Saskatchewan, Ugandan refugees in Toronto, and fishermen in Newfoundland, they come to share a certain national identity that overrides variation in lifestyles.

In a very basic sense, "modern" means "not traditional." Implicit is the idea of replacement; a new tool, idea, or style of behavior replaces an old and customary one. But modernization is not just change by substitution, such as a radio substituting for folk tales and ballads as a form of entertainment. To become modern is to experience reorganization, rearrangement of priorities, and a new set of values and felt needs.

For the individual, becoming modern means a change in thinking. Modernizing people actively try to master the environment and are open to new ideas and new ways of doing things, including new approaches to health problems. They seek to increase their level of competence and to use knowledge to gain control over the environment.

A person who believes in scientific knowledge and technology can accept the idea that illness has a natural cause and a natural cure, and she or he will trust doctors to use their technical expertise to her or his benefit even if the techniques are strange and frightening. Fatalism about sickness and death begins to fade as modernizing people discover the effectiveness of antibiotics, immunizations, and surgery. Although people do not abandon traditional ethnomedicine altogether, the traditional connection between religion and healing weakens as evidence mounts that both the causes and prevention of illness can be understood in a secular framework. Folk healers who use religious ritual for psychotherapeutic purposes practice alongside Western-trained physicians and medical auxiliaries who perform secular healing functions. Thus modernization expands the range of health care alternatives and raises expectations that a cure can be found.

For a whole society, and ultimately for each individual, modernization also means changes in basic institutions, and each change affects physical and emotional health. Extended family bonds diminish, and individuals or nuclear families are more on their own. As limitation of family size becomes technically possible, more women are able to enter the wage labor force. The rearing of children changes with earlier weaning, substitute caretakers, and dependence on schools for socialization. The aged are also more likely to be handled by institutions and to be excluded from meaningful roles.

Economically, a modernizing society reorganizes itself around consumerism and a cash economy. The mass media urge people to buy household goods, clothing, commercial foods, bicycles and motorscooters, radios and televisions. Advertising offers easy credit and emphasizes that by purchasing modern goods, one is "in style" and "progressive."

The impetus for modernization comes from the cities, diffusing to small towns and remote villages when development workers enter rural areas as agents of change. In Iran, for example, national service is required of all young people, and those who qualify may enter the Teachers Corps, Health Corps, or Development Corps. These young women and men, mostly from middle-class urban backgrounds, introduce many innovative ideas to the rural classrooms and clinics. And their own lives are examples for village children. For example, the idea that a twenty-year-old Persian woman might be still unmarried, employed, and living apart from her parents amazes traditionally reared village girls. They wonder if there are alternatives to early marriage and farm labor in their own lives, and they look to the city for opportunities.

Migration to cities is a key aspect of modernization in most countries. The reasons for migrating are called "push-pull" factors. What pushes people into the city is rapid population growth without increase in land, mechanization in agriculture, and the need for cash because of land reform and taxation. What pulls villagers is the opportunity for industrial wage labor in the cities and suburbs. Medical care is better in cities, and young people must go to cities for advanced schooling and vocational training. Further, as the applied medical anthropologist George Foster has observed (1973:47), people like to go to the city because there are more interesting things to do there. Even though housing is not adequate and they must squeeze into squatter settlements and slums, migrants find the city exciting and full of opportunities that are not available in home villages. Even those who find no housing stay on. In Teheran, the capital of Iran, thousands have no place to live and must sleep on the sidewalk, trusting that late-night pedestrians will simply walk around them. Some of these people are beggars, others are wage-employed, and yet others are sidewalk vendors of crafts and produce.

The contrast between the increasingly affluent middle class and the urban poor in developing countries lends a sense of deprivation and frustration to the lives of squatters. Poverty is proof of inferiority and powerlessness within the modernizing context; material goods lend an illusion of competence and mastery in a stratified and impersonal social environment. Modernized societies are economic, class-structured systems. Individual material wealth is as important as family prestige or kinship relations, and upward mobility through economic improvement is more possible in a modernizing society than in a traditional one. The sidewalk resident can hope to find a shack to live in; the squatter may move into an apartment; the small merchant saves to buy a car. All these persons expect their children to be even better off.

If there is any one single theme of modernization, "raised aspirations" comes closest to describing it. An Inuit child dreams of becoming an airplane pilot; Iranian parents consider permitting their daughter to apply to medical school; a Spanish village teen-ager envies her sister in town who "doesn't have to feed pigs or go around in sloppy work clothes all the time like we do around here . . . [but] dresses up every day and spends afternoons walking the children and promenading [de paseo] with her friends" (Spindler 1977:70).

ECONOMIC
DEVELOPMENT

Politicians and statesmen have aspirations as well, and economic development programs reflect these aspirations. Modernization is rarely "planned" in a narrow sense, but development is. A minimal definition of development would be "conscious and deliberate intervention" to change conditions (Hughes and Hunter 1970:444). Usually the agent of intervention is the national and regional government, frequently in conjunction with foreign advisers who provide financial assistance and advice.

In theory, economic development is a rational, controlled process that balances economic progress against political advantage for a government or a socioeconomic class. The plans for development may well be rational, but responses to change programs often show that the plans are unrealistic. Persons responsible for initiating change discover that villagers are not always motivated to cooperate in a health project. Some Peruvian women are reluctant to boil water because it is considered unnecessary for healthy people to consume "cooked" water and also wasteful of fuel and a woman's time. Water is not considered the source of disease, so the women see no reason to boil it (Wellin 1955). In India, attempts to reduce fecal contamination of water by providing latrines have met with limited success in rural areas. Women especially dislike the latrines, preferring their custom of defecating in the fields because it gives them a chance to relax from chores and talk with friends (Paul 1977:235).

If there is resistance to change at the local level (and this is certainly not always the case, as the rapid shift to bottle-feeding has shown), there is often too quick an acceptance of ill-conceived development programs at the regional and national level. The expansion of export cash crops such as coffee, tea, and sugar reduces self-sufficiency. Small nations such as Sri Lanka must import most of their food and are precariously dependent on the world economy. In Jamaica, dependence on the export of bauxite, sugar, and bananas and the import of 47 percent of all food (and 67 percent of all protein) consumed has contributed to serious malnutrition, especially in children (Marchione 1977:61).

Malnourished children are certainly not one of the expected outcomes of a rational development plan. Even with the most careful planning, modernizing nations face unexpected problems because they do not take all ecological and social variables into account. They also face the difficulty of limited capital and a shortage of trained personnel for ecologically sound management of development projects.

What characteristics define a country as developing? In economic terms, nations with per capita annual incomes of less than $300 are classified as developing, while those with incomes of more than $1500 per capita are considered developed (Sorkin 1976:1–2). By this economic criterion, two-thirds of the nations of the world are still developing. Ecologically, a person in a developed country consumes between thirty and fifty times as many nonrenewable resources as those consumed by someone in a developing country (Owen 1973:179). In terms of health, life expectancy is low in a developing country. Infant mortality is very high, and population growth is also high, usually exceeding 2 percent per year. Between 35 and 60 percent of all deaths are of children under age 5; in the United States, mortality in this age group is less than 7 percent of all deaths (Bryant 1969:35).

Table 9.1 illustrates some of the health differences among eight selected nations in the late 1960s, contrasting four industrial and affluent nations with four countries at different stages of development. These statistics indicate that a developing country is severely disadvantaged in terms of medical care, population growth, nutrition, and life expectancy in contrast to developed countries. While "developing" is an appropriate term in a political sense, these nations are *underdeveloped* financially and medically.

The reasons for underdevelopment lie largely within international economic relations and the history of contact and colonialism. Although it is beyond the scope of this chapter to explore these reasons fully, it is important to recognize that nations do not become underdeveloped in isolation, but rather through economic and political relationships with the developed nations to which they are invidiously compared. The developed countries of North America and Europe as well as Japan and the Soviet Union have their own interests in maintaining their markets, sources of cheap labor and raw materials, and alliances.

TABLE 9.1 Selected health indicators in four developed and underdeveloped nations in 1969.

	Representative developed countries				Representative underdeveloped countries			
	USA	Sweden	USSR	Japan	UAR (Egypt)	Brazil	India	Chad
Annual Per Capita Income ($U.S.)	3,578	2,905	—	1,122	156	271	73	60
Population density (per sq. mile)	55	44	26	702	78	26	398	8
No. of inhabitants per physician	670	910	460	930	2,380	2,290	5,780	73,330
Life expectancy at birth females males	74 67	76 71	70 70	74 68	53 51	45 39	40 41	35 29
Live birth rate per 1000	17	14	17	18	36	41	41	45
Infant deaths, under 1 year, per 1000 births	21	12	26	14	83	—	139	160
Daily food intake per capita calories proteins (grams)	3,200 96	2,850 80	— —	2,460 75	2,810 81	2,690 66	1,810 45	— —
% of animal origin	40	41	—	13	7	14	5	—

SOURCE: Extracted from Allan Chase, *The Biological Imperatives: Health, Politics and Human Survival* (Baltimore: Penguin Books, 1971), pp. 379–380, 381–382.

APPROACHES
TO EVALUATING
MODERNIZATION AND
HEALTH

How shall we evaluate the relationship between modernization and the health of populations? Is the promise of longer life and freedom from hunger an illusion for most of the developing world? To attempt to answer this question, we need to look at both sides of the issue. We will use two approaches here, the first emphasizing the unexpected consequences or negative repercussions of development projects, the second considering the contribution of modernization to attempts to cope with health problems. We begin with efforts to improve agricultural productivity and consider some of the side effects of these efforts.

Agriculture and Development

The most serious problem facing all developing nations is food shortage. At least 2 billion people in the world are undernourished or malnourished, and agricultural production can barely keep up with population growth. In the 1960s, it became clear that world food production would have to increase by about 50 percent by 1985 to feed the expected population, even if fertility were reduced by 30 percent (Ehrlich, Ehrlich, and Holdren 1973:70–73).

International efforts to increase production have been called the Green Revolution, emphasizing high-yield varieties of grains and the increased use of fertilizers, irrigation water, and pesticides. The initial results of these efforts were encouraging. After fifty years of dependence on imports, the Philippines were finally able to grow enough rice to feed their population. Between 1965 and 1972, India's wheat production increased from 11 million to 27 million tons (Sorkin 1976:6). With the construction of the Aswan High Dam in Egypt, productivity also increased, but the soil fertility was diminished because the flow of silt was interrupted. In irrigation, there is danger of waterlogging and salt accumulation in soil; in fact, 5 million acres of farmland in Pakistan have been ruined by irrigation (Ehrlich, Ehrlich, and Holdren 1973:92).

There are also health risks in developing irrigation systems. Reservoirs and canals are suitable habitats for scores of parasites and their intermediate hosts, especially mosquitoes, tsetse flies, and snails. A severe fungus disease, madura foot or mycetoma, has increased in areas of the Sudan with irrigation projects. One of the best documented examples of increase in disease due to irrigation is schistosomiasis, a parasitic disease transmitted by snails. The reasons for the increase in schistosomiasis are discussed in the following health profile.

PROFILE: IRRIGATION AND SCHISTOSOMIASIS

The Egyptians of ancient times describe in their medical records an ailment called *â a â*, written in hieroglyphics as

The glyph on the lower right is a penis, symbolizing blood in the urine, one of the primary symptoms of the disease. This condition was a problem for many Egyptians, and no fewer than twenty remedies for *â a â* are recorded in the 3500-year-old fragments of papyrus scrolls. Perhaps the most imaginative prescription is to shape cake dough like a penis, wrap it in meat, say a magic formula, and give the pastry to a cat (Farooq 1973:2).

What caused this disease? Clues have been found in the kidneys of mummies of Egyptians who died around 1000 b.c.—a large number of calcified eggs of a parasitic blood fluke called a schistosome. The parasite was first identified in Cairo in 1851 by

Theodor Bilharz. The disease is called bilharziasis in recognition of Bilharz's discovery, or schistosomiasis, after the parasite causing it.

Schistosomiasis affects Egyptians today even more than it did 3000 years ago. Almost half the total population of Egypt had schistosomiasis in 1967 (Sandbach 1975:517); young people between the ages of 10 and 15 were most severely affected (Wright 1973:44–45). In fact, the disease is now a serious public health problem in seventy-two countries, mostly in Africa but also in China, Japan, Puerto Rico, Brazil, Venezuela, Israel, Turkey, and a number of other countries (Weisbrod et al. 1973:48). The disease has even been introduced to California by Arab farm workers. Altogether, about 200 million persons in the world are infected (Sandbach 1975:517).

For thousands of years, schistosomiasis has troubled humans, but only in the last century has it become a worldwide problem. The main factor in the increase and spread of the disease is the increase in irrigation projects in Egypt and in other developing nations. The schistosomes that cause the disease live part of their life cycle in the tissues of snails that thrive in slow-moving streams and canals of irrigation projects.

The basin of the Upper Nile River has always provided favorable habitats for these snails, as have the irrigation systems of the Tigris and Euphrates rivers in present-day Syria and Iraq. It is said that in countries like Egypt "one can stand with one foot in the desert and with the other in a garden," so critical is irrigation for food production (Patai 1971:73). But survival for humans in arid regions has also meant survival for vector snails, and consequently the disease has long been endemic in agricultural societies that depend on irrigation.

Since the Second World War, nations of the Middle East and North Africa have placed high priority on new irrigation schemes in an effort to overcome food deficits. Faced with rising birth rates and doubling of the population every generation, the United Arab Republic (Egypt) is a prime example of a developing nation that has invested much in the control of water resources. The Aswan High Dam, which impounds part of the Nile River, has increased by one-third the amount of land available for cultivation. The shift from seasonal basin or flood irrigation to year-round irrigation has undoubtedly increased agricultural productivity, but it has also increased the snail population and, with it, the prevalence of schistosomiasis. When only seasonal irrigation was employed, some of the snails and many of the schistosomes did not survive the dry period (Wolstenholme and O'Connor 1962:10–11). In the southern provinces of Egypt, the prevalence of the disease rose from 3 percent in 1935 to 42 percent in 1955 (Wright 1973:44). In four villages, for example, the infection rate in 1934 was 7.5. Only four years later, after the introduction of perennial irrigation, the rate had risen to an average of 58 percent (Lanoix 1958:1013). Hospital records for 1955 showed that of patients coming from perennially irrigated districts, between 56 and 69 percent had the disease, while only 9 to 17 percent of those from basin-irrigation districts tested positively (Wright 1973:44–45).

While irrigation systems have provided new habitats for snails, the disease would not be increasing if humans did not enter the canals and streams where the snails live. To understand the disease transmission, we need to trace the life cycle of the schistosomes (figure 9.1) and show how human customs influence the transmission of the disease.

A larval form of the parasite, called a miracidium, penetrates the snail through its soft tissues. The miracidium then goes through two asexual generations within sporocysts in the snail. Some snails die from the infection; if this happens, the schistosome dies, too. If the snail is living in a favorable habitat such as a poorly drained, marshy, sunlit pond or canal, more miracidia will succeed in finding snail hosts. When humans create these habitats, they unknowingly help the schistosomes survive (Hairston 1973:289).

Within the sporocysts develop male and female cercariae, forms of the parasite that are adapted for penetrating a human or other animal host. After leaving the snail, cercariae must find a host within one to two days. They are most likely to be released from the snails in the hours just before and after noon. This timing is one of the reasons why schistosomiasis is more prevalent among men than among women in Egypt. They go to the water at different times of the day, the women mostly in early morning to draw water, wash pots, and bathe children, the men to do

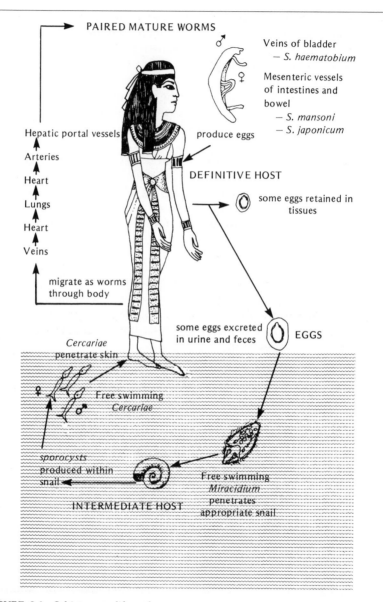

PAIRED MATURE WORMS

♂

Veins of bladder
— *S. haematobium*

Mesenteric vessels
of intestines and
bowel
— *S. mansoni*
— *S. japonicum*

♀

Hepatic portal vessels

Arteries

Heart

Lungs

Heart

Veins

produce eggs

DEFINITIVE HOST

some eggs retained in
tissues

migrate as worms
through body

some eggs excreted
in urine and feces

EGGS

Cercariae
penetrate skin

Free swimming
Cercariae

♀

♂

sporocysts
produced within
snail

Free swimming
Miracidium
penetrates
appropriate snail

INTERMEDIATE HOST

FIGURE 9.1   Schistosome life cycle.

ritual ablutions in the afternoon when the probability of being infected is greater (Stirewalt 1973:24; Hairston 1973:329). Also, whereas Egyptian women bathe without removing any clothes, the men bathe and swim in the nude, which makes them more susceptible to penetration by the cercariae (Farooq and Mallah 1966:379).

Once the cercariae penetrate the human host, they change into a wormlike form and travel through the blood vessels to the heart, the lungs, and then to the liver, where they mate and mature. The adult schistosomes then migrate to the veins associated with the bladder or intestines and produce thousands of eggs. There are three species: *Schistosoma haematobium* affects the urinary bladder, and *S. japonicum* and *S. mansoni* affect the upper and lower mesenteric veins.

The eggs themselves damage the body, producing lesions and hemorrhage, blocking digestion, and disturbing the functioning of the ureter. *Schistosoma haematobia* causes bladder discomfort, fever, headache, and damage to the kidneys and ureter. The intestinal forms cause dysentery, abdominal pain, liver fibrosis, and enlargement of the liver and spleen. Whatever the form of the disease, the victim loses weight and has lower resistance to other illnesses (MacDonald 1973:361–363).

The adult schistosomes stay in the human host for about four years and continue to produce eggs at a phenomenal rate, anywhere from 100 to 1400 eggs per female worm per day. Some of these eggs are excreted in the feces or urine. If they are excreted into water, they will develop into miracidia, thus completing the life cycle. When humans excrete in or near water where snails live, they facilitate this life cycle. It makes a difference which age group is involved in contaminating the water, because adolescents are more severely infected through repeated exposure while adults develop immunities to and tolerance of the eggs. If modern sanitary practices such as the use of latrines are observed only by adults, while young boys urinate while swimming, the transmission cycle will not be broken.

At each stage in the schistosome's life cycle, survival depends on maintenance of contact with its two hosts and successful transmission in water between hosts. There are three critical factors in the transmission process: the availability of snails, the availability of humans or other animals, and the deposition of egg-containing excrement near water. Human technology and customs enhance each of these conditions. The construction of any kind of water reservoirs in which drainage is slow and weeds are not controlled enhances the cycle. This includes artificial fish ponds developed for protein supplements, hydroelectric projects, and any road building and construction that do not provide for adequate drainage. Mosquitoes also thrive in such habitats and serve as vectors for other diseases.

The second factor, the availability of human hosts, is enhanced by the use of canals and streams in communities lacking plumbing or central laundries and bathhouses. Further, people working or playing near water are likely to urinate into it or into vegetation nearby where runoff from rains is likely. In Islamic societies, excretion near water is particularly common because the religion dictates that one should cleanse oneself with flowing water, if possible, after defecation and urination. Muslim males are most strictly enjoined to do this. They also go through ritual cleansing (washing the body, the nostrils, and gargling) ideally five times a day before prayers. Thus people make themselves available for penetration by the cercariae and continue to perpetuate the disease through excreting the eggs.

Another human practice indirectly affecting transmission is the migration of infected persons into areas where schistosomiasis had not previously been a problem. The disease is being spread by migratory workers through Uganda, the Sudan, and Nigeria (Hughes and Hunter 1970). Irrigation schemes constitute a double risk: snail populations increase because of this technological change, and increased numbers of infected laborers come into the region looking for work.

Attempts to control the transmission of schistosomiasis have focused on decreasing the availability of snail hosts. The use of molluscicides to control snails has been most popular, but there is a risk that these toxins will build up in the food chain. A predator Marisa snail has been used in Puerto Rico with success, but these snails could become a threat to agricultural products also (Sandbach 1975:520). Mass chemotherapy of infected people has been tried, but the success rate is only between 35 and 65 percent (Sandbach 1975:519). It is difficult to get patients to complete the course of treatment, and there is concern that chemotherapy causes the worms to shift to another part of the body such as the liver or lungs, where they do more damage (Wolstenholme and O'Connor 1962:65–68).

Health education for change in sanitation patterns faces the difficulty of persuading people to change religiously prescribed behaviors. Also, without alternative water sources, people are not likely to stop using canals and streams even if they know such places are infested. Simply being told by public health workers of the risks may not change villagers' behavior if they do not share the same concepts of disease.

For these cultural reasons, engineering and ecological management are considered more effective approaches to control. Public health workers may not easily dissuade people from using canals, but it is possible to line the canals with cement, to keep the water free of weeds, to maintain a rapid flow of water, or to simulate wet–dry cycles through the control of irrigation systems. What has worked best, though, is to provide piped water and sewage facilities. This has led to a significant decline in schistosomiasis in Puerto Rico (Sandbach 1975:520). Wherever projects have provided well water, latrines, and central laundries, the success rate has been most satisfactory, with reduction of other infectious diseases as well.

REPERCUSSIONS OF TECHNOLOGICAL CHANGE

The schistosomiasis study illustrates how technological change can disrupt a population's ecological stability. Change itself does not cause disease, but it can reorganize relationships of organisms in a habitat, and there is always the risk that this reorganization will affect humans adversely. At the same time, the reorganization of relationships allows for the achievement of specific developmental goals such as raising agricultural productivity.

Each change has some positive results and some negative repercussions. Like a pebble thrown into a pond, the repercussions of increased parasitic infection on a population expand outward. Infected people need more food because of fever and nutrient absorption by worms. They have lower physical and emotional resistance to new stressors than do healthy individuals; infected women are more likely to have a miscarriage. Children with high worm burdens are less able to cope with food shortage. These are some of the debilitating repercussions of new irrigation systems.

Disease eradication efforts provide other examples of how economic development creates new health problems or revives old ones. Insecticides have reduced the incidence of malaria, but the disease continues to be endemic in many underdeveloped nations. Why has the disease not been brought under better control?

One reason is that mosquitoes have remarkable adaptive potential. They breed quickly and prolifically, and there is rapid selection for insecticide-tolerant strains. They also adapt behaviorally by changing habits, for example, by leaving a house right after biting a person rather than resting on the walls of the house and being exposed to DDT.

Antimalarial measures are expensive and have become even more so as the cost of petroleum products increases. Thus government health teams may stop spraying as soon as the malaria rate goes down (Burnet and White 1972:240). Often within a year, however, the malaria rates are as high as before. For example, after the disease rate was decreased to 5 percent in Tanzania, the spraying stopped. Within thirteen months, the rate had risen to 30 percent among children (Hughes and Hunter 1970:464).

When the disease is essentially eradicated and populations are not exposed for some period, people do not develop immunity. Then there is the threat of epidemics among nonimmune adults and children when infected migrants enter the region. In addition, when the disease is brought under control, population increases as the death rate drops. Because malaria increases the risk of miscarriage, the live birth rates rise after eradication. On Mauritius, an island off East Africa, birth rates rose and infant mortality rates fell after the vector mosquitoes were eliminated. The rate of population increase rose to 3 percent per year, a serious problem for an island of less than 800 square miles (2222 square km) (Burnet and White 1972:241). Figure 9.2 shows a similar pattern of population increase in Sri Lanka after malaria control was initiated in the 1930s.

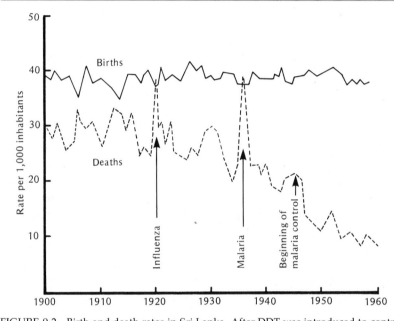

FIGURE 9.2   Birth and death rates in Sri Lanka. After DDT was introduced to control malaria, the death rate lowered and population increased.

SOURCE: Reprinted from Albert Damon, *Human Biology and Ecology* (New York: W. W. Norton & Co.), p. 334. Copyright © 1977 by W. W. Norton & Company, Inc. Damon's sources for this graph: Population Reference Bureau (1954) *Population Bulletin* 10:60–61; *American Journal of Public Health*, January 1972.

Work productivity increases when people are not suffering periodic attacks of malaria. In the Philippines, absenteeism from work due to malaria was 35 percent before eradication programs. Now the absenteeism rate is between 2 and 4 percent and the required labor force has been reduced by one-fourth, thus increasing unemployment (Sorkin 1976:45).

When regional development includes efforts to increase cash crop yields, subsistence farming and nutrition suffer. In West Africa, the best lands are used to grow cocoa and coffee, and cash from the sale of these products is spent on goods rather than on food. In cocoa-producing regions of Nigeria, there are food shortages each year before harvest. The small amount of land used to grow food is becoming eroded, and people are moving into cities to seek nonagricultural work (Collis, Dema, and Omololu 1962).

The export of cash crops often leads to a shortage of sources of protein in poor nations. These countries export to developed nations 3.5 million tons of high-quality protein per year in the form of fish meal, presscakes of oilseeds, and soybeans. How do importing countries use these products? To feed poultry, livestock, and pets (Ehrlich, Ehrlich, and Holdren 1973:89)!

City dwellers are even more dependent on commercial food. The urban poor, like rural cash-croppers, buy the cheapest food available with the little cash they have. Their diet lacks the diversity that would protect them from nutritional deficiencies. Lower-class urban Guatemalans, for example, live mostly on tortillas, bread, black beans, and rice. They consume small amounts of vegetables and meat two or three times a week. They cannot afford to buy more meat, and they save the few chickens, ducks, and pigs they raise to sell when they need cash in an emergency. They do not have the space or the water supply to keep a garden (Gonzalez 1964).

The Native Canadians of Kenora, Ontario, have enough to eat in the still plentiful supply of fish, ducks, and deer, but industrial wastes have polluted the lakes and contaminated the animals with mercury. In fact, there is a danger that the Japanese Minamata disease tragedy will be repeated in northern Canada. Visiting Japanese scientists have found signs of neurological damage in cats and dogs in the area, and blood tests have shown mercury levels of residents to be considerably higher than those of southern Ontarians (*Akwesasne Notes* 1975:16–17). Gold mining in Yellowknife, another northern Canadian town, has led to arsenic pollution of the soil, vegetation, and water. Arsenic is carcinogenic and leads to respiratory debilitation (*Inuit Today*, March/April 1977:23–24). The risk of exposure to toxic substances is another significant repercussion of industrial development.

STRATEGIES FOR HEALTH CARE DEVELOPMENT

The previous section discussed some problems created by modernization; here we consider ways in which developing nations have sought to address those problems. Most nations' development programs include plans to improve the organization and delivery of health care. Scarce resources, including trained personnel, must be carefully and rationally allocated. Decisions about priorities must be made—for example, are resources to be put into preventive medicine, or health education, or curing of disease? These decisions and plans may be considered "strategies"—responses to health problems that draw on modern ideas and technical skills.

The most serious health care problem in developing countries, even more basic than the need for hospitals and medical schools, is the critical need for health personnel in rural areas. Western-trained physicians often leave to practice in other countries. If indeed they remain in their home countries rather than immigrating to the developed countries, they prefer to practice in urban centers and to administrate agencies and clinics. Many countries are trying to counter such rural shortages by training health auxiliaries. The Sudan, in northeastern Africa, has a dispersed population of 15 million and less than 1000 physicians. Health care in the Sudan depends on auxiliary personnel, who have had four to eight years of basic education and three years of special training to become nurses, medical assistants, and health visitors. Training is planned and administered by physicians, who teach both diagnosis and treatment methods (Bryant 1969:66–70).

Since there is resistance in this Muslim country to sending women to remote rural areas away from their families, male medical assistants are assigned to supervise the desert village dispensaries. The staff includes a certified nurse and two midwives. About 150 patients per day are treated. Cases range in severity from meningitis and fractured skull to diarrhea, malaria, and childbirth. Patients needing specialized

FIGURE 9.3   This child in the Sudan is held by her father while being vaccinated to
prevent meningitis.
Photo: World Health Organization.

care are referred to hospitals. With little supervision and no further
training, the medical assistants' technical understanding of the diseases they treat does not increase over time. They tend to use a
"cookbook approach" to treating each case, giving medicines and
injections even when they are not needed and carefully following a
diagnostic sequence that is not always appropriate for the patient. Yet
despite these drawbacks, health auxiliaries have proved valuable aids
in rural health programs in the Sudan. Given the shortage of physicians in many countries, the use of auxiliaries is a practical alternative.
    Colombia has a very modern health care system compared to the
Sudan's. There are adequate numbers of doctors and hospital beds,
but there is still a shortage of nurses since most nurses prefer to work

in the major cities. Some 10,000 auxiliary nurses, with four to five years of basic education and a year of training, do the jobs of nurses in emergency rooms, in maternal and child health clinics, and in home visits.

Despite the availability of health care in Colombia, less than half the people needing care were reached in the 1960s, in large part because of resistance by the population. Less than one-third of pregnant women came to clinics for delivery by trained midwives; dying children were not brought to clinics. One of the reasons was the "social distance" barrier between the rural poor and the city doctors and nurses. This distance was due not only to class differences but also to differences in conceptions of disease and treatment (Bryant 1969:82–90). All segments of a nation do not modernize at the same pace; there is always a lag between middle-class urbanites' and rural peasants' acceptance of new ideas and values.

To deal with this lag, many developing nations have invested part of their limited funds and personnel in health education. An immediate problem is that medically trained personnel must learn how to communicate new concepts of disease, and so considerable effort has gone into training health *educators* first. A manual written for Kenyan development workers explains that villagers will neither understand nor believe a health worker who declares that flies transmit disease, for how can such small creatures hurt anyone? The approach recommended by the manual is vividly illustrated through a sample question-and-answer session in which the educator builds up a series of facts that villagers do know to a logical conclusion that proves that flies transmit disease:

> "Have you feet?" "Yes!" Feet are shown with laughter.
>
> "If you step in the excreta from one of your cows do you get the excreta on your feet?" "Yes!"
>
> "When you enter your house afterwards does any of the excreta get on your floor?" "Oh, yes! . . ."
>
> "Do flies have feet?" . . . "Oh, yes! We have seen them."
>
> "Have you seen flies settle on human excreta?" "Yes, many times."
>
> "Can you see that in the same way that you get cows' excreta on your feet, the fly gets human excreta on his?"

Pause for thought, then comes the answer, "Yes, we can see that."

"Good!" . . . "Have you ever seen flies settle on your food?" "Yes, very often."

"Do you now see that just as you left some of the cows' excreta on the floor, the fly leaves a little human excreta on your food?"

A longer pause, followed by somewhat reluctant nodding. Final question, "Do you think it is a good thing to eat excreta?"*

Visual aids must also accommodate to cultural differences in perception. If a poster, movie cartoon, or model form depicts a larger-than-life fly or mosquito, the villager is likely to say to the health educator, "It can't be, we don't have flies that size in Kenya" (Holmes 1964:65).

A combination of health education and mass promotion has been attempted in several developing countries to limit population growth. India's birth rate is one of the highest in the world, and as table 9.1 showed, its population density is high and its calorie intake very low. To disseminate the idea of family planning, the Indian government has established birth control clinics, temporary camps, and even mobile vasectomy clinics, buses that travel both to cities and to isolated villages. Men who undergo vasectomy, as well as anyone who persuades a man to do so, are paid a fee. Rural people have occasionally shown resistance to these programs for religious or political reasons and have rioted against them, even destroying the camps and buses (Ehrlich, Ehrlich, and Holdren 1973:242).

Resistance to family planning was a problem throughout the 1940s and 1950s in Puerto Rico also (Stycos 1955). The birth rate was twice that of the U.S. mainland, while the death rate dropped sharply because of improved sanitation and medical care. More than a hundred birth control clinics were established, but most Puerto Ricans did not use these facilities, even though they approved of small families. The Catholic Church's official position on birth control did not prevent them from considering methods of family planning, but other attitudes

---

* Reprinted by permission from Alan C. Holmes, *Health Education in Developing Countries* (London: Thomas Nelson and Sons Ltd., 1954), p. 48.

pikinini na i tok, "Dispela pikinini em i sik nogut tru. Mi laik yu

bringim dispela pikinini i kam insait na bai mi givim marasin long en. "

Ol i bringim Piring i go insait na ol i putim em antap long tebol.

Doktaboi i askim ol, "Hamas de dispela pikinini i bin stap sik?"

Dabi i bekim tok, "Fopela de tasol em i bin stap sik . "

Ol i putim Piring antap long tebol

Dokta i bekim tok olsem, "Bilong wanem yu no bringim em kwiktaim?"

Dabi em i bekim tok long doktaboi olsem, "Mipela tingting marasin

6

FIGURE 9.4 This malaria education booklet was written for beginning readers of
Neo-Melanesian, a lingua franca used in Papua New Guinea. Because
much of this vocabulary of Neo-Melanesian is derived from English, by
reading this page of the booklet aloud you will understand much of the
conversation between the health auxiliary and the father of the sick child.

SOURCE: Roy Gwyther-Jones, "Piring Em I Kisim Sik/Malaria," third edition,
(Ukarumpa, Papua New Guinea: Summer Institute of Linguistics, 1972), p. 6.

deterred them from using certain contraceptives. Most important was
the fear that contraceptives would undermine a man's authority and
promote his wife's infidelity. Some people also believed that contraceptives cause cancer and sterilization makes a woman chronically ill.

FIGURE 9.5   This research team in India includes doctors, nurses, social workers, and
             statisticians. They are collecting information in a poor part of Bombay on
             women's views of family planning, the difficulties they may have had in
             using contraceptives, and the effects of their many pregnancies on their
             children's health.
             Photo: World Health Organization.

Puerto Rican men felt that using a condom with one's wife would
"degrade a pure and sacred relationship." As one man said, "Those
things I don't use with my wife, because it debases my wife to use
something that is used with prostitutes" (Stycos 1955:199). A woman
wishing to limit family size found it difficult to discuss the matter with
her husband because it violated the cultural notion of how a "good"
woman was supposed to behave and might lead the husband to
suspect her of wanting to have an affair (Stycos 1955:200).

Before health education can be effective, the beliefs and attitudes of
a population must be understood, and this information can best be
discovered and explained by someone with anthropological training.
Health workers have not always taken community organization and
values into account in planning and implementing change programs,
and anthropologists have showed how important it is to consider these
factors in designing projects.

ANTHROPOLOGISTS IN DEVELOPING AREAS

Health personnel often find that villagers and urban migrants do not welcome their advice or flock to their clinics. Do people resist health programs because they find the disadvantages and risks greater than promised benefits? Because of the cost? Or because of a fear of new and strange ideas? They readily acquire radios and new clothing styles and reorganize their lives around wage labor, and so their apparent conservatism in matters of health is puzzling both to Westerners and to educated native elites.

Applied anthropologists have also been concerned with these questions. Working on foreign advisory teams, in government agencies, or with university projects, they have been involved in assessing the barriers and avenues to change.

Values and Change

One of the tenets of cultural anthropology is that values—deeply rooted codes that direct choices and order priorities—always affect human behavior. Before a change program can be successful, the basic values of a people must be known. Americans place a high value on the maintenance of health through technological means, but not all societies place such a high value on health. Some may be more concerned with religious virtue, or with meeting family obligations, or with maintaining a hierarchical, stratified society. Others who do consider health of highest importance, such as the Navaho Indians, believe that health is best maintained not through technology but through social and ecological harmony.

Health programs can be geared to implementing community values rather than conflicting with them. A sanitation program was started in Thailand when a Buddhist priest was persuaded to organize citizens to build latrines at the temples. Rather than trying to convince laborers that better sanitation was worthwhile, the project stressed that religious merit would be earned by working for the temple, and the latrines were completed in only two days (Paul 1969:34)!

Health workers must also be aware of social structure, that is, the system of relationships and roles organizing the behavior of individuals and groups in a community. A medical project can fail because it threatens the authority and prestige of local politicians, clergy, and folk healers. A health team attempting to establish a clinic in Tepotzlan, Mexico, encountered such problems, leading the anthropologist Oscar Lewis to comment as follows:

> Those who enter a community to engage in an action program must recognize the implications of the fact that they are not entering a power vacuum. In every human community there exists a network of relations between individuals. . . . Any group of outsiders moving into the community will be seen by some as potentially disruptive, even if they plan no action. If they do plan action, whatever positive measures they undertake, no matter how benign, will be perceived by some community members as a threat to their own status and interests.*

Anthropologists can clarify the community perception of what is illness. This is evident in how they have learned to deal with the hip problems of the Navaho. Navaho Indians have a high prevalence of congenital dislocation of the hip, and treatment of school-age children usually requires surgery to create a shelf of bone to keep the head of the femur in the pelvic joint. If this does not work, the hip joint must be fused to prevent serious and painful arthritis later in life.

A fused hip is a minor handicap for an urban American, but it creates major problems for the Navaho. With a fused hip, the person cannot ride a horse or sit on the ground at family meals in the hogan. Moreover, a dislocated hip is not considered a disease worth treating. There is no stigma attached to it; disabled individuals marry and raise children normally and carry out the usual work roles. A dislocated hip is less of a handicap than having a fused hip. As medical personnel became aware of Navaho attitudes toward this disorder, they shifted from surgical treatment to prevention and early nonsurgical correction in infants (McDermott et al. 1969:127–130).

---

* From "Medicine and Politics in a Mexican Village," by Oscar Lewis, in *Health, Culture, and Community: Case Studies of Public Reactions to Health Problems,* edited by Benjamin D. Paul, © 1955 Russell Sage Foundation, New York.

In some cases, anthropologists participate in the earliest stages of health programs. Isabel Kelly and Hector Garcia Manzanedo assisted in planning a malaria eradication program in Mexico in the 1950s, recommending ways to improve efficiency and budget planning. Because many monolingual Indian populations would be affected, Kelly and Manzanedo urged that communication costs be increased. They explained that opposition to taking blood samples could be anticipated because of witchcraft beliefs, and that some groups would consider blood as nonrenewable and would fear loss of strength and sexual vigor. Justifiable fear of the effects of DDT was also anticipated; in other areas, resistance had developed after people observed that spraying led to deaths of chicks, bees, and cats. The anthropologists recommended not only a careful explanation of the side effects of DDT, but also extreme care in reducing the risk of side effects. Finally, they suggested that health teams collaborate with other development agents at the National Indian Institute, many of them Indians themselves, who had gained the confidence of the isolated rural populations in previous projects (Foster 1973:218–220).

Anthropologists as Community Mediators

Anthropologists also are called on to intervene when a health project has run into difficulties and to "diagnose," as it were, the reasons for community opposition. One example is an experiment in nutritional change in five Guatemalan villages in the 1950s (Adams 1955). The experiment involved assessing the effects of vegetable protein supplements on the health of malnourished children. Control groups were given placebos, and all groups had to be examined periodically, with blood samples and X rays taken and weight gains recorded. In one village, parents became antagonistic to the project and threatened to kick the health team out. The project workers did not understand the reasons for opposition, and an anthropologist, Richard Adams, was brought in to study the situation.

Adams tried to look at the project through the eyes of the villagers and to understand the fears they had about outsiders testing their children. Eventually he discovered four factors working together to create opposition. First, the village was divided into neighborhoods, or *barrios,* one more progressive than the other. By befriending people from the progressive barrio and ignoring the more conservative group, the health workers had alienated half the village without realizing it. The villagers feared that the health workers supported pro-Communist forces in Guatemala, and so the second reason for opposition was political factionalism between pro- and anti-Communists in the town. The small landholders especially feared the health project, believing that it was part of a plot to take over their land. The third factor was the belief that taking blood weakened a person because blood did not regenerate. Parents were amazed that medical personnel would purposefully weaken their children. In truth, the health team was taking too much blood because of inefficiency and spoilage, and the anthropologist urged them to change laboratory procedures and to take fewer samples. The most unexpected and serious factor was the rumor that the children were being fed to fatten them up for shipment to the United States, where they would be eaten. Periodic blood sampling and weighing reinforced this belief.

Adams recommended that community leaders be invited to visit the laboratories and be shown how and why blood was processed. The anthropologist himself attempted to address these rumors directly by talking with villagers about the program's goals, and he helped ease the villagers' doubts and fears. All too often, development projects do not communicate adequately with community residents. When modernizing pressures come from outsiders, without the full participation or interest of those supposedly benefiting from these efforts, anthropologists can easily predict the nature of misunderstanding and opposition. Unfortunately, often they are called in too late and can give only a postmortem analysis of what went wrong.

Sometimes villagers do welcome the presence of health facilities, but interaction between patients and medical personnel is still hindered by misunderstandings. The anthropologist tries to understand the expectations of both groups and to promote better communication between staff and patients. A project to eliminate hookworm in Sri Lanka, sponsored by the Rockefeller Foundation, encountered many problems of conflicting expectations. First, the people considered hookworm less serious than other complaints such as leg ulcers, and they were irritated that the public health workers put more emphasis on prevention than on cure. The health team in turn felt "shock and annoyance" at this lack of gratitude and enthusiasm (Foster 1973:231). A second problem in communication arose because American personnel interacted with patients in ways Americans find most comfortable, with egalitarian, warm, outgoing mannerisms. The Sri Lankans expected educated people to be more formal and authoritarian and were confused by their friendliness. A third problem was that treatment for hookworm makes villagers feel weak, and since they needed several days to recover, they felt they could not afford the time away from work. Because it was difficult for middle-class personnel to understand the narrow margin of poverty of these people, they failed to see how only two days' income was more important than being cured of hookworm (Foster 1973:29).

Evaluating Economic Development—No Free Lunch?

The efforts of applied anthropologists to assist development projects have met with varying success. When anthropologists themselves play a central role in planning and carrying out projects, they can take sociocultural factors into account at each step. But all too often, development workers proceed to introduce rapid change without cautiously evaluating possible repercussions, ignoring or misunderstanding anthropological principles. In such cases, the anthropologist feels rather powerless, a fifth wheel in the midst of engineers, medics, and politicians and reduced to a conflict mediator and mender of hurt or threatened egos. Over the course of time, anthropologists have seen many communities and ecosystems disrupted by the impact of development, and so they remain skeptical of the notion of "progress." They recognize the inevitability of modernization but usually take the position that people should have a choice of modernizing or remaining traditional, fully informed of the relative costs, risks, and benefits of either course.

The late Albert Damon, who had an M.D. with a Ph.D. in biological anthropology, believed that economic development is always a trade-off. He emphasized that "anything you do or refrain from doing has a cost"; in other words, there is "no free lunch" (Damon 1977:330). One way of looking at the principle of tradeoff is through the idea of **minimax strategies,** introduced in chapter 3, in which "behavior which produces economic gain is balanced against hazards to health generated either directly or indirectly by such behavior" (Alland 1970:184). A population learns to minimize potential risks and maximize potential gain over time through feedback mechanisms. If the use of feces as fertilizer increases soil fertility but also increases human exposure to parasites, then the maximization factor (use of feces) must be modified. One modification is to store the manure for several days, thus reducing the parasite count (Alland 1970:95, 131).

Cost-benefit analysis is a second approach to the tradeoff idea. It is particularly useful for health economists who must assess whether a proposed health project will pay off in the long run. For example, malnutrition has certain real dollar costs in addition to causing human suffering. These include direct costs of treating diseases of malnutrition and the indirect costs of lowered productivity of hungry and sick workers. But is it worthwhile to feed these people, and how does one calculate the answer in other than humanitarian terms? Health economists argue, in fact, that a hard-nosed approach demonstrates that nations cannot develop economically unless the population's health needs are met first. They consider the expense of alleviating hunger to be an investment in human capital. In return, increase in human energy, overall health, intelligence, and productivity is anticipated. The demand for health services theoretically should lessen, thus lowering medical costs. Each person should live longer, have more productive working years, and thus earn more money overall. And even if jobs are not available to everyone year-round, seasonal labor-intensive agricultural production should benefit from increased numbers of workers (Sorkin 1976:33–37).

The trouble with cost-benefit analysis is that it is built on Western economic theory. The reduction of mortality in the United States and Europe has been associated with economic growth and has led to a lowered birth rate. This is the model that economists expect developing nations to follow, but many nations do not conform to the patterns that came out of decades of slow industrial growth in the Western world. They grow rapidly in population size without concomitant economic growth. Even if economic opportunities are available, better health does not necessarily improve individual productivity on the job as long as other noneconomic goals are more highly valued.

One example is St. Lucia, a West Indies island, where health economists studied how parasitic infection affected work behavior and school performance. People free of parasitic infection were generally no more productive on plantations than were those who have schistosomiasis and other diseases. Although men infected with schistosomiasis earn about 30 percent less money on a daily basis than do healthy men, they compensate for their lowered productive capacity by working more days each week and actually earning more money than noninfected workers. Similarly, children infected with schistosomiasis are absent from school less than are healthy children, although there was no difference recorded in school performance. Why don't the healthier individuals work harder and produce more? Because the culture emphasizes the enjoyment of leisure and family ties and adequate food is available, the St. Lucians rarely work longer hours than is necessary to maintain the customary standard of living (Weisbrod et al. 1973:71, 87).

A third way to evaluate development, through the assessment of environmental impact, has been stressed throughout this chapter. This approach illustrates the "ecologic surveillance and sensitivity" that Hughes and Hunter recommend (1970:445) in regard to development activities. From an anthropological perspective, ecological surveillance means focusing not only on relationships between human populations and their environment, but also on relationships between societies. Being deprived of freedom and autonomy can be as stressful for a population as being deprived of traditional subsistence; human groups can do violence to one another as much as to the natural environment through development activities. Just to obtain more electrical power for Quebec and the United States, for example, it has been necessary to flood thousands of square miles of territory in the James Bay region of northern Canada. Flooding has altered the ecosystem radically. Many Cree and Inuit have been displaced from their hunting and trapping lands and plunged into the modern world because of urban North America's energy needs. Sometimes one segment of a pluralistic society benefits from development, while another segment must pay the social and ecological costs involved. This has happened with the Alaskan pipeline, with strip mining in the Dakotas, and with the Kinzua Dam on Iroquois lands. There are many other cases, each illustrating the immense environmental impact of exploitation by an industrial society.

MINORITY HEALTH IN DEVELOPED NATIONS

The most striking physical findings on these children
were distended abdomens in 41 percent. This disten-
tion is most likely due to varying degrees of malab-
sorption, secondary to the presence of the intestinal
roundworm, Ascaris lumbricoides.
— Taylor (1973:159–160)

The three-to-six-year-olds were getting only 800
calories (daily). This caloric insufficiency is certainly
not enough to support the patient and barely enough
to support the worms.
— Taylor (1973:160)

This time of year we see a lot of anemias, low-grade
anemias. You get the picture of a pale, fat baby, behind
in development, sometimes irritable, subject to fre-
quent infections and prolonged colds.
— Taylor (1973:156)

Each of these doctors' reports read like field notes from a health project
in an underdeveloped nation. If you were to learn that the average life
expectancy for these children is age 49, that half of them have received
no immunizations, and that 10 percent have never seen a doctor, you
could make an educated guess that these doctors were surveying a
Latin American or Asian country. But your guess would be wrong,
because these are children of migrant farm workers in South Carolina
and California.

A key feature of the poor in a developing nation is their optimism.
Raised aspirations pull them to the city, attract them to school, and
make their hardships seem tolerable. But in a developed, affluent
country like the United States, the poor retain little optimism in the
1970s. Among the poor, the migrant workers have the greatest hardships. Their health problems resemble those of all groups under
stress—a rate of pneumonia and tuberculosis twice the national
average, infant mortality almost twice the national average, and
children suffering from rickets, pellagra, and kwashiorkor.

Health care is also generally inadequate for migrants and complicated with red tape. For example, one woman wrote from Florida:

> Now if any of us old migrants gets bad sick, we must hunt up
> one of our commissioners to get his approval to go to a doctor
> and you might as well forget it, for the county don't want to
> pay and to them we are just dirty old farm workers and not
> human . . . . You would think the Government with all the
> millions of dollars they send to other countries and shoot to
> the moon, they could spare a little to help us.*

It is disturbing to find people in the United States who are as hungry
and poor as those in the most underdeveloped countries of the world.
Because their migrant lifestyle keeps them invisible in many ways, the
U.S. public finds it more comfortable to minimize the problem. To
consider the dynamics of an affluent class extracting resources and
labor from an impoverished class, one would have to examine the
political and historical issues. Politics affect a group's access to resources and ultimately its chances for health care; this is true on the
national as well as the international level.

One striking fact about the health of U.S. migrants is that by simply
changing the names and places, you would be describing the health
problems of any U.S. minority group at some point. In the 1950s, the
average life expectancy of Native Americans was below 50; by 1970 it
was 64 (Michal et al. 1973:6). Kwashiorkor and marasmus were found
among reservation children in the 1960s. Public health workers, many
of them natives who understand community problems, now monitor
child development, urge mothers to breast-feed, and refer undernourished individuals (mothers as well as children) to outpatient care
before clinical symptoms develop. For almost a century, the health
status and care facilities of Native Americans on reservations were
even worse than those of migrant farm workers. Why has change
occurred? Certain logistical problems in health care delivery have been
met, and political relations between Native Americans and Euro-
americans are being redefined, with increased Indian participation in
planning and supervising their own community health services.

There were many barriers to health care for reservation communi-

---

* *The New York Times,* November 1, 1973. © 1973 by The New York Times Company.
Reprinted by permission.

ties. Native Americans were thinly dispersed in rural homesteads over large areas of land. Physicians and nurses could not regularly get to the homesteads because of treacherous roads and long distances, and Native Americans were reluctant to come to hospitals for treatment and childbirth. Linguistic and cultural barriers made communication very difficult.

These problems were particularly critical for the Navaho Indians of the Southwest, about 80,000 people living on a 15-million-acre reservation. The first step toward a solution, taken in 1956, was to train Navaho health visitors who would travel around the reservation, keeping in touch by two-way radio with the clinic to transmit and receive information about patients (McDermott et al. 1969:131). Thirteen years later, the training of health auxiliaries became a regular aspect of a Project HOPE program intended to develop a completely Navaho-run health system. These auxiliaries were known as DDNs, "Dine Dabinighango Natinii," which means "home-to-home teacher of the people." They were trained in preventive medicine, emergency care, and interpretation of health terminology. Like the home visitors earlier, they reached isolated families for preventive and follow-up work (Hudson and Kauffman 1974:9).

The use of bilingual medical assistants, which was so important in improving health care for the Navaho, had not yet been organized when Margaret Clark studied Chicano health problems in San Jose, California, in the 1950s. One of the first medical ethnographies of a minority group in an urban setting, the Clark study (1970) dealt with linguistic and cultural barriers that impeded health care delivery. The problem of language blocked Chicano access to health information in many ways—in telephone calls to clinics, in reading labels, in understanding the instructions of doctors. Even people who knew English found it difficult to understand the technical language used by doctors. A patient planning to wean her child would not understand "apply a tight pectoral binder and restrict your fluid intake" (Clark 1970:220), and she would be too shy or proud to ask for an explanation.

Treatment prescribed at clinics and sanitoriums often conflicted with Chicano beliefs about illness. One belief was that illness can be caused by exposure to air currents. People being treated for pulmonary tuberculosis with pneumothorax (use of oxygen to collapse the lung by injecting air into the chest, thereby resting a diseased lung) were fearful of this procedure and likely to leave the hospital when it was prescribed (Clark 1970:224). Problems of modesty conflicted with clinical procedures also. Because Chicano girls were taught never to expose their bodies, not even to other women, clinical examination was difficult even when women doctors or nurses were available.

Perhaps the greatest source of difficulty was the social distance between Chicano clients and Anglo staff. While this distance was due partly to ethnic differences in medical beliefs and communication styles, socioeconomic differences also affected social distance. Although placing Chicano physicians and nurses in the clinics would improve communication, the problem of class differences remained. The attitudes of San Jose Chicanos toward their own status and living conditions was indicated by the name of one of their barrios: Sal si Puedes ("get out if you can"). Chicano health professionals had moved up to a higher status in San Jose, and the residents of this barrio both envied and resented them (Clark 1970:234).

What factors affect the health of minority groups in urban settings? Health facilities and good medical information are theoretically available to all groups in a city, and transportation problems such as those faced by the Navaho are less of a problem. And yet for political and cultural reasons, to be poor in the city leads to a higher rate of illness, inadequate nutrition, and the extra stressor of relative deprivation and frustration. As the following health profile of two minority groups in an industrial suburb shows, however, health reflects not only objective factors but also the subjective responses of a group to environmental stressors.

PROFILE: ARABS AND BLACKS IN AN INDUSTRIAL AMERICAN CITY

On a clear day, and especially in the evenings, one sees curls of white and red-brown smoke puffing into the air at a very rapid and constant rate . . . . Whatever the direction of air and wind currents, this community

*is in the way of pollutants . . . . One young Black
man, standing and watching a grey dark cloud curling
in the air and forming an overcast near the apartments
sarcastically exclaimed, "This must be the promised
beauty of the great north expectations of my people!
The great trek to the north has been fulfilled at last!"*
—Chilungu (1974:24–25)

To a person reared in a North American city, the Arctic seems full of dangers with its blizzards and polar bears, and the tropics seems dangerous with its snakes and insects. The canals of a Middle Eastern village are full of schistosomiasis-causing cercariae, and new roads in Africa increase the spread of tsetse flies and sleeping sickness. It is easy to recognize the dangers of rural ecosystems, but every human environment has certain health hazards. We might ask how a medical anthropologist coming from a developing nation would perceive a typical U.S. city. What would a person from East Africa, for example, consider to be the greatest stressors of living next to a steel mill?

In 1972–1973, a Kenyan medical anthropologist, Simeon W. Chilungu, did carry out such a study in the Lake Erie city of Lackawanna, New York. Chilungu did doctoral dissertation research with two ethnic groups, American blacks and Arab immigrants, comparing their perceptions of the quality of life in an industrial environment.

Lackawanna, a city of about 28,000, is a southern suburb of Buffalo, in western New York. The city grew through the immigration of steel workers in the early part of the century, including large numbers of Poles, blacks, and Italians. In the last few decades, Puerto Ricans and Arabs have been the last groups to move to Lackawanna.

In 1972, Chilungu arranged to observe the Lackawanna Community Health Center. He talked with patients, attended medical team meetings, and observed weight watchers' meetings. He also participated in community activities and social clubs, and he read metropolitan and local newspapers to get a sense of community organization and history. Chilungu also consulted published statistical data and neighborhood census tracts.

Environmental pollution was a major concern expressed by residents. They feared lung damage and pointed to rusting cars,

FIGURE 9.6 Simeon Chilungu and his daughter Nelima and son Michael at the Lackawanna Community Health Center.

Photo by Kathleen E. Chilungu.

dirt particles on clothes, and peeling paint as evidence of pollution. They saw themselves as caught in a bind: the steel mill and other heavy industries provided employment but also endangered their health. One solution was to move to another suburb and to commute to work, but doing so was not always possible.

One of Chilungu's first questions was: To what extent did general discontentment with work and home conditions increase negative perceptions of air pollution? He acknowledged that the fear of pollution was valid, and indeed the Sierra Club was soon to publish a report showing that Lackawanna industry was a major source of pollution in the county, emitting dangerous amounts of sulfuric acid and sulfur dioxide. Both chemicals increase the incidence of bronchitis, emphysema, and asthma.

But the central question of the study was not whether there was evidence of physical damage due to pollution, but rather how residents perceived health hazards. While an epidemiologist is best qualified to answer the first question, a study of community opinions and individual attitudes is best done with the special interviewing and observation skills of the cultural anthropologist.

To answer the question of how cultural background affects a group's perception of health problems, Chilungu chose to compare blacks with Arabs. The 2700 blacks of the First Ward are a part of the steady northward flow of southern blacks since the 1930s. Poles and Italians have mostly moved out of this ward, but housing discrimination in other wards has not made it easy for blacks to move out, and many feel trapped. The 500 Arabs who live in the First Ward of Lackawanna immigrated from Yemen via Saudi Arabia. Some have lived there for ten years, others for only one year. Many of them came individually, sending for families after getting settled. Unlike the blacks, the Arabs have chosen to live in the First Ward.

The Arabs came from an ethnomedical system that contrasted sharply with what the clinic offered. Arabs traditionally believe that when a person covets or envies another, the "evil eye" they cast on the victim brings sickness or misfortune. Evil spirits, *jinn*, also bring trouble. Traditional Arabic medicine has many empirical techniques, but of equal significance are prayers, protective amulets, and divination rituals. Even modern medicine in Saudi Arabia is not completely modeled after Western metropolitan medicine. Doctors have religious rules as well as medical procedures to follow, and they avoid negative prognoses because no one but Allah really knows if a person will die. Because of modesty rules for women, gynecologists and obstetricians should be middle-aged women. Chilungu wondered whether these ethnomedical differences would create problems for the immigrants. Would they encounter communication blocks at the clinic? Would they distrust male gynecologists?

Chilungu did not anticipate unusual medical beliefs in the black community, but he was interested in cultural factors that affected mental and physical health. One important set of factors was the symbolic system of pride. Traits of pride that give a sense of positive self-identity include fashionable dress, prowess in dance and sports, musical ability, and a unique style of personal interaction that reinforces identity and group support. Traits of "no pride" include prostitution, pimping, and drug abuse, all a part of negative community identity. Chilungu discovered considerable ambivalence rather than pride among blacks about soul food, representing rural food traditions going back to the time of slavery. This ambivalence is unfortunate because these foods are very nutritious. While soul food was consumed at special family dinners, the more usual diet included a large proportion of fried food—fried chicken and fish, french fries, hamburgers, potato chips, and the like.

After studying qualitative aspects of black and Arab health concerns and expectations, Chilungu drew a random sample of names from a city directory for a quantitative epidemiological survey. He designed a questionnaire that included questions about the interviewees' socioeconomic background; 27 open-ended questions such as "What do you understand by the word 'illness'?"; listed items (such as a set of reasons for choosing a doctor) that the interviewees were asked to rank; and finally, a set of 195 yes-or-no questions from the Cornell Medical Index (CMI) that ask about symptoms of physical health problems, social habits, and psychological states. Arabic speakers translated the questionnaires and assisted in interviewing the sample of thirty Arabs. Black community residents worked as research aides also.

Table 9.2 gives some of the health problems indicated by answers to the Cornell Medical Index. Two types of comparisons can be made by looking at the table: differences between ethnic groups and differences between males and females in each group and between groups. Remember that these are not illnesses but rather reports of symptoms and feelings. For example, a "yes" answer to "Do you often wish you were dead and away from it all?" would be a response in the "depression" category.

Problems of the digestive tract are reported frequently by both groups but twice as much for blacks as for Arabs. In view of complaints about pollution, it is interesting that the figures for respiratory ailments are not as high as those for digestive prob-

TABLE 9.2 Percentage of black and Arab responses to Cornell Medical Index, by symptom category.

	Blacks		Arabs	
Type of health problem	Males % (N = 24)	Females % (N = 30)	Males % (N = 20)	Females % (N = 10)
Digestive	88	97	40	50
Nervous system	71	84	15	30
Respiratory	67	64	40	50
Skin	63	50	20	10
Eye and ear problems	55	67	30	60
Cardiovascular	55	77	10	30
Genitourinary	50	87	10	10
Psychological states				
Anger	63	63	30	10
Inadequacy	37	53	40	40
Anxiety	37	53	20	20
Sensitivity	37	70	30	00
Tension	37	67	20	40
Depression	29	43	10	10

SOURCE: Data extracted from statistical tables in Simeon W. Chilungu, "A Study of Health and Cultural Variants in an Industrial Community" (Ph.D. diss., SUNY at Buffalo, 1974).

lems. Symptom reporting is generally higher for blacks than for Arabs. Either the Arabs are actually healthier, or else they do not consider their health problems important enough to report. Black females also report more symptoms than do black males; this pattern of sex differences does not occur in the Arab sample.

How do these data compare with actual medical histories? Chilungu found that the proportion of people being treated for specific ailments was considerably lower than those reporting symptoms on the CMI. Table 9.3 gives a partial list of the more frequent disorders. Blacks have more medical problems than Arabs, and black women have more than black men. Notice how the illnesses differ by sex and ethnic group. Hypertension is almost exclusive to black females in this small sample, venereal disease exclusive to black males, and psychiatric problems ("mental breakdown" requiring hospitalization) exclusive to the Arab sample. The Arab responses to psychological questions on the CMI were generally lower than black responses, and yet their rate of treated psychiatric problems is higher. This discrepancy raises a number of questions. Does denial of negative feelings

TABLE 9.3 Percentage of blacks and Arabs treated for specific disorders.

Treated health problem	Blacks		Arabs	
	Males % (N = 24)	Females % (N = 30)	Males % (N = 20)	Females % (N = 10)
Venereal disease	33	0	0	0
Major injury	21	0	0	10
Hay fever	21	16	5	0
Overweight	16	33	20	20
Underweight	16	6	5	0
Unspecified surgery	12	33	0	10
Kidney or bladder	12	0	0	0
Hypertension	8	26	0	0
Hemorrhoids	8	20	0	0
Hernia	8	0	10	0
Asthma	4	6	10	0
Anemia	0	20	0	0
Varicose veins	0	20	0	0
Tumor or cancer	0	13	0	0
Mental breakdown	0	0	20	10
Tuberculosis	0	0	10	0

SOURCE: Data extracted from statistical tables in Simeon W. Chilungu, "A Study of Health and Cultural Variants in an Industrial Community" (Ph. D. diss., SUNY at Buffalo, 1974).

contribute to poor mental health? Does expression of anger and tension reduce stress for blacks? Or do blacks simply "channel" stress responses into physical symptoms rather than emotional disorders? We do not know the answers, but these would be interesting questions for a medical anthropology student to explore.

Another part of the study probed the perception of which health disorders seriously affected the community. The results are shown in table 9.4. It is interesting that no blacks listed obesity or digestive problems, perhaps because they did not consider them health problems. Arabs have a very different perception of community health than do blacks, and their perception only partially reflects their actual illnesses.

When asked to rank various causes of illness, 48 percent of the blacks gave first rank to "bad germs, bacteria, and viruses," 22 percent to "lack of personal hygiene," and 15 percent to "individual self negligence." No one put "pollution" at first rank. The Arabs ranked the causes of disease very much the same way as did the blacks. No one checked "evil eye" or "punishment by

TABLE 9.4   Major community health problems as identified by blacks and Arabs.

Blacks		Arabs	
Problem	% (N = 54)	Problem	% (N = 30)
venereal disease	48	cancer	27
hypertension	29	colds and flu	23
drug addiction	22	headaches	20
heart disease	18	venereal disease	16
cancer	15	air pollution	16
sickle cell anemia	15	stomach aches	13
arthritis	11	tuberculosis	7
air pollution	11		

SOURCE: Data extracted from statistical tables in Simeon W. Chilungu, "A Study of Health and Cultural Variants in an Industrial Community" (Ph. D. diss., SUNY at Buffalo, 1974).

 God" as a major cause of illness, even those who had lived in Lackawanna for only a year.

Chilungu also asked persons to rank valued attributes of a medical doctor. He thought that a doctor's understanding of their way of life might be of prime importance to the Arabs, or that perhaps the sex of the doctor would be important to women patients. In addition, he expected blacks to prefer black doctors. Given the differences in the ethnomedical backgrounds of the two groups, the results of this test were surprising. The groups are almost identical in their ranking of criteria for choosing a doctor. Of highest importance was the doctor's field of specialization; second, his or her reputation, fame, and popularity; and third, proximity to one's residence. Cost, understanding attitudes, sex, religion, and ethnicity were all of lesser importance to both groups.

Blacks and Arabs are similar in expectations of health care and perceptions of illness. But blacks are less healthy, objectively and in their own perception, than the Arabs. Why is this the case? Both groups live in a similar physical environment, but their social and emotional environments differ.

The blacks feel they are overcrowded, discriminated against, and held back by what one man in Lackawanna called "a chain of ill health, frustration, of self perpetuation and of destruction" (Chilungu 1974:225). In conversations, they blame pollution and racism for their problems, but on questionnaires they list germs, viruses, and poor hygiene as more important. Lung cancer worries them, but poor digestion, hypertension, and venereal disease affect them more directly. They do not designate emotional disorders as a community problem, and yet they check off a high number of psychological symptoms. Chilungu suggests that depression, anger, feelings of inadequacy, and mistrust are in fact common responses to the life conditions of a black person in the United States.

Chilungu believes that the Arabs' adjustment and general health are better partly because they are relatively satisfied with their life situation. They say that life in Lackawanna is better in many ways than in their native country, and they do not often meet racial discrimination. Perhaps most important, they reduce the stress of adjustment by sharing homes as extended families, participating in the Yemenite Benevolent Social Club, and eating traditional food as much as possible.

Chilungu's study demonstrates that environmental stress is not a fixed variable. The perceptions and expectations of a group add to or lessen the impact of pollution, crowding, and low income. Negative expectations and disillusionment add to the emotional problems of blacks, while changes in their traditional diet raise the incidence of digestive disorders. The expectations of Arab immigrants, on the other hand, have not been crushed. They maintain a balanced diet and personal hygiene standards derived from an empirically sound ethnomedicine. Despite the environmental stressors that both groups share, Arabs have maintained enough cultural continuity for physical and emotional resistance, while blacks find the industrial environment a truly dangerous place to live.

CONCLUSIONS

No one denies the disadvantages of living near massive industrial plants, highways, and a railroad, and we can empathize with the young man's bitter statement that "the great trek to the north has been

fulfilled at last!" Modernization has not given the blacks of Lackawanna the level of opportunities they expected. The Arabs have been
more fortunate, and their expectations are also derived from comparisons with conditions in Saudi Arabia and Yemen. Moving toward a
more modern life has meant a chance for economic security for these
Arab immigrants, a goal shared by modernizing people all over the
world. Changes brought by population growth, by the mechanization
of agriculture, and by industrialization have both pushed and pulled
people from traditional relationships with the environment and forced
them to try new adaptive alternatives. But are these alternatives
working? What are the effects of modernization on the individual, on
populations, and on the global ecosystem?

On the individual level, the technological progress intrinsic to
modernization allows an Inuit child to watch satellite-transmitted
television. It provides a bus service through Iranian mountains and
allows a worried mother to take her sick child to a government health
clinic. It divides African families when husbands go off to work in
cities and mines a hundred miles away while wives and children stay
home to tend the farms. Modernization brings both rewards and
problems; above all, it brings changes in lifestyles. Depending on a
country's income structure, the benefits of modernization may be
distributed more unequally than the costs. Even for the elite who
benefit the most materially, the loss of traditional anchor points in
belief, ritual, and social ties may bring alienation and anomie, a sense
of normlessness.

On the national level, development may also mean raised and
unfulfilled aspirations. When foreign investors profit most heavily
from industrialization and the mechanization of agriculture, "development" becomes a dirty word in the eyes of nationalists. Development and modernization are concepts that originated in a capitalist
vision of how change occurs, and critics have viewed the processes
described in this chapter simply as manifestations of a new phase of
imperialism and colonialism.

Despite development efforts, the gap between the rich and poor
nations has been steadily widening. In the light of this gap, many
developing nations are exploring alternative types of planned change
to improve health and prosperity. Rather than emphasizing capital-
intensive industrial development, they may choose to emphasize

agriculture. Instead of investing in the most advanced, large-scale technology, they can create more jobs by developing intermediate technology, which creates small cottage industries (Schumacher 1973).

These kinds of choices about the course of economic development have their analogue in the health care system. Nations must choose how to allocate limited resources, and these decisions must take place against the background of a rapidly changing health picture. Migration is changing the epidemiology of infectious disease. Urbanization and cash-cropping increase the risk of malnutrition. Mental illness, degenerative diseases, and the occupational injuries and diseases associated with industrialization claim attention at the same time that infectious disease and malnutrition remain of paramount concern.

In response to these health problems, developing nations look to models provided by the health care systems of developed nations, but the emphasis on medicine rather than on prevention and ecological management poses a dilemma. If the limited personnel and money of health agencies are concentrated on treatment efforts, inadequate attention is given to limiting population growth, improving nutrition, and assessing the risks of new development projects. With a conventional emphasis on medicine rather than on health, there will always be new cases to treat, new public health problems, and a continuing spiral of rising health costs and personnel shortages.

On a global scale, the price of modernization along the lines followed by the Western industrial nations may be too great for our planet's resources. The idea that the finite natural resources of our planet cannot support the present rate of industrial growth, nor the rate of population growth in underdeveloped countries (see figure 9.7), for more than a few decades is now widely heard. This idea was forcefully presented by an international and interdisciplinary team of consultants reporting to the United Nations Conference on the Human Environment (Ward and Dubos 1972). Computer simulations that project the collapse of our industrial system by A.D. 2100 as a result of pollution, resource depletion, or food shortage, depending on what assumptions are made, have been a widely publicized finding of the report *Limits to Growth* (Meadows et al. 1974).

Although talk of a retreat from industrialism is heard in some parts of the industrial world, few in these countries seem eager to give up any comforts already won, despite the acknowledged health costs of

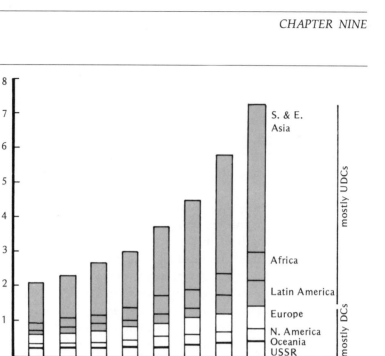

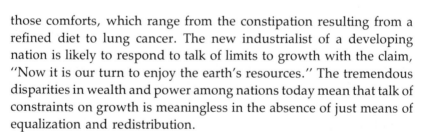

FIGURE 9.7   Past and projected world population growth for developed and under-developed countries. Projections are from United Nations estimates.

SOURCE: Reprinted from Albert Damon, *Human Biology and Ecology* (New York: W. W. Norton & Co.), p. 317. Copyright © 1977 by W. W. Norton & Company, Inc.

those comforts, which range from the constipation resulting from a refined diet to lung cancer. The new industrialist of a developing nation is likely to respond to talk of limits to growth with the claim, "Now it is our turn to enjoy the earth's resources." The tremendous disparities in wealth and power among nations today mean that talk of constraints on growth is meaningless in the absence of just means of equalization and redistribution.

Yet the prospect of unlimited growth and its predicted consequences of overpopulation and pollution invites science fiction fantasies of universal chaos, scenes in which food is as precious as gold, human life is worth little, and human dignity is worth less. But *is* this science fiction? What would a beggar in India think? Do we already have a preview of approaching conditions when we see people sleeping on sidewalks, "housing projects" that are nothing more than tin-roofed lean-tos to shelter people from sun and rain, and children fighting with monkeys over scraps of food in the streets of Calcutta? Do we have another kind of preview when families living near a chemical or nuclear dump in the United States suffer illness and birth defects before being evacuated from their homes?

These are difficult, uncomfortable questions, but they are not to be ignored. We live in a global ecosystem, and our lives touch in many ways. Modernization has brought all of us many problems, but as a process of cultural adaptation it also offers ways of dealing with these problems. Modernization has renewed our awareness of how fragile this global ecosystem is and how we must work to restore and preserve a balance between human beings and the rest of the biosphere.

RESOURCES

Readings

Bryant, John
  1969   Health and the Developing World. Ithaca, New York: Cornell University Press.
  This book deals with the management of medical resources and the training of health teams in developing nations. Its basic approach is economic, but the six long case studies of health care delivery problems are directly relevant to medical anthropology.
Foster, George M.
  1973   Traditional Societies and Technological Change. Second ed. New York: Harper & Row.
  A classic of applied anthropology and culture change studies, Foster's book emphasizes understanding types of barriers and stimulants to change and provides numerous examples of anthropologists and technical teams doing projects in developing countries.
Holmes, Alan C.
  1964   Health Education in Developing Countries. London: Thomas Nelson.
  A delightful manual for health educators in Kenya, this small text is complete with diagrams on making puppets, home-made film projectors, flannelgraphs, flicker books, and a variety of other teaching props and visual aids.

Lynch, L. Riddick, ed.
   1969   The Cross-Cultural Approach to Health Behavior. Rutherford,
   New Jersey: Fairleigh Dickinson University Press. (Distributed through
   Associated University Presses, Cranbury, New Jersey.)
   This is a book of readings on anthropology and community health
   especially appropriate for beginning students. Of particular value are five
   articles on changing Navaho health, including one by Annie Wauneka, a
   distinguished public health worker and member of the Navaho Tribal
   Council.
Markandaya, Kamala
   1954   Nectar in a Sieve. New York: New American Library.
   This novel shows the costs of modernization for an impoverished family
   in village India. It is one of the many fine novels and life histories coming
   out of developing nations that powerfully present the impact of modernization on the individual.
Meadows, Donella H., et al.
   1974   The Limits to Growth. Second ed. New York: New American
   Library.
   The Limits to Growth is a study of the world's economic future using
   computer simulations that show that industrial collapse is likely by the
   year 2100 unless humans decide to stop economic growth, stabilize
   population, and decrease capital investment.
Cole, H. S. D., et al.
   1973   Models of Doom: A Critique of the Limits to Growth. New York:
   Universe Books.
   This study is one of many responses elicited by the original 1972 version
   of The Limits to Growth study. Although the authors may disagree on
   assumptions and methods, all are agreed on the seriousness of the
   problems facing the global ecosystem.

APPENDIX:
PROJECTS IN
MEDICAL ANTHROPOLOGY

An excellent way to learn about medical anthropology is to design and carry out a research project, working either individually or as a team. In this section we briefly describe a few of the projects our students have chosen and enjoyed. In most types of projects, it is preferable that the final paper be different from the typical term paper. A personal, subjective account of why the student chose the project, how she or he proceeded, methods attempted, and evaluation of what was learned is often the most effective kind of reporting. Some class time should be devoted to a discussion of research techniques, problems encountered in field work situations, and issues of ethics and confidentiality. It is especially important that students come to understand how to safeguard the rights of those they interview or observe and to secure permission in any projects involving individuals in health settings.

1. Ask two or three elderly people, preferably relatives or neighbors, to talk about health and illness in the nineteenth century and early twentieth century as they experienced and remember it. Ask them to recall types of prevalent illness, kinds of treatment and practitioners, what childbirth was like, and how medical care changed

over the decades. If the conversations go well and your informant is willing to discuss more sensitive issues, ask about the causes of death, attitudes toward death, attitudes toward mental illness, and other possibly stigmatized conditions.

2. Choose a current health problem that has been covered in general media such as newspapers or in specialized journals or published government documents. Examples are drought and famine in Africa and India, chemical waste deposits in North America, lead and arsenic pollution in the Arctic and Subarctic. Prepare a report that looks at the health problem holistically, as an anthropologist would, considering the medical, economic, sociocultural, and psychological components of the impact of this health problem on a community or a population.

3. Using the Human Relations Area Files or ethnographies suggested by your instructor, look comparatively at the ethnomedicine of ten or more societies, noting differences and similarities in beliefs about illness, use of herbs, nutritional rules, childbirth practices, care of the elderly, trance and possession, and beliefs relating ecology and health.

4. Carry out approximately fifteen hours of observation or participation in a community health setting, keeping a confidential record of your experiences. The identity of all individuals must be guarded in your record. If possible, work as a volunteer in the health setting such as a Veterans' Administration hospital, a workshop for the mentally retarded, a center for the elderly, or a children's hospital. You may also be able to arrange permission to observe at Lamaze classes in prepared childbirth, at well-baby clinics, at meetings of Alcoholics Anonymous and Overeaters Anonymous open to the public, and other self-help organizations.

5. Choose a disease that once had a great impact on human societies, such as smallpox, and trace the history of how humans regarded the disease, attempted cures and prevention, and treated victims. What effect did the disease have on history? What is the status of the disease today?

6. Choose a health problem that affects one particular age group in North American society, for example, heart attacks among middle-aged men or crib death in infants, and look through journals and medical reports for recent research findings that link ecological or nutritional factors to these problems. If possible, compare differences in various regions and differences over time in reported rates. If you were to design field research as a medical ecologist on this health problem, how would you proceed?

7. Interview people who practice Yoga, Transcendental Meditation, Scientology, or a similar system, or who follow macrobiotic principles in their diet. Discuss the health benefits and therapeutic components of the system being explored, and ask about the history of the organization and the philosophy behind the system.

8. Interview students whose families represent different cultural traditions about how they classify, explain, and respond to minor illnesses such as colds. Chicken soup, mustard plasters, and hot rum toddies each come from a different subcultural tradition of folk medicine.

9. Identify a problem of concern to you that is related to health, think through possible solutions, and take action that contributes to solving the problem. The problem may be a local one, such as need for a blood pressure screening program or the lack of nutritious snacks in dorm vending machines, or it may be a world problem, such as legislation needed to help make Third World nations more self-sufficient in food production. After investigating the issue, you may wish to write letters to newspapers and legislators suggesting a course of action.

REFERENCES CITED

Abramson, Harold, John F. Bertles, and Doris L. Wethers, eds.
1973   Sickle Cell Disease. St. Louis: C. V. Mosby.

Adams, Richard N.
1955   A Nutritional Research Program in Guatemala. *In* Health, Culture, and Community. Benjamin D. Paul, ed. Pp. 435–458. New York: Russell Sage Foundation.

Akinkugbe, O. O.
1972   High Blood Pressure in the African. Edinburgh: Churchill Livingstone.

Akwesasne Notes, Mohawk Nation, via Rooseveltown, New York.
Published by the Program in American Studies, State University of New York at Buffalo.

Alland, Alexander, Jr.
1970   Adaptation in Cultural Evolution: An Approach to Medical Anthropology. New York: Columbia University Press.

Alpers, Michael
1970   Kuru in New Guinea: Its Changing Pattern and Etiologic Elucidation. American Journal of Tropical Medicine and Hygiene 19:133–137.

American Society of Anesthesiologists
1974   Occupational Disease among Operating Room Personnel: A National Study. Anesthesiology 41:321–340.

Anderson, James N.
1976   Dietary Changes of West Coast Malays: Context and Consequences. Paper delivered to annual meeting of the American Anthropological Association, Washington, D. C.

Ansari, N., ed.
1973   Epidemiology and Control of Schistosomiasis (Bilharziasis). Baltimore: University Park Press.

Appley, Mortimer H., and Richard Trumbull
1967   Psychological Stress. New York: Appleton-Century-Crofts.

Arnott, Margaret L., ed.
1975   Gastronomy: The Anthropology of Food and Food Habits. The Hague: Mouton.

Ashburn, Percy M.
1947   The Ranks of Death: A Medical History of the Conquest of America. New York: Coward-McCann.

Azumi, Koya
1968   The Mysterious Drop in Japan's Birth Rate. TransAction 5 (May):46–48.

Baker, Paul T.
1969   Human Biological Variation as an Adaptive Response to the Environment. *In* Evolutionary Anthropology. Hermann K. Bleibtreu, ed. Pp. 305–321. Boston: Allyn and Bacon.
1978   The Biology of High-Altitude Peoples. Cambridge, England: Cambridge University Press.

Baker, P. T., and Michael A. Little, eds.
1976   Man in the Andes: A Multidisciplinary Study of High Altitude Quechua. Stroudsburg, Pennsylvania: Dowden, Hutchinson, and Ross.

Baker, Paul T., and J. S. Weiner, eds.
1966   The Biology of Human Adaptability. Oxford: Clarendon Press.

Balikci, Asen
1970   The Netsilik Eskimo. Garden City, New York: Natural History Press.

Bang, H. O., J. Dyerberg, and N. Hjørne
1976   The Composition of Food Consumed by Greenland Eskimos. Acta Medica Scandinavica 200:69–73.

Barth, Fredrik
1974   On Responsibility and Humanity: Calling a Colleague to Account. Current Anthropology 15:99–102.

Benet, Sula
1974   Abkhasians: The Long-Living People of the Caucasus. New York: Holt, Rinehart and Winston.
1976   How to Live to Be 100: The Life-Style of the People of the Caucasus. New York: Dial Press.

Bennett, F. J., et al.
1973   Studies on Viral, Bacterial, Rickettsial and Treponemal Diseases in the Hadza of Tanzania and a Note on Injuries. Human Biology 45:243–272.

Berg, Alan
1973   The Nutrition Factor: Its Role in National Development. Washington D.C.: Brookings Institution.

Berg, Gösta, ed.
1973 Circumpolar Problems: Habitat, Economy, and Social Relations in the Arctic. Wenner-Gren Center, International Symposium Series, Vol. 21. New York: Pergamon Press.

Binford, Lewis R., and W. J. Chasko, Jr.
1976 Nunamiut Demographic History: A Provocative Case. *In* Demographic Anthropology: Quantitative Approaches. A School of American Research Advanced Seminar Book. Ezra B. W. Zubrow, ed. Pp. 63–143. Albuquerque: University of New Mexico Press.

Birdsell, Joseph B.
1968 Some Predictions for the Pleistocene Based on Equilibrium Systems among Recent Hunter-Gatherers. *In* Man the Hunter. Richard B. Lee and Irven DeVore, eds. Pp. 229–240. Chicago: Aldine.
1972 Human Evolution. Chicago: Rand McNally.

Black, Francis L.
1975 Infectious Diseases in Primitive Societies. Science 187:515–518.

Boas, Franz
1921 Ethnology of the Kwakiutl, Based on Data Collected by George Hunt. 35th Annual Report of the Bureau of American Ethnology, 1913–1914, Part 1.
1940 Changes in the Bodily Form of Descendants of Immigrants. *In* Race, Language and Culture. Pp. 60–75. New York: Macmillan.
1964 The Central Eskimo. Lincoln: University of Nebraska Press. (First published in Sixth Annual Report of the Bureau of Ethnology, Smithsonian Institution, Washington D.C., 1888.)

Bolton, Ralph
1973 Aggression and Hypoglycemia Among the Qolla: A Study in Psychobiological Anthropology. Ethnology 12:227–257.
1976 Andean Coca Chewing: A Metabolic Perspective. American Anthropologist 78:630–634.

Boserup, Ester
1965 The Conditions of Agricultural Growth: The Economics of Agrarian Change Under Population Pressure. Chicago: Aldine.

Boughey, Arthur S.
1973 Man and the Environment. Second ed. New York: Macmillan.

Bowman, James E.
1974 Sickle Cell Screening—Medical-Legal, Ethical, Psychological, and Social Problems: A Sickle Cell Crisis. DHEW Publication No. (HSM)73-9141. First International Conference on the Mental Health Aspects of Sickle Cell Anemia, Nashville, 1972. Pp. 40–54.

Brewer, George J.
1976 A View of the Current Status of Antisickling Therapy. American Journal of Hematology 1:121–128.

Briggs, L. Cabot
1975 Environment and Human Adaptation in the Sahara. *In* Physiological Anthropology. Albert Damon, ed. Pp. 93–129. New York: Oxford University Press.

Brodie, Jessie Laird
    1975   Medical and Social Problems of Sickle Cell Anemia: The Patient
    and the Bearer of the Trait. Journal of the American Medical Women's
    Association 30:453–455.
Brues, Alice M.
    1969   Population Genetics of the A-B-O Blood Groups. In Evolutionary
    Anthropology. Hermann K. Bleibtreu, ed. Pp. 292–301. Boston: Allyn
    and Bacon.
Bryant, John H.
    1969   Health and the Developing World. Ithaca, New York: Cornell
    University Press.
Bryant, Vaughn M., and Glenna Williams-Dean
    1975   The Coprolites of Man. Scientific American 232(1):100–109.
Buchbinder, Georgeda
    1977   Endemic Cretinism among the Maring: A By-Product of Culture
    Contact. In Nutrition and Anthropology in Action. Thomas K. Fitzger-
    ald, ed. Pp. 106–116. Assen: Van Gorcum.
Buck, Alfred A., et al.
    1968   Coca Chewing and Health. American Journal of Epidemiology
    88:159–177.
Bullough, Bonnie, and Vern L. Bullough
    1972   Poverty, Ethnic Identity, and Health Care. New York: Apple-
    ton-Century-Crofts.
Burchard, Roderick E.
    1975   Coca Chewing: A New Perspective. In Cannabis and Culture. Vera
    Rubin, ed. Pp. 463–484. The Hague: Mouton.
Burkitt, Denis P.
    1973   Some Diseases Characteristic of Modern Western Civilization.
    British Medical Journal 1:274–278.
Burnet, Sir MacFarlane, and David O. White
    1972   Natural History of Infectious Disease. Fourth ed. London: Cam-
    bridge University Press.
Butler, Judy, et al.
    1978   Dying for Work: Occupational Health and Asbestos. NACLA
    Report on the Americas 12(2):2–39.
Cannon, Walter B.
    1929   Bodily Changes in Pain, Hunger, Fear and Rage. Second ed. New
    York: D. Appleton.
    1932   The Wisdom of the Body. New York: W. W. Norton.
    1942   "Voodoo" Death. American Anthropologist 44:169–181.
Carneiro, Robert L.
    1968a   Cultural Adaptation. In International Encyclopedia of the Social
    Sciences, Vol. 3. Pp. 551–554.
    1968b   The Transition from Hunting to Horticulture in the Amazon
    Basin. 8th Congress of Anthropological and Ethnological Sciences,
    Proceedings, Tokyo and Kyoto, 1968. Pp. 244–248.

Carson, Rachel
  1962   Silent Spring. Boston: Houghton Mifflin.
Cassel, John
  1955   A Comprehensive Health Program among South African Zulus. *In* Health, Culture, and Community. Benjamin D. Paul, ed. Pp. 15–41. New York: Russell Sage Foundation.
  1970   Physical Illness in Response to Stress. *In* Social Stress. Sol Levine and Norman A. Scotch, eds. Pp. 189–209. Chicago: Aldine.
  1977   Social and Cultural Implications of Food and Food Habits. *In* Culture, Disease, and Healing. David Landy, ed. Pp. 236–242. New York: Macmillan.
Castro, Josué de
  1952   Geography of Hunger. London: Victor Gollancz.
Cawte, John
  1978   Gross Stress in Small Islands: A Study in Macropsychiatry. *In* Extinction and Survival in Human Populations. Charles D. Laughlin, Jr., and Ivan A. Brady, eds. Pp. 95–121. New York: Columbia University Press.
Center for Disease Control
  1972   Ten State Nutrition Survey, 1968–70. U.S. Department of Health, Education, and Welfare.
Cerami, Anthony, and Charles M. Peterson
  1975   Cyanate and Sickle-Cell Disease. Scientific American 232(4):44–50.
Chagnon, Napoleon A.
  1977   Yanomamo: The Fierce People. Second ed. New York: Holt, Rinehart and Winston. Case Studies in Cultural Anthropology. George Spindler and Louise Spindler, gen. eds.
Chase, Allan
  1971   The Biological Imperatives: Health, Politics and Human Survival. Baltimore: Penguin Books.
Chilungu, Simeon W.
  1974   A Study of Health and Cultural Variants in an Industrial Community. Ph.D. dissertation, Anthropology Department, State University of New York at Buffalo.
Citizen's Board of Inquiry into Hunger
  1968   Hunger, U.S.A. Washington D.C.: New Community Press.
Clark, Margaret
  1970   Health in the Mexican-American Culture. Berkeley: University of California Press.
Cockburn, Aidan
  1963   The Evolution and Eradication of Infectious Diseases. Baltimore: Johns Hopkins Press.
  1977   Infectious Diseases in Ancient Populations. *In* Culture, Disease, and Healing. David Landy, ed. Pp. 83–95. New York: Macmillan.
Cohen, B. M., and M. Z. Cooper
  1954   A Follow-up Study of World War II Prisoners of War. V. A.

Medical Monograph. Washington, D.C.: U.S. Government Printing Office.

Cole, H. S. D., et al.
1973 Models of Doom: A Critique of the Limits to Growth. New York: Universe Books.

Collis, W. R. F., J. Dema, and A. Omololu
1962 On the Ecology of Child Health and Nutrition in Nigerian Villages. Tropical and Geographical Medicine 14:140–162.

Cook, Earl
1971 The Flow of Energy in an Industrial Society. Scientific American 225(3):134–144.

Cook, S. F.
1972 The Epidemic of 1830–1833 in California and Oregon. In The Emergent Native Americans: A Reader in Culture Contact. Deward E. Walker, Jr., ed. Pp. 172–192. Boston: Little, Brown.
1973 The Significance of Disease in the Extinction of the New England Indians. Human Biology 45:485–508.

Cosminsky, Sheila
1977 Childbirth and Midwifery on a Guatemalan Finca. Medical Anthropology 1:69–104.

Crapanzano, Vincent
1973 The Hamadsha: A Study in Moroccan Ethnopsychiatry. Berkeley: University of California Press.

Cravioto, Joaquin, E. R. DeLicardie, and H. G. Birch
1966 Nutrition, Growth and Neurointegrative Development: An Experimental and Ecologic Study. Pediatrics 38:319–372.

Crick, F. H. C.
1966 The Genetic Code: III. Scientific American 215(4):55–62.

Crosby, Alfred W., Jr.
1969 The Early History of Syphilis: A Reappraisal. American Anthropologist 71:218–227.
1972 The Columbian Exchange: Biological and Cultural Consequences of 1492. Westport, Connecticut: Greenwood.

Cruz-Coke, Ricardo, Hugo Donoso, and Radek Barrera
1973 Genetic Ecology of Hypertension. Clinical Science and Molecular Medicine 45:55s–65s.

Dahl, L. K.
1972 Salt and Hypertension. American Journal of Clinical Nutrition 25:231–244.

Damon, Albert
1977 Human Biology and Ecology. New York: W. W. Norton.

Dewalt, Kathleen M., and Gretel H. Pelto
1977 Food Use and Household Ecology in a Mexican Community. In Nutrition and Anthropology in Action. Thomas K. Fitzgerald, ed. Pp. 79–93. Assen: Van Gorcum.

Dimsdale, Joel E.
1976 The Coping Behavior of Nazi Concentration Camp Survivors. In

Human Adaptation. Rudolf H. Moos, ed. Pp. 350–360. Lexington, Massachusetts: D. C. Heath.

Divale, William Tulio, and Marvin Harris
1976 Population, Warfare, and the Male Supremacist Complex. American Anthropologist 78:521–538.

Dobzhansky, Theodosius
1960 The Present Evolution of Man. Scientific American 203(3):206–217.

Dols, Michael W.
1977 The Black Death in the Middle East. Princeton, New Jersey: Princeton University Press.

Dornstreich, Mark D., and George E. B. Morren
1974 Does New Guinea Cannibalism Have Nutritional Value? Human Ecology 2:1–12.

Douglas, Mary
1972 Deciphering a Meal. Daedalus 101:61–82.

Draper, H. H.
1977 The Aboriginal Eskimo Diet. American Anthropologist 79:309–316.

Dublin, Louis I.
1965 Factbook on Man from Birth to Death. Second ed. New York: Macmillan.

DuBois, Cora
1961 The People of Alor: A Social-Psychological Study of an East Indian Island. 2 vols. New York: Harper. (First ed., University of Minnesota Press, 1944.)

Dubos, René
1959 Mirage of Health: Utopias, Progress, and Biological Change. New York: Harper.
1965 Man Adapting. New Haven, Connecticut: Yale University Press.

Dunn, Frederick L.
1968 Epidemiological Factors: Health and Disease in Hunter-Gatherers. In Man the Hunter. Richard B. Lee and Irven DeVore, eds. Pp. 221–228. Chicago: Aldine.

Eaton, Cynthia
1977 Diabetes, Culture Change, and Acculturation: A Biocultural Analysis. Medical Anthropology 1:42–63.

Eckenfels, Edward J., et al.
1977 Endemic Hypertension in a Poor, Black Rural Community: Can It Be Controlled? Journal of Chronic Diseases 30:499–518.

Edgerton, Robert B.
1967 The Cloak of Competence: Stigma in the Lives of the Mentally Retarded. Berkeley: University of California Press.

Edgerton, Robert B., and Sylvia M. Bercovici
1976 The Cloak of Competence: Years Later. American Journal of Mental Deficiency 80:485–497.

Edozien, Joseph C.
1970 Malnutrition in Africa: Need and Basis for Action. In Malnutrition

Is a Problem of Ecology. P. György and O. L. Kline, eds. Pp. 64–72. Basel, Switzerland: S. Karger.

Ehrlich, Allen S.
1974 Ecological Perception and Economic Adaptation in Jamaica. Human Organization 33:155–161.

Ehrlich, Paul R., Anne H. Ehrlich, and John P. Holdren
1973 Human Ecology. San Francisco: W. H. Freeman.

Fabrega, Horacio, Jr.
1974 Disease and Social Behavior: An Interdisciplinary Perspective. Cambridge, Massachusetts: M.I.T. Press.

Farb, Peter
1968 Man's Rise to Civilization. New York: Avon Books.

Farooq, M.
1973 Historical Development. In Epidemiology and Control of Schistosomiasis (Bilharziasis). N. Ansari, ed. Pp. 1–16. Baltimore: University Park Press.

Farooq, M., and M. B. Mallah
1966 The Behavioral Pattern of Social and Religious Water Contact Activities in the Egypt–49 Bilharziasis Project Area. Bulletin of the World Health Organization 35:377–387.

Fields, Suzanne
1976 Storefront Psychotherapy Through Seance. Innovations, Winter 1976, pp. 3–11.

Fischer, Ann, and J. L. Fischer
1961 Culture and Epidemiology: A Theoretical Investigation of Kuru. Journal of Health and Human Behavior 2:16–25.

Fitzgerald, T. K.
1976 Ipomoea Batatas: The Sweet Potato Revisited. Ecology of Food and Nutrition 5:107–114.

Flatz, Gebhard, and Hans Werner Rotthauwe
1973 Lactose Nutrition and Natural Selection. The Lancet ii:76–77.

Food and Agriculture Organization
1970 Amino-acid Content of Foods and Biological Data on Proteins. Rome.

1973 FAO/WHO Energy Requirements and Protein Requirements. WHO Technical Report Series No. 522.

Foster, George M.
1973 Traditional Societies and Technological Change. Second ed. New York: Harper & Row.

1978 Medical Anthropology: Some Contrasts with Medical Sociology. In Health and the Human Condition. Michael H. Logan and Edward E. Hunt, Jr., eds. Pp. 2–11. North Scituate, Massachusetts: Duxbury Press.

Foulks, Edward F.
1972 The Arctic Hysterias of the North Alaskan Eskimo. Anthropological Studies #10. Washington D.C.: American Anthropological Association.

Frake, Charles O.
1961 The Diagnosis of Disease Among the Subanun of Mindanao. American Anthropologist 63:113–132.

Fraser, Judy
1974 The Female Alcoholic. Toronto: Addiction Research Foundation of Ontario. (Reprinted from Addictions, Fall 1973.)

Frisch, Rose E.
1971 Does Malnutrition Cause Permanent Mental Retardation in Human Beings? Psychiatria, Neurologia, Neurochirurgia 74:463–479.
1978 Population, Food Intake, and Fertility. Science 199:22–30.

Frisch, R. E., and J. W. McArthur
1974 Menstrual Cycles: Fatness as a Determinant of Minimum Weight Necessary for their Maintenance or Onset. Science 185:949–951.

Gajdusek, D. Carleton
1977 Urgent Opportunistic Observations: The Study of Changing, Transient and Disappearing Phenomena of Medical Interest in Disrupted Primitive Human Communities. In Health and Disease in Tribal Societies. Ciba Symposium #49. Pp. 69–102. Amsterdam: Elsevier.

Gajdusek, D. Carleton, Clarence J. Gibbs, Jr., and Michael Alpers
1967 Transmission and Passage of Experimental 'Kuru' to Chimpanzees. Science 155:212–214.

Gardner, Lytt I.
1972 Deprivation Dwarfism. Scientific American 227(1):76–82.

Garn, Stanley M., and Walter D. Block
1970 The Limited Nutritional Value of Cannibalism. American Anthropologist 72:106.

Garn, Stanley M., and Diane C. Clark
1974 Economics and Fatness. Ecology of Food and Nutrition 3:19–20.

Garrison, Vivian
1977 Doctor, Espiritista or Psychiatrist?: Health-Seeking Behavior in a Puerto Rican Neighborhood of New York City. Medical Anthropology 1:65–180.

Gary, Lawrence E.
1977 The Sickle-Cell Controversy. In Heredity and Society: Readings in Social Genetics. Second ed. Adela S. Baer, ed. Pp. 361–373. New York: Macmillan.

Geertz, Clifford
1963 Agricultural Involution: The Process of Ecological Change in Indonesia. Berkeley: University of California Press.

Gillie, R. Bruce
1971 Endemic Goiter. Scientific American 224(6):92–101.

Glass, David C., and Jerome E. Singer
1975 Effects of Noise on Human Performance. In Physiological Anthropology. Albert Damon, ed. Pp. 335–359. New York: Oxford University Press.

Glasse, Robert
    1967   Cannibalism in the Kuru Region of New Guinea. Transactions of
    the New York Academy of Sciences 29:748–754.
Gonzalez, Nancie L. S.
    1964   Beliefs and Practices Concerning Medicine and Nutrition Among
    Lower-Class Urban Guatemalans. American Journal of Public Health
    54:1726–1734.
Gopalan, C.
    1975   Protein Versus Calories in the Treatment of Protein-Calorie Mal-
    nutrition: Metabolic and Population Studies in India. In Protein-Calorie
    Malnutrition. Robert E. Olson, ed. Pp. 330–351. New York: Academic
    Press.
Gordon, J. E., J. B. Wyon, and W. Ascoli
    1967   The Second Year Death Rate in Less Developed Countries.
    American Journal of the Medical Sciences 254:357–380.
Gorst, D. W.
    1976   Sickle Cell Disease. Nursing Times 72:1436–1438.
Gould, Richard A.
    1969   Yiwara: Foragers of the Australian Desert. New York: Charles
    Scribner's Sons.
Graham, Saxon
    1963   Social Factors in Relation to the Chronic Illnesses. In Handbook of
    Medical Sociology. H. E. Freeman, S. Levine, and L. G. Reeder, eds.
    Pp. 65–98. Englewood Cliffs, New Jersey: Prentice-Hall.
Greene, Lawrence S.
    1973   Physical Growth and Development, Neurological Maturation and
    Behavioral Functioning in Two Ecuadorian Andean Communities in
    Which Goiter Is Endemic. American Journal of Physical Anthropology
    38:119–134.
Gross, Daniel R., and Barbara A. Underwood
    1971   Technological Change and Caloric Costs: Sisal Agriculture in
    Northeastern Brazil. American Anthropologist 73:724–740.
Gubser, Nicholas J.
    1965   The Nunamiut Eskimos: Hunters of Caribou. New Haven, Con-
    necticut: Yale University Press.
Guemple, Lee
    1972   Eskimo Band Organization and the DP Camp Hypothesis. Arctic
    Anthropology 9:80–112.
Haas, Jere D., and Gail G. Harrison
    1977   Nutritional Anthropology and Biological Adaptation. Annual
    Review of Anthropology 6:69–101.
Hairston, N. G.
    1973   The Dynamics of Transmission. In Epidemiology and Control of
    Schistosomiasis (Bilharziasis). N. Ansari, ed. Pp. 250–333. Baltimore:
    University Park Press.

Hall, Richard C. W., and Patrick T. Malone
1976 Psychiatric Effects of Prolonged Asian Captivity: A Two-Year Follow Up. American Journal of Psychiatry 133:786–790.

Hammel, H. T.
1969 Terrestrial Animals in Cold: Recent Studies of Primitive Man. In Evolutionary Anthropology. Hermann K. Bleibtreu, ed. Pp. 322–344. Boston: Allyn and Bacon.

Hanna, Joel M.
1974 Coca Leaf Use in Southern Peru: Some Biosocial Aspects. American Anthropologist 76:281–296.

Harlow, Harry F.
1971 Learning to Love. New York: Ballantine Books.

Harner, Michael
1977 The Ecological Basis for Aztec Sacrifice. American Ethnologist 4:117–135.

Harris, Marvin
1977 Cannibals and Kings: The Origins of Cultures. New York: Random House.

Harrison, Gail G.
1975 Primary Adult Lactase Deficiency: A Problem in Anthropological Genetics. American Anthropologist 77:812–835.

Harrison, Gail G., W. L. Rathje, and W. W. Hughes
1975 Food Waste Behavior in an Urban Population. Journal of Nutrition Education 7:13–16.

Haviland, William A.
1967 Stature at Tikal, Guatemala: Implications for Ancient Maya Demography and Social Organization. American Antiquity 32:316–325.

Heber, Rick
1961 Modifications in the Manual on Terminology and Classification in Mental Retardation. American Journal of Mental Deficiency 65:499–500.

Henry, James P., and John C. Cassel
1969 Psychosocial Factors in Essential Hypertension: Recent Epidemiologic and Animal Experimental Evidence. American Journal of Epidemiology 90:171–200.

Hern, Warren M.
1976 Knowledge and Use of Herbal Contraceptives in a Peruvian Village. Human Organization 35:9–19.

Heyden, Siegfried, et al.
1969 Elevated Blood Pressure Levels in Adolescents, Evans County, Georgia. Journal of the American Medical Association 209:1683–1689.

Hirst, L. Fabian
1953 The Conquest of Plague: A Study of the Evolution of Epidemiology. Oxford: Clarendon Press.

Hobart, Charles W.
1975 Socioeconomic Correlates of Mortality and Morbidity Among Inuit Infants. Arctic Anthropology 12:37–48.

Hochstein, Gianna
  1968 Pica: A Study in Medical and Anthropological Explanation. *In* Essays on Medical Anthropology. Thomas Weaver, ed. Pp. 88–96. Southern Anthropological Society Proceedings, No. 1.

Hock, Raymond J.
  1970 Physiology of High Altitude. Scientific American 222(2):52–62.

Hodges, R. E.
  1971 Nutrition and the Pill. Journal of the American Dietetic Association 59:212–217.

Holmberg, Allan R.
  1969 Nomads of the Long Bow: The Siriono of Eastern Bolivia. Garden City, New York: Natural History Press.

Holmes, Alan C.
  1964 Health Education in Developing Countries. London: Nelson.

Holmes, Thomas H.
  1956 Multidiscipline Studies of Tuberculosis. *In* Personality, Stress, and Tuberculosis. Phineas J. Sparer, ed. Pp. 65–152. New York: International Universities Press.

Honigmann, John J.
  1967 Personality in Culture. New York: Harper & Row.

Howell, Nancy
  1976 The Population of the Dobe Area !Kung. *In* Kalahari Hunter-Gatherers. R. B. Lee and I. DeVore, eds. Pp. 137–151. Cambridge, Massachusetts: Harvard University Press.

Howells, William W.
  1960 The Distribution of Man. Scientific American 203(3):112–127.

Hudson, James I., and George E. Kauffman
  1974 Development of an Indian-operated Health System Through the Process of Interim Management by a Non-local Organization. People-to-People Health Information Project Hope. Washington, D.C.: Department of Information Services.

Hughes, Charles Campbell
  1965 Under Four Flags: Recent Culture Change Among the Eskimos. Current Anthropology 6:3–69.

Hughes, Charles C., and J. M. Hunter
  1970 Disease and "Development" in Africa. Social Science and Medicine 3:443–493.

Hulse, Frederick S.
  1957 Exogamie et hétérosis. Archives Suisses D'Anthropologie Générale 22:103–125.

Hunt, Edward E., Jr.
  1978a Ecological Frameworks and Hypothesis Testing in Medical Anthropology. *In* Health and the Human Condition: Perspectives on Medical Anthropology. Michael H. Logan and Edward E. Hunt, Jr., eds. Pp. 84–100. North Scituate, Massachusetts: Duxbury Press.
  1978b Evolutionary Comparisons of the Demography, Life Cycles and Health Care of Chimpanzee and Human Populations. *In* Health and the

Human Condition. Michael H. Logan and Edward E. Hunt, Jr., eds. Pp. 52–57. North Scituate, Massachusetts: Duxbury Press.

Hunter, Edna J.
1976 The Prisoner of War: Coping with the Stress of Isolation. *In* Human Adaptation. Rudolf H. Moos, ed. Pp. 322–331. Lexington, Massachusetts: D. C. Heath.

Hunter, John M.
1973 Geophagy in Africa and the United States: A Culture-Nutrition Hypothesis. Geographical Review 63:171–195.

Hurlich, Marshall
1976 Environmental Adaptation: Biological and Behavioral Response to Cold in the Canadian Subarctic. Ph.D. dissertation, Anthropology Department, State University of New York at Buffalo.

Hurlich, M. G., and A. T. Steegmann, Jr.
1979 Contrasting Laboratory Response to Cold in Two Subarctic Algonkian Villages: An Admixture Effect? Human Biology, in press.

Imperato, Pascal James
1976 Health Care Systems in the Sahel: Before and After the Drought. *In* The Politics of Natural Disaster: The Case of the Sahel Drought. Michael A. Glantz, ed. Pp. 282–302. New York: Praeger.

Inuit Today. Inuit Tapirisat of Canada, Ottawa. Leah d'Argencourt, ed.

Isaac, Barry
1977 The Siriono of Eastern Bolivia: A Reexamination. Human Ecology 5:137–154.

Jelliffe, Derrick B.
1957 Social Culture and Nutrition: Cultural Blocks and Protein Malnutrition in Rural West Bengal. Pediatrics 20:128–138.
1966 The Assessment of the Nutritional Status of the Community. Geneva: World Health Organization.
1968 Infant Nutrition in the Subtropics and Tropics. Geneva: World Health Organization.

Jelliffe, D. B., and E. F. P. Jelliffe
1972 Lactation, Conception, and the Nutrition of the Nursing Mother and Child. Journal of Pediatrics 81:829–833.

Jelliffe, D. B., et al.
1962 The Children of the Hadza Hunters. Tropical Pediatrics 60:907–913.

Jerome, Norge W.
1968 Food Consumption Patterns in Relation to Life-Styles of In-Migrant Negro Families. University of Wisconsin, Institute for Research on Poverty, Discussion Papers.
1975 On Determining Food Patterns of Urban Dwellers in Contemporary U.S. Society. *In* Gastronomy: The Anthropology of Food and Food Habits. Margaret L. Arnott, ed. Pp. 91–111. The Hague: Mouton.

Johnson, Stanley B.
1974 The Problem of Sickle Cell Disease: Unawareness among Medical Personnel. DHEW Publication No. (HSM)73-9141. First International

Conference on the Mental Health Aspects of Sickle Cell Anemia, Nashville, 1972. Pp. 58–61.

Jones, David E.
1972 Sanapia: Comanche Medicine Woman. New York: Holt, Rinehart and Winston.

Jones, K. L., and D. W. Smith
1975 The Fetal Alcohol Syndrome. Teratology 12:1–10.

Jurmain, Robert D.
1977 Paleoepidemiology of Degenerative Knee Disease. Medical Anthropology 1:1–14.

Kahn, Robert L., and John R. P. French, Jr.
1970 Status and Conflict: Two Themes in the Study of Stress. *In* Social and Psychological Factors in Stress. Joseph E. McGrath, ed. Pp. 238–263. New York: Holt, Rinehart and Winston.

Katz, S. H., M. L. Hediger, and L. A. Valleroy
1974 Traditional Maize Processing Techniques in the New World. Science 184:765–773.

Kemp, William B.
1971 The Flow of Energy in a Hunting Society. Scientific American 225(3):104–115.

Kent, Saul
1976 What Nutritional Deprivation Experiments Reveal about Aging. Geriatrics 31:141–144.

Kimble, George H. T.
1960 Tropical Africa. Vol. I. New York: Twentieth Century Fund.

Kiste, Robert C.
1974 The Bikinians: A Study in Forced Migration. Menlo Park, California: Cummings.

Knutsson, Karl Eric, and Ruth Selinus
1970 Fasting in Ethiopia: An Anthropological and Nutritional Study. American Journal of Clinical Nutrition 23:956–969.

Kroeber, Theodora
1961 Ishi in Two Worlds. Berkeley: University of California Press.

Kroeber, Theodora, and Robert F. Heizer
1968 Almost Ancestors: The First Californians. San Francisco: Sierra Club/Ballantine Books.

Kummer, Hans
1971 Primate Societies. Chicago: Aldine.

Kunitz, Stephen J.
1974 Some Notes on Physiologic Conditions as Social Problems. Social Science and Medicine 8:207–211.

Landy, David, ed.
1977 Culture, Disease, and Healing: Studies in Medical Anthropology. New York: Macmillan.

Langer, William L.
1964 The Black Death. Scientific American 210(2):114–121.

1972 Checks on Population Growth: 1750–1850. Scientific American 226(2):92–99.

Lanoix, Joseph N.
1958 Relation Between Irrigation Engineering and Bilharziasis. Bulletin of the World Health Organization 18:1011–1035.

Laughlin, Charles D., Jr.
1978 Adaptation and Exchange in So: A Diachronic Study of Deprivation. In Extinction and Survival in Human Populations. Charles D. Laughlin, Jr., and Ivan A. Brady, eds. Pp. 76–94. New York: Columbia University Press.

Laughlin, William S.
1964 Genetical and Anthropological Characteristics of Arctic Populations. In The Biology of Human Adaptability. Paul T. Baker and J. S. Weiner, eds. Pp. 469–497. Oxford: Clarendon Press.

1969 Eskimos and Aleuts: Their Origins and Evolution. In Evolutionary Anthropology. Hermann K. Bleibtreu, ed. Pp. 633–645. Boston: Allyn and Bacon.

Leaf, Alexander
1973 Getting Old. Scientific American 229(3):45–52.

Lee, Richard B.
1967 Trance Cure of the !Kung Bushmen. Natural History 76(a):31–37.

1968 What Hunters Do for a Living, or How to Make Out on Scarce Resources. In Man the Hunter. R. B. Lee and I. DeVore, eds. Pp. 30–48. Chicago: Aldine.

1972 Population Growth and the Beginnings of Sedentary Life among the !Kung Bushmen. In Population Growth: Anthropological Implications. Brian Spooner, ed. Pp. 329–342. Cambridge, Massachusetts: M.I.T. Press.

1973 Mongongo: The Ethnography of a Major Wild Food Resource. Ecology of Food and Nutrition 2:307–321.

LePontois, Joan
1975 Adolescents with Sickle-Cell Anemia Deal with Life and Death. Social Work in Health Care 1(1):71–80.

Lerner, Michael, and William J. Libby
1976 Heredity, Evolution and Society. Second ed. San Francisco: W. H. Freeman.

Lévi-Strauss, Claude
1969 The Raw and the Cooked. New York: Harper & Row.

Levinson, F. James
1974 Morinda: An Economic Analysis of Malnutrition among Young Children in Rural India. Cornell/M.I.T. International Nutrition Policy Series.

Levy, Jerrold E., and Stephen J. Kunitz
1974 Indian Drinking: Navajo Practices and Anglo-American Theories. New York: John Wiley.

Lewis, Oscar
1955 Medicine and Politics in a Mexican Village. In Health, Culture, and

Community. Benjamin D. Paul, ed. Pp. 403–434. New York: Russell Sage Foundation.

Lex, Barbara W.
1977   Voodoo Death: New Thoughts on an Old Explanation. In Culture, Disease, and Healing. David Landy, ed. Pp. 327–331. New York: Macmillan.

Lieban, Richard W.
1973   Medical Anthropology. In Handbook of Social and Cultural Anthropology. John J. Honigmann, ed. Pp. 1031–1072. Chicago: Rand McNally.

Lindenbaum, Shirley
1971   Sorcery and Structure in Fore Society. Oceania 41:277–287.
1977   The "Last Course": Nutrition and Anthropology in Asia. In Nutrition and Anthropology in Action. Thomas K. Fitzgerald, ed. Pp. 141–155. Assen: Van Gorcum.

Livingstone, Frank B.
1958   Anthropological Implications of Sickle Cell Gene Distribution in West Africa. American Anthropologist 60:533–562.

Lizot, J.
1977   Population, Resources, and Warfare among the Yanomami. Man 12:497–517.

Logan, Michael H.
1978   Humoral Medicine in Guatemala and Peasant Acceptance of Modern Medicine. In Health and the Human Condition: Perspectives on Medical Anthropology. Michael H. Logan and Edward E. Hunt, Jr., eds. Pp. 363–375. North Scituate, Massachusetts: Duxbury Press.

MacAndrew, Craig, and Robert B. Edgerton
1969   Drunken Comportment. Chicago: Aldine.

McArthur, Margaret
1960   Report of the Nutrition Unit. In Records of the American–Australian Scientific Expedition to Arnhem Land, Vol. 2. Pp. 1–143. Melbourne: Melbourne University Press.

McCarthy, F. D., and Margaret McArthur
1960   The Food Quest and the Time Factor in Aboriginal Economic Life. In Records of the American–Australian Scientific Expedition to Arnhem Land, Vol. 2. Pp. 145–194. Melbourne: Melbourne University Press.

McCracken, Robert D.
1971   Lactase Deficiency: An Example of Dietary Evolution. Current Anthropology 12:479–517.

McDermott, Walsh, et al.
1969   Introducing Modern Medicine in a Navaho Community. In The Cross-Cultural Approach to Health Behavior. L. Riddick Lynch, ed. Pp. 111–145. Rutherford, New Jersey: Fairleigh Dickinson University Press.

MacDonald, G.
1973   Measurement of the Clinical Manifestations of Schistosomiasis. In

Epidemiology and Control of Schistosomiasis (Bilharziasis). N. Ansari, ed. Pp. 354–387. Baltimore: University Park Press.

McDonough, John R., Glen Earl Garrison, and Curtis G. Hames
1967 Blood Pressure and Hypertensive Disease among Negroes and Whites in Evans County, Georgia. In The Epidemiology of Hypertension. J. Stamler, et al., eds. Pp. 167–187. New York: Grune & Stratton.

McElroy, Ann P.
1977 Alternatives in Modernization: A Study of Styles and Strategies in the Acculturative Behavior of Baffin Island Inuit. New Haven, Connecticut: HRAFlex Books, ND5-001, Ethnography Series.

1975 "Arctic Modernization and Change in Inuit Family Organization," In S. Parvez Wakil, ed., Marriage, Family and Society: Canadian Perspectives. Pp. 379–400. Scarborough: Butterworths.

McKeown, Thomas
1976 The Modern Rise of Population. New York: Academic Press.

McNeill, William H.
1976 Plagues and People. Garden City, New York: Anchor Press/Doubleday.

Malcolm, L. A.
1970 Growth and Development of the Bundi Child of the New Guinea Highlands. Human Biology 42:293–328.

Marchione, Thomas J.
1977 Food and Nutrition in Self-Reliant National Development: The Impact on Child Nutrition of Jamaican Government Policy. Medical Anthropology 1:57–79.

Martin, Paul S.
1973 The Discovery of America. Science 179:969–974.

Martin, Richard T.
1970 The Role of Coca in the History, Religion, and Medicine of South American Indians. Economic Botany 24:422–437.

Marx, Jean L.
1976 Hypertension: A Complex Disease with Complex Causes. Science 194:821–825.

Mason, J. B., et al.
1974 Nutritional Lessons from the Ethiopian Drought. Nature 248:646–650.

Mathews, John D., Robert Glasse, and Shirley Lindenbaum
1968 Kuru and Cannibalism. The Lancet ii:449–452.

May, David A., and David M. Heer
1968 Son Survivorship Motivation and Family Size in India: A Computer Simulation. Population Studies 22:199–210.

May, Jacques M.
1957 The Geography of Food and Cooking. International Record of Medicine 170:231–239.

Mayer, J.
1967 Nutrition and Civilization. Transactions of the New York Academy of Science II:29:1014–1032.

Mazess, Richard B.
    1975   Human Adaptation to High Altitude. *In* Physiological Anthropology. Albert Damon, ed. Pp. 167–209. New York: Oxford University Press.
Mead, Margaret
    1943   The Problem of Changing Food Habits. Committee On Food Habits. Bulletin of the National Research Council, No. 108.
Meadows, Donella H., et al.
    1974   The Limits to Growth. Second ed. New York: New American Library.
Mercer, Jane R.
    1973   Labeling the Mentally Retarded: Clinical and Social System Perspectives on Mental Retardation. Berkeley: University of California Press.
Messiant, Christine
    1975   La Situation Sociale et Matérielle des Populations. *In* Secheresses et Famines du Sahel. Jean Copans, ed. Pp. 61–73. Paris: Maspero.
Meyer, Herman F.
    1968   Breast Feeding in the United States. Clinical Pediatrics 7:708–715.
Michal, Mary L., et al.
    1973   Health of the American Indian. Publication #HSM 73-5118. Rockville, Maryland: Department of Health, Education, and Welfare.
Milner, Paul F.
    1973   Functional Abnormalities of Sickle Cells: Uptake and Delivery of Oxygen. *In* Sickle Cell Disease. Harold Abramson, John F. Bertles, and Doris L. Wethers, eds. Pp. 155–163. St. Louis: C. V. Mosby.
Monckeberg, Fernando
    1970   Factors Conditioning Malnutrition in Latin America with Special Reference to Chile. *In* Malnutrition Is a Problem of Ecology. Paul György and O. L. Kline, eds. Pp. 23–33. Basel, Switzerland: S. Karger.
Montague, Katherine, and Peter Montague
    1971   Mercury. San Francisco: Sierra Club.
Moos, Rudolf H., ed.
    1976   Human Adaptation. Lexington, Massachusetts: D. C. Heath.
Moran, Emilio
    1975   Food, Development, and Man in the Tropics. *In* Gastronomy: The Anthropology of Food and Food Habits. Margaret L. Arnott, ed. Pp. 169–186. The Hague: Mouton.
Motulsky, Arno G.
    1971   Metabolic Polymorphisms and the Role of Infectious Diseases in Human Evolution. *In* Human Populations, Genetic Variation, and Evolution. Laura Newell Morris, ed. Pp. 222–252. San Francisco: Chandler.
Mouratoff, George J., Nicholas V. Carroll, and Edward M. Scott
    1967   Diabetes Mellitus in Eskimos. Journal of the American Medical Association 199:107–112.

Muñoz de Chavez, Miriam, et al.
1974 The Epidemiology of Good Nutrition in a Population with a High Prevalence of Malnutrition. Ecology of Food and Nutrition 3:223–230.

Nag, Moni, Benjamin N. F. White, and R. Creighton Peet
1978 An Anthropological Approach to the Study of the Economic Value of Children in Java and Nepal. Current Anthropology 19:293–306.

Naroll, Frada, Raoul Naroll, and Forrest H. Howard
1961 Position of Women in Childbirth: A Study in Data Quality Control. American Journal of Obstetrics and Gynecology 82:943–954.

National Research Council. Food and Nutrition Board.
1968 Recommended Dietary Allowances. Washington, D.C.: National Academy of Sciences.

Neel, James V.
1970 Lessons from a "Primitive" People. Science 170:815–822.

1971 Genetic Aspects of the Ecology of Disease in the American Indian. *In* The Ongoing Evolution of Latin American Populations. Francisco M. Salzano, ed. Pp. 561–590. Springfield, Illinois: Charles C Thomas.

Neel, James V., and William J. Schull
1958 Human Heredity. Chicago: University of Chicago Press.

Neel, James V., et al.
1970 Notes on the Effect of Measles and Measles Vaccine in a Virgin-Soil Population of South American Indians. American Journal of Epidemiology 91:418–429.

Nerlove, Sara B.
1974 Women's Workload and Infant Feeding Practices: A Relationship with Demographic Implications. Ethnology 13:207–214.

Neumann, Thomas W.
1977 A Biocultural Approach to Salt Taboos: The Case of the Southeastern United States. Current Anthropology 18:289–308.

Newman, Lucile F.
1972 Birth Control: An Anthropological View. Reading, Massachusetts: Addison-Wesley Modular Publications, No. 27.

Newman, Marshall T.
1975 Nutritional Adaptation in Man. *In* Physiological Anthropology. Albert Damon, ed. Pp. 210–259. New York: Oxford University Press.

Newman, Russell W.
1975 Human Adaptation to Heat. *In* Physiological Anthropology. Albert Damon, ed. Pp. 80–92. New York: Oxford University Press.

Nietschmann, Bernard
1973 Between Land and Water: The Subsistence Ecology of the Miskito Indians, Eastern Nicaragua. New York: Seminar Press.

Norgan, N. G., A. Ferro-Luzzi, and J. V. G. A. Durnin
1974 The Energy and Nutrient Intake and the Energy Expenditure of 204 New Guinean Adults. Philosophical Transactions of the Royal Society (London) 268:309–348.

Olafson, Freya, and Alberta W. Parker, eds.
    1973   Sickle Cell Anemia—The Neglected Disease: Community Approaches to Combating Sickle Cell Anemia. Berkeley: University Extension Publications, University of California.
O'Laughlin, Bridget
    1974   Mediation of Contradiction: Why Mbum Women Do Not Eat Chicken. In Woman, Culture, and Society. M. Z. Rosaldo and L. Lamphere, eds. Pp. 301–318. Stanford, California: Stanford University Press.
Oliver, William J., Edwin L. Cohen, and James V. Neel
    1975   Blood Pressure, Sodium Intake, and Sodium Related Hormones in the Yanamamo Indians, a "No-Salt" Culture. Circulation 52:146–151.
Oomen, H. A. P. C.
    1970   Interrelationship of the Human Intestinal Flora and Protein Utilization. Proceedings of the Nutrition Society 29:197–206.
Ortiz de Montellano, Bernard R.
    1978   Aztec Cannibalism: An Ecological Necessity? Science 200:611–617.
Oswalt, Wendell H.
    1967   Alaskan Eskimos. Scranton, Pennsylvania: Chandler.
Owen, D. F.
    1973   Man in Tropical Africa. New York: Oxford University Press.
Page, Lot B.
    1976   Epidemiologic Evidence on the Etiology of Human Hypertension and its Possible Prevention. American Heart Journal 91:527–534.
Patai, Raphael
    1969   Society, Culture and Change in the Middle East. Third ed. Philadelphia: University of Pennsylvania Press.
Patton, Robert Gray, and Lytt I. Gardner
    1963   Growth Failure in Maternal Deprivation. Springfield, Illinois: Charles C. Thomas
Paul, Benjamin D.
    1969   Anthropological Perspectives of Medicine and Public Health. In The Cross-Cultural Approach to Health Behavior. L. Riddick Lynch, ed. Pp. 26–42. Rutherford, New Jersey: Fairleigh Dickinson University Press.
    1977   The Role of Beliefs and Customs in Sanitation Programs. In Culture, Disease, and Healing. David Landy, ed. Pp. 233–236. New York: Macmillan.
Pearson, Howard A.
    1973   Sickle Cell Anemia: Clinical Management during the Early Years of Life. In Sickle Cell Disease. Harold Abramson, John F. Bertles, and Doris L. Wethers, eds. Pp. 244–251. St. Louis: C. V. Mosby.
Pelletier, Omer
    1970   Vitamin C Status of Smokers and Non-Smokers. American Journal of Clinical Nutrition 23:520–524.
Pincus, Walter
    1978   Bikini Islanders Must Evacuate Atoll Homes. Buffalo Evening News, May 23, p. 3.

Platt, B. S.
   1962   Table of Representative Values of Foods Commonly Used in Tropical Countries. Medical Research Council, Special Report Series, No. 302. London.

Price, Barbara J.
   1978   Demystification, Enriddlement, and Aztec Cannibalism: A Materialist Rejoinder to Harner. American Ethnologist 5:98–115.

Price, Weston A.
   1939   Nutrition and Physical Degeneration: A Comparison of Primitive and Modern Diets and Their Effects. New York: Paul B. Hoeber.

Prothero, R. Mansell
   1965   Migrants and Malaria in Africa. Pittsburgh: University of Pittsburgh Press.

Rappaport, Roy A.
   1968   Pigs for the Ancestors: Ritual in the Ecology of a New Guinea People. New Haven, Connecticut: Yale University Press.

Reed, William P., et al.
   1970   Bubonic Plague in the Southwestern United States: A Review of Recent Experience. Medicine 49:465–486.

Ricci, Larry J.
   1976   Kepone Tragedy May Spur Tough Toxic-Chemicals-Control Law. Chemical Engineering 83(6):53–54.

Richards, Audrey I.
   1939   Land, Labour, and Diet in Northern Rhodesia. London: Oxford University Press.

Richter, Curt P.
   1957   On the Phenomenon of Sudden Death in Animals and Man. Psychosomatic Medicine 19:191–198.

Robson, John R. K.
   1972   Malnutrition: Its Causation and Control with Special Reference to Protein Calorie Malnutrition. 2 vols. New York: Gordon and Breach.

Rodahl, K.
   1963   Nutritional Requirements in the Polar Regions. WHO Public Health Paper 18, Medicine and Public Health in the Arctic and Antarctic. Pp. 97–115.

Roe, Daphne A.
   1973   A Plague of Corn: The Social History of Pellagra. Ithaca, New York: Cornell University Press.

Rosenhan, D. L.
   1973   On Being Sane in Insane Places. Science 179:250–258.

Ross, W. Gillies
   1977   Whaling and the Decline of Native Populations. Arctic Anthropology 14(2):1–8.

Rubel, Arthur J.
   1964   The Epidemiology of a Folk Illness: Susto in Hispanic America. Ethnology 3:268–283.

Ruddle, Kenneth, et al.
    1978   Palm Sago: A Tropical Starch from Marginal Lands. Honolulu: University of Hawaii Press.
Russell, Paul F., et al.
    1963   Practical Malariology. London: Oxford University Press.
Sandbach, F. R.
    1975   Preventing Schistosomiasis: A Critical Assessment of Present Policy. Social Science and Medicine 9:517–527.
Schaefer, Otto
    1971   When the Eskimo Comes to Town. Nutrition Today 6:8–16.
    1977   When the Eskimo Comes to Town: Follow Up. Nutrition Today 12(3):21, 33.
Schlenker, E. D., et al.
    1973   Nutrition and Health of Older People. American Journal of Clinical Nutrition 26:1111–1119.
Schumacher, E. F.
    1973   Small Is Beautiful: Economics as if People Mattered. New York: Harper & Row.
Scotch, Norman A.
    1963   Sociocultural Factors in the Epidemiology of Zulu Hypertension. American Journal of Public Health 53:1205–1213.
Scrimshaw, Nevin S., Carl E. Taylor, and John E. Gordon
    1968   Interactions of Nutrition and Infection. Geneva: World Health Organization.
Seaman, John, et al.
    1973   An Inquiry into the Drought Situation in Upper Volta. The Lancet ii:774–778.
Segal, Julius, Edna J. Hunter, and Zelda Segal
    1976   Universal Consequences of Captivity: Stress Reactions Among Divergent Populations of Prisoners of War and Their Families. International Social Sciences Journal 28:593–609.
Selye, Hans
    1956   The Stress of Life. New York: McGraw-Hill.
    1974   Stress without Distress. Philadelphia: Lippincott.
    1976   Stress in Health and Disease. Boston: Butterworths.
Sever, Lowell E.
    1975   Zinc and Human Development: A Review. Human Ecology 3:43–57.
Sheets, Hal, and Roger Morris
    1976   Disaster in the Desert. In The Politics of Natural Disaster: The Case of the Sahel Drought. Michael A. Glantz, ed. Pp. 25–76. New York: Praeger.
Silberbauer, George B.
    1972   The G/wi Bushmen. In Hunters and Gatherers Today. M. G. Bicchieri, ed. Pp. 271–326. New York: Holt, Rinehart and Winston.

Simoons, Frederick J.
    1970 Primary Adult Lactose Intolerance and the Milking Habit: A Problem in Biologic and Cultural Interrelations. II. A Culture Historical Hypothesis. American Journal of Digestive Diseases 15:695–710.
Simpson, George G.
    1969a Organisms and Molecules in Evolution. *In* Evolutionary Anthropology. Hermann K. Bleibtreu, ed. Pp. 78–88. Boston: Allyn and Bacon.
    1969b The Study of Evolution: Methods and Present Status of Theory. *In* Evolutionary Anthropology. Hermann K. Bleibtreu, ed. Pp. 3–23. Boston: Allyn and Bacon.
Sorenson, E. Richard
    1976 The Edge of the Forest: Land, Childhood, and Change in a New Guinea Protoagricultural Society. Washington, D.C.: Smithsonian Institution Press.
Sorkin, Alan L.
    1976 Health Economics in Developing Countries. Lexington, Massachusetts: Lexington Books, D. C. Heath.
Spaulding, Raymond C., and Charles V. Ford
    1976 The Pueblo Incident: Psychological Reactions to the Stresses of Imprisonment and Repatriation. *In* Human Adaptation. Rudolf H. Moos, ed. Pp. 308–321. Lexington, Massachusetts: D. C. Heath.
Spindler, Louise S.
    1977 Culture Change and Modernization. New York: Holt, Rinehart and Winston.
Spitz, René
    1954 Unhappy and Fatal Outcomes of Emotional Deprivation and Stress in Infancy. *In* Beyond the Germ Theory. I. Galdston, ed. Pp. 120–131. New York: Health Education Council.
Spradley, James P.
    1970 You Owe Yourself a Drunk: An Ethnography of Urban Nomads. Boston: Little, Brown.
Spuhler, James N.
    1976 The Maximum Opportunity for Selection in Some Human Populations. *In* Demographic Anthropology. Ezra B. W. Zubrow, ed. Pp. 185–226. A School of American Research Advanced Seminar Book. Albuquerque: University of New Mexico Press.
Srole, Leo, et al.
    1975 Mental Health in the Metropolis. Revised ed. New York: Harper & Row.
Steegmann, A. T., Jr.
    1975 Human Adaptation to Cold. *In* Physiological Anthropology. Albert Damon, ed. Pp. 130–166. New York: Oxford University Press.
    1977 Finger Temperatures During Work in Natural Cold: The Northern Ojibwa. Human Biology 49:349–362.

Stemmermann, Grant N.
  1970   Patterns of Disease Among Japanese Living in Hawaii. Archives of Environmental Health 20:266–273.
Steward, Julian H.
  1955   Theory of Culture Change: The Methodology of Multilinear Evolution. Urbana: University of Illinois Press.
Stini, William A.
  1971   Evolutionary Implications of Changing Nutritional Patterns in Human Populations. American Anthropologist 73:1019–1030.
  1975a   Adaptive Strategies of Human Populations under Nutritional Stress. In BioSocial Interrelations in Population Adaptation. E. S. Watts, F. E. Johnston, and G. W. Lasker, eds. Pp. 19–41. The Hague: Mouton.
  1975b   Ecology and Human Adaptation. Dubuque, Iowa: Wm. C. Brown.
Stirewalt, M. A.
  1973   Important Features of Schistosomes. In Epidemiology and Control of Schistosomiasis (Bilharziasis). N. Ansari, ed. Pp. 17–31. Baltimore: University Park Press.
Stycos, J. Mayone
  1955   Birth Control Clinics in Crowded Puerto Rico. In Health, Culture, and Community. Benjamin D. Paul, ed. Pp. 189–210. New York: Russell Sage Foundation.
Swift, Jeremy
  1977   Sahelian Pastoralists: Underdevelopment, Desertification, and Famine. Annual Review of Anthropology 6:457–478.
Tanaka, Jiro
  1976   Subsistence Ecology of Central Kalahari San. In Kalahari Hunter-Gatherers. R. B. Lee and I. DeVore, eds. Pp. 98–119. Cambridge, Massachusetts: Harvard University Press.
Tanner, J. M.
  1968   Earlier Maturation in Man. Scientific American 218(1):21–27.
Taylor, Ronald B.
  1973   Sweatshops in the Sun: Child Labor on the Farm. Boston: Beacon Press.
Taylor, Ronald L.
  1975   Butterflies in My Stomach: Or: Insects in Human Nutrition. Santa Barbara, California: Woodbridge Press.
Todhunter, E. N.
  1976   Life Style and Nutrient Intake in the Elderly. In Nutrition and Aging. Myron Winick, ed. Current Concepts in Nutrition 4:119–127.
Topley, Marjorie
  1970   Chinese Traditional Ideas and the Treatment of Disease: Two Examples from Hong Kong. Man 5:421–437.
Townsend, Patricia K.
  1971   New Guinea Sago Gatherers: A Study of Demography in Relation to Subsistence. Ecology of Food and Nutrition 1:19–24.

1974 Sago Production in a New Guinea Economy. Human Ecology 2:217–236.

Travers, Robert
1968 The Tasmanians: The Story of a Doomed Race. Melbourne: Cassell Australia.

Truswell, A. Stewart, and John D. L. Hansen
1976 Medical Research Among the !Kung. In Kalahari Hunter-Gatherers. R. B. Lee and I. DeVore, eds. Pp. 166–194. Cambridge, Massachusetts: Harvard University Press.

Turnbull, Colin M.
1972 The Mountain People. New York: Simon and Schuster.

Underwood, Jane H.
1973 The Demography of a Myth: Depopulation in Yap. Human Biology in Oceania 2:115–127.

United Nations
1977 Demographic Yearbook: 1976. New York.

United States Senate. Select Committee on Nutrition
1973 "Hunger 1973" and Press Reaction. Washington, D.C.: U.S. Government Printing Office.

1977 Dietary Goals for the United States. Washington D.C.: U.S. Government Printing Office.

Usher, Peter J.
1971 The Bankslanders: Economy and Ecology of a Frontier Trapping Community. Vol. 2: Economy and Ecology. NSRG 71-2. Ottawa: Northern Science Research Group, Department of Indian Affairs and Northern Development.

van Amelsvoort, V. F. P. M.
1964 Culture, Stone Age and Modern Medicine. Assen: Royal Van Gorcum.

Van Arsdale, Peter W.
1975 Population Correlates of Induced Culture Change among Asmat Hunters-and-Gatherers. Paper delivered to Annual Meeting of the American Anthropological Association, San Francisco.

1978 Population Dynamics Among Asmat Hunter-Gatherers of New Guinea: Data, Methods, Comparisons. Human Ecology 6:435–467.

van der Walt, L. A., et al.
1977 Endocrine Studies on the San ("Bushmen") of Botswana. South African Medical Journal 52:230–232.

Van Stone, James W.
1972 New Evidence Concerning Polar Eskimo Isolation. American Anthropologist 74:1062–1065.

Van Veen, A. G., and Marjorie Scott Van Veen
1974 Some Present-Day Aspects of Vitamin A Problems in Less Developed Countries. Ecology of Food and Nutrition 3:35–54.

Vavasseur, June
1977 A Comprehensive Program for Meeting Psychosocial Needs of

Sickle-Cell Anemia Patients. Journal of the National Medical Association 69:335–339.

Vayda, Andrew P.
1976   War in Ecological Perspective: Persistence, Change, and Adaptive Processes in Three Oceanian Societies. New York: Plenum.

Vayda, Andrew P., and Roy A. Rappaport
1968   Ecology, Cultural and Noncultural. *In* Introduction to Cultural Anthropology. James A. Clifton, ed. Pp. 477–497. Boston: Houghton Mifflin.

Vimokesant, S. L., et al.
1975   Effects of Betel Nut and Fermented Fish on the Thiamin Status of Northeastern Thais. American Journal of Clinical Nutrition 28:1458–1463.

Wallace, Anthony F. C.
1969   The Death and Rebirth of the Seneca. New York: Random House/Vintage Books.
1972   Mental Illness, Biology and Culture. *In* Psychological Anthropology. Francis L. K. Hsu, ed. Pp. 362–402. Cambridge, Massachusetts: Schenkman.

Wallace, Robert K., and Herbert Benson
1972   The Physiology of Meditation. Scientific American 226(2):84–91.

Ward, Barbara, and René Dubos
1972   Only One Earth: The Care and Maintenance of a Small Planet. New York: W. W. Norton.

Watt, Kenneth E. F.
1973   Principles of Environmental Science. New York: McGraw-Hill.

Wellin, Edward
1955   Water Boiling in a Peruvian Town. *In* Health, Culture, and Community. Benjamin D. Paul, ed. Pp. 71–103. New York: Russell Sage Foundation.

Wells, Calvin
1964   Bones, Bodies, and Disease: Evidence of Disease and Abnormality in Early Man. New York: Praeger.

White, Leslie
1969   Energy and the Evolution of Culture. *In* The Science of Culture. Pp. 363–393. New York: Farrar, Straus and Giroux.

Whiting, John W. M.
1964   Effects of Climate on Certain Cultural Practices. *In* Explorations in Cultural Anthropology. W. H. Goodenough, ed. Pp. 511–544. New York: McGraw-Hill.

Whyte, Robert Orr
1974   Rural Nutrition in Monsoon Asia. Kuala Lumpur: Oxford University Press.

Wiesberg, Laurie
1976   An International Perspective on the African Famines. *In* The Politics of Natural Disaster: The Case of the Sahel Drought. Michael A. Glantz, ed. Pp. 101–127. New York: Praeger.

Weisbrod, Burton A., et al.

1973 Disease and Economic Development. Madison: University of Wisconsin Press.

Wiesenfeld, Stephen L.
1967 Sickle-Cell Trait in Human Biological and Cultural Evolution. Science 157:1134–1140.

Wilmsen, Edwin N.
1978 Seasonal Effects of Dietary Intake on Kalahari San. Federation Proceedings 37:65–72.

Wilson, Christine S.
1973 Food Taboos of Childbirth: The Malay Example. Ecology of Food and Nutrition 2:267–274.

1977 Comment to Thomas W. Neumann, A Biocultural Approach to Salt Taboos: The Case of the Southeastern United States. Current Anthropology 18:303–304.

Wilson, Peter, et al.
1975 More Thoughts on the Ik and Anthropology. Current Anthropology 16:343–358.

Winick, Myron
1976 Malnutrition and Brain Development. New York: Oxford University Press.

Wolf, Stewart, and Helen Goodell, eds.
1968 Stress and Disease. Second ed. Springfield, Illinois: Thomas.

Wolstenholme, Gordon E. W., and Maeve O'Connor, eds.
1962 Ciba Foundation Symposium: Bilharziasis (Proceedings) Boston: Little, Brown.

Wood, Corinne Shear
1978 Syphilis in Anthropological Perspective. Social Science and Medicine 12:47–55.

Woods, Clyde M.
1975 Culture Change. Dubuque, Iowa: Wm. C. Brown.

World Health Organization
1973 Energy and Protein Requirements. WHO Technical Report No. 522. Geneva.

1977 The Five Principal Deficiency Diseases in the World Today. World Health (May 1977):16–17.

Wright, W. H.
1973 Geographical Distribution of Schistosomes and Their Intermediate Hosts. In Epidemiology and Control of Schistosomiasis (Bilharziasis). N. Ansari, ed. Pp. 32–247. Baltimore: University Park Press.

Wynder, Ernest L., et al.
1954 Study of Environmental Factors and Cancer of the Cervix. American Journal of Obstetrics and Gynecology 68:1016–1052.

Yellen, John E., and Richard B. Lee
1976 The Dobe-/Du/da Environment. In Kalahari Hunter-Gatherers. R. B. Lee and I. DeVore, eds. Pp. 27–46. Cambridge, Massachusetts: Harvard University Press.

Index

Abkhasians (U.S.S.R.): 244–248
Aborigines (Australia): 300–301;
  extinction of, 333; hunting and
  gathering, 183–184; infanticide
  by, 147; sorcery of, 289; sub-
  incision of, 105
Abortion: 133, 149; in Japan, 160;
  among !Kung, 181; spontaneous, 164
Abstinence: sexual, 127. *See also*
  Postpartum sex taboo
Accidents: among Hazda, 128; of
  hunters-gatherers, 146; in industrial society, 161; Inuit, 27,
  28, 340, 345; and stress, 166, 271
Acclimation: 94
Acclimatization: 94, 95
Acculturation: 335–336; health
  risks of, 351–354; Siriono and
  Ik, 262–263
Achondroplastic dwarfs: 80–81
ACTH: 281
Adams, Richard N.: Guatemala
  nutrition study of, 407–408
Adaptation: and blood groups,
  7–8; to cold, 25–26, 74–75,
  96–97, 202, 203, 205, 352; concept of, 12–13; coping strategies, 297; cultural, 73, 74,
  100–106, 126, 332–333; defined,
  12, 72–76; in diet, 195–196; and
  ecosystem, 15, 16; and evolution, 10, 76–85; general adaptation syndrome, 280–281; and
  genetic changes, 72, 73, 74, 75;
  health as measure of, 2, 13;
  high altitude, 94–96, 119,
  202–205; individual, 101–104; of
  Inuit, 16–28; limits to, 117–119;
  of mentally retarded persons,
  62, 64; physiological, 72–73, 74,
  75–76, 93–97; of skid road
  bums, 11; and stress, 268, 272,
  273, 298
Adrenaline: 285; and adrenal hormones, 302
Adrenocorticotrophic hormone
  (ACTH): 281
Africa: cash cropping and drought
  in, 206, 398; disease in, 380; ge-

netic adaptation in, 74–75; hypertension in, 56–58; lactose intolerance in, 98; malaria in, 87, 90; nutrition in, 199–200
African peoples. *See* Ik; Mbum Kpau; San; So; Zulu
Aging: 147, 161, 264, 293; and nutrition, 208, 243–250
Agricultural societies: disease in, 147–149; natality in, 131, 149–151; nutrition in, 185–195
Agriculture: cash cropping, 206, 253, 385, 398; cereal crops, 190–194; child workers in, 150; and city growth, 153; development of, 129; and disease, 87, 90, 93, 117, 148, 169–170; economic development and, 388–395, 398; family size and, 149–150; food crops in, 187–194; in Indonesia, 150; peasant farmers in, 190–195; population patterns and, 147–148, 150; techniques of, 117, 175, 185–187, 188, 190–191, 363–367; and subsistence farming, 185–195; in United States, 215; Zulu, 363–365
Air pollution: and automobile, 161; and disease, 159
Alarm reaction: 280
Alcohol: in healing rituals, 295; and infant mortality, 336
Alcoholism: 199; fetal, 224; of Inuit, 306, 338–339, 347, 348–349; of Native Americans, 337, 338; of skid road bums, 11–12; and stress, 320–322
Alienation: 310
Alland, Alexander, Jr.: on minimax strategies, 117–118, 121
Allele: 77, 79
Allergies: and stress, 274
Alor (Indonesia): 228
Amahuaca (Peru): 184

Amazonian peoples: diet of, 189, 195; hunting-gathering, 185
Amino acids: 77, 176, 192, 193
Amniocentesis: 110
Amok hysteria: 312, 314
Anaclitic depression: 315
Andes Mountains: coca chewing in, 200–205; longevity in, 249
Anemia: and coca chewing, 204; and dietary taboos, 108; infant, 348; iron deficiency, 204, 209, 216, 225. *See also* Sickle cell anemia
Anesthetics: as occupational hazard, 164
Animals, domesticated: 21, 148, 189, 191, 255–256
Anopheles species: 354
Anthropology: 7–11; applied, 10, 405–409. *See also* Medical anthropology; Nutritional anthropology
Anthropometry: 7, 251
Antibiotics: 4, 158, 159; gastrointestinal effects of, 200
Antibodies: testing for, 49
Anxiety: 270, 295; and disease, 107; and stress, 288, 311; Zulu, 364
Appendicitis: 213, 281
Arabs: in Lackawanna, N.Y., 416, 418–423, 424
Archaeology: 8–9, 211; and paleopathology, 51, 165–168
Arctic ecosystems: 18–21, 27, 74–75; climatic stress in, 299
Arctic hysteria: 268, 302–307, 323, 324
Arsenic pollution: 398
Arterial disease: 215
Arteriosclerosis: 83, 165. *See also* Atherosclerosis
Arthritis: osteo, 27, 166; rheumatoid, 273, 282, 283, 310–311
Artifacts: defined, 15; Inuit, 19–20;

Artifacts (*cont.*)
  inventory, 129; and paleopath-
  ology, 168
Asbestos: 164
Ascorbic acid: 24. *See also* Vita-
  min C
Asmat (Irian Jaya): 135, 329,
  359–361
Aspirin: herbal equivalent of, 108
Assimilation: 336–337
Asthma: and pollution, 418; and
  stress, 274
Atherosclerosis: 213, 287
Australia: 144. *See also* Aborigines
Autism: 68
Automobile: and accidents, 161
Aymara (Bolivia): 202, 218
Aztecs (Mexico): 190, 357–358

Bacteria: intestinal, 39, 85
Baffin Island: 340–341
Banana: 188
Bangladesh: 238, 242
Banting, Sir Frederick: 280
Barley: 191, 195
Bears: polar, 16–17, 21, 26, 28, 39
Bee sting: 282
Beef consumption: 188, 214, 215
Beer: millet, 199, 363
Benet, Sula: longevity study of,
  244–248
Berg, Alan: *The Nutrition Factor,*
  259
Beriberi: 194, 197
Betel nut: 197
Bikini Island: forced migration
  from, 369–370, 373
Bilharz, Theodor: 390
Bilharziasis: 390. *See also* Schisto-
  somiasis
Biofeedback: 324
Biomass: 41
Biorhythms: 268, 301–302,
  305–307

Birdsell, Joseph B.: aborigine
  study of, 121, 147
Birth control: 169; and breast feeding, 227–228; cultural constraints to, 131–134; by hunters-
  gatherers, 127; in India, 403;
  by Inuit, 352, 353; in Japan,
  160; pill, 200; in Puerto Rico,
  403–404; taboos, 105; by sterilization, 338; techniques, 149. *See
  also* Birth spacing; Contraception; Postpartum sex taboo
Birth defects: 166; and anesthetics,
  164; and nutrition, 224
Birth spacing: 42, 105, 134, 229; by
  Asmat, 360–361; by !Kung,
  181–182; by Sanio-Hiowe, 137
Black Death: 153–158
Blacks (United States): clay or
  starch eating by, 199; hypertension of, 51, 52–58, 420; in
  Lackawanna, N.Y., 415–423,
  424; lactose intolerance in, 98;
  natality of, 133; nutrition of,
  209, 419; sickle cell disease in,
  108–116
Blindness: hysterical, 295; snow,
  20, 27; Vitamin A deficiency
  and, 216, 259; and xerophthalmia, 195
Blistering: 108
Blood: coagulability, 286, 287;
  groups, 7–8; in high altitude
  adaptation, 96; hyperventilation
  and, 304–305; pressure, 53, 61,
  273, 308; tests, 49. *See also* Sickle
  cell trait
Bloodletting: 108, 269, 294–295
Blumberg, Baruch: 48
Boas, Franz: on increasing body
  size, 235–237; Inuit study of,
  36, 344; Kwakiutl salmon recipes of, 197–198
Body type: and climate adapta-

tion, 74–75; and increasing size, 235–237, 261

Bolivia: 203, 218

Bolton, Ralph: on coca chewing, 203–204

Bonding behavior: 102–103

Boredom: as stressor, 319

Boserup, Ester: on population and agriculture, 150

Bottle-feeding: infant, 225–227, 346

Botulism: 27

Brain, human: 102, 103; evolution of size of, 82–83; nutrition and, 225, 260–261

Brazil: 144, 206, 387

Breast feeding: 225–228; in agricultural society, 149–150; assimilation and, 337; breast cancer and, 371; decline of, 233; immunity and, 84; infanticide and, 134; Inuit, 23, 24, 346, 348; !Kung, 181–182; nutrition and, 108, 364; postpartum taboos and, 132; weaning and, 149–150, 228–230, 232–233

Breeding periods: 42

Bronchitis: chronic, 161; and Inuit, 345; and pollution, 418

Bubonic plague: 153–158; symptoms of, 155

Burchard, Roderick E.: on coca chewing, 203

Burns: herbal treatments for, 107

Bushmen (southern Africa): 178, 182; blood pressure of, 54; hunting by, 175. *See also* San

Caffeine: 288

Calcium: 176; and arctic hysteria, 304–305, 306; deficiency, 214, 268, 294, 304–305, 306; and Inuit, 24; and lactose, 99; and sickle cell anemia, 116

California Indians: contact of with settlers, 330–332; malaria of, 354–358

Caloric needs: of Inuit, 23

Canada: 144, 398, 411. *See also* Cree; Hutterites; Inuit; Ojibwa

Cancer: 161; bladder, 164; breast, 371; and carcinogens, 398; cervical, 105; colon, 213, 214; lung, 50, 164, 334–335, 336; from operating room work, 164; and prejudice, 61; and selection, 83; stomach, 371; and stress, 271, 288

Canker sores: 145

Cannibalism: of Inuit, 21; and *kuru*, 47, 49; in New Guinea, 44–45, 46, 47, 49; as protein source, 189–190; and *wiitiiko*, 302

Cannon, Walter B.: on fight or flight response, 283–286, 322; on magical death, 291, 293

Carbohydrates: 176, 345, 348; and birth rate, 151; and Inuit, 23, 24, 352; in tropics, 188; and Zulu, 363, 366, 367

Cardiovascular disease: 24, 161, 213, 249, 336; and stress, 271, 274, 287, 288. *See also* Hypertension; Stroke

Caribou: 21, 24, 25, 39, 41

Carneiro, Robert L.: on Amazonian diet, 189; measurement of subsistence economies by, 184

Carnivores: 41

Carriers: of disease, 356

Carrying capacity: 41

Carson, Rachel: *Silent Spring,* 163

Cassava: 105, 187, 188, 197

Cassel, John: 67, 336; Zulu study of, 362–367, 373

Castro, Josué de: *The Geography of Hunger,* 261

Cathartics: 107
Caucasus Mountains: longevity in, 244–248
Celibacy: 159
Cercariae: 391, 392, 393
Cereal crops: 188, 190–194, 195
Cerebral hemorrhage: 371
Chad: 253, 254, 387; famine in, 256; food taboos in, 242. *See also* Mbum Kpau
Chagnon, Napoleon A.: 3, 4
Change: social and cultural, 196–197, 334–338, 363–367, 372–373
Cherokee (United States): diet of, 241; forced march of, 368–369
Chicanos: health problems of, 414–415. *See also* Mexican-Americans
Chicken pox: 148, 233, 359
Childbirth: and dietary taboos, 106, 108, 241; and high altitude adaptation, 96; and malaria, 87–88; and obstetric procedures, 133–134; and pelvic structure, 81, 83
Child care: 42, 138, 147, 150, 342; by Inuit, 20, 23, 25–26; by !Kung, 181–182; and modernization, 383
Children: abuse of, 316, 357; cold adaptation of, 96; diseases of, 148; as laborers, 150, 235; malaria in, 93; nutrition of, 216, 229–238, 260–261, 298–299, 385–386; and sickle cell anemia, 110–113; skeletal growth of, 167
Chile: birth rate in, 133; breast feeding in, 226; hypertension in, 56
Chilungu, Simeon W.: Lackawanna study of, 416–423
Chimpanzees: birth spacing of, 42; in *kuru* research, 47
Chinese: and measles, 108

Chlorinated hydrocarbons: 162–163
Cholera: 149; control of, 359; and sanitation, 153
Cholesterol: and Inuit, 24; nutrition and, 213; stress and, 287–288, 323
Chromosomes: 77–78; and hallucinogens, 165
Circadian rhythms: 301–302, 305–306
Circannual rhythms: 301
Circumcision: 104–105, 230
Cirrhosis: liver, 199, 271
Cities: health and disease in, 152–164; and nutrition, 206–207; preindustrial, 152–153. *See also* Urbanization
Clark, Margaret: on Chicano health problems, 414
Clay: eating of, 199–200
Climate: adaptation to, 17–18, 74–76, 96–97; and epidemiology, 43; and natural selection, 80; as stressor, 299–301
Clinical medicine: defined, 48–50
Clinics: 359, 362–366, 414–416. *See also* Hospitals; Medical practitioners
Clothing: and climate, 299–300; Inuit, 20, 25; in New Guinea, 335
Coca leaves: chewing of, 174, 200–205
Cocaine: 201–202
Cold adaptation: 17, 74–75, 96–97; and coca chewing, 202, 203, 205; and Inuit, 25–26; and nutrition, 352
Colombia: health care system, 400–401
Colonialism: 332, 386
Comanche (United States): healing rituals of, 294
Communication, mass: 382–383;

public health projects and, 408–409
Comparative studies: 58
Competition: between populations, 39
Concentration camp survivors: and stress, 297–298
Conjunctivitis: among Hazda, 128
Consumerism: 383
Contraception: 159, 160, 403–404; herbal, 133; Inuit, 352, 353
Coping: 270, 275, 297, 308, 321, 324–325
Copper: 176
Coprolites: 167–168
Corn. *See* Maize
Cornell Medical Index: 419–420
Cortez, Hernando: and smallpox, 357–358
Cosmopolitan medicine: 106–107, 108
Cost-benefit analysis: 259–260, 410
Cravioto, Joaquin: Mexican nutrition study of, 261
Cree (Canada): cold adaptation of, 96; and economic development, 411; and *wiitiiko*, 10
Cretinism: endemic, 196–197, 260
Cross resistance: 283, 294
Crowding: as stressor, 143, 307, 308, 309, 310
Culture: and adaptation, 13, 73, 74, 100–106, 126; and birth rate, 42, 131–134, 160; and diet, 195–198, 239–241; and evolution, 104, 169; and health, 104–106; and innovations, 103–104; and physiological adaptation, 97; stressors in, 307–322; transmission of, 101–102, 103, 120; variability and change in, 103–104
Culture contact: 331–374; acculturation in, 335–336; assimilation in, 336–337; and diffusion, 334–335; and ethnic revitalization, 337–338; health repercussions of, 328–373; Zulu and, 362–367
Customs: adaptive functions of, 105

Dairy: farming, 194; products, 215
Damon, Albert: 8, 122; on economic development, 409
Dancing: 269; in healing rituals, 295; trances, 276–277
Darwin, Charles: and Darwinian fitness, 80, 81, 92; evolution theory of, 80, 129; natural selection theory of, 119
DDT: 162–163, 407
Deafness: hysterical, 295; and noise, 309
Death: and sorcery, 288–293; submissive, 325. *See also* Mortality
Demography: 131–144, 171; and culture contact, 351–352, 359–361; demographic change model, 362; demographic transition, 159–160, 410
Dental health: 27; and fluorine, 43; and loss of teeth, 249; and nutrition, 196, 352; and periodontal disease, 214
Deoxyribonucleic acid (DNA): 77, 78, 79
Depression: anaclitic, 315; of Eskimos, 306
Deprivation dwarfism: 314–319
Desert ecosystems: 182–183, 299–300
Desertification: 256
Desynchronization: 268, 301–302; and arctic hysteria, 306
Developing countries: 386; anthropologists in, 405–411; health care in, 399–404, 425; malnutrition in, 259

Development, economic: defined, 385; environmental impact of, 411, 424–427; evaluating costs and benefits of, 380, 409–411; and health, 385–411; nutrition and, 174, 387–389; in Sahel, 253–258

Developmental acclimatization: 94

Diabetes: 249; and Inuit, 24; in Japan, 371; mellitus, 348, 366, 367; and nutrition, 352; and selection, 83; and stress, 275, 323

Diarrhea: herbal treatments for, 107; in humoral medicine, 107; weanling, 233

Diastolic pressure: 53–54

Diffusion: of cultural traits, 334–335

Diphtheria: 340, 344, 351

Disasters: natural, 268, 328

Discrimination: and cancer patients, 61; and sickle cell screening, 115, 116

Disease: and adaptation, 13; and agriculture, 148; causes of, 15–16; childhood, 148; defined, 48, 49; degenerative, 160–161, 243–244, 287; eradication of, 396; etiology of, 51; evolution of, 165–168; and extinction, 331, 333; and famine, 256; iatrogenic, 164–165; incidence of, 50; infectious, 148–149, 158–159, 161; and Inuit, 27, 340, 344–345; labeling of, 60–62; and migration, 425; and natural selection, 80, 83–85; and nutrition, 169, 213, 216; occupational, 162–164; prevalence of, 50; resistance to, 5, 83–84, 90; and stress, 268–324; transmission of, 148, 155; of Zulu, 363. *See also* under specific disease names

Diverticular disease: 213

Division of labor: sexual, 238, 240

DNA: 77, 78

Dogs: and Inuit, 21–22, 35, 39

Douglas, Mary: on British diet, 198

Down's syndrome: 63

Dropsy: 61

Drought: adaptation to periodic, 118, 255; on Bentinck Island, 300–301; Sahel, 256

Drugs: addiction to, 224, 307; effects of on nutrition, 199–200

Dubos, René: *Man Adapting*, 97; on tuberculosis decline, 160, 170

Dwarfism: 166; achondroplastic, 80–81; deprivation, 314–319

Dye industry: and bladder cancer, 164

Dysentery: 107, 117, 140, 363

Ear infections: 339, 345

Earthquakes: 128

Ecology: defined, 37–38; ecological anthropology, 10; ecological niche, 38, 39, 41, 74, 76, 87, 90, 119; ecological pyramid, 40–41; and health model, 13–16; medical, 10, 15; and nutrition, 174, 176–185

Ecosystem: and adaptation, 76, 120; arctic, 17, 19, 21, 27, 28; desert, 182–183, 299–300; and energy flow, 39–40; grasslands, 74–75, 253–255; and health, 14, 15–16; and industrial pollution, 161; tropical, 146, 184–190

Ecuador: longevity in, 249

Eczema: and stress, 274

Edema: 230, 231

Edgerton, Robert B.: *Cloak of Competence*, 64–66, 68; *Drunken Comportment*, 321

Education: health care, 363–366, 401–403, 404, 427

Eggs: 188, 229

Egypt: Aswan High Dam, 388, 390–391; mummies of, 165, 166; schistosomiasis in, 389–393

Ehrlich, Allen S.: Jamaican sugar plantation study, 206
Electrophoresis: 115
Elephantiasis: 359
Embolisms: 294
Emetics: 107, 297
Emotional deprivation: 314–319
Emphysema: 161, 418
Endemic disease: 50; among hunters-gatherers, 127, 145
Energy: for adaptation to stress, 271; flow, 18–25, 39–41, 130; and nutrition, 21, 176
Environmental factors: and adaptation, 72, 73, 74, 75; and carrying capacity, 41–42; and development, 411; and energy flow, 39–41; environmental trauma, 128; and health, 5, 13–16, 37–43; and population interactions, 39–41; and stress, 298–307, 423
Epidemic disease: 50; among Asmat, 359; bubonic plague as, 140, 153–158; childhood diseases as, 148; and culture contact, 350, 351, 352; among hunters-gatherers, 145; among Inuit, 27, 340, 344–345; among Native Americans, 140; pneumonic plague as, 43; and population patterns, 127; smallpox as, 140, 357, 358; among Yanomamo, 3–5, 151; among Zulu, 363
Epidemiology: 34, 50–51; and culture contact, 350–351, 354–358; and disease labeling, 61; of hypertension, 52; of *kuru*, 46–48; and malaria, 354–358; and mental retardation, 63–64; of schistosomiasis, 390–394; and statistics, 67
Epinephrine: 285, 291; and stress, 323
Eskimos: 16–29, 334–353, 359, 373; and arctic hysteria,

302–307; and arthritis, 166; cultural artifacts of, 334–336; and lice, 39; natality of, 133. *See also* Inuit; Netsilik; Nunamuit
Estrus: 42
Ethiopia: 243, 259
Ethnic psychoses: 10
Ethnic revitalization: 337–338
Ethnocide: 354
Ethnography: 9, 59; and ethnographies, 197–198
Ethnomedicine: 9–10, 106–108, 129; Arab, 418; and attitudes about sickness, 382–383; in childbirth, 133–134; defined, 106; Egyptian, 389; and malaria, 85–86; and public health work, 408; and rituals, 294, 383; use of coca in, 204; use of stress in, 276–277, 294–297
Ethnoscience: 11, 59–60
Ethnosemantics: 11–12
Etiology of disease: 51
Europe: dairying and lactose tolerance in, 98–99; ecology of food in, 195, 215; historical demography of, 141, 158–159; plague in, 153–157
Evolution: 10, 102–103, 129; and adaptation, 73, 74, 76–85; cultural, 104, 120, 126, 129, 130, 372–373; of hand and brain, 102; and mutations, 79; of pathogenic organisms, 84–85, 87, 148–149; of pelvis, 83; and natural selection, 79–80; and selective compromise, 80–83; Spencerian, 129. *See also* Darwin, Charles
Exercise: and disease, 288; and longevity, 247–248; and stress, 323, 324
Experiments: on diet and aging, 243–244; on genetic resistance to disease, 84; on hypertension, 56; on stress, 279–284, 291–292

Extinction: of animals, 147; of
  peoples, 329–330, 330–333

Fabrega, Horacio, Jr.: 68; on medi-
  cal ecology, 6
Family: and modernization, 383
Famine: 252–263; and natural se-
  lection, 80; and plague, 155,
  157; Sahel, 206, 253–258
Fasting: 242–243, 269, 295
Fats: 176, 212–213; and Inuit, 23,
  24
Fava beans: and anemia, 91
Fear: 285, 291
Feces: and coprolites, 167–168;
  contamination by, 385; as fertil-
  izer, 117, 148, 410; and para-
  sites, 393, 394
Fertility. See Natality
Fertilizer: feces as, 117, 148, 410
Fetal nutrition: 223–225
Fiber: dietary, 194, 213
Fieldwork: 58–60, 64; among
  Abkhasians, 244; among Ik and
  Siriono, 262–263; methods of in
  nutrition, 250–252; in Papua,
  New Guinea, 46–47, 135–136;
  and participant observation, 59,
  64; in student projects, 68,
  429–431; in United States, 11,
  64–66, 416–423; among Yano-
  mamo, 3–5
Fight-or-flight response: 284–286
Fiji: 234
Fish: as protein source, 188, 189
Fitzgerald, Thomas R.: nutrition
  study of, 198, 217
Flea: and bubonic plague, 154, 155
Flukes: and schistosomiasis, 148
Fluorine: 43, 176
Folic acid: deficiency, 216
Folk illnesses: 10, 302–304,
  311–314. See also Amok; Arctic
  hysteria; Kayak phobia;
  Pibloktoq; Susto

Folk medicine. See Ethnomedicine;
  Herbal medicine; Medical practitioners
Food: and nutritional needs,
  175–176; processing of, 215;
  superfoods, 191–192; supply
  and economic development,
  217, 387–389
Food aid programs: 100, 252,
  256–259
Food chain: and energy flow,
  40–41; and pesticides, 163
Food taboos: 105–106, 228, 229,
  239–242; in infancy, 229; in
  pregnancy and lactation, 108,
  139, 223, 241; among Zulu:
  363–365
Fore (Papua, New Guinea): 43–49,
  135
Foster, George M.: on cultural anthropology, 9, 427; on rural-
  urban migration, 384
Foulks, Edward F.: on arctic hysteria, 303–307, 324
Fractures: and osteoporosis, 24; in
  paleopathology, 166
Frake, Charles O.: Subanun,
  study of, 59–60
France: diet of, 215
Frobisher Bay (Canada): 338–345
Frostbite: treatment for, 107
Fulani (Africa): 255
Fuller, Ozella Keys: 109–115
Functionalism: 105–106

Gajdusek, D. Carleton: on kuru,
  46, 48
Gall bladder disease: 213, 348
Gardner, Lytt I.: infant depriva-
  tion studies of, 315–319
Gastritis: 281–282
Gastroenteritis: 227, 233
Gastrointestinal diseases: infant,
  232, 348
Gastronomy: 198

Geertz, Clifford: on Indonesian agriculture, 186–187

Genetic adaptation: 72, 73, 74, 75, 76–93; and disease, 83–85, 160; and evolution, 76–85; and increase in human size, 238; and lactose intolerance, 99–100; of mosquitoes, 164; and selective compromise, 80–83

Genetic factors: and genes, 8, 77–79; genetic codes, 77–80; genetic counseling, 115; genetic disease, 54, 109–116, 320; genetic inheritance, 3, 5; genotype, 77, 79, 80; and hypertension, 54; and screening, 115–116

Genocide: 333

Geophagy: 199–200

Geronticide: 147

Gerontology. See Aging

Glasse, Robert: on *kuru*, 47

Glaucoma: and stress, 274

Glucose: intolerance, 371; metabolism, 24; and stress, 286, 287

Goiter: endemic, 196–197, 216, 259–260

Graburn, Nelson H.H.: on Inuit, 373

Grassland ecosystems: adaptation to, 74–75, 253–255

Great Basin, Nevada: Shoshoneans of, 182–183

Green Revolution: 388

Growth and development: 230–232, 234–238; critical periods of, 225; Inuit, 345; retarded, 315–318

G6PD deficiency: 91–92

Guatemala: humoral medicine in, 107; nutrition in, 398, 407–409

Habitat: 38

Hadza (Tanzania): diet of, 238–239; and environmental hazards, 128

Hallucinogens: 165; and healing rituals, 295

Hamadsha (Morocco): healing rituals of, 295, 296

Hand: prehensile, 102

Hand-foot syndrome: 110–111

Handsome Lake: religion of, 337

Hanna, Joel M.: on coca chewing, 202

Harlow, Harry F.: monkey deprivation study, 319

Harris's lines: 167

Harvard Kalahari Research Group: 178

Hashish: as medicine, 108

Hawaii: migration to, 371, 372

Hay fever: and stress, 274, 282

Health: and adaptation, 2, 13, 104–106; and culture, 104–106, 351–354; and environment, 13–16, 43; and modernization, 378–427

Health care resources: and culture contact, 350–353; in developing nations, 399–404; and education, 363–366, 401–404, 427; and Mexican-Americans, 414–415; and Native Americans, 413–414

Heart: and high altitude adaptation, 96; and sickle cell anemia, 112. See also Cardiovascular disease

Heat: adaptation to, 74–75, 299–300, 301

Helminthic diseases: 145

Hematomas: 294

Hemoglobin: and malaria, 85, 88–93; and sickle cell anemia, 110–111

Hemorrhage: herbal treatment of, 107

Hemorrhoids: 213

Hepatic disease: 164

Herbal medicine: 9, 107–108, 129, 204, 294, 295, 297; and contraception, 133, 137
Herbivores: and food chain, 41
Herding: in Sahel, 255–256
Heroin: infant addiction to, 224
Herpes virus: 145
Heterozygote: 77, 79; and sickle cell trait, 89–90, 92, 93
High altitude adaptation: 94–96, 119, 202
Hippocrates: on healing, 294
Holism: 6, 7, 15, 66
Holmberg, Allan R.: Siriono study of, 261, 262
Homeostasis: 93, 285
Homicide: 27, 146
Hominids: evolution of, 81–83
Homozygote: 78, 79; in sickle cell anemia, 90, 92
Hong Kong: measles in, 108
Honigmann, John J.: on stress, 273
Hookworm: 117, 204–205, 408–409
Hormones: and deprivation dwarfism, 317–318; prolactin, 132–133; and stress, 96, 279, 281–284, 285, 322, 323; and sugar consumption, 348
Hospitals: 61, 64–65, 335–336, 338–339, 353
Housing: 26, 75–76, 128, 155, 343
Hulse, Frederick: on Swiss stature, 238
Humoral medicine: 107, 229, 241
Hunger: 26–27, 205–211; Inuit, 340; seasonal, 184; in United States, 207–211. See also Famine
Hunting: 118, 147, 177–185, 189, 242, 262; by Inuit, 17–21, 23, 26, 27, 35, 36; by !Kung, 175, 181–185; by Yanomamo, 38
Hunting and gathering societies: and culture contact, 330; health and disease in, 127, 144–147,

169; migration by, 142; natality in, 131, 146–147; nutrition in, 176–185
Hunza, Pakistan: longevity in, 249
Hurlich, Marshall: cold adaptation study of, 96–97
Hutterites (Canada): natality of, 131–133
Hypertension: 49, 51, 52–58; of blacks, 116, 420; and disease labeling, 61; and salt, 106, 214; and stress, 268, 273, 307; of Zulu, 366
Hyperthyroidism: and stress, 274
Hyperventilation: and arctic hysteria, 304–305; and healing rituals, 295
Hypocalcemia: 304
Hypoglycemia: and coca chewing, 203, 204
Hypoxia: 94
Hysteria: *amok*, 312; arctic, 302–307; and blindness, 295; and *kuru*, 49

Iatrogenic disease: 164–165
Igluit: 26, 75
Ik (Africa): 261–263
Illness: defined, 49. See also Folk illness
Immunity: 84, 396; of infants, 88; to malaria, 356; and tuberculosis, 160
Immunization programs: 159, 379
Incas (Peru): coca chewing by, 201–202; and smallpox, 358
India: 144, 385, 387, 388; disease in, 149, 157; natality and birth control in, 140, 403–404; nutrition in, 196, 228–229, 231–234, 238
Indians. See Native Americans
Indonesia: 144; agriculture in, 150, 186–187. See also Alor
Industrial societies: 237–238, 411;

and effects of industrialization, 425–426; health and disease in, 158–164; natality in, 131, 159–160; nutrition in, 207–215
Infant mortality: 134–139, 140, 153, 159, 233, 300, 336, 386–387; Asmat, 359–360; Inuit, 336, 337, 340; of migrant farmworkers, 412; Sanio-Hiowe, 137–139; Zulu, 363, 366
Infanticide: 27–28, 134, 149, 169; Asmat, 359; female, 27–28, 134, 137–139, 151, 301, 361; and hunters-gatherers, 147; in industrial society, 159; by Inuit, 27–28, 352; !Kung, 181; and population control, 127; Sanio-Hiowe, 137–139; Yanomamo, 151
Infants: abandonment of, 159; and bonding, 102; emotional deprivation of, 269, 314–319; and heat stress, 300; immunity of, 88; nutrition of, 208, 216, 225–229; sickle cell anemia in, 110. *See also* Breast feeding
Infection: defined, 281
Inflammation: and hormones, 281–284
Influenza: 262, 340, 345, 357, 358; in Native Americans, 331, 333; and virus evolution, 149
Insecticides: 162–163, 394, 396
Insects: as food, 189, 234–235; as parasites, 39, 145; as vectors of disease, 39, 86–87, 154–155
Insulin: 280; and deprivation dwarfism, 317–318; and rheumatoid arthritis, 283; and sugar consumption, 348, 366
Intestinal bacteria: 39, 85, 200
Inuit; 2, 16–30, 107, 274–275, 338–349; and alcohol, 337, 338, 340, 348–349; arctic hysteria of, 302–307; and child care,

274–275, 348; cold adaptation by, 25–26, 96; culture contact stresses of, 334–336, 338–349, 349–354; dietary patterns of, 22–25, 41, 177, 345–348, 352; diseases of, 340, 344–345, 351, 352; ethnic revitalization of, 337–338; folk illnesses of, 303–307, 313–314; and genetic adaptation, 74–75; kayak phobia of, 313–314; modernization and, 335–336, 338–347, 373, 382, 411; mortality of, 340, 344, 345; natality of, 340, 345, 348, 351–352; population control by, 26–28; tobacco use by, 334–335, 338, 345, 352; traditional cultural adaptation of to Arctic, 15–30, 35–36, 39–41, 177
Iodine: 216; goiter and, 259–260; in salt, 196–197
IQ: and mental retardation, 61–62; and nutrition, 260
Iran: modernization in, 383, 384
Ireland: population growth in, 158
Irian Jaya (New Guinea): 135, 359
Iron: 176; deficiency, 209, 216
Iroquois: religion of, 337
Irrigation: and agriculture, 186–187, 191; and disease, 388–395; and parasites, 148, 379; and schistosomiasis, 390–391, 394
Ishi: 330–331, 374
Islam: 157, 242, 394

Jamaica: agriculture in, 206; economy of, 385; hypertension in, 56
Japan: 144, 387; birth rate in, 160; diet of, 214, 215; hypertension in, 56, 57; mercury poisoning in, 161; and migration to Hawaii, 371, 372
Java: child labor in, 150
Jelliffe, Derrick B.: infant nutrition

Jelliffe, Derrick B. (cont.)
  study of, 228, 264
Jerome, Norge: nutrition study of,
  198
Jet lag: 304
Jogging: and stress, 276

Kaiadilt (Australia): 300–301
Kalahari Desert: 178–179
Kayak phobia: 313–314, 323
Kelly, Isabel: and malaria eradica-
  tion program, 407
Kepone poisoning: 162–163
Kiste, Robert C.: Bikini study of,
  373
Kroeber, A.L.: and Yahi, 330
Kroeber, Theodora: and Yahi, 354,
  374
Kummer, Hans: on adaptability,
  120–121
!Kung. See San
Kunitz, Stephen J.: on Navaho al-
  cohol use, 321
Kuru: 34, 35, 43–49, 161; causes
  of, 293
Kwashiorkor: 216, 230–231, 232,
  234, 260, 264, 363, 412, 413; of
  Zulu, 366

Labeling: diagnostic, 63; of dis-
  eases, 60–62
Laboratory tests: use of, 49
Lackawanna, New York: Arabs
  and blacks in, 415–423
Lactation. See Breast feeding
Lactose intolerance: 97–100
Lappé, Frances Moore: on world
  hunger, 217
Langer, William C.: on European
  population growth, 158–159
Language: acquisition of, 102, 103
Latah psychosis: 10
Latrines: 393, 405
Lead poisoning: 161

Leaf, Alexander: longevity studies
  of, 248–249
Learning: as basis for culture,
  101–104
Lee, Richard B.: !Kung study of,
  178, 180, 181, 183, 184, 324
Lentils: 188
Leukemia: 164
Lévi-Strauss, Claude: The Raw and
  the Cooked, 198
Levy, Jerrold E.: on Navaho
  drinking styles, 321
Lex, Barbara W.: on voodoo
  death, 292–293
Lice: 39, 145, 168
Life cycle: and longevity, 140–141,
  386–387; and nutrition, 222–263
Limiting factor: 40–41, 256
Limits to Growth: 425, 428
Lindenbaum, Shirley: on kuru, 47
Linguistics: 11, 136
Lipids: blood, 348; and stress, 286,
  287
Liver disease: 199
Livingstone, Frank B.: on malaria,
  87
Locus (genetic): 77
London, England: plague in, 155,
  156
Longevity: 386–387; and degener-
  ative disease, 161; male, 287;
  and nutrition, 244–250; in
  United States, 140
Lung diseases: 161
Lysine: 192, 193

MacAndrew, Craig: Drunken Comportment, 321
McArthur, Margaret: Aborigine
  study of, 183
McCarthy, J.D.: Aborigine study
  of, 183–184
McCay, Clive: nutrition study of,
  243

McElroy, Ann P.: 28, 340–342,
347, 382
Madura foot: 389
Magical death: 288–293. *See also*
Sorcery
Maize: 188, 190, 191, 192, 193,
194, 197, 363; lime treatment of,
192, 196
Malaria: 145, 151; and agriculture,
85–93, 148; in Americas, 331,
354–358; control of, 359,
396–397, 407; and sickle cell
trait, 88–93, 115
Malaysia: 207, 241
Mali: 253, 254
Malnutrition: 167, 169, 174–175,
217, 259–264, 298, 363, 366,
385–386; in infancy and early
childhood, 227, 230–236,
260–261; in United States,
208–211
Manioc: 187, 189, 197
Marasmus: 216, 227, 230–231, 234,
315, 413
Marijuana: as medicine, 108
Maring (Papua, New Guinea):
189, 196–197
Marriage practices: 131, 136, 151,
159, 229–230
Mauritania: 253, 254
Mauritius: 396–397
May, Jacques: on French cuisine,
215
Mayans (Central America): 9
Mbum Kpau (Chad): food taboos
of, 223, 242
Mead, Margaret: on United States
diet, 198
Measles: 3, 4–5, 108, 148, 151,
233, 256, 340, 345, 358, 359
Meat: eating of, 24, 177, 180–181
Medical anthropology: 2–3, 6–11,
13, 29–30, 58; fieldwork in,
58–60, 405–411; multidiscipli-

nary nature of, 35–37, 43,
66–67
Medical ecology: 2–3, 5–6, 10, 15;
interdisciplinary approach of,
35–36
Medical practitioners: folk psychotherapists as, 371; health auxiliaries as, 399–401; occupational
health of, 164–165; ratio of to
population, 387; in research
team, 4, 46; role of in labeling
mentally ill and retarded, 61–62;
San trance dancers as, 276–277;
and Selye's early work, 278–279
Medical treatment: diseases
caused by, 164–165
Medicine, clinical: 34, 48–49, 68;
biomedical perspective in, 48; in
nutrition surveys, 251
Medicine, cosmopolitan: 106–107,
108
Medicine, humoral: 107, 229, 241
Meditation: 292, 295
Men: differential exposure to infection in, 45–46, 391–393; food
taboos of, 239, 242; nutritional
status of, 210–211
Menarche: 136, 151, 237, 364; and
heat stress, 300; and menopause, 246
Mental illness: 306–314, 371; and
Arab immigrants, 420–421; arctic hysteria as, 302–307; and
crowding, 310; and disease labeling, 61; and ethnic psychoses, 10; hysteria as, 49; and
noise, 309; and stress, 268, 309,
323
Mental retardation: 61–66, 315
Mercury poisoning: 161, 163, 224,
398
Metabolism: basal, 25; glucose, 24,
203–204
Methodology: ethnoscientific,

Methodology (*cont.*)
59–60; in nutrition studies,
250–252. *See also* Epidemiology;
Experiments; Fieldwork
Mexican-Americans: 98, 414–415
Mexico: 207, 238, 261, 357–358,
407
Miasma: 157
Middle East: 98, 104–105, 153,
157, 194
Migrant workers: 208, 412–413
Migration: 142–143, 159, 329,
368–372, 394, 425; involuntary,
368–370; and stature, 235–238;
urban, 58, 207, 256, 258, 363,
366–367, 384
Milk: 188, 194, 196, 364–366; in
infant feeding, 225–226; and
lactose intolerance, 97–100
Millet: 105, 191
Minerals: nutritional, 176, 189,
194, 195, 200, 213–214
Minimata disease: 161, 224, 398
Minimax strategies: 117–118, 121,
410
Mining: and lung disease, 164
Miracidium: 391, 392, 393
Miskito (Nicaragua): 206, 218
Mites: 168
Modernization: defined, 381; and
economic development,
385–386; health effects of,
378–427
Mongolism: 63
Mongongo nut: 178–180
Monkeys: chimpanzees, 42, 47;
rhesus, 319
Monotony: as stressor, 319
Moors (Bedouin Arabs): 255
Moran, Emilio: on Amazonian
diet, 189
Morbidity: defined, 51
Morocco: 295–296
Mortality: 139–142; Asmat,
359–360; defined, 51; disease

and, 127, 158–159; and economic development, 410; and
heat stress, 300; and hypertension, 116; Inuit, 344, 355; from
malaria, 87–88; from measles,
108; Native American, 369; and
population regulation, 42; of
prisoners of war, 270–271; social, 26, 27; and warfare,
151–152, Zulu, 363. *See also* Infant mortality
Mosquitoes: 86–87, 148, 163–164,
354–356, 389, 394, 396
Multicausal model: and arctic hysteria, 306–307; in hypertension,
57; in medical ecology, 13–15
Mummies: and paleopathology,
165–166, 389
Mumps: 148
Musk ox: arctic, 21
Musselmann syndrome: 297
Mutation: 77; and sickle cell trait,
88, 90, 92; of viruses, 149
Mycetoma: 389
Myxomatosis: 84–85

Narcotics: coca leaves, 205
Natality: 42, 131–134, 159, 160,
351–352; Asmat, 360–361; Inuit,
340, 345, 348; !Kung, 181–182;
and nutrition, 195, 242, 261;
Sanio-Hiowe, 136–137
Native Americans: alcohol use by,
321, 337, 338; cold adaptation
of, 96; and culture contact, 140,
330–332, 349–354, 368–369, 411;
disease in, 148, 357–358;
ethnomedicine of, 294, 297;
health care of, 413–414; lactose
intolerance in, 98; nutrition of,
106, 142, 177, 183, 192, 196, 208,
241; tuberculosis in, 166–167;
wiitiiko psychosis in, 302. *See
also* under specific tribal names
Natural disasters: 268, 328

Natural selection: 79–80, 104; and
    adaptation, 72, 119–120; and
    Darwin, 129; and disease,
    83–85; and selective compro-
    mise, 80–83
Naturopath: 107
Navaho (United States): 107, 158,
    321; and health, 405, 406, 414
Neel, James V.: Yanomamo study
    of, 3–4, 5, 8
Negritos (Southeast Asia): 185
Nepal: child labor in, 150; Sherpa
    of, 95
Nervous system: parasympathetic,
    286, 292, 293, 322; sympathetic,
    285–286, 322
Netherlands: 144, 259
Netsilik (Canada): 27–28
Neumann, Thomas W.: on dietary
    taboos, 106, 241
Neuroses: 292
New Guinea: 135, 186, 335; agri-
    culture in, 189, 195; cannibalism
    in, 45, 190; magical death in,
    289–291; nutrition in, 190, 252.
    See also Asmat; Fore; Irian Jaya;
    Maring; Papua, New Guinea;
    Sanio-Hiowe
Niacin: 192, 194
Nicaragua: diet in, 206
Niche, ecological: 38, 39, 41, 74,
    76, 119; and malaria, 87, 90
Nicotine: 288
Niger: 253, 254
Nigeria: 56, 235, 236, 398
Noise: 274–275, 307, 308, 309
Nomadic people: diet of, 256
Norepinephrine: 285, 287
Nuclear weapons: 370
Nunamiut (Canada): 39
Nutrition: 172–264; of aging,
    243–250; of ancient peoples, 9,
    167–168; of Andes peoples, 204;
    of Bikini Islanders, 370; and
    birth rate, 151; and brain

damage, 260–261; and cold
    adaptation, 97; culture and, 175,
    195–199; and dietary taboos,
    105–106, 108, 139; and disease,
    161, 348; and diversity in diet,
    184, 189, 191, 192, 216; and
    ecology, 174, 175–185; and heal-
    ing, 107; human requirements
    for, 175–176, 237, 251–252; of
    hunters-gatherers, 184; and hy-
    pertension and, 56–57; in in-
    fancy, 137, 153, 225–229; of
    Inuit, 17, 19, 21–25, 340, 341,
    345–348, 352; !Kung, 177–182;
    in later childhood, 229–238; and
    life cycle, 222–263; Mayan, 9;
    methodology of, 250–252; and
    nonfood substances, 199–205;
    and overnutrition, 211–215; and
    peasant agriculture, 191–195;
    prenatal, 223–225; Sanio-Hiowe,
    135; and sexual differences,
    210–211, 238–242; in soul food,
    419; and stature, 9, 261; and
    stress, 298, 323; in tropics, 185;
    and tuberculosis, 84; in under-
    developed nations, 398; and ur-
    banization, 425; as variable in
    culture contact, 350, 352,
    362–367; Zulu, 363–367
Nutritional anthropology: 198,
    217, 252

Oats: 191, 195
Obesity: 24, 175, 210–211,
    211–215, 226, 246, 298–299, 348
Occupational safety and disease:
    162–164, 171
Oils: curative functions of, 107
Ojibwa (Canada): 96; and wiitiiko,
    10, 302
O'Laughlin, Bridget: on Chad
    food taboos, 242
Opium: medical uses of, 108
Osteomalacia: 99, 305

Osteoporosis: 24, 27, 214, 249
Otitis media: 345, 348
Overlaying: 159

Pakistan: 249, 389
Paleopathology: 51, 165–168, 389
Pancreatitis: 274
Pandemic: 153, 157
Pangnirtung, Northwest Territories, Canada: 340, 341, 345
Papua New Guinea: 135; health education in, 402; magical death in, 289–291; menarche in, 237. *See also* Fore; Maring; New Guinea; Sanio-Hiowe
Paralysis: hysterical, 295; in kayak phobia, 313
Parasites: 21, 127; agriculture and, 117, 148; and economics, 411; and geophagy, 199–200; and host-vector relationship, 39; of hunters-gatherers, 145–146; irrigation and, 389; malaria, 85–93; in paleopathology, 168; schistosomiasis, 391–393; and stress, 323
Parasympathetic nervous system: 286, 291–292, 322
Participant observation: 59, 64
Pastoralists: 255
Pathology: 48
Patton, Robert Gray: and deprivation dwarfism, 315–317, 318–319
Peary, Robert: on arctic hysteria, 303
Pellagra: 192, 196, 363, 412
Pelvis: evolution of, 83
Penicillin: and humoral medicine, 107
Personality: and cardiovascular disease, 287–288; and culture, 10; and nutrition, 261–262
Peru: coca chewing in, 200–205; high altitude adaptation in, 119;

modernization and, 385; mummies in, 165
Pesticides: 162–164, 394, 396
Pharmacopoeia: 129
Phenotype: 77
Philippines: 60, 388
Phosphorus: 176, 214
Photosynthesis: 40
Phthisis: 61
Phylogenetic patterns: 301
Physical anthropology: 7
Physiological adaptation: 72–73, 74, 75–76, 93–97
Phytate: 194
Pibloktoq: 303–307, 314
Pigs: 189
Pinta: 149
Pinworms: 145, 168
Pizarro, Francisco: 358
Plague, bubonic: 140, 153–158; resistance to, 84
Plantain: 188
Plants: as producers, 40
Plasmodium genus: 86, 87, 89, 90
Pneumonia: 333, 340, 344, 359, 412
Pneumonic plague: 43
Pneumothorax: 414
Point mutation: 79, 88
Polar bear: 16–17, 21, 26, 28, 39
Polgar, Steven: 170
Polio: 340, 345
Pollution: industrial, 159, 161–164, 398, 416–418, 419, 421–422; and Inuit, 337; as stressor, 274, 307
Polygyny: 151, 229–230
Polymorphism: 78–79, 92
Polyps: 213
Population: 143–144; and agriculture, 149–150, 187, 195; and culture, 130, 169, 350, 351; defined, 38, 77; and demographic transition, 159–160; density, 143–144; and disease eradication, 396–397; equation, 131–134; exponential growth of, 41; and in-

dustrialization, 142, 158–161, 425–426; interactions and energy flow, 39–41; and migration, 142–143; and modernization, 379

Population limitation: 26–28, 42, 146, 169; of hunters-gatherers, 146–147; and mortality, 139–142; and parasites, 41, 42; and predator-prey relationship, 39; and social mortality, 26, 27–28; techniques of, 149; and warfare, 151–152. *See also* Birth control; Infanticide

Postpartum sex taboo: 105, 132, 137, 140, 146–147, 169, 181, 229–230

Potassium: 200

Potato: 158, 188, 197; sweet, 43, 187, 188, 189, 195, 198

Poverty: 384; and health, 412–413; and nutrition, 174, 204–211; and stress, 307

Predation: 17–19; and predator-prey relationship, 39, 42

Pregnancy: 132; and geophagy, 199; and malaria, 87–88; and nutrition, 28, 223–225; and osteomalacia, 305; and salt restriction, 106

Prehistory: and disease, 165–166

Preventive medicine: 49

Price, Weston A.: dental study of, 196

Primates: 42, 47, 82, 319

Prisoners of war: and stress, 270–271

Procaine: 116

Protein: 176, 387; and caloric needs, 23, 188–190; complementarity, 192–194, 196; deficiency, 192, 366; in insects, 235; protein calorie malnutrition (PCM), 231; protein energy malnutrition (PEM), 231; and weaning, 230

Protozoan parasites: 145, 146

Psychogenic illnesses: 351

Psychological factors: in acculturation, 342; in adaptation to industrial environment, 420–423; in sickle cell anemia, 112–114

Psychoses: 10, 292

Public health projects: 362–367, 395, 399–409

Pueblo (United States): 166

Puerto Rico: birth control in, 403–404; migration from, 371; schistosomiasis in, 394, 395

Purgatives: 108, 297

Pygmies (Africa): 185

Quarantine: 157

Quechua (Peru): 202–205

Radiation: 370

Radiology: and leukemia, 164

Rappaport, Roy A.: *Pigs for the Ancestors,* 189

Rats: 148, 154–155

Rauwolfia: 108

Religion: birth control and, 403; fasting and, 242–243; and health, 139, 393–394, 405; Iroquois, 337; and plague, 155, 157; stress in, 277, 325. *See also* Ritual

Research methods. *See* Experiments; Fieldwork; Paleopathology

Respiratory alkalosis: 295

Respiratory disease: 159, 348

Rheumatic fever: 282, 283

Rheumatoid arthritis: 273

Rhythms: biological, 301–302, 305–306

Riboflavin: 209

Rice: 186–187, 188, 190, 191, 194, 206

Richards, Audrey I.: *Land, Labour, and Diet in Northern Rhodesia,* 198

Richter, Curt P.: on sudden death, 291–292

Rickets: 99, 305, 412; and Inuit, 24

Ritual: 189; adaptive functions of, 105; Arab, 418; and cannibalism, 190; cleansing, 394; coca chewing, 202; and disease, 145; divination, 45; and fasting, 242–243; foods, 228, 229; healing, 9, 77, 107, 269, 294–297, 383; and measles, 108; of So, 118; and stress process, 276

Roads: and disease, 380–381

Robson, John R.K.: on malnutrition, 217

Rodents: 148, 153–158

Role conflict: 306, 311–314, 323

Rongerik (Micronesia): 370

Roundworm: 117

Rubella: 148

Rye: 195

Sago: 135, 186, 188, 189

Sahel: drought in, 253–258

St. Lucia (West Indies): 411

Salt: 56–57, 106, 196–197, 213–214, 241, 295

San (southern Africa): 145, 177–185, 217, 218; blood pressure of, 54; diet and nutrition of, 23, 177–182, 242, 251; natality, 133, 181–182, 242; trance dance of !Kung, 276–277, 324, 325

Sanio-Hiowe (Papua, New Guinea): 134–139; child nutrition of, 234–235; food taboos of, 239–240; healing rituals of, 297; and yaws, 149

Sanitation: and city growth, 153; and disease control, 159; and parasites, 393, 394, 395; in Thailand, 405; and village settlement, 148

Scabies: 335

Scandinavia: diet of, 215

Schaefer, Otto: on Inuit nutrition, 345, 348

Schistosomiasis: 148, 165, 379, 389–395, 411

Scotch, Norman A.: on Zulu blood pressure, 57–58

Seals: and Inuit, 35, 36

Secular trend: defined, 50

Selective compromise: 80–83

Selye, Hans: on homeostasis, 285; inflammatory pouch test of, 282–283, 284; on stress, 276, 278–281, 298, 322, 325

Seneca (United States): 166–167, 337

Senegal: 253, 254

Sensory deprivation: 275, 314–319

Sensory overload: 27, 276, 295

Settlement patterns: and disease, 145, 148

Sex differences in epidemiology: of hypertension, 52; of *kuru,* 46; of schistosomiasis, 391–393

Sexual intercourse: cultural variation in, 133; and hunger, 261–262. *See also* Postpartum sex taboo

Shamans: 9, 152, 165, 350, 351

Sherpa (Nepal): 95

Shoshoni (United States): 142, 182–183

Sickle cell anemia: 90, 91, 92, 105, 108–116, 122

Sickle cell trait: 88–93, 115; distinguished from sickle cell anemia, 90, 115

Sickness: defined, 49

Sierra Club: 417–418

Simpson, George C.: on natural selection, 79

Siriono (Bolivia): 261–262
Skeletal system: maturation of, 235; and paleopathology, 9, 51, 166–167
Skin disease: 149
Slash-and-burn cultivation: 185
Sleep: 274–275, 302, 318–319
Sleeping sickness: 380
Smallpox: 140, 158, 165, 262, 357–358, 363; eradication of, 148–149; in Native Americans, 331, 357–358; resistance to, 84
Smoking: 334–335; and fetal size, 224; by Inuit, 345, 352; and Vitamin C, 200
Snails: and schistosomiasis, 148, 389–395
So (Uganda): 118, 120
Sociocultural factors: and plague, 157; and public health programs, 406, 415; social alienation, 309, 310–311; social bonding, 102, 103; social distance, 415; social stratification, 153; as stressors, 307–322, 323
Sodium cyanate: 116
Somatotrophic hormone (STH): 281
Somatotrophin: 317, 318–319
Sorcery: and death, 45, 288–293; and food, 262; and hypertension, 58; and illness, 45, 294, 295; and *kuru*, 49
Sorghum: 105, 191, 197
Soul food: 419
South Africa: and stress in blacks, 57–58
South American Indians. *See* Amahuaca; Quechua; Siriono; Yanomamo
Soybeans: 188, 198
Species: defined, 38
Spencer, Herbert: on evolution, 129
Spinal defects: 27, 166, 167

Spitz, René: on institutionalized infants, 315, 319
Spleen: enlarged, 111
Spradley, James P.: on fieldwork, 68; *You Owe Yourself a Drunk*, 11–12, 30
Sri Lanka (Ceylon): economy of, 385; hookworm in, 408–409; malaria in, 356–357; population, 397
Statistics: and epidemiology, 50, 51, 67
Stature: and nutrition, 9, 235–237, 261
Steegman, A.T.: cold adaptation study of, 96
Sterilization: 403
Steward, Julian H.: Shoshoni study of, 142, 183; *Theory of Cultural Change*: 129
STH: 281
Stigma: 61, 63, 65
Stimulants: 269
Stini, William A.: 119, 122, 235
Strain: defined, 273
Stress: 268–325; acute, 274; and adaptation, 93, 94; and alcoholism, 320–322; in blacks, 420–421; chronic, 274; climatic, 299–301; concept of, 269–278; and cross resistance, 283, 294; and culture, 166, 262–263, 307–322, 323–324, 357; cumulative, 300–301; and disease, 84, 107, 161, 208–324; of emotional deprivation, 314–319; environmental, 97, 298–307, 423; and fight-or-flight response, 284–286, 322; and healing, 294–298; and hormones, 281–284, 285; hypertension and, 56, 57–58; model of, 271–274; physiology of, 278–288; and role conflict, 311–314; and weaning, 232

Stroke: 52, 54, 109, 371
Subanun (Philippines): 60
Subincision: 105
Subsistence economies: 184
Sudan: 255, 389, 399–400
Sugar: 212–213, 288, 345, 348, 363, 366
Suicide: 27, 271, 297, 338, 345
Superfoods: 191
Surgery: 108, 134
Survival processes: 5
Susto psychosis: 10, 312
Sweat baths: 107, 297
Sweating: 299, 300; and adaptation, 74, 75
Sweden: 387
Sweet potato: 43, 187–189, 195, 198
Swiddens: 186–187, 189
Switzerland: 144, 238
Symbiosis: defined, 39; and hunters-gatherers, 146
Sympathetic nervous system: 285, 291–293
Synergism: of malnutrition, infection and stress, 169, 232, 252–253
Syphilis: 149, 166, 224, 344, 353, 363
Systems approach: 15–16. *See also* Ecosystem
Systolic blood pressure: 53–54

Taboos: and death, 289, 291; and hunger, 261. *See also* Food taboos; Postpartum sex taboo
Tannic acid: 197
Tannins: 107
Tanzania: 396
Tapeworm: 21, 27, 168
Taro: 187, 188, 189, 195
Tasmanians: 333
Tea: 197
Technology: evolution of, 129–130; intermediate, 425; repercussions

of, 395–398; and schistosomiasis, 390–391, 395
Tetany: 304, 305
Thailand: 197, 405
Thalassemia complex: 91
Thiamine: 194, 197
Ticks: 168
Tools: making and use of, 102, 103
Townsend, Patricia K.: 37, 135–138
Toxic substances: 161–164, 398
Tramps: 11–12
Trances: 9, 269, 276–277; and healing rituals, 295, 296; and kayak phobia, 313
Transamazonian highway: 189
Trauma: environmental, 128; and paleopathology, 166
Treponemas: 149
Trichinosis: 21, 27
Tropics: agriculture in, 185–190; diet in, 229–230; ecosystems, 146
Trypanosomiasis: 380
Tryptophan: 192, 193
Tsembaga Maring (New Guinea): 189, 196–197
Tsetse fly: 380, 389
Tuberculosis: 158, 412; and air pollution, 159; control and treatment of, 359, 414; decline in, 160; and extinction, 333; in Inuit, 336, 338, 340, 345, 351; and mortality, 140; in paleopathology, 166, 167; and phthisis, 61; resistance to, 84; and social alienation, 310; and stress, 271, 274; in Zulu, 363
Tubers: 187
Tumors: 164
Tundra: 18–19, 27
Tuning: concept of, 292–293
Turnbull, Colin: *The Mountain People*, 262–263
Typhoid: 153, 357, 363

Typhus: 159, 358, 363

Ulcerative colitis: 213
Ulcers: and concentration camps, 297–298; herbal treatment of, 107; and high altitude adaptation, 96; and stress, 268, 273, 279, 283
Underdevelopment, economic: 386–387
Unemployment: and stress, 307
Union of Soviet Socialist Republics: 244–248, 387
United Arab Republic: 387–397
United States: aging in, 249–250; anthropological studies of, 11–12, 62–66, 415–423; birth rates, 160; energy use in, 130; ethnomedical systems of, 106–108; health indicators, 387; hunger in, 207–211; hypertension in, 52–55; immigrants to, 235–237, 371, 415, 418; longevity in, 140, 287; mobility and health in, 336; mortality, 288; nutrition in, 198, 207–215, 237; plague in, 157–158; pollution, 162–163; population variables, 133, 140–141, 144; and Sahel famine, 256, 257–258; salt consumption, 56–57; and sickle cell disease, 115–116. *See also* Native Americans
Upper Volta: 253, 254
Urbanization: 56, 143, 308–311; and diet, 202, 398; 425; and disease, 336; and hypertension, 58; and migration, 207, 256, 258, 363, 366–367, 384; and stress, 307, 308–311

Vaccination: 4
Values, cultural: and change, 405–407
Variability: cultural, 103

Varicose veins: 213
Vasoconstriction: 202
Vasodilatation: 74, 75
Vector-host relationship: 39, 159, 379; in bubonic plague, 154–155; in malaria, 85, 86–87, 148, 354, 355–356; in schistosomiasis, 390–394
Venereal disease: 50, 142, 149, 339–340, 344, 345, 357, 420
Vietnam: 158
Villages: life cycle in, 147–152
Viruses: 48, 224; evolution of, 148–149; resistance to, 84–85; and stress, 268
Vitamins: 176, 189, 195, 209–210, 213, 246; thiamine, 194, 197; Vitamin A, 21, 24, 195, 198, 209, 213, 216, 259; Vitamin B-12, 216; Vitamin C, 24, 200, 210, 305; Vitamin D, 24, 213, 268; Vitamin E, 352
Voodoo: 291, 292–293

Wallace, Anthony F.C.: on arctic hysteria, 304–305, 306
Warfare: 27, 46, 140, 143, 146, 151–152, 190, 301, 330–331, 359–361
Washington, George: death causes of, 108, 294
Waste disposal: and disease, 153, 393–394
Water: 176, 385
Weaning: 228–234. *See also* Breast feeding
Wheat: 188, 190, 191, 194, 195
Whiting, John W.M.: child nutrition study of, 229–230
Whooping cough: 359
Wiitiiko psychosis: 10, 302–303
Willow: as herbal medicine, 107–108
Wilson, Christine S.: Malay nutrition study of, 241

Windigo psychosis: 302
Women: alcoholism of, 320–321;
    fractures among ancient Egyp-
    tian, 166; and infanticide of fe-
    males, 27–28, 134, 137–139,
    151, 301, 361; labor by, 149, 150,
    180, 181, 183; as medical practi-
    tioners, 399; modesty and clini-
    cal examination of, 415, 418; nu-
    trition of, 210–211, 223,
    238–243; smoking by, 334–335;
    and warfare, 301
Woods, Clyde N.: 374
Work: by children, 150, 235; coca
    chewing and, 202–205; and pro-
    ductivity and schistosomiasis,
    411; and time in producing
    food, 181, 183–184
World Health Organization: 148,
    216, 251
Worms: 107, 145, 146

Xenopsylla cheopis: 155
Xerophthalmia: 195, 216

Yahi (United States): 330–333, 354,
    374
Yams: 105, 187, 188, 189, 195
Yanomamo (Venezuela): 3–6, 8,
    29–30, 38, 41–42, 54; shamans,
    152, 165; and war, 151
Yap (Micronesia): 140–142
Yaws: 142, 149, 359
Yellow fever: 84, 145, 353

Zigas, Vincent: on *kuru,* 46
Zinc: 176, 194; and sickle cell
    anemia, 116
Zoonosis: 145
Zulu (South Africa): 57–58, 329,
    362–367

ABOUT THE BOOK AND AUTHORS

This is the first text to present medical anthropology within an ecological and adaptational framework. Written for students who have little background in anthropology, the book provides a biomedical introduction to the field and examines human health, disease, and coping patterns from an evolutionary perspective.

Drs. McElroy and Townsend comprehensively cover the theory and methodology of medical anthropology, the role of disease in human evolution, comparative demography and epidemiology, nutrition, stress and disease, and health problems related to culture contact, modernization, and development.

Health profiles appearing throughout the book illustrate the methods and findings of researchers studying specific issues like hypertension, sickle-cell anemia, deprivation dwarfism, aging and the environment, schistosomiasis, the neurological disease, *kuru*, as well as fourteen other topics. An extensive bibliography and lists of recommended readings, films, and other resources for each chapter enhance the book's use as a reference and as a text.

Ann McElroy is associate professor at the State University of New York at Buffalo. **Patricia K. Townsend** teaches anthropology at Houghton College and is doing evaluation research for the American Lung Association of Western New York.